This edition published by Parragon in 2007

Parragon
Queen Street House
4 Queen Street
Bath BA1 1HE, UK

Copyright © Parragon Books Ltd 2003

ISBN 978-1-4054-9922-4

Printed in Malaysia

This edition was created by
Starry Dog Books

Authors
Keith Lye and Philip Steele

Editorial consultant
Brian Williams

ATLAS
OF THE WORLD

PaRragon

Bath · New York · Singapore · Hong Kong · Cologne · Delhi · Melbourne

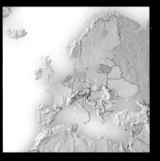

INTRODUCTION

EUROPE

Planet Earth
6
The Earth in Space
8
Land and Sea
10
The Changing Earth
12
Shaping the Land
14
Weather and Climate
16
Plants and Animals
18
Population
20
Industry and Economy
22
The Environment
24
World Facts
26
Countries of the World
28

Europe: Introduction
30
Scandinavia and the
Far North
32
The Low Countries
38
The British Isles
44
France
52
Germany
60
Iberian Peninsula
68
Italy and its Neighbors
76
Central Europe and
the Baltic
84
The Balkans
92

CONTENTS

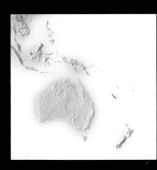

THE AMERICAS

ASIA

AFRICA

OCEANIA

The Americas:
Introduction
98
Canada
100
United States of
America
106
Mexico and
Central America
116
The Caribbean
122
Northern Andean
Countries
128
Brazil and its
Neighbors
134
Argentina and its
Neighbors
142

Asia: Introduction
148
Russia and its
Neighbors
150
Southwest Asia
158
Southern Asia
166
Eastern Asia
174
Japan
182
Southeast Asia
188

Africa: Introduction
196
North Africa
198
West Africa
204
Central, Eastern, and
Southern Africa
210

Oceania: Introduction
218
Australia
220
New Zealand and the
Pacific Islands
228

OCEANS

Pacific Ocean
235
Atlantic Ocean
236
Indian Ocean
237

POLAR LANDS

Arctic Ocean
238
Antarctica
240

Glossary 242
Index of Place Names
246
General Index 251
Acknowledgements
256

PLANET EARTH

The Earth is a huge sphere of rock, surrounded by air and partly covered by water. The North Pole is the point at the top of the sphere, while the South Pole is at the bottom. The imaginary line connecting the North Pole, the center of the Earth, and the South Pole is called the Earth's axis. It is tilted by about 23.5 degrees.

Another imaginary line runs around the Earth exactly halfway between the two poles. This line is called the Equator. It divides the world into two halves, called hemispheres. The Equator appears on globes, together with other lines that run around the globe parallel to the Equator. These are called parallels, or lines of latitude. Latitude is measured in degrees between the Equator (0 degrees latitude) and the poles (90 degrees latitude). The latitude of any place between them is the angle formed at the center of the Earth between the place and the Equator.

axis

prime meridian (longitude)

Equator (latitude)

Other lines on the globe run at right angles to the parallels. These are called meridians, or lines of longitude.

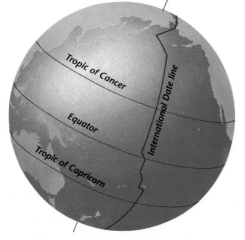

Tropic of Cancer

International Date line

Equator

Tropic of Capricorn

⟳ SPECIAL LINES OF LATITUDE
The hottest part of the world, called the tropics, lies between two special lines of latitude: the Tropic of Cancer, which is 23.5 degrees north and the Tropic of Capricorn, which is 23.5 degrees south. The coldest parts of the world lie north of the Arctic Circle, which is 66.5 degrees north, and south of the Antarctic Circle, which is 66.5 degrees south.

⟳ FINDING THE WAY
Explorers use compasses to work out directions. Compass needles point toward the magnetic North Pole.

The prime meridian (0 degrees longitude) runs through Greenwich, in London, England. Other lines of longitude are measured 180 degrees east and 180 degrees west of the prime meridian. On athe opposite side of the world from the prime meridian, around 180 degrees east or west, lies the International Date Line.

◑ MAPPING THE LAND
Land surveyors measure the positions and heights of places on the Earth's surface. Their measurements are used to make maps.

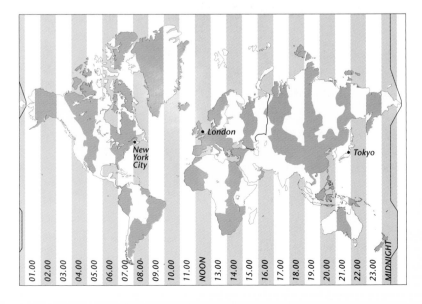

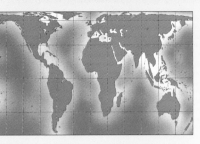

◑ PETER'S PROJECTION
Map projections are ways of showing the Earth's curved surface on a flat piece of paper. The Peter's projection (top) shows the areas of land masses accurately, but distorts their shapes.

◑ MERCATOR'S PROJECTION
No map projection is completely accurate. Gerardus Mercator's 16th-century projection shows directions accurately and ships' navigators used it to find their way. But this projection distorts areas.

To map any area, people called surveyors measure the exact latitude and longitude of a network of points on the Earth's surface. Then they measure the positions of all the land features between the points. With this information, they draw maps of the area. Drawing maps of large areas is made difficult by the fact that the Earth's surface is curved. World maps, which show the entire surface of the globe on a flat piece of paper, must be distorted to ensure that certain things, such as correct areas, distances, and directions, are preserved. The only true world map is the globe, because it has a curved surface.

◑ TIME ZONES
Because the Earth rotates once every 24 hours, clocks in various parts of the world show different times. Time zones are measured east and west of the prime meridian. Canada and the United States each have six standard time zones.

01.00 02.00 03.00 04.00 05.00 06.00 07.00 08.00 09.00 10.00 11.00 NOON 13.00 14.00 15.00 16.00 17.00 18.00 19.00 20.00 21.00 22.00 23.00 MIDNIGHT

New York City · London · Tokyo

THE EARTH IN SPACE

◯ **HUBBLE TELESCOPE**
Launched into space in 1990, the Hubble telescope has sent back amazing pictures. These show distant galaxies that could not be seen through telescopes on Earth.

The Earth is a tiny speck in space. It is the fifth-largest of the nine planets that rotate around the Sun in the Solar System. The Sun is one of millions of stars that make up the Milky Way galaxy, which, in turn, is one of the billions of galaxies that form the Universe.

Most scientists believe that the Universe was formed between 10 and 20 million years ago, in a huge explosion called the Big Bang. The Sun was formed about 4.7 billion years ago, while the Earth and the planets were formed about 4.6 billion years ago from a flattened disk of gas and dust rotating around the Sun.

◯ **GLOWING GALAXY**
Galaxies are astronomical systems consisting of millions of stars. Our sun is one of the stars in a galaxy called the Milky Way. The Universe contains billions of galaxies.

◯ **THE SOLAR SYSTEM**
Nine planets and their moons rotate around the Sun. Together with other bodies, such as asteroids, comets, and meteors, they make up the Solar System.

1	Sun	6	Jupiter
2	Mercury	7	Saturn
3	Venus	8	Uranus
4	Earth	9	Neptune
5	Mars	10	Pluto

EQUINOXES AND SOLSTICES

On two days every year, on March 20th or 21st, and again on September 22nd or 23rd, the Sun is overhead at noon at the Equator. These two days are called equinoxes, a term meaning "equal night." This is because everywhere on our planet has 12 hours of darkness and 12 hours of daylight.

However, after March 21st, the northern hemisphere leans increasingly toward the Sun. On June 20th or 21st, the Sun is overhead at noon at the Tropic of Cancer. This day is called the summer solstice in the northern hemisphere and the winter solstice in the southern hemisphere.

After September 23rd, the southern hemisphere leans increasingly toward the Sun until, on December 21st or 22nd, the Sun is overhead at the Tropic of Capricorn. This is the summer solstice in the southern hemisphere and the winter solstice in the northern hemisphere.

Our planet is always on the move. It rotates on its axis once every 24 hours, giving us night and day. It also orbits around the Sun once every 365 days, 5 hours, 48 minutes, and 46 seconds. This is called the solar year. Our calendar includes some leap years of 366 days to allow for the difference between the solar and calendar year.

○ THE FOUR SEASONS

Places in the middle latitudes experience four seasons in the year as the Earth rotates once around the Sun.

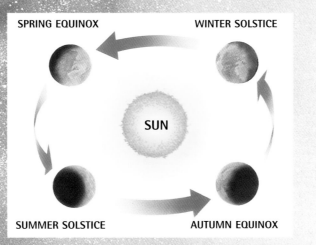

SPRING EQUINOX

WINTER SOLSTICE

SUN

SUMMER SOLSTICE

AUTUMN EQUINOX

○ SWIRLING CLOUDS

Photographs of our planet taken from space show swirling clouds and blue oceans. Water covers most of the Earth.

Neap tides occur when the Moon and Sun form a right angle with the Earth.

SUN

MOON

EARTH

○ DAY AND NIGHT

The Earth spins on its axis, taking 24 hours, or one day, to complete one revolution. The term day is also used for the period when the Sun is shining on our part of the Earth. But the night, when it is dark because our part of the Earth faces away from the Sun, is also part of the whole 24-hour day.

○ TIDES

The gravitational pull of the Moon and, to a lesser extent, the Sun, causes bulges in the waters of the oceans. These bulges cause tides. Two high tides and two low tides occur every 24 hours and 50 minutes. The highest tides are called spring tides. These occur when the Moon, Earth, and Sun are in a straight line so the pull of the Moon and Sun is combined. The smallest tidal range (the difference between the levels of high and low tides) occurs when the Moon, Earth, and Sun form a right angle. The gravitational pull of the Moon and Sun are then opposed, causing neap tides. Spring and neap tides occur about twice every month.

9

LAND AND SEA

Land covers about 29.1 percent of the Earth's surface. Most of the land is grouped into seven continents. Water covers nearly 71 percent of the Earth's surface. The largest of the four oceans is the Pacific, which covers about a third of the Earth's surface. People sometimes describe the waters around Antarctica as a fifth ocean, called the Southern or Antarctic Ocean. Most geographers, however, regard these waters as the southern parts of the Atlantic, Indian and Pacific oceans.

☼ CORAL ISLANDS
Oceanic islands rise from the deep ocean bed. These islands are active or extinct volcanic mountains. The tops of many ancient volcanoes are capped by coral. Coral is a hard rock built up by tiny creatures called coral polyps in warm, shallow seas. By contrast, continental islands, such as the British Isles, are parts of the continental shelf which lie above sea level.

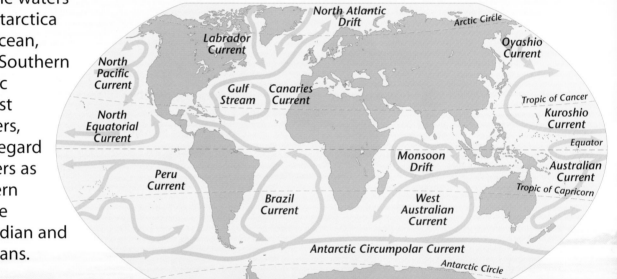

North Atlantic Drift

Arctic Circle

Labrador Current

Oyashio Current

North Pacific Current

Gulf Stream

Canaries Current

Tropic of Cancer

Kuroshio Current

North Equatorial Current

Equator

Monsoon Drift

Australian Current

Tropic of Capricorn

Peru Current

Brazil Current

West Australian Current

Antarctic Circumpolar Current

Antarctic Circle

☼ INTREPID SUB
This submersible craft, called Alvin, has carried scientists down to the dark ocean floor. The scientists took photographs and collected samples. Unmanned subs are also used to explore the ocean bed. They collect video film for the scientists.

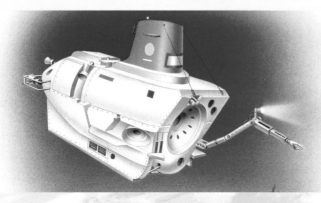

☼ MOVING SEAWATER
Seawater is always on the move. Waves, which make the water move up and down, are caused by the wind. Wind-driven currents carry warm water from the tropics toward the cold polar regions, while cold currents flow back toward the Equator. The Gulf Stream is a warm current which begins in the Gulf of Mexico. It runs up the coast of the eastern United States and then crosses the Atlantic toward Europe.

☼ AROUND A BLACK SMOKER
Hot water bubbles from a chimney on the ocean floor. Minerals feed tiny bacteria, which in turn provide food for giant clams and tubeworms.

Around most of the continents are shallow seas, covering areas called continental shelves. The continental shelves are flooded parts of the continents. The gently-sloping continental shelves end at the continental slope, which descends steeply to the abyss.

The abyss contains vast muddy plains and huge volcanic mountains, some of which rise from the ocean floor and emerge as islands. Other features are ocean ridges, which are long, underwater mountain ranges. In the middle of these ridges are rift valleys, where earthquakes are common. Scientists have discovered "black smokers" in the rift valleys. Black smokers are places where hot, mineral-rich water reaches the surface through cracks in the rocks. Minerals are deposited around the cracks to form tall "chimneys," around which strange creatures live. Molten lava also flows on to the surface in the rift valleys, creating new crustal rock. The other main feature of the oceans are enormous trenches. They are the deepest places in the oceans.

↻ VOLCANIC ISLAND
When an undersea volcano erupts, it may spell the birth of an island, if enough molten rock is flung up.

↻ THE OCEAN BED
Running through the Atlantic Ocean from north to south is a huge, mostly submerged mountain range called the Mid-Atlantic Ocean Ridge.

FACTS

MAJOR MOUNTAINS OF THE WORLD

AFRICA
Kilimanjaro 19,340 ft

ANTARCTICA
Vinson Massif 16,863 ft

ASIA
Mount Everest 29,029 ft

AUSTRALIA
Mount Kosciusko 7,310 ft

EUROPE
Mount Elbrus 15,510 ft

NORTH AMERICA
Mount McKinley 20,322 ft

SOUTH AMERICA
Aconcagua 22,831 ft

continent
continental shelf
continental slope
abyssal plain
ocean ridge
oceanic crust
magma

11

THE CHANGING EARTH

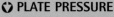

◊ PLATE PRESSURE
Earthquakes are most likely to happen where the edges of two plates that are moving in different directions grind against each other.

For millions of years after the Earth was formed, its surface was probably covered by molten rocks. Heavy elements, such as iron, sank to the center of the Earth to form a solid inner core and a molten outer core. Around the core was a thick mantle, composed of dense (heavy) rocks. Light material rose to the surface, while gases, released from the rocks by volcanic explosions, formed the beginnings of an atmosphere.

As the Earth cooled, the surface hardened to form a thin crust, while rain from the atmosphere filled hollows to form the first oceans and seas. The oldest rocks found on Earth are about 3.9 billion years old. No one knows exactly when life began.

◊ CONTINENTAL DRIFT
About 280 million years ago, the land formed just one supercontinent, Pangaea.

◊ By 180 million years ago, Pangaea began to split into Laurasia (to the north) and Gondwanaland (to the south).

◊ About 65 million years ago, the Atlantic was widening, India was moving toward Asia, and Australia and Antarctica were still joined.

◊ LIFE ON EARTH
Imagine all of the Earth's history compressed into 24 hours. On this scale, the first-known fossils would have formed at 05.45. However, the first creatures with backbones (the fishes) would not appear until 21.20. The first land plants would have appeared at 21.50 and the first land animals (amphibians) at 22.00. The first dinosaurs would have appeared at 22.50, but they would have become extinct at 23.40. People would have evolved only in the last 40 seconds!

million years ago	up to 540	540–505	505–433	433–410	410–360	360–286	286–245	245–202	202–144	144–65	65 mya – present

But the oldest fossils of simple organisms found so far were in rocks about 3.5 billion years old.

From a study of fossils, scientists have discovered that the surface of our planet is always changing. This is because the Earth's hard outer layers, consisting of the crust and the top, rigid layer of the mantle, are split into huge blocks called plates. These plates are moved around by currents in the partly-molten mantle beneath them. Plates do not move smoothly. Their jagged edges are locked together for most of the time. But pressure makes the rocks break. They then lurch forward, causing earthquakes.

⊙ These very gradual plate movements have changed the face of the Earth, and are still going on today.

inner core

outer core

mantle

crust

⊙ INSIDE THE EARTH
The Earth's crust is a thin shell, averaging 22 to 25 miles under the continents and 4 miles under the oceans. The crust encloses the 1,802-mile-thick mantle, the liquid outer core and the solid inner. The core is mostly iron.

⊙ EARTHQUAKE HOT SPOT
The San Andreas Fault, California, is where the Northern Pacific plate and the North American plate are sliding past each other in opposite directions. There have been many serious quakes along this fault, including the devastating ones that hit San Francisco in 1906 and 1989.

The plates do not join up neatly. There are three main kinds of "join." Along the rift valleys in the ocean ridges, plates are moving apart. Molten rock, called magma, rises to fill the gaps and new crust is formed. Along ocean trenches, one plate is sinking beneath another. The edge of the sinking plate, called the subduction zone, melts into magma. The third kind of plate edge is called a transform fault, such as the San Andreas Fault in the western United States. This is a long crack between two plates that are moving alongside each other. Sudden movements along the fault cause severe earthquakes, with devastating results.

SHAPING THE LAND

Plate movements create land features. For example, chains of volcanoes form where one plate is sinking beneath another. Also, when two plates carrying land areas collide, the rocks along the plate edges are buckled upward into folds. Such collisions create long fold mountain ranges, such as the Alps, Himalayas, and Rockies. Plate movements also stretch and crack rocks, creating long faults. Sometimes, blocks of rock are pushed upward between faults to form block mountains. Blocks that sink between faults form steep-sided rift valleys.

☼ BUILDING MOUNTAINS
Plate movements form fold and block mountains. Dome mountains are pushed up by hot molten rock in the Earth's mantle.

☼ FOLD MOUNTAIN

☼ DOME MOUNTAIN

☼ FOLD MOUNTAINS
The Alps formed when plate movement squeezed rock up into folds.

The land is also shaped by erosion. For example, when water freezes in cracks in rocks, the ice occupies more space than the water. Constant freezing and thawing gradually enlarges cracks until the rocks split apart. Shattered rocks tumble downhill.

Some rock fragments are carried away by huge bodies of ice, called glaciers, which slide downhill. Rocks frozen in the base or sides of glaciers give the ice "teeth," enabling glaciers to wear away the land and carve out deep, U-shaped valleys.

Rivers also carry away rock fragments. They wear away V-shaped valleys as the moving rock fragments on the riverbed rub against the land, eroding other rocks.

☼ GRANITE
The ancient Egyptians mined granite and used it to build statues and other monuments. This igneous rock is hard-wearing and easy to carve.

☼ AMMONITES
Many fossil ammonites were formed after the dead animals were buried on the seabed. The remains decayed, leaving holes, or molds, in the rocks. The molds were later filled by minerals to form fossil casts.

◊ SEDIMENTARY ROCKS
Most sedimentary rocks formed in layers at the bottom of the sea or a lake. Weathering forms them into shapely mountains.

Waves and currents create bays, headlands, cliffs, and caves along coasts. In dry areas, wind-blown sand scours rocks, whittling them into strange shapes.

Worn fragments of rocks, ranging from pebbles to fine particles of sand and mud, often pile up on the beds of lakes and seas. They squash together to make layers of rocks. These rocks often contain the fossils of ancient creatures that were buried at the bottom of the lake or sea.

Rocks formed from rock fragments are called sedimentary rocks. The other two main kinds of rocks

◊ DEEP CANYON
The Yellowstone River has worn a deep, V-shaped valley in the Yellowstone National Park in Wyoming, USA.

◊ BLOCK MOUNTAIN

◊ GIANT'S CAUSEWAY, IRELAND
Basalt, a rock formed on the surface from molten lava, sometimes hardens to form six-sided columns.

◊ THE GREAT RIFT VALLEY
This valley, stretching from Turkey to Mozambique, was caused by plate movements.

are igneous and metamorphic rocks. Igneous rocks are formed from molten material. Some, such as granite, form when magma cools underground. Others, such as basalt, form when lava hardens on the surface.

Metamorphic rocks are rocks that have been changed by great heat or intense pressure. For example, heat and pressure change the sedimentary rock limestone into marble.

◊ MOVING ICE
Glaciers are rivers of ice that form in cold mountain regions. They carry pieces of rock called moraine, which wear away the land as they move along.

glacier

snout

moraine

meltwater

15

WEATHER AND CLIMATE

tundra
coniferous forest
temperate deciduous forest
savanna
grassland
rainforest
chaparral (scrubland)
desert

☼ SOLAR HEAT
The Sun's heat is most intense around the Equator. Near the poles, the Sun's rays are spread over a much larger area.

☼ LIVING COMMUNITIES
Scientists divide the world into several biomes—plant and animal communities that cover large areas. The largest influence on what lives in a biome is the climate. For example, the treeless tundra is a biome in the north polar region.

Weather is the state of the air around the Earth. It may be hot or cold, wet or dry, windy or calm. Most of the weather that affects us occurs in the lowest layer of the atmosphere—the troposphere. The troposphere is about 110 miles thick above the Equator and about 6 miles thick over the poles. It contains more than 75 percent of the air in the atmosphere.

The atmosphere includes other layers, such as the stratosphere, directly above the troposphere. The stratosphere contains a layer of a gas called ozone, which blocks out most of the Sun's harmful ultraviolet rays.

The atmosphere is always moving. Near the Equator, the Sun heats the ground and hot air rises. The rising air eventually cools and spreads out north and south. Around latitudes 30 degrees north and south, the air sinks back to the surface. Some of this air flows back to the Equator, forming trade winds, while some forms the westerly winds. These are called prevailing (main) winds. The other prevailing winds are the cold polar easterlies that flow from the poles.

☼ LAND AND SEA BREEZES
1. During the day, cool winds from the sea blow over the hot land.

2. At night, the land cools more quickly than the water and cool winds blow from the land over the warmer sea.

☼ EYE OF THE STORM
The center of a hurricane, known as the eye, is an area of calm surrounded by violent, swirling winds.

◐ SPLITTING THE SKY
Flashes of lightning are huge discharges of electricity in clouds. The intense heat created by lightning causes thunderclaps.

Air contains moisture in the form of invisible water vapor. Hot air can contain more moist water vapor than cold air. Hence, when warm air rises and cools, it releases the water vapor in the form of droplets of water or ice crystals. Billions of droplets and ice crystals form clouds.

Clouds are the source of rain and snow. Huge cumulonimbus clouds form in thunderstorms. Thunderstorms, which bring heavy rain, are the most common storms. Many occur in the rising air near the Equator. Others occur in the depressions that form along the polar front, the boundary between the cold polar easterlies and the warm westerly winds.

Other storms called hurricanes form over the oceans north and south of the Equator. When hurricanes reach land, they cause tremendous damage. The strongest winds of all occur in relatively small storms, called tornadoes.

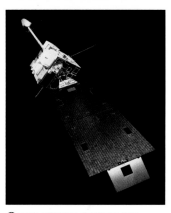

◐ WEATHER SATELLITE
Satellites send back images of cloud systems and other weather information, such as temperatures in the upper air.

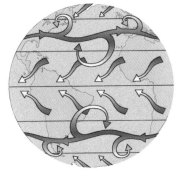

◑ PREVAILING WINDS
Trade winds, westerlies, and polar easterlies are the world's prevailing winds. Around the Equator, winds blow from east to west. Local winds often blow in different directions from the prevailing winds.

rain
cloud

river carries
water back
to ocean

FACTS

Climate is the usual, or average, weather of a place. The five main climatic types are tropical rainy climates, dry climates, warm temperate (or middle latitude) climates, cold forest climates, and polar climates. Each of these is further subdivided according to special features of temperature and rainfall. Some scientists recognize a sixth, mountain climate type, because on mountains temperatures fall the higher you climb. As a result, the tops of high mountains near the Equator are as cold as polar regions.

◐ THE WATER CYCLE
There is only so much water on the Earth. Because we cannot make new water, clouds and rain are important parts of the water cycle. Heat from the Sun changes water from oceans, lakes, seas, trees, the soil, and other moist surfaces into water vapor, which forms the rain clouds. Most rain falls back directly into the oceans. The water that falls on land also finds its way back to the oceans in the end, by draining into rivers that lead to the sea. Then it is ready to go round the water cycle all over again.

PLANTS AND ANIMALS

Climate affects the soils, plants, and animals found in any area. Soils store heat, food, and water for plants. They also support plant roots. Scientists have divided the world into regions of different types of vegetation.

Around the icy polar regions are cold, treeless zones called tundra. Snow covers the tundra in winter, but during the short summer, the snow melts and plants grow in the swampy soil. Animal migrants, such as reindeer and caribou, arrive to feed on the plants. Birds also nest there, feeding on the swarms of insects that fill the air.

MOUNTAINS
Temperatures fall at higher altitudes, so plant and animal habitats in mountain regions vary according to the height of the land.

▶ MOUNTAIN GOAT

GRASSLANDS
Prairies are mid-latitude grasslands that are too dry for trees to grow.

TROPICAL RAINFORESTS
Hot, steamy rainforests are rich in plant and animal species. Scientists believe that they contain many species yet to be discovered.

◀ GIRAFFE, AFRICAN SAVANNA

▼ TREE FROG

There are many different types of forest. In the far north, south of the tundra, there are vast, cold coniferous forests, which are home to evergreen trees such as fir, pine, larch, and spruce. The forests contain animals such as bears, mink, moose, and wolves. By contrast, warm temperate regions support forests of deciduous trees, such as ash, beech, chestnut, and oak, which shed their leaves in winter. Much forest has been cut down to create farmland, though wild boars, deer, foxes, and weasels survive in some areas. Mediterranean regions are covered with large areas of heathland, with their wiry grasses and trees such as cork oaks, myrtles, and olives. Tropical rainforests contain more than half of the world's species. Monkeys, snakes, and many birds live in the leafy canopy.

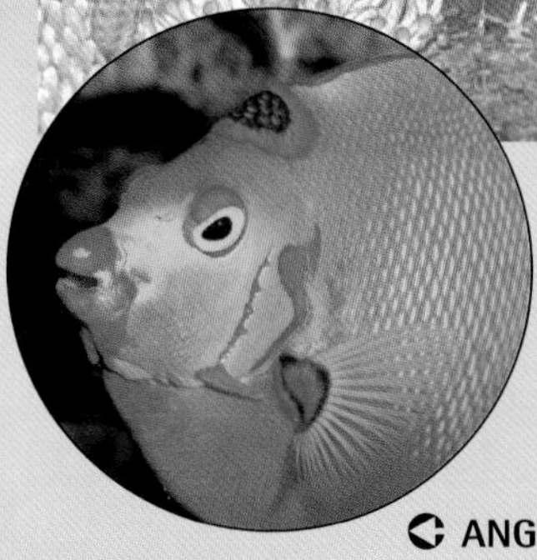

⟲ CORAL REEFS
The world's coral reefs, which thrive in clean, warm seas, are threatened by human activities, including pollution and tourism.

⟳ ANGELFISH

⟲ CROCODILE

⟲ WETLANDS
Lakes, rivers, and swamps form habitats for many plants and animals. Each species is adapted to its environment.

Savanna (grassland with scattered trees) borders the rainforests. The African savanna is especially rich in wildlife, including elephants, giraffes, lions, rhinoceroses, and zebras. Other kinds of grassland are much drier. They include the prairies of North America and the dry steppes of southeastern Europe and Central Asia.

Desert plants and animals must survive long periods without water. For example, cacti in North America's deserts store water in their swollen stems. Similarly, camels can go for several days without drinking.

⟳ SAGUARO CACTUS

Mountains have varied plant and animal zones. Only sure-footed animals, such as yaks, ibexes, and wild sheep can scale the steepest rocky slopes. Other plant and animal regions include lakes and rivers, and the oceans.

⟲ TUNDRA
During the short summer, the empty tundra becomes a breeding area for many migrating birds. In winter, the ground is frozen.

⟲ POLAR BEAR

⟲ DESERTS
Following a rare rain shower, a desert may be carpeted with flowers.

19

POPULATION

About 10,000 years ago, life on Earth was hard and most people lived by hunting animals and gathering plant foods. But once people had learned how to farm the land, food supplies increased and so also did the number of people.

⟳ HUMAN EVOLUTION
Humanlike creatures evolved on Earth over the last four million years, but modern people appeared only recently.

4–1.5 million years ago	2.5–1.5 million years ago	1.5 million– 200,000 years ago	120,000– 30,000 years ago	Modern man From 15,000 years ago

⟳ IT TAKES ALL KINDS
The world's people are an exciting mix of different races, languages and cultures.

By 8000 BC, the world population was still only about eight million (today there are cities with more people than that!), but it steadily increased, reaching 300 million by AD 1000. The billion mark was reached in about 1850, and the two billion mark in the 1920s.

In 1975, the world population reached four billion, and the six billion mark was passed in 1999. The rapid increase in the 20th century, called the "population explosion," is expected to continue during the 21st century.

The world's people are divided by several factors, including race, language, and religion. All people belong to one species, called *Homo sapiens*. However, most people identify three main groups: Caucasoids (whites); Negroids (blacks); and Mongoloids, such as Chinese and Japanese. Racial discrimination has caused much conflict between peoples around the world.

⟳ OFFICIAL LANGUAGES
Europeans started traveling to other parts of the world from the 14th century. Later on, they set up colonies overseas. When such countries won their independence, they often adopted the language of the former colonial power as their official language. This is why English is now the official language of about 27 percent of the world's population. It is also the language for most international business. Other major official and business languages are Chinese, Hindi, Spanish, Russian, and French.

⟳ URBAN LIFE
People in cities face many problems, including pollution, gridlock, and high crime rates. Yet cities are growing throughout the world, because city people usually get better jobs and services than their country cousins.

Language and religion also divide peoples. Experts argue about the number of languages in the world today, with estimates ranging between 3,000 and 6,500. The largest language group is the Indo-European family,

☉ POPULATION CONTROL

China has more people than any other country. To control its rapid population growth, the government encourages families to have only one child. Posters explain to people why population control is good for China. But some people oppose this policy. They want many sons to support them when they are old.

which includes most European languages, as well as Persian and Hindi in Asia. The second-largest language family is Sino-Tibetan, which includes Chinese.

The world's chief religions are Christianity (about 1.9 billion followers), Islam (about 1.1 billion), Hinduism (780 million), and Buddhism, which is followed by 324 million people.

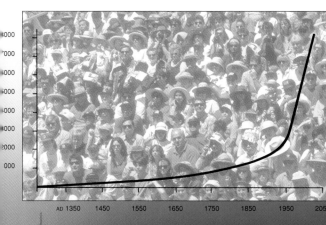

☉ POPULATION GROWTH

In 1999, the world's population passed six billion. It is expected to level out at around 11 billion in 2200.

FACTS

RELIGIONS OF THE WORLD

CHRISTIANITY
Christians believe in one God and in the teachings of Jesus Christ. Christianity is the chief religion of the Americas, Europe, and Australia.

ISLAM
Islam was founded by the prophet Muhammad in Arabia in AD 622. It is widely practiced in northern Africa and parts of Asia, and also has followers in North America and Europe.

HINDUISM
Hindus worship many gods. Hinduism is one of the world's oldest religions—it began 3,500 years ago. Today, it is the main religion of India.

BUDDHISM
Buddhism developed in India from the teachings of Gautama Buddha (the Enlightened One).

CONFUCIANISM AND TAOISM
Confucianism is based on the teachings of Confucius, a Chinese philosopher born about 550 BC. Taoism is another Chinese religion. It is based on the teachings of Lao Tzu about 300 BC.

JUDAISM
Judaism is an ancient "one-god" religion that developed in southwest Asia. Its followers are known as Jews.

SIKHISM
Sikhism was founded in India in the 1400s by Guru Nanak. The word "Sikh" means "disciple."

SHINTOISM
Shintoism is the oldest surviving religion of Japan. Shintoists worship forces in nature, including rocks and trees.

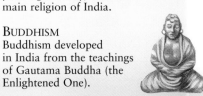

INDUSTRY AND ECONOMY

⟳ SAXON FARMERS
Until about 200 years ago, most people depended on farming. Even today, agriculture employs about half of the world's population.

Farming supplies most of the world's food and the raw materials to make clothes and other products. It is the world's biggest employer. But its relative importance has declined as manufacturing and the service industries have grown. The United States is the world's leading trading nation, followed by Germany, Japan, France, and the United Kingdom.

⟳ MINING
Some underdeveloped countries have large deposits of oil or valuable minerals. But only a few people benefit and many people remain poor.

One of the most important industries is mining. It produces fuels—mainly coal, oil, natural gas, and uranium for use in nuclear power plants—together with metals and many other materials used in manufacturing industries. When reserves run out, we may have to mine other planets or moons.

The modern world divides into developed countries, where many people live in luxury, and developing countries, where many people are very poor.

⟳ SUBSISTENCE FARMING
Many people in Africa and Asia produce little more than they need to support their families.

⟳ INDUSTRIAL REVOLUTION
The Industrial Revolution began in Britain in the late 18th century and spread rapidly. Today, manufacturing is a major employer, although in some countries it has become automated and employs fewer people. This has led to an expansion of the number of people in service industries.

PER CAPITA GNPS

The per capita GNP, or gross national product, is the total value of all the goods and services produced by a country in one year, divided by the population. It is usually expressed in US dollars. The average per capita GNP in developed countries with high-income economies, such as the United Kingdom, is about US$23,500. In developing countries with middle-income economies it is $2,500. In developing countries with low-income economies, it is less than $400.

◊ STOCK EXCHANGE
The economies of countries have become increasingly involved with each other because of trade and financial links.

◊ STRUCTURE OF PRODUCTION
In India, agriculture (red), is still more important than industry (yellow). But services (blue) provide most income. In the United States, services and industry are far more important than agriculture.

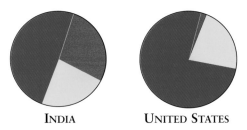

INDIA   UNITED STATES

◊ COMMUNICATIONS SATELLITE
Service industries such as television boomed in the 20th century.

They may live in poor housing, often at some distance from a supply of clean water. Experts divide developing countries into those with middle-income economies, and those with low-income economies.

Developed countries with high-income economies import food and raw materials and export manufactured products. By contrast, developing countries with low-income economies have few manufacturing industries and most people work on farms, often at subsistence level. Countries with low-income economies include many nations, such as Mozambique (Africa) and Bangladesh (Asia), where per capita GNP (see panel) is less than US$500 a year. In a country such as Argentina, with a middle-income economy, GNP is around US$8,000 a year.

◊ WHEN RESOURCES RUN OUT...
Biosphere was an artificial world created in Arizona, USA, to study how people might live within carefully controlled environments, such as a colony on the Moon.

GROSS NATIONAL PRODUCT
The map shows how countries are divided into poor developing economies, middle-income economies, and the wealthy high-income economies.

- Low
  $785 or less
- Lower middle
  $786–3115
- Upper middle
  $3,116–9,635
- High
  $9,636 or more

THE ENVIRONMENT

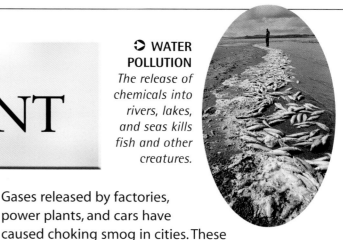

WATER POLLUTION
The release of chemicals into rivers, lakes, and seas kills fish and other creatures.

The development of the world's natural resources has brought great wealth to many people, especially in developed countries. However, economic development has caused great damage to the natural world. Because of the huge population explosion, people have flooded into areas of wasteland, cutting down forests and digging up grasslands to create farmland. This has led to soil erosion and massive reductions in wildlife. In some areas, fertile land has been turned into desert.

The growth of industrial cities has polluted the land, sea, and air. Rivers and lakes have been left lifeless by poisonous industrial wastes; air pollution has affected wildlife and caused health problems.

MOUNTAINS OF RUBBISH
Unsightly refuse dumps can also be a health hazard. They provide homes for disease-carrying creatures, such as rats.

Gases released by factories, power plants, and cars have caused choking smog in cities. These gases are sometimes dissolved in water droplets in the air. This creates acid rain, which kills trees and most living things in lakes. The gases that pollute the atmosphere include carbon dioxide, which is released by the burning of fossil fuels—coal, oil, and natural gas. Carbon dioxide is called a "greenhouse gas," because it prevents the heat that rises from the ground escaping into space. As the amount of carbon dioxide in the air increases, so also does the temperature of the air. This process, called "global warming," has already begun to change world climates. In the future, it may melt the ice sheets around the poles and raise the level of the sea. Low-lying islands would disappear, and fertile or densely populated coastal lowlands would be flooded.

FILTHY AIR
Car exhaust fumes pollute the air. Air pollution causes smog, which harms people and plants.

FAREWELL TO THE FORESTS
The destruction of rainforests in South America, Africa, and Asia is a major environmental disaster.

☼ WIND POWER
The burning of fossil fuels (coal, gas, and oil) causes pollution. Wind turbines can harness the power of the wind to produce "clean" energy.

☼ SOLAR PANELS
Energy from the Sun can be harnessed by solar panels. In the future it may replace fossil fuels as a source of environmentally friendly power.

Gases called chlorofluorocarbons, or CFCs for short, have damaged the layer of ozone in the stratosphere, which protects the Earth from the Sun's burning ultraviolet radiation. Since the 1980s, governments have worked together to reduce the release of CFCs into the air to halt this danger. Such international action is required on many fronts to halt the damage being done by human activities to the Earth's fragile environment.

☼ GREENHOUSE EFFECT
Greenhouse gases in the atmosphere retain heat that is reflected from the Earth's surface. This used to be a helpful thing, but the steady increase of these gases due to human activities has warmed the planet to dangerous levels over the last 150 years.

☼ RECYCLING
Many waste materials, including metals, glass, and paper, can be recycled. Re-use reduces the amount of garbage that must be dumped or burned.

WORLD FACTS

EARTH SEEN FROM SPACE

FACTS

THE PLANET EARTH

AGE: About 4,600 million years
DIAMETER: 7,926 miles
EQUATOR: 24,902 miles
MASS: 5,980 billion billion tons
TILT: 23.4° from the upright
DISTANCE FROM SUN: 92,000,000 miles
TIME TAKEN TO SPIN ON AXIS:
23 hrs 56 min
TIME TAKEN TO ORBIT SUN:
365 days 6 hrs
NUMBER OF MOONS: 1

FACTS

CLIMATE AND WEATHER

HIGHEST-KNOWN TEMPERATURE:
136°F (Libya, 1922)
LOWEST KNOWN TEMPERATURE:
-192°F (Antarctica, 1983)
WETTEST PLACE:
Mawsynram, India
(average rainfall of 467 inches a year)
DRIEST PLACE:
Atacama Desert, Chile
(average rainfall 0 inches per year)
MOST POWERFUL TORNADO:
280 mph (Texas,1958)

TORNADO

FACTS

SOARING PEAKS

1 Everest or Qomolangma, Himalaya
(29,029 ft)
2 K2 or Qogir Feng, Himalaya (28,251 ft)
3 Kanchenjunga, Himalaya (28,208 ft)
4 Lhotse, Himalaya (27,923 ft)
5 Yalung Kang, Himalaya (27,893 ft)
6 Makalu 1, Himalaya (27,788 ft)
7 Dhaulagiri 1, Himalaya (26,663 ft)
8 Manaslu 1, Himalaya (26,758 ft)
9 Cho Oyu, Himalaya (26,748 ft)
10 Nanga Parbat 1, Himalaya
(26,660 ft)

MOUNT EVEREST

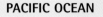

PACIFIC OCEAN

FACTS

OCEANS AND SEAS

1 Pacific Ocean: 64,187,000 sq mi.
2 Atlantic Ocean: 33,420,000 sq mi.
3 Indian Ocean: 28,351,000 sq mi.
4 Arctic Ocean: 5,106,000 sq mi.
5 South China Sea: 1,149,000 sq mi.
6 Caribbean Sea: 1,063,000 sq mi.
7 Mediterranean Sea: 969,000 sq mi.
8 Bering Sea: 873,000 sq mi.
9 Sea of Okhotsk: 610,000 sq mi.
10 Gulf of Mexico: 596,000 sq mi.

NILE DELTA

FACTS

MIGHTY RIVERS

1 Nile, North Africa (4,160 miles)
2 Amazon, South America (4,049 miles)
3 Chang Jiang, China (3,964 miles)
4 Mississippi-Missouri, USA
(3,740 miles)
5 Ob-Irtysh, Russia (3,461 miles)
6 Yenisey-Angara, Russia (3,449 miles)
7 Huang He, China (3,395 miles)
8 Congo, Central Africa (2,900 miles)
9 Paraná, South America (2,796 miles)
10 Mekong, Southeast Asia (2,750 miles)

FACTS

A RESTLESS PLANET

WORST VOLCANIC ERUPTIONS:
Thíra, Greece (c.1500 BC)
Tambora, Indonesia (1815)
Krakatoa, Indonesia (1883)
HIGHEST ACTIVE VOLCANO:
Ojos del Salado, Chile-Argentina (22,595 ft)
MOST MASSIVE ACTIVE VOLCANO:
Mauna Loa, Hawaii, USA (1,500,875 cu ft)
HIGHEST GEYSER:
Waimangu, New Zealand (1,509 ft, 1903)
MOST POWERFUL KNOWN EARTHQUAKES:
Assam, India (Richter scale 9, in 1950)
HIGHEST TSUNAMI:
Alaska, USA (1,719 ft, in 1958)

VOLCANO

FACTS

EARTH'S LANDSCAPES

BIGGEST DESERT:
Sahara, North Africa (about 3,579,000 sq mi.)
BIGGEST RAINFOREST:
Amazon basin, South America
(about 965,000 sq mi.)
BIGGEST RIVER GORGE:
Grand Canyon, Arizona, USA
(277 miles long, about 5,300 ft deep)
LONGEST CAVE SYSTEM:
Mammoth Cave, Kentucky, USA
(about 348 miles)
HIGHEST WATERFALL:
Angel Falls, Venezuela (3,212 ft)

DESERT

COUNTRIES
OF THE WORLD

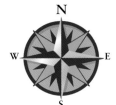

The world is divided into about 192 independent countries, which have control over their own affairs, and more than 40 dependencies, which rely to some extent on an independent country.

The largest independent countries are Russia, Canada, China, the United States, and Brazil. The smallest are Vatican City, Monaco, Nauru, Tuvalu, and San Marino. The numbers of independent countries and dependencies often change. For example, the Indonesian province of East Timor became an independent nation in 2002.

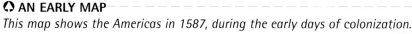

○ **AN EARLY MAP**
This map shows the Americas in 1587, during the early days of colonization.

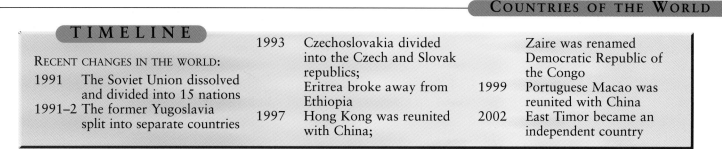

TIMELINE

RECENT CHANGES IN THE WORLD:

1991   The Soviet Union dissolved and divided into 15 nations

1991–2   The former Yugoslavia split into separate countries

1993   Czechoslovakia divided into the Czech and Slovak republics;
Eritrea broke away from Ethiopia

1997   Hong Kong was reunited with China;

Zaire was renamed Democratic Republic of the Congo

1999   Portuguese Macao was reunited with China

2002   East Timor became an independent country

ICELAND

NORWAY

SWEDEN

FINLAND

ESTONIA

LATVIA

LITHUANIA

RUSSIA

BELARUS

POLAND

UKRAINE

SCOTLAND

IRELAND

WALES

ENGLAND

DENMARK

NETHERLANDS

BELGIUM

GERMANY

CZECH REP.

SLOVAKIA

MOLDOVA

Key to Numbered Countries

1 LUXEMBOURG
2 LIECHTENSTEIN
3 SAN MARINO
4 VATICAN CITY
5 MONACO
6 ANDORRA

FRANCE

SWITZ.

AUSTRIA

HUNGARY

ROMANIA

SLOVENIA

CROATIA

SERBIA & MONTENEGRO

BOS.-HERZ.

PORTUGAL

SPAIN

ITALY

BULGARIA

ALBANIA

MACEDONIA

GREECE

MALTA

EUROPE

⚫ Oil rig,
NORTH SEA

⚫ Mt Triglav,
SLOVENIA

⚫ Bluebell wood,
BRITISH ISLES

⚫ Mt St Michel,
FRANCE

Europe's western shores face the North Atlantic Ocean. The restless sea has gnawed away at this coastline over the ages, creating chains of islands, headlands, and channels. Ocean currents warm the northwest of the continent, giving a moist and mild climate. Southern European lands border the Mediterranean and Black Seas, and are mostly warm and dry. However, Europe's northern borders are formed by the ice-bound coasts of the Arctic Ocean. In the east, the continental border with Asia runs overland along the Ural Mountains, the shores of the Caspian Sea, and the Caucasus Mountains. Europe and Asia are part of the same vast landmass.

Thousands of years of farming and hundreds of years of industrialization have completely changed the European landscape. Dense woodlands have been cut down and steppes (natural grasslands) have been given over to farming. Great cities and ports have grown up, linked by highways and railroads. Wilderness survives only in a few areas, such as the forests of the far north.

The European Union (EU), currently with 15 member nations, aims to bring increasing economic and political unity to the continent, particularly with the launch of a single currency, the euro. Europe is home to many different peoples, cultures, and languages. English, French, and Spanish are now spoken in many other parts of the world.

⊃ GRAY
HERON

31

SCANDINAVIA
AND THE FAR NORTH

Iceland is a northwestern outpost of Europe, lying just below the Arctic Circle. The island is volcanic, with warm springs and eruptions of lava in a bleak, moorland landscape.

◌ NORTHERN LIGHTS
The aurora borealis (northern lights) flicker eerily across the night sky in Arctic regions. They are caused by particles streaming from the Sun.

To the east, the Atlantic Ocean extends into the Norwegian and North Seas. The ocean sweeps on through the windy channels of the Skagerrak and Kattegat, into the shallow Baltic Sea. To the south lies Denmark, which takes in the flat lands of the Jutland peninsula and about 500 islands. The biggest of these are Sjælland, Fyn, Lolland, and Falster.

To the north lies the Scandinavian peninsula, occupied by Sweden and Norway. This stretches all the way to North Cape, beyond the Arctic Circle, where the sun lights up midsummer nights and the winters remain long and dark. Northern winters are severe, but southern regions have a more moderate climate. Lowland plains, covered in birch and spruce, rise to a backbone of rugged mountains. The landscape has been scarred by ancient glaciers. These have created many lakes, as well as the deep sea inlets or fjords that indent the Norwegian coast.

Finland lies on the freezing lands between the Scandinavian and Russian Arctic, with coasts on the Gulfs of Bothnia and Finland. Pitted with over 55,000 lakes, this is the most densely forested country in Europe.

DENMARK
Kongeriget Danmark
AREA: 16,638 sq mi.
POPULATION: 5.3 million
CAPITAL: Copenhagen
OTHER CITIES: Århus, Odense
HIGHEST POINT:
Yding Skovhøj (568 ft)
OFFICIAL LANGUAGE: Danish
CURRENCY: Danish krone

FINLAND
Suomen Tasavalta – Republiken
Finland
AREA: 130,559 sq mi.
POPULATION: 5.1 million
CAPITAL: Helsinki
OTHER CITIES: Tampere, Turku
HIGHEST POINT:
Haltiatunturi (4,357 ft)
OFFICIAL LANGUAGES: Finnish, Swedish
CURRENCY: Euro

◌ GUSHING GEYSERS
Iceland's geysers are caused by hot rock inside the Earth. The rock heats up pockets of water underground and makes spouts of steam gush up to the surface.

◌ NORWEGIAN FJORD
A fjord is a deep valley that was carved by a glacier during the Ice Age. When the glacier melted, the valley flooded with salty sea water.

ICELAND

NORWAY

SWEDEN

FINLAND

DENMARK

⊙ BEAVER
Scandinavia is one of the last strongholds of the European beaver. This species was once common in northern lands.

⊙ HELSINKI PORT
The Finnish capital has a fine natural harbor that has to be cleared of ice during the winter months.

⊙ DOWNHILL SKIING
Both Alpine (mountain) and Nordic (cross-country) skiing are popular during snowy Scandinavian winters. A wooden ski found in Sweden is believed to date back to about 2500 BC.

⊙ WOLVERINE
The wolverine lives in the forests of the cold north. It is a fierce predator, and will even attack deer or bear cubs.

○ ROYAL GUARD

A soldier stands guard outside the Amalienborg palace, Copenhagen. The palace is the home of the Danish royal family.

The term "Scandinavia" commonly refers to three northern European monarchies—Sweden, Norway, and Denmark—but it sometimes also includes the republics of Iceland and Finland. All these countries are democracies that have enjoyed a high standard of living in the last 50 years. Denmark, Sweden, and Finland are members of the European Union (EU). Denmark's self-governing overseas territories include the Faeroe Islands and Greenland, which geographically is part of North America. Norwegian territories include the Arctic islands of Jan Mayen and the Svalbard archipelago.

The development of these lands on the rim of Europe has been conditioned by harsh northern winters and by remote and difficult terrain, much of it covered in dense forests. The population is concentrated in the milder southern and coastal regions, where most

○ GRUNDTVIG'S CHURCH

This modern Danish church is named for Nikolai Grundtvig (1783–1872), who founded the Evangelical Lutheran People's Church of Denmark.

farming, industry, and trade is located. Only eight percent of Finland is suitable for agriculture, and only three percent of Norway. To the south, Denmark is a major producer of bacon and dairy items such as butter, cheese, and yoghurt. In volcanic Iceland, underground heat has been harnessed to warm greenhouses, where flowers and vegetables are grown for export.

The forests of northern Scandinavia provide timber for paper-making, construction, and furniture.

○ OIL FROM THE SEA

Large reserves of oil beneath the North Sea have made Norway Europe's largest oil producer. Norway also has major industries based on natural gas and petrochemicals.

○ LEGOLAND, DENMARK

Denmark exports the most famous toy in the world, Lego. Tourists flock to Legoland, where a tiny model of every major city has been built from the brightly coloured plastic bricks.

○ WIND TURBINES

Danish engineers pioneered wind turbine technology and today groups of windmills are a familiar sight in the Danish countryside. They may be up to 100 feet high, generating enough electricity for export as well as for local needs.

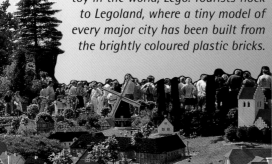

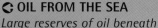

These lands also produce vehicles, machinery, and scientific and electrical equipment. Sweden has rich reserves of iron ore and uranium, and both Denmark and Norway have profited from North Sea oil and natural gas. Northern mountain streams and lakes generate hydroelectric power, and Denmark has been at the forefront of developing wind power. Fisheries have always provided food and a livelihood for people in each one of these northern lands.

Reykjavík, in Iceland, is the world's most northerly capital city. The capitals of the region are all old seaports that grew up on the trading routes between the Baltic, the North Sea, and the North Atlantic.

◯ TIMBER!

Timber is an important resource in Norway and Sweden. Some 65 percent of Finland is forested, and wood products make up 40 percent of Finnish exports.

◯ STOCKHOLM

Stockholm, the Swedish capital, lies on a strait between Lake Malar and the Baltic coast. The city's waterfronts also take in a number of small islands linked by bridges.

FACTS

ICELAND
Lyðveldið Ísland
AREA: 39,768 sq mi.
POPULATION: 0.3 million
CAPITAL: Reykjavík
OTHER CITIES: Kópavogur, Hafnarfjörður
HIGHEST POINT: Hvannadalshnúkur (6,951 ft)
OFFICIAL LANGUAGE: Icelandic
CURRENCY: Icelandic króna

NORWAY
Kongeriket Norge
AREA: 125,050 sq mi.
POPULATION: 4.5 million
CAPITAL: Oslo
OTHER CITIES: Bergen, Trondheim
HIGHEST POINT: Galdhøppigen (8,100 ft)
OFFICIAL LANGUAGE: Norwegian
CURRENCY: Norwegian krone

SWEDEN
Konungariket Sverige
AREA: 173,732 sq mi.
POPULATION: 8.8 million
CAPITAL: Stockholm
OTHER CITIES: Göteborg, Malmö
HIGHEST POINT: Kebnekaise (6,926 ft)
OFFICIAL LANGUAGE: Swedish
CURRENCY: Swedish krona

Scandinavia is home to several different peoples. The Saami have lived there since prehistoric times. Their modern homeland, known as Lapland, stretches through Arctic Norway, Sweden, and Finland and into Russia. Their language is related to Finnish and Estonian. Traditionally, the Saami are nomadic reindeer herders, but many now live and work in towns.

The Finns make up the majority of people living in Finland. They too speak their own language. Their ancestors moved into the region from what is now Russia, about 2,000 years ago. About the same time, other peoples were moving north into Scandinavia from Germany. These were the ancestors of today's Swedes (some of whom also live in Finland), Danes, Norwegians, and Icelanders. Swedish, Danish, Icelandic, and the two spoken versions of Norwegian (Bokmål and Nynorsk) are separate languages that have developed from similar Germanic roots.

About 1,200 years ago, the Scandinavians began to take to the sea to seek their fortune abroad. Known as Vikings or Northmen, they attacked coastal settlements all over the British Isles and Western Europe.

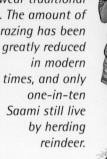

STAVE CHURCH
During the 11th century, Christianity began to spread across Norway. About 600 wooden stave churches were built there during the Middle Ages. Today, only about twenty-four remain standing. They are named for their corner-posts, or staves.

SAAMI TRIBESMAN
The Saami from Sweden still wear traditional costume for special occasions. The amount of Arctic pasture available for grazing has been greatly reduced in modern times, and only one-in-ten Saami still live by herding reindeer.

A BRAVE LEADER
King Gustavus Adolphus of Sweden (1611–32) died after the battle of Lützen, in the Thirty Years' War. The Protestant Swedes were fighting Spain and the Holy Roman Empire.

TOLLUND MAN
Discovered at Tollund Fen, Denmark, in 1950, the Tollund Man is over 2,000 years old. His body had been preserved in a peat bog since Iron Age times. The peat also dyed his skin brown.

VIKING RAIDERS
The Vikings set sail from Scandinavia to trade, and also to raid the coasts of Europe. Armed with fearsome iron swords and axes, they looted towns, seized land, and took captives.

○ GARDEN OF CULTURE

Tivoli pleasure gardens in Copenhagen provide the venue for open-air theaters, pavilions, and a concert hall. In daylight, the flowerbeds are a sea of color while at night, colored floodlights and firework displays brighten the sky.

○ ST LUCY'S DAY

In Sweden, where northern winters are dark and long, it is small wonder that people like to honor St Lucy, a Christian saint associated with light. Her feast day falls on December 13th. Girls dress in white and wear a crown of fairy lights or candles.

They sailed westward to settle Iceland and Greenland, and even discovered North America. They founded new states in Russia and traded with the Arabs in the Middle East. By the 1100s the Viking homelands had become Christian kingdoms, which grew rich by trading in fish, timber, and furs.

In 1397 Sweden was united with Norway and Denmark by the Union of Kalmar. Sweden broke away in 1523 and over the next two centuries became a powerful nation. Norway regained independence in 1905 and Iceland in 1944. Finland was ruled by Russia from 1809 to 1917. After World War II (1939–45), Europe's far north enjoyed peace and increasing prosperity under a series of liberal governments. Most Scandinavian Christians are Protestants.

○ CLEAN DESIGN

Scandinavian design is admired around the world for its unfussy look. This chair by Esko Pajamies was inspired by the renowned Finn, Alvar Aalto (1898–1976).

TIMELINE

AD

c.200	Germanic tribes control most of Scandinavia; Finns settle Finland
c.750	The Viking age (until c.1100): overseas raids, trade, settlement
872	King Harald Finehair of Norway conquers Scandinavia
874	Norwegian Vikings settle Iceland
930	Establishment of Althing, one of the world's oldest parliaments, in Iceland
982	Danes colonize Greenland
1397	Union of Kalmar unites mainland Scandinavia under Danish rule
1523	Sweden leaves the Union
1540	Sweden rules Finland (until 1809)
1618	Thirty Years' War (until 1648): Scandinavia supports Protestants
1700	Great Northern War (until 1721): Sweden invades Russia, but is defeated
1809	Russia rules Finland (until 1917)
1905	Norway becomes independent
1919	Finland recognized as independent republic
1920	Iceland becomes independent
1939	World War II (until 1945): Germany invades Denmark and Norway; Sweden remains neutral; Finland invaded by Russia, allies itself to Germany in 1941
1944	Iceland becomes a republic
1973	Denmark joins EEC (later EU)
1994	Sweden and Finland vote to join EU; Norway votes against joining

THE LOW COUNTRIES

FACTS

BELGIUM
Royaume de Belgique –
Koninkrijk België
AREA: 11,783 sq mi.
POPULATION: 10.3 million
CAPITAL: Brussels
OTHER CITIES: Antwerp,
Ghent
HIGHEST POINT: Botrange
(2,276 ft)
OFFICIAL LANGUAGES:
Flemish, French
CURRENCY: Euro

LUXEMBOURG
Grand-Duché de Luxembourg
AREA: 999 sq mi.
POPULATION: 0.4 million
CAPITAL: Luxembourg City
OTHER CITIES: Esch-sur-
Alzette
HIGHEST POINT: Buurgplatz
(1,843 ft)
OFFICIAL LANGUAGES: French,
German, Letzebuergesch
CURRENCY: Euro

NETHERLANDS
Koninkrijk der Nederlanden
AREA: 15,770 sq mi.
POPULATION: 16 million
CAPITAL: Amsterdam
OTHER CITIES: Rotterdam,
the Hague
HIGHEST POINT: Vaalser Berg
(1,053 ft)
OFFICIAL LANGUAGE: Dutch
CURRENCY: Euro

The Netherlands, Belgium, and Luxembourg lie in northwestern Europe, between France and Germany. They mostly enjoy a mild and moist climate.

The sand dunes of the West Frisian islands and the North Sea coast fringe a low plain. For thousands of years these marshy lands were flooded by the great rivers that spill across them—the Rhine, Schelde, and Meuse—and by wind-whipped tides powering in from the sea. Over the centuries, the peoples of the lowlands learned to build sea and river defences—dykes, dams, and barriers. They also became expert at draining marshes and flooded land. The large windmills that powered the drainage pumps may still be seen in many places. Areas reclaimed from the sea, known as polders, now form wide areas of green farmland. A network of canals crosses the countryside.

◯ RIVER TOWN
On a wooded bend in the Sûre River, Luxembourg, is the old town of Esch-sur-Sûre, which attracts tourists and hikers.

To the south, the flat lands give way to sandy heaths and fertile plateaus, rising to the Ardennes. This wooded range of hills, some of which rise to over 1,970 feet, crosses southeastern Belgium, northern Luxembourg, and part of eastern France. Southern Luxembourg is taken up by rolling farmland, bordered by the Sûre and Moselle Rivers and crossed by the Alzette River.

◯ COPPER BUTTERFLY

◯ GRAY HERON

◐ DUTCH WINDMILL
As you cycle alongside Dutch canals, you are sure to see beautiful old windmills rising above the fields. Some are still in working order.

○ HOLDING BACK

At 20 miles long, the Afsluitdijk, between North Holland and Friesland, is the world's longest sea dam. Completed in 1935, it created a huge new lake, the Ijsselmeer.

BELGIUM

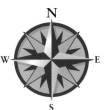

LUXEMBOURG

○ SPACE–AGE LANDMARK

The Atomium was built for the World Fair, held in Brussels in 1958. It was a symbol of scientific progress.

NETHERLANDS

Map labels

Westfriesische Inseln
Ameland
Terschelling
Vlieland
Westfriesische Inseln
Texel
Waddenzee
Barrier Dam
Leeuwarden
Groningen
Sneek
Assen
Emmen
Ijsselmeer
Nordoost-polder
Meppel
Alkmaar
Markermeer
Zwolle
Zaanstad
Flevoland Polder
Almelo
Haarlem
Amsterdam
NIEDERLANDE
Enschede
Hilversum
Leiden
Apeldoorn
Amersfoort
's-Gravenhage (Den Haag)
Gouda
Utrecht
Ijssel
Delft
Lek
Arnhem
Rotterdam
Waal
Nijmegen
Dordrecht
Maas
s'Hertogenbosch
DEUTSCHLAND
Oosterschelde
Breda
Tilburg
Vlissingen
Eindhoven
Westerschelde
Venlo
Zeebrugge
Ostend
Bruges
Antwerpen
Sint-Niklaas
Genk
Gent
Mechelen
Roeslare
Hasselt
Heerlen
Kortrijk
Brussel/Bruxelles (Brüssel)
Aalst
Leuven (Louvain)
Maastricht
Schelde
Waterloo
Liège (Lüttich)
Vaalserberg 321 m
BELGIEN
Verviers
Tournai
La Louvière
Namur
Huy
Meuse
Spa
Botrange 694 m
Mons
Sambre
Charleroi
ARDENNEN
FRANKREICH
Dinant
Buurgplatz 559 m
DEUTSCHLAND
Bastogne
Libramont
LUXEMBURG
Letzebuerg/Luxembourg/ Luxemburg
Esch-sur-Alzette

○ THE AMSTEL RIVER

Amsterdam is the capital city of the Netherlands. It lies on the Amstel River, which has been channeled into canals to prevent flooding.

○ THE GRAND-PLACE

At the heart of Brussels, the Belgian capital, is the Grand-Place. Here, flower-sellers display their wares. Every other year a special floral display is held and the square is carpeted with begonias.

Belgium, the Netherlands, and Luxembourg are all small countries lying in a densely populated part of northern Europe. Together they are sometimes referred to as Benelux, the name of an economic union they formed in 1948. In 1957 the same three countries went on to become founder members of the European Economic Community (EEC), the ancestor of today's European Union (EU). All three are democracies. The Netherlands and Belgium are kingdoms, while Luxembourg is a grand duchy.

◯ MELT IN THE MOUTH
Belgium is famous for its luxurious chocolates. Each truffle is handmade, using the finest cocoa.

◯ LIGHT BULBS
Eindhoven is a major industrial center in the central southern Netherlands. It is dominated by Phillips, a Dutch-founded multinational firm that specializes in electrical goods for the home and in electronic technology.

The two most populous provinces of the Netherlands are North and South Holland, and the whole country is often referred to as Holland. The capital is Amsterdam, an old trading port where tall merchants' houses from the 1600s line the canals. It is a center of business and the arts, with a lively youth culture. The government sits at The Hague.

◯ TRAMS IN AMSTERDAM
Amsterdam's trams speed across the old city, crossing rings of canals. They connect Central Station, Dam Square, the old Mint, and the shops of Vijzelstraat, among other important sites.

The Netherlands is a wealthy country. It produces beers, vegetables, and dairy products, and is particularly well known for its cheeses. The fields are brightly colored with tulips in the spring. Bulbs and cut flowers are important exports.

◯ BELGIAN LACEMAKER
A Belgian lacemaker in traditional dress skillfully moves bobbins across a pillow. Cities such as Bruges have been famous for their lace since medieval times.

◯ BRUGES
Known as "the Venice of the north," the port of Bruges in northern Belgium has many picturesque canals and a thriving tourist industry.

○ BELGIAN BEER

Belgium grows more than 400 tons of barley every year. Much of it goes to the brewing industry.

○ ROTTERDAM PORT

Rotterdam, in the Dutch province of South Holland, was destroyed by bombing during World War II (1939–45). It was rebuilt and today is Europe's most important seaport.

○ TULIP BULBS

In spring, when the tulips are blooming, the Dutch bulb fields take on the appearance of a child's coloring book. The Dutch passion for tulips dates back to the 1500s.

The industrial south produces household and electrical goods. Rotterdam is the world's busiest seaport, sprawling across a vast area of 40 sq miles.

○ EUROPE UNITED

Luxembourg City is home to the EU Parliament and Court of Justice. The flags of EU members fly outside.

Belgium has been famous for its cloth since the Middle Ages and is still a major textile producer. It manufactures steel and chemicals, but coal mining is no longer the great industry it once was. Popular food products include beers, chocolates, and cooked meats from the Ardennes. The Belgian capital is Brussels—the chief administrative center of the EU.

Tiny Luxembourg is home to both the European Parliament and the European Court of Justice. In terms of income per head, it is the world's richest country. Its wealth comes from banking and finance. Wine-making is also important.

Most people in the Netherlands are Dutch, and the Dutch language is spoken everywhere. The Frisians, who live in the north and on the offshore islands, also speak their own language. Many Dutch cities are home to people whose ancestors

VINCENT VAN GOGH
The Dutch artist Vincent van Gogh painted this self-portrait after cutting off part of his ear. His landscapes and still-life paintings display the same boldness and original use of color.

THE BIG RACE
The Elfstedentocht, or 11 Towns' Tour, dates back to the 1600s. At 124 miles, it is the longest ice-skating race in the world. It is also the biggest, with as many as 16,000 competitors. The race is normally held in the Netherlands, but if the weather is too warm, it is held somewhere else.

came from countries formerly ruled by Holland, such as Surinam and the Dutch East Indies (now Indonesia), as well as workers from other parts of Europe.

The two peoples native to Belgium are the Flemings of the north, who in their language and customs are very close relatives of the Dutch, and the French-speaking Walloons of the south. There have been violent clashes between the two communities over language and culture. French and German are widely spoken in Luxembourg, along with a local language called Letzebuergesch.

A TRADING EMPIRE
The Dutch East India Company was founded in 1602. Its ships sailed to the Dutch East Indies (now Indonesia) to buy coffee, tea, and spices. On the way, the merchants would stop off at the Cape of Good Hope in southern Africa to stock up on supplies for their voyage.

In ancient times, this region of northern Europe was occupied by both Germanic and Celtic peoples, and lay on the edge of the Roman empire. In the 700s and 800s, it became part of the Frankish empire. During the Middle Ages, rule passed from one family of European nobles to another. As wars of religion tore Europe apart in the 1500s, the Protestant Dutch fought against rule by Roman Catholic Spain. By the 1600s the Netherlands was a wealthy, independent sea power, trading with the Far East. The year 1806 saw the region under French rule, but independence was soon restored.

GOUDA CHEESES
Round, yellow Dutch cheeses are laid out and weighed at Alkmaar in North Holland—a glimpse of tradition that is always popular with the many tourists that visit the area.

LANGUAGE RIGHTS DEMONSTRATION
Language rights are a live political issue in Belgium. The Flemings of the north speak Vlaams or Flemish, a dialect of Dutch. The Walloons of the south are French-speakers.

☉ SOCCER CRAZY
Dutch soccer teams, such as Ajax, have won fans all over Europe and the national team is always a major contender in World Cup events.

Belgium broke away from the Netherlands in 1830, and Luxembourg in 1867.

Since the Middle Ages, the region has been a center of scholarship and the arts. Famous philosophers included Erasmus (1466–1536) and Spinoza (1632–77), while great painters included Pieter Breughel (c.1520–69), Rembrandt van Rijn (1606–69), Vincent van Gogh (1863–90), and Piet Mondrian (1872–1944).

☉ ANNE FRANK
Anne Frank (1929–45) was a young Jewish girl who spent two years living in a secret annexe in this house in Amsterdam, when the Germans occupied the Netherlands. In 1944 her family was discovered and deported. Anne died in a concentration camp. Her moving diary of the time spent in hiding has been published in at least 50 languages.

TIMELINE

AD

c.50	River Rhine becomes border of Roman empire
714	Franks rule most of Low Countries
922	Counts of Holland rule Low Countries (until 1384)
963	Luxembourg part of Holy Roman Empire
1384	Burgundy rules Low Countries and Luxembourg (until 1487)
1519	Low Countries part of Habsburg empire
1568	Start of Eighty Years' War against Spanish rule in Netherlands; Belgium remains Spanish
1602	Founding of Dutch East India Company
1648	Netherlands recognized as independent
1700	France rules Belgium (until 1713)
1713	Austria rules Belgium (until 1789)
1795	France rules Low Countries (until 1815)
1815	United Kingdom of the Netherlands
1830	Belgium breaks away from the Netherlands
1867	Luxembourg independent under Dutch monarch
1890	Luxembourg has its own grand duke
1914	World War I (until 1918): Germany invades Belgium; Netherlands neutral
1939	World War II (until 1945): Germany invades Belgium and Netherlands
1948	Benelux economic union formed
1957	Belgium, Netherlands, Luxembourg founder members of EEC (later EU)

THE
BRITISH ISLES

FACTS

UNITED KINGDOM
United Kingdom of Great Britain
and Northern Ireland
AREA: 94,251 sq mi.
POPULATION: 58.8 million
CAPITAL: London
HIGHEST POINT: Ben Nevis
(4,408 ft)
OFFICIAL LANGUAGES: English,
Welsh
CURRENCY: Pound sterling

REPUBLIC OF IRELAND
Eire
AREA: 27,137 sq mi.
POPULATION: 3.8 million
CAPITAL: Dublin
OTHER CITIES: Cork,
Limerick
HIGHEST POINT:
Carrauntoohil (3,414 ft)
OFFICIAL LANGUAGES: Irish,
English
CURRENCY: Euro

The British Isles rise from a continental shelf, an underwater ledge of land extending into the Atlantic Ocean from northwestern Europe. They include about 5,000 small islands and two large ones, Great Britain and Ireland. Warm ocean currents keep the climate moderate, with winds bringing the heaviest rainfall to western coasts. The British Isles are occupied by two nations, the United Kingdom (a union of England, Scotland, Wales, and Northern Ireland) and the Republic of Ireland.

Southern England includes low chalk hills and plains of fertile clay. The River Thames flows into the North Sea, to the south of the flat lands of East Anglia. The rugged peninsula of Cornwall extends southwest toward the Scilly Isles. Northern England includes bleak moors rising to the Pennines—a chain of low mountains—and the Lake District of Cumbria.

To the west, Wales is a country of hills, green valleys, and mountains, bordering the Irish Sea. Across the Scottish border lie fertile lowlands, the island's highest mountain chains, and lakes known as "lochs." Scotland is fringed by the island chains of the Hebrides, Shetlands, and Orkneys.

Ireland is a land of lakes, river estuaries, peat bogs, and green farmland rising to low mountain chains. In the west, tall cliffs and long, sandy beaches meet the Atlantic breakers.

✪ LOCHS AND ISLES
This castle lies on a tiny island in the middle of Loch Linnhe, on the west coast of Scotland, just south of Ben Nevis.

✪ BLUEBELL WOODS
In early May, large areas of woodland in the British Isles are carpeted with sweetly scented wild flowers—bluebells.

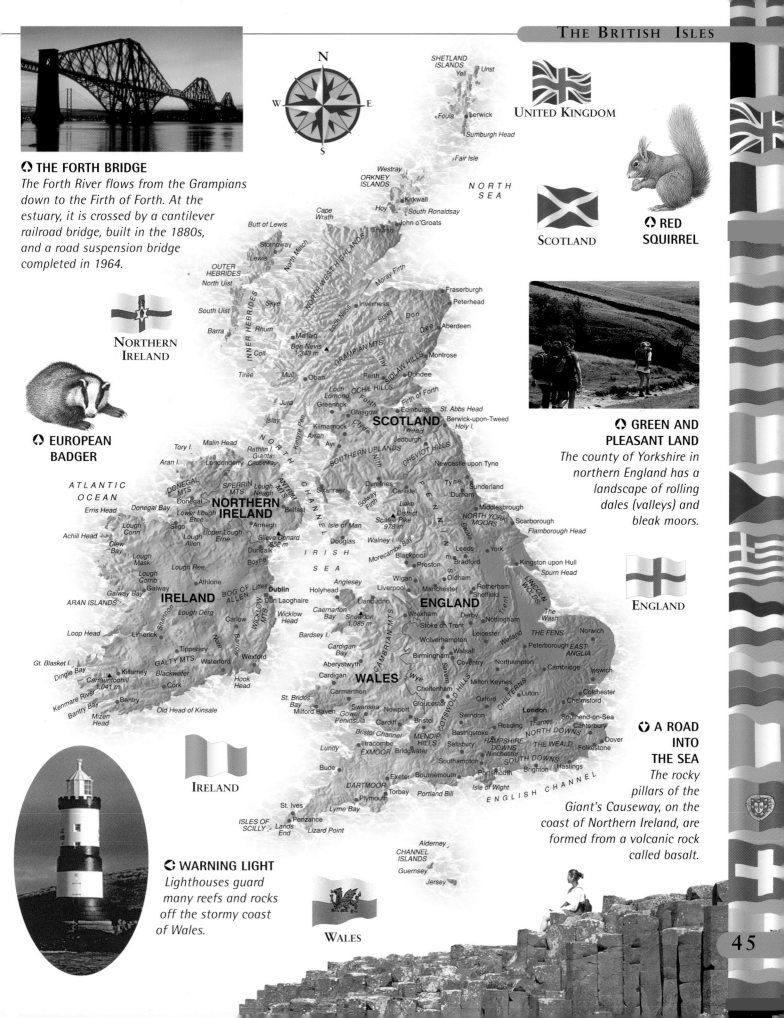

○ THE FORTH BRIDGE
The Forth River flows from the Grampians down to the Firth of Forth. At the estuary, it is crossed by a cantilever railroad bridge, built in the 1880s, and a road suspension bridge completed in 1964.

UNITED KINGDOM

SCOTLAND

○ RED SQUIRREL

NORTHERN IRELAND

○ EUROPEAN BADGER

○ GREEN AND PLEASANT LAND
The county of Yorkshire in northern England has a landscape of rolling dales (valleys) and bleak moors.

ENGLAND

IRELAND

○ A ROAD INTO THE SEA
The rocky pillars of the Giant's Causeway, on the coast of Northern Ireland, are formed from a volcanic rock called basalt.

○ WARNING LIGHT
Lighthouses guard many reefs and rocks off the stormy coast of Wales.

WALES

Map labels:
SHETLAND ISLANDS, Yell, Unst, Foula, Lerwick, Sumburgh Head, Fair Isle, Westray, ORKNEY ISLANDS, Kirkwall, Hoy, South Ronaldsay, John o'Groats, Cape Wrath, Thurso, Butt of Lewis, Stornoway, Lewis, North Minch, OUTER HEBRIDES, North Uist, NORTH-WEST HIGHLANDS, Moray Firth, Fraserburgh, Peterhead, Inverness, Loch Ness, Spey, Don, Dee, Aberdeen, South Uist, Skye, Barra, Rhum, Mallaig, Coll, Ben Nevis 1,343 m, GRAMPIAN MTS., Tay, Montrose, Tiree, Mull, Oban, Perth, SIDLAW HILLS, Dundee, Loch Lomond, OCHIL HILLS, Firth of Forth, Jura, Greenock, Forth, Edinburgh, St. Abbs Head, Islay, Glasgow, SCOTLAND, Berwick-upon-Tweed, Holy I., Kilmarnock, Clyde, Tweed, Kintyre Pen., Arran, Jedburgh, CHEVIOT HILLS, Tory I., Malin Head, Ayr, SOUTHERN UPLANDS, Newcastle upon Tyne, Aran I., Londonderry, Rathlin I., Giants Causeway, NORTH CHANNEL, ANTRIM MTS., Stranraer, Dumfries, Tyne, Sunderland, DONEGAL MTS., SPERRIN MTS., Lough Neagh, Carlisle, Durham, Donegal, NORTHERN IRELAND, Belfast, Solway Firth, Middlesbrough, ATLANTIC OCEAN, Lower Lough Erne, Sligo, Armagh, IRISH CHANNEL, Lake District, NORTH YORK MOORS, Scarborough, Erris Head, Donegal Bay, Lough Conn, Upper Lough Erne, Slieve Donard 852 m, Isle of Man, Scafell Pike 978 m, Swale, Flamborough Head, Achill Head, Clew Bay, Lough Allen, Dundalk, Douglas, Walney I., IRISH SEA, Morecambe Bay, Leeds, York, Lough Mask, Lough Ree, Boyne, Blackpool, Preston, Bradford, Kingston upon Hull, Lough Corrib, Galway, Athlone, Anglesey, Wigan, Liverpool, Manchester, Oldham, Rotherham, Sheffield, Spurn Head, Galway Bay, BOG OF ALLEN, Liffey, Dublin, Holyhead, Llandudno, LINCOLN WOLDS, ARAN ISLANDS, IRELAND, Dún Laoghaire, WICKLOW MTS., Caernarfon Bay, Snowdon 1,085 m, ENGLAND, Wrexham, Derby, Nottingham, The Wash, Loop Head, Lough Derg, Carlow, Wicklow Head, Stoke on Trent, Leicester, Welland, Norwich, Limerick, Nore, Barrow, Bardsey I., CAMBRIAN MTS., Wolverhampton, THE FENS, Tipperary, Birmingham, Walsall, Peterborough, EAST ANGLIA, Gt. Blasket I., GALTY MTS., Waterford, Wexford, Cardigan Bay, Coventry, Northampton, Cambridge, Ipswich, Dingle Bay, Carrauntoohill 1,041 m, Killarney, Blackwater, Hook Head, Aberystwyth, Milton Keynes, Kenmare River, Cork, Cardigan, WALES, Wye, Cheltenham, COTSWOLD HILLS, Oxford, CHILTERNS, Luton, Colchester, Bantry, Carmarthen, Gloucester, Swindon, London, Chelmsford, Bantry Bay, St. Brides Bay, Swansea, Newport, Bristol, Reading, Thames, Southend-on-Sea, Mizen Head, Milford Haven, Gower Peninsula, Cardiff, Bristol Channel, Basingstoke, NORTH DOWNS, Canterbury, Lundy, MENDIP HILLS, Salisbury, HAMPSHIRE DOWNS, THE WEALD, Dover, Ilfracombe, Bridgwater, Winchester, SOUTH DOWNS, Folkestone, EXMOOR, Southampton, Portsmouth, Brighton, Hastings, Bude, DARTMOOR, Exeter, Bournemouth, Isle of Wight, ENGLISH CHANNEL, Plymouth, Torbay, Portland Bill, St. Ives, Lyme Bay, ISLES OF SCILLY, Penzance, Lands End, Lizard Point, Alderney, CHANNEL ISLANDS, Guernsey, Jersey

The United Kingdom (UK) brings together the two kingdoms of England and Scotland, the principality of Wales, and the province of Northern Ireland. All are ruled by a single monarch and have a long history of democracy. In 1997 both Wales and Scotland voted to have their own parliaments.

◑ CROWN JEWELS
The Crown Jewels of the British kings and queens include a dazzling array of gold and precious stones dating back over 1,000 years.

The UK is a member of the European Union (EU). The Isle of Man and the Channel Islands are self-ruling states associated with the UK.

◑ PEAT BOG
Over many thousands of years, large peat bogs have formed in Ireland. This waterlogged turf is cut and dried for fuel in the home and for use in power stations.

The most densely populated area of the UK centers around the capital, London, in southeast England. London is home to about 6.8 million people. On the south coast, a rail tunnel links England with northern France. Other large industrial cities are found in the Midlands and the north. The traditional industries of these regions—coal, textiles, and shipbuilding—have all declined. The economy today is based on finance, services, chemicals, and telecommunications.

Wales is sheep-farming country. The capital, Cardiff, is in the industrialized south, where foreign-owned factories produce goods such as electronic components.

◑ BLACKPOOL LIGHTS
England's most popular seaside resort is Blackpool, on the northwest coast of Lancashire in northern England. Its attractions include the Blackpool Tower, the famous illuminations (lights) and many amusement parks.

◐ LIVERPOOL SKYLINE
Liverpool is a lively city on the River Mersey, in northwest England. During the 1800s and early 1900s it was one of the busiest seaports in the world.

◑ PRIME BEEF
The Aberdeen Angus is a breed of cattle from northeast Scotland, prized for its meat. Its long coat protects it from the cold.

⟳ SCOTTISH TRAWLERS
At Mallaig harbor in Scotland, fishing boats return to unload the day's catch. Scottish trawlers bring in over 65 percent of all the fish and shellfish caught in the United Kingdom.

⟳ ALL ABOARD!
Southern England and northern France, separated by the waters of the Channel about 10,000 years ago, were linked by a rail tunnel in 1994.

The Scottish capital is the city of Edinburgh. Heavy industry has always been based around Glasgow and the River Clyde. The most important resource is oil, drilled from under the North Sea. Important exports include salmon and Scotch whisky.

Northern Ireland has the industrial city of Belfast as its capital. The province has seen long years of conflict between those who wish to remain within the UK and those who wish to be part of the Republic of Ireland. A 1998 peace agreement set up a devolved Northern Ireland assembly.

The capital of the Republic of Ireland is Dublin, on the River Liffey. Ireland's green fields are ideal for dairy farming, while the coasts and rivers provide fishing. Ireland's industries include brewing, glass-making, and computer manufacture. With a long history of poverty, the Irish economy has been transformed in recent years by membership of the EU.

⟳ MILKING TIME
A cow is milked by hand on a small farm in Ireland. Irish dairy products include delicious butter and cheeses.

⟳ SALMON LEAP
Scotland is famous for its freshwater fish. Wild salmon head upriver each year to their spawning grounds.

FACTS

ENGLAND
AREA: 50,332 sq mi.
CAPITAL: London
OTHER CITIES: Birmingham, Manchester, Liverpool

NORTHERN IRELAND
AREA: 5,463 sq mi.
CAPITAL: Belfast
OTHER CITIES: Derry, Armagh

SCOTLAND
AREA: 30,406 sq mi.
CAPITAL: Edinburgh
OTHER CITIES: Glasgow, Aberdeen

WALES
AREA: 8,015 sq mi.
CAPITAL: Cardiff
OTHER CITIES: Swansea, Wrexham, Bangor

SELF-GOVERNING ISLANDS
Isle of Man, Guernsey (with six dependencies), Jersey

◑ GODDESS OF THE CELTS

The Irish have a strong tradition of story-telling. Many myths date back to the days of the Celts. This statue shows the Celtic horse goddess, Epona, who was worshiped in Europe about 400 BC.

◑ GLOBE THEATER

The Globe was originally built in 1599, on the south bank of the River Thames in London. Many of Shakespeare's plays were first performed there. Now a new Globe has been built.

The English are descended from the many different peoples who settled in the southern part of the United Kingdom over the ages—British Celts, Germanic peoples such as the Angles, Saxons, and Danes, and French-speaking Normans. The English language developed from Anglo-Saxon, but includes many words based on Latin and Norman French. It is the language of some of the world's greatest works of literature, such as the plays of William Shakespeare (1564–1616) and the poetry of John Keats (1795–1821).

The Welsh and Cornish are mostly the descendants of British Celts and are closely related to the Bretons. They have their own languages. Welsh is spoken by about half a million people in Wales and has a literature dating back about 1,400 years. Festivals of music and poetry called *eisteddfodau* are held throughout Wales, where there is a strong tradition of choral singing.

Scots are descended from both Gaelic and British Celts, from a people called the Picts, and from Norse invaders. The Scottish version of the Gaelic language may still be heard in the Highlands and islands, while the Anglo-Scots dialect of the Lowlands was the language of Scotland's national poet Robert Burns (1759–96).

◑ A HINDU TEMPLE

Britain has many Hindu and Sikh temples, Islamic mosques, and Jewish synagogues in addition to its Christian churches.

◑ THE GAME OF CRICKET

The game of cricket was invented in England in the 1700s. It spread from there to Australia, New Zealand, India, Pakistan, South Africa, and the Caribbean.

◑ NATIONAL FLOWERS

Each country in the British Isles has its own national flower. There are the Scottish thistle (1), the Irish shamrock (2), the Welsh daffodil (3), and the English rose (4).

(1)

(2)

◐ TOWERING ANGEL
Unveiled by artist Antony Gormley in 1998, the much-loved Angel of the North rises 65 feet into the sky. It is the largest sculpture in Britain.

◑ WELSH ARTS FESTIVALS
At an eisteddfod, poets, musicians, dancers, and actors of all ages compete in front of judges for honors.

The Manx people from the Isle of Man, which lies midway between England, Ireland, Scotland, and Wales, are of mixed Celtic and Norse descent, while the Channel Islanders have English, Norman, and French roots.

The Irish are mostly descended from Gaelic Celts, along with some Viking, Norman, English, and Scottish ancestry. The Irish language, a version of Gaelic, is still spoken in some rural areas. Irish authors and poets have used both the Irish and English languages to great effect.

Many other peoples have settled the British Isles over the ages, contributing to the richness and variety of its culture. They include Roma (gypsies), Jews, Italians, Greek and Turkish Cypriots, Afro-Caribbeans, Chinese, Indians, Pakistanis, and Bangladeshis.

◑ COWES WEEK
Cowes, on the Isle of Wight off southern England, is the setting for an annual yacht race, the Fastnet Cup.

◑ MANX CAT
The Manx is a tailless breed of cat from the Isle of Man.

◑ CHINATOWN
Chinese people see in the Chinese New Year in style. Cities such as London, Liverpool, and Manchester all have lively Chinese districts.

(3)   *(4)*

49

About 2,000 years ago, most of Great Britain was occupied by a group of Celtic tribes—the Britons. Picts lived in parts of Scotland, while Ireland was the home of another Celtic group, the Gaels. The Romans invaded in 55 BC and 54 BC and again from AD 43. They failed to conquer the far north and Ireland, but stayed for nearly 400 years.

☼ SACRED STONES
Massive stones, lined up with the midsummer sunrise, were raised at Stonehenge in southern England between about 3200 and 2000 BC.

After the Romans left, the Britons came under attack from the west by groups of Gaels known as Scots, and from the south and east by Angles and Saxons—Germanic peoples who founded a number of small kingdoms that later became England.

☼ THE BAYEUX TAPESTRY
In 1066 William, Duke of Normandy, defeated King Harold of England near Hastings. The story of the Norman invasion was recorded in the Bayeux Tapestry.

☼ WARRIOR QUEEN
Boudicca was queen of a Celtic tribe called the Iceni. In AD 60 she led an uprising against the Roman conquerors of Britain. She captured London, but was then defeated in battle and killed herself.

Gradually the Britons were driven into Wales, Cornwall, and across the Channel to Brittany. Wales, Scotland, and Ireland flourished as centers of Celtic Christian civilization. Large areas of Britain and Ireland were later invaded by Vikings and then by Normans. The Norman kingdom founded in England in 1066 became very powerful, ruling large parts of France.

Wales was formally annexed by England in the 1500s, and the Scottish and English thrones were united in 1603. The United Kingdom, largely Protestant, tightened its grip on Roman Catholic Ireland, which was made part of the union in 1800.

☼ EDINBURGH CASTLE
Edinburgh, the Scottish capital, was settled over 5,000 years ago. In 1997 the Scots voted to have their own parliament, based in Edinburgh.

By this time, the United Kingdom was becoming the world's first industrialized nation. It ruled a vast overseas empire, from India to Africa and Australia, which gave it raw materials and new markets. Not until the 20th century did the power of the British empire begin to fade, exhausted by two world wars (1914–18 and 1939–45).

◑ TUDOR KING
Henry VIII (1491–1547) was the second Tudor king of England. He made himself head of the Church in England, and married six times.

◐ DEATH OF A KING
In 1649 the whole of Europe was shocked when Parliament ordered the execution of King Charles I, after the English Civil War. Britain returned to being a monarchy in 1660, when Charles II was restored to the throne.

Southern Ireland became a Free State in 1922 and a fully independent republic in 1949.

During the 1960s, most of Britain's remaining colonies became independent, as Commonwealth members. By 2000, the UK and Irish Republic had moved closer to their European trade partners, within the expanding European Union.

◑ POWER TO THE NORTH
After nearly 30 years of communal strife in Northern Ireland, a peace agreement in 1998 devolved power to a new Assembly, with members from Unionist and Nationalist parties.

◑ EAMON DE VALERA
Eamon de Valera (1882–1975) took part in the Easter Rising in Dublin in 1916. He later became President of the Irish Republic.

◑ DOMESDAY BOOK
In 1086 King William I (c. 1028–87) ordered a great survey of people and property in the lands he had conquered 20 years earlier. It was used for legal and taxation purposes until 1522.

TIMELINE

AD

43	Roman occupation of Britain (until 446)
795	Start of Viking raids on British Isles
844	Kenneth MacAlpin unites the Picts and the Scots
1066	Norman invasion of England
1175	England claims Ireland
1284	England conquers Wales
1338	Hundred Years' War (until 1453) between England and France
1536	(and 1542) Acts of Union, England–Wales
1603	Scotland and England unite under one monarch
1649	Republican commonwealth until 1660
1707	Act of Union, England–Scotland
1776	American colonies declare independence
1801	Act of Union, Great Britain–Ireland
1914	World War I (until 1918): against Central powers (including Germany and Austria)
1917	Easter Rising, Ireland
1922	Irish Free State (republic 1949)
1939	World War II (until 1945): against Axis powers (including Germany and Japan)
1973	UK and Ireland join EEC (later EU)
1997	Scots and Welsh vote for own devolved parliaments
1998	Northern Ireland Assembly set up
2003	UK allies with USA to invade Iraq and overthrow dictator Saddam Hussein

FRANCE

FACTS

FRANCE
République Française
AREA: 212,936 sq mi.
POPULATION: 59 million
CAPITAL: Paris
OTHER CITIES: Marseille, Lyon
HIGHEST POINT: Mont Blanc (15,770 ft)
OFFICIAL LANGUAGE: French
CURRENCY: Euro

MONACO
Principauté de Monaco
AREA: 0.75 sq mi.
POPULATION: 0.03 million
CAPITAL: Monaco
OTHER CITIES: Monte Carlo
OFFICIAL LANGUAGE: French
CURRENCY: Euro

France lies at the center of western Europe, between Germany and Spain. To the north it is bordered by the sandy shores and chalk cliffs of the Channel coast and the rocky headlands of Brittany. In the southwest, pine forests and dunes face the stormy Atlantic Ocean. The sun-baked hills of southern France descend to the Mediterranean Sea.

Along the Spanish border, the snowy peaks of the Pyrenees form a high barrier. The Alps, which straddle the border with Italy and Switzerland, soar to 15,770 feet at Mont Blanc. Northward lie the forested slopes of the Jura, Vosges, and Ardennes.

✪ CITY OF ARTISTS
The Montmartre district of the French capital, Paris, is famed for its street artists.

Most of northern France is a rolling plain, now cultivated. It is crossed by the winding River Seine. The volcanic rocks of the Massif Central dominate south-central France, to the west of the Rhône valley. The River Rhône flows south to form a delta on the southern coast, creating the wetland region of the Camargue. The Mediterranean island of Corsica is also French territory. It is mountainous, with olive groves and dry scrubland, called maquis.

Monaco is a tiny state on the Mediterranean coast, surrounded by France. It is a built-up zone, which includes new land reclaimed from the sea.

✪ WATER CARRIER
The Pont du Gard aqueduct in southern France was built 2,000 years ago by the Romans to carry water to the city of Nîmes.

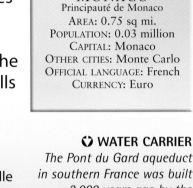

✪ ISLAND OF THE MONKS
Mont-Saint-Michel is linked to the Normandy coast by a tidal causeway. Crowning the island is a Benedictine abbey, built in AD 966 and fortified by thick walls.

A SNOWY PEAK
Mont Blanc in the Alps is western Europe's tallest mountain. A 7.5-mile-long road tunnel was dug beneath the mountain in the 1960s.

ESTEREL, SOUTHERN FRANCE
The southern coast of France borders the Mediterranean. The inviting blue waters and sunny climates make the coast a popular tourist destination.

WILD BOAR

FRANCE

INSECT-EATER
The hoopoe, with its striking crest, is found in southern Europe. Its curved bill is tailor-made for teasing out insects from the bark of trees.

Map labels

Dunkerque, Calais, Boulogne, Lille, BELGIUM, Montreuil, Arras, Douai, LUXEMBOURG, Abbeville, Valenciennes, Cambrai, Dieppe, St. Quentin, Hirson, Charleville-Mézières, GERMANY, Cherbourg, Fécamp, Bolbec, Amiens, Montdidier, Compiègne, Reims, Verdun, Metz, Bay of the Seine, Le Havre, Rouen, Beauvais, Châlons-sur-Marne, Meuse, Pont à Mousson, Carentan, Caen, Louviers, Evreux, Meaux, Paris, Marne, Nancy, Strasbourg, St. Lô, Lisieux, Argentan, St. Germain-en-Laye, Versailles, St. Dizier, Toul, Moselle, Gulf of St-Malo, Granville, Rambouillet, Fontainebleau, VOSGES, Epinal, Colmar, Morlaix, St.-Malo, Dinan, Alençan, Chartres, Nemours, Sens, Troyes, Langres, Rhine, Mulhouse, Brest, St-Brieuc, Fougeres, Mayenne, Laval, Orléans, Montargis, Auxerre, LANGRES PLATEAU, Montbéliard, Douernenez, Quimper, Pontivy, Rennes, Vitre, Le Mans, Gien, Avallon, Dijon, Besançon, SWITZERLAND, Lorient, Vannes, Redon, Angers, Tours, Blois, Vierzon, Loire, Autun, Dôle, Doubs, JURA, St. Nazaire, Belle-Ile, Nantes, Saumur, Châtellerault, Cher, Bourges, Nevers, Le Creusot, Pontarlier, Chalon-sur-Saône, La Roche-sur-Yon, Isle d'Yeu, Poiters, Châteauroux, La Châtre, Moulins, Montceau les Mines, St.Claude, Les Sables-d'Olonne, Niort, Montluçon, Mâcon, Saône, Ré I., La Rochelle, Rochefort, Oléron I., Civray, FRANCE, Vichy, Bourg-en-Bresse, Annecy, Cognac, Angoulême, Limoges, Clermont-Ferrand, Villefranches, Chamonix, Mont Blanc 4,807m, Royan, Nontron, Puy de Sancy 1,886m, MASSIF CENTRAL, St.-Etienne, Lyon, Villeurbanne, Chambéry, Val d'Isère, Pauillac, Barbezieux, Périgueux, Annonay, Vienne, Grenoble, Libourne, Bergerac, Souillac, Aurillac, Cère, Romans-sur-Isère, Valence, Bordeaux, Dordogne, Lot, Privas, Montélimar, Gap, Durance, Marmande, Rodez, Mende, Montélimar, Cère, Cahors, Aveyron, Millau, CÉVENNES, Carpentras, ITALY, LES LANDES, Agen, Gaillac, Albi, Tarn, Alès, Avignon, Monte-de-Marsan, Montauban, Nîmes, Arles, Nice, MONACO, Bayonne, Toulouse, Castres, Montpellier, Aix-en-Provence, Cannes, Biarritz, Pau, Auch, Garonne, Sète, Marseille, Brignoles, St.Raphael, St.Tropez, Côte d'Azur, Tarbes, Carcassonne, Aude, Béziers, Toulon, Lourdes, St. Gaudens, Foix, Narbonne, PYRENEES, Ariège, Perpignan, SPAIN, ANDORRA

Inset map
Cape Corse, Bastia, CORSICA, Gulf of Sagone, Ajaccio, Bonifacio, Strait of Bonifacio

MONACO

THE LAP OF LUXURY
One of the world's smallest countries, Monaco, attracts very wealthy visitors. The port of its capital, Monaco, is crammed with luxury yachts from around the world.

LOIRE RIVER
Straddling the Loire is the castle, or château, of Chenonceaux. The Loire is France's longest river. It stretches for about 630 miles from the Cévennes Mountains to the coast of Brittany.

France is a democratic republic and a founder member of the European Economic Community (EEC), now the European Union (EU). It is one of the world's wealthier countries, and through its former overseas colonies, still has considerable international influence.

The capital, Paris, has a metropolitan population of over nine million people. It is in the center of northern France, on the River Seine. France's second city is Marseille, a large seaport on the coast of the Mediterranean Sea. The country is divided into 22 regions.

The coalfields of northern France have mostly run out. To generate power for industry, France depends heavily on nuclear power and hydroelectric schemes. Alternative energy sources that are harnessed include the sun and tides. French factories produce chemicals, aircraft, cars, and high-speed trains.

Traditionally, France is an agricultural country, and many people across the region still work as farmers. Normandy produces apples and dairy products.

♦ FASHION CAPITAL
A model at the Chanel catwalk show in Paris. Chanel was founded by the great French couturier, Coco Chanel (1883–1971).

♦ SUNFLOWERS
In the fields of southern France, bright yellow sunflowers ripen in the sun. The seeds of the flowers are harvested and then pressed to make sunflower oil.

♦ CHAMPAGNE

♦ HIGH-SPEED TRAIN
The TGV (train à grande vitesse) is a feat of French engineering. This high-speed train can top 310 mph.

♦ FINE WINES
The region of Bordeaux produces some of the world's finest red wines. Many vineyards are attached to a stately home, or château, which gives the wine its name.

The wide range of climates makes it possible to grow many kinds of crops, from wheat and maize to rice.

The warm hillsides of Provence in southern France provide flowers for the perfume industry, particularly lavender. The Loire, Burgundy, and Champagne regions are renowned for their fine wines. Forests in many areas provide timber and there are large fishing fleets in the west.

French cooking is generally thought to produce some of the best dishes in the world—indeed, French is the language of cooking. The catwalks of Paris are the

C FATTENING UP

Pâté de foie gras is a rich pâté made from goose liver. The birds are fattened up on plenty of corn. Every region of France has its own pâté recipe.

○ SOFT CHEESES

ultimate achievement of any career as a fashion model. Tourists bring wealth to France too, visiting the Alpine ski resorts, the castles or châteaux of the Loire, and the beaches and yachting marinas of the south.

Although Monaco is such a small country, its tax laws attract many wealthy residents. It is a center of finance, tourism, and gambling, in the famous casino at Monte Carlo.

○ APPLES

In Normandy in northern France, farming is smallscale. Dairy farms and apple orchards predominate. The apples are used to make cider and calvados (apple brandy).

○ TIDAL BARRIER AT RANCE

France is a major exporter of electricity. Most is generated in nuclear power stations, but the French have also tried "greener" ways to make electricity. Here at St Malo, a massive tidal barrier harnesses the power of the River Rance.

○ INTO THE FUTURE

At Futuroscope, a theme park and high-tech college near Poitiers, French architects were given a free reign to create bold, imaginative designs for the 21st century.

C FAST CARS

Motor racing is an important source of income to Monaco. Each year, the Monaco Grand Prix is held, with cars racing around its narrow streets.

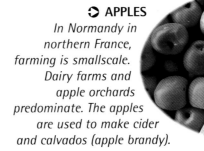

The French are descended from many different peoples, including the ancient group of Celtic tribes known as Gauls, and the Franks, a Germanic people. The French language mostly comes from Latin, the language of the Roman empire. It is spoken everywhere in France, although there are great historical differences between French as spoken in the north and the Provençal version of the south.

Since the Middle Ages, the French language has been celebrated by poets, playwrights, storytellers, and philosophers. France has also produced great philosophers, movie-makers, painters, and composers.

◑ FATHER OF COMEDY
Jean Baptiste Poquelin (1622–73) was known as Molière. Many of his plays were performed for King Louis XIV.

◐ ENLIGHTENED TIMES
During the 1700s, France was a center of learning. The writer Denis Diderot (1713–84) compiled a massive 28-volume encyclopedia, which aimed to further all knowledge.

Playwrights such as Corneille (1606–84), Molière (1622–73), and Racine (1639–99), painters such as Monet (1840–1926) and Dégas (1834–1917), and composers such as Debussy (1862–1918) are admired around the world.

Within the French borders there are other peoples besides the French. The Basques and Catalans of the southwest have their own languages and traditions. The homelands of both these peoples extend across the border into Spain. The Corsicans have their own language, and along the eastern borders there are speakers of Italian and German.

The Bretons of the northwest are descended from British Celts who settled the region about 1,500 years ago. Their language is related to Welsh and Cornish.

◖ SACRÉ COEUR
Overlooking the French capital, Paris, is the domed Roman Catholic church of Sacré Coeur ("sacred heart"). Although France does not have an official state religion, most French people follow the Catholic faith.

◑ UP, UP AND AWAY
The Montgolfier brothers, Joseph and Jacques, pioneered the use of hot-air balloons in the 1780s.

C A GAME OF BOWLS
Pétanque is a popular game played all over France; most towns have a square of gravel set aside for the game. Players aim to bowl their ball as close as possible to a smaller ball.

The Normans are descended from Viking (Norsemen) invaders, who settled in the region of northern France that became known as Normandy.

Also living in France there are Roma (gypsies) and Jews. North Africans, descended from the citizens of France's former colonies, make up three percent of the French population. Many of these are Muslim, but nine-out-of-ten French people are Roman Catholic.

A hundred years ago the French were mostly a nation of country-dwellers. Today nearly 75 percent of the population live in towns and cities, leaving many rural areas deserted or given over to holiday homes and tourism.

C THE NAUGHTY NINETIES
In the 1890s, Paris had a reputation for being a city of fun, wild dances such as the can-can, pretty girls, artists, and poets.

C TOUR DE FRANCE
Every year, France hosts the world's most famous cycle race, the Tour de France. The grueling course stretches for about 2,500 miles and takes about three weeks to complete.

C MILITARY TRAINING
France has a military tradition dating back to the Middle Ages. Most men must spend some time in the army doing military service.

C A TREASURE–TROVE OF ART
The Louvre museum, Paris, houses one of the world's greatest art collections. In the 1980s, a stunning pyramid of steel and glass was built at the entrance to the old museum.

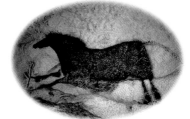

⟲ ICE AGE ART
There are about 600 cave paintings at Lascaux. They show the animals that prehistoric people hunted— bison, stags, and horses.

France has been inhabited since prehistoric times— cave paintings discovered at Lascaux date back to 15,000 BC. The ancient Greeks founded the port of Marseille in about 600 BC, when most of the country was home to a group of Celtic tribes known as the Gauls.

The Gauls were conquered by the Romans between 58 and 48 BC, and the Latin language became widely spoken. Germanic-speaking peoples from beyond the Rhine River began to attack the Roman empire, and by AD 476 it had collapsed. Power passed to the Franks, after whom the modern country is named.

⟲ STANDING STONES
Sited at Carnac, on the coast of Brittany, over 3,000 stone monuments are arranged in avenues and circles. They were erected in Stone Age times.

INTO BATTLE
Fierce Frankish armies defeated the Romans, Gauls, and Visigoths in their quest for land. By AD 540 they controlled most of Roman Gaul.

OFF WITH THEIR HEADS!
In the 1780s, the French people, tired of paying exorbitant taxes to their king, rose up in revolt. In the Reign of Terror that followed the Revolution, over 17,000 aristocrats were guillotined.

The Franks beat back invasion attempts by the Moors (Muslim Berbers and Arabs) and founded a great Western European empire under Charlemagne (768–814). Vikings took control of Normandy in 911, but the French kings became very powerful during the later Middle Ages. They battled with their neighbors, especially the English, and expanded the frontiers of their kingdom. From the Middle Ages until the death in 1715 of Louis XIV, the "Sun King," France was seen as the center of European civilization, despite a series of fierce religious wars.

⟲ BURNED AT THE STAKE
After hearing voices from God, Joan of Arc led the French into battle in the Hundred Years' War. The English burned her as a witch in 1431.

◑ MEDIEVAL FRANCE
A code of fine manners, known as chivalry, grew up in the castles and great houses of France in the Middle Ages.

◑ LOUIS XIV (1638–1715)
The "Sun King" ruled France for 72 years, during which time French power in Europe was at its height. He built the magnificent palace of Versailles near Paris.

◑ THE EMPEROR
From his revolutionary beginnings, Napoleon Bonaparte (1769–1821) became the most powerful ruler in Europe. He was a great soldier and law-maker.

◑ GENERAL DE GAULLE
Charles de Gaulle (1890–1970) led the French resistance to the Nazi occupation in World War II.

France began to build up a large empire overseas, but injustice at home led to the outbreak of the French Revolution in 1789. Out of the ruins of this dream of freedom arose a Corsican general named Napoleon Bonaparte, who was crowned emperor in 1804. He led brilliant military campaigns from Spain to Russia and Egypt, but was finally defeated by British and Prussian forces at Waterloo in 1815.

France then suffered a series of invasions by Germany—in 1870, in 1914, and in 1940. After World War II, France lost most of its overseas empire, but encouraged economic and political union in Western Europe.

◑ WE WILL REMEMBER THEM
To this day, the fields of northeastern France are planted with poppies in remembrance of the soldiers who died there in the trenches during World War I. Millions of Allied and German soldiers lost their lives.

TIMELINE

AD

560	Frankish kingdom covers most of France
911	Vikings settle region of France now called Normandy
1297	Grimaldi dynasty rule Monaco
1337	Hundred Years' War against England (until 1453)
1491	France and Brittany united
1638	Birth of Louis XIV, France becomes major European power
1789	Start of the French Revolution
1804	Napoleon Bonaparte crowned emperor
1815	Napoleon defeated by British and Prussians at Waterloo
1848	France becomes a republic again
1852	France returns to being an empire
1870	Prussia defeats France. Revolution of the Paris Commune. The Third Republic
1914	World War I against Germany (until 1918)
1939	World War II against Germany (until 1945): France occupied 1940; Liberation 1944
1957	France founder member of EEC (later EU)
1958	Charles de Gaulle president until 1969
1968	Uprisings by students and workers
1995	Jacques Chirac becomes president

FACTS

GERMANY
Bundesrepublik Deutschland
AREA: 137,820 sq mi.
POPULATION: 82.3 million
CAPITAL: Berlin
OTHER CITIES: Hamburg,
Munich, Cologne
HIGHEST POINT: Zugspitze
(9,720 ft)
OFFICIAL LANGUAGE: German
CURRENCY: Euro

GERMANY

Germany is a country of contrasts. Famous for its busy cities and industrial regions, it also has some of Europe's most spectacular scenery with lakes, steep-sided river valleys, large forests, and snow-capped mountains.

Northern Germany, crossed by the rivers Weser and Elbe, lies on the windy coasts of the North Sea and the Baltic. These are linked by the Kiel Canal, which cuts through Schleswig-Holstein on the Danish border. The land is mostly a wide, flat plain. In central Germany rise the Harz Mountains and Swabian Jura, which drop away to sandy heath and flat farmland, part of the Great Plain that stretches eastward into Poland and Russia. Germany's eastern border lies on the rivers Oder and Neisse. The southwest of Germany is covered by woodland, the Black Forest, while the Bohemian Forest covers the southeast. The busy River Rhine winds northward from the French border, to be joined by the Main at Mainz and the Moselle at Koblenz. It flows through steep valleys covered in vineyards. In the far south are Germany's highest peaks—the Bavarian Alps—an extension of the Alps, the highest mountain chain in Europe. These mountains form a natural barrier between Germany and its southern neighbors.

The climate of the region varies greatly, being generally mild in the west, with harsh winters in the Alps and across the northeastern plains.

○ ON THE PISTE
Skiing—both downhill and cross-country—is a very popular winter pastime in Germany. The winter resorts attract tourists from all over Europe.

○ ALONG THE RHINE
The source of the River Rhine is high in the Swiss Alps. Flowing northwest, it passes through Germany and the Netherlands. It is Europe's busiest river. Here, the wine-producing town of Bacharach overlooks the river.

NATURE'S PALETTE
Named for its dark spruces, the Black Forest also includes deciduous trees, that put on a colorful show each fall.

EDELWEISS

WHITE GRAPES
Some of Germany's best wines are made from white grapes grown along the sunny banks of the River Rhine.

GERMANY

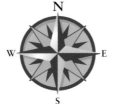

KAFFEE UND KÜCHEN
Coffee and cakes like these are a special treat in cafés across Germany. A particular favorite is Black Forest gateau, which is coated with dark chocolate.

FAITHFUL FRIEND
The German Shepherd dog is brave and loyal, which makes it an ideal breed for police work. Originally from Germany, it is now found worldwide.

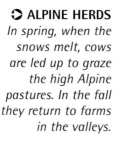

ALPINE HERDS
In spring, when the snows melt, cows are led up to graze the high Alpine pastures. In the fall they return to farms in the valleys.

Map labels

NORTH SEA
BALTIC SEA
Sylt · Flensburg
Schleswig · Kiel Bay
Helgoland · Kiel · Fehmarn · Rügen
Rendsburg · Neumünster · Mecklenburg Bay · Stralsund
Cuxhaven · Itzehoe · Lübeck · Rostock
Elmshorn · Norderstedt · Wismar · Güstrow
Wilhelmshaven · Bremerhaven · Hamburg · Schwerin · Neubrandenburg
Emden · Buxtehude · Müritz Lake
Papenburg · Oldenburg · Bremen · Lüneburg · Neustrelitz
Delmenhorst · Weser · Uelzen · Elbe · Wittenberge · Eberswalde-Finow
Nordhorn · Vechta · Nienburg · Celle · Stendal · Berlin
Rheine · Osnabrück · Hannover · Aller · Wolfsburg · Brandenburg · Oder
Gronau · Minden · Hildesheim · Brunswick (Braunschweig) · Potsdam · Frankfurt (an der Oder)
Münster · Bielefeld · Hameln · Salzgitter · Magdeburg · Eisenhüttenstadt · POLAND
Bocholt · Hamm · Holzminden · Bad Harzburg · Halberstadt · Dessau · Cottbus · Neisse
Duisburg · Dinslaken · Dortmund · Paderborn · Göttingen · HARZ MTS. · Halle · Hoyerswerda
Mönchen-Gladbach · Krefeld · Essen · Wuppertal · Arnsberg · Kassel · Münden · Nordhausen · Leipzig · Meissen · Görlitz
Düsseldorf · Remscheid · Solingen · GERMANY · Mühlhausen · Weimar · Dresden
Cologne (Köln) · Bergisch-Gladbach · Erfurt · Jena · Gera · Freiberg
Aachen · Bonn · Siegen · Marburg · Alsfeld · Chemnitz
Neuwied · Giessen · Fulda · Suhl · Zwickau
Daun · Koblenz · Werra · Hof · Plauen
Trier · Mosel · Rhine · Wiesbaden · Frankfurt am Main · Coburg · BOHEMIAN FOREST
HUNSRÜCK · Mainz · Offenbach · Schweinfurt · Bayreuth · CZECH REPUBLIC
Saar · Darmstadt · Main · Würzburg · Bamberg
Ludwigshafen · Worms · Kitzingen · STEIGERWALD
Kaiserslautern · Mannheim · Jagst · Fürth · Nuremberg (Nürnberg)
Saarbrücken · Heidelberg · Regensburg
Karlsruhe · Heilbronn
FRANCE · Baden-Baden · Pforzheim · Stuttgart · Aalen · Ingolstadt · Passau
Rhine · Neckar · Tübingen · SWABIAN JURA · Ulm · Danube
BLACK FOREST · Reutlingen · Augsburg · Inn · Braunau
Freiburg · Memmingen · Lech · Munich (München) · Salzach
Konstanz · Kempten · Rosenheim · Kufstein
Lake Constance (Bodensee) · Zugspitze 2,963 m
SWITZERLAND · LIECHTENSTEIN · AUSTRIA
NETHERLANDS · TEUTOBURG FOREST · THURINGIAN FOREST
BELGIUM · LUXEMBOURG

Germany is a democratic republic, with a federal system of government. This means that its regions, called Länder, have considerable local power. Until 1871 Germany was made up of many different small countries, and it was divided again from 1949 until 1990.

◊ EAU DE COLOGNE

Germany has the strongest economy in Europe and was a founder member of the European Economic Community (today's European Union or EU). It produces electrical goods, optical instruments, chemicals, and cars, and is world-famous for company names such as Bayer, Bosch, Volkswagen, Mercedes, and BMW. German regions are known for their beers, white wines, and sausages.

Germany has to import much of its food. Most farms in Germany are small and run by part-time farmers, who have other jobs as well. The country's industrial growth in the 19th century was boosted by mining of coal reserves near the Ruhr River, but these reserves are almost used up, and Germany now relies on imported oil and gas for much of its energy needs.

◊ FRUIT OF THE VINE
Vineyards were planted in Germany in Roman times. The chief wine-growing areas are in the southwest and the sunny valleys of the Rhine and Moselle rivers.

◊ ROWS OF BEET
Sugar beet is a major crop in this part of Europe. Traditionally, farms in southern Germany are small family businesses, while on the plains of eastern Germany they are often very large.

◊ MEDIEVAL COSTUME
In Baden Württemberg, a festival in medieval costume celebrates the history of the region. Germany in the Middle Ages was made up of many small states.

◊ EUROPEAN GRAY WOLF
Once thought to be extinct in most central European countries, the European gray wolf is making a comeback in Germany. The wolves cross into the country from Poland across the Oder and Neisse rivers.

German demonstrators protest against the transportation of nuclear waste. Environmental issues came to the fore in German politics between the 1970s and 90s, with a party called the Greens gaining wide support.

○ COMPACT DISKS
Germany today is a major exporter of CDs, high-quality audio systems, radios, and electrical goods for the home, such as refrigerators.

○ BEER FESTIVALS
Every October a famous beer festival is held in Munich, capital of Bavaria. Regional dress is still common in Bavaria—for women this is often a laced bodice, puffed sleeves, and a wide skirt, often decorated with ribbons.

The country has a fine network of railroads, including high-speed lines, and of highways (autobahns), the construction of which began in the 1930s. The River Rhine and a network of canals are used by freight barges, on a scale greater than anywhere else in Europe.

Germany has many large cities, such as Hamburg, Munich, Cologne, and Frankfurt am Main, which is a center of banking and international trade. Many foreign workers have sought employment in Germany, although the economy suffered from the high costs of reunification and modernizing East German industries in the 1990s. With the collapse of Communism in East Germany, Berlin once again became the capital of the whole country.

○ THE VOLKSWAGEN
In German, Volkswagen means "people's car." Founded in 1936 to produce cheap, tough family cars, the company had worldwide success from the 1960s onward. Its works at Wolfsburg remain the world's largest.

⊙ THE PROTESTANT
Martin Luther (1483–1546) was a German monk who condemned corruption in the Roman Catholic Church and wrote a new translation of the Bible. He led the Protestant Reformation.

⊙ FOLK COSTUME
These dancers wear the traditional costume of Bavaria in southern Germany. The man wears lederhosen *(leather shorts) and the woman a dress called a* dirndl.

⊙ OBERAMMERGAU
In 1633 a terrible plague struck this village in Bavaria. The survivors vowed to thank God by staging a play about the sufferings of Christ. The play is still put on every 10 years.

For a long time in its history, the German language was the only unifying element in German culture. German culture was thought of as being that of all those people who spoke German, and this included Austrians.

The standard form of the German language, called Hochdeutsch, is spoken throughout Germany, but there are also many regional dialects that vary greatly from north to south. In the last forty years or so, many workers from southern Europe and Turkey have also settled in German cities. The north is a stronghold of the Protestant faith, while the south is largely Roman Catholic. There are many traditional festivals and customs, with carnival being celebrated as a major festival from Cologne southward into Bavaria and Austria.

Germany has a long cultural history, dating from before the emergence of a single German state. It was the birthplace of the painter Albrecht Dürer (1471–1528), one of the great artists of the European Renaissance. Though German art has never rivaled that of France or Italy, German painters have produced works of striking individuality, among them those of the 19th-century Romantic painter Caspar David Friedrich and 20th-century Expressionists such as Max Beckmann.

⊙ LIFE OBSERVED
Fine detail characterizes the drawings of Albrecht Dürer, the greatest German artist of his day. Born in 1471, Dürer produced hundreds of paintings, engravings, and woodcuts.

SPEAK... GERMAN

hello	guten Tag
goodbye	auf Wiedersehen
thank you	danke
please	bitte
yes	ja
no	nein
school	schule
children	kinder

◯ KARL MARX
Born at Trier in 1818, Marx showed how history is driven by economic forces and called on workers to seize power. His ideas inspired Communists long after his death in 1883.

Germany is particularly noted for its music. It has produced many of the finest composers: Bach, Handel, Beethoven, Mendelssohn, Schumann, Brahms, Wagner, and Richard Strauss. German orchestras, conductors, instrumentalists, and singers have achieved international renown.

◯ PRINTING PIONEER
Johannes Gutenberg was a pioneer of printing with movable type. Born at Mainz in 1400, he moved to Strasbourg and set up a printing press there, perhaps as early as 1439.

◯ THE YOUNG MOZART
German culture flowered outside what is today Germany. The composer Mozart, born in Salzburg (Austria) in 1756, spoke German. In the 18th century, imperial Austria with its rich artistic life at Vienna, where Mozart was court musician, began losing ground to Prussia, the emerging military power among the German states.

Germany has also produced a number of great writers and thinkers, among them Kant (1724–1804), Goethe (1749–1832), and Schiller (1759–1805). In the 19th century, Germany was a center for new technology and new political ideas. The founder of Communist theory, Karl Marx, was German. So too were the pioneers of the motor car, Karl Benz and Gottfried Daimler, and Wilhelm Roentgen who discovered X-rays in 1895. In the field of medicine, Germany's Robert Koch made discoveries about the links between bacteria and disease.

German architecture ranges from the medieval magnificence of cathedrals at Cologne and Ulm to the 20th-century innovations of the Bauhaus school, founded in 1919 by the architect Walter Gropius and influential far beyond Germany.

⟳ **THE THIRTY YEARS' WAR**
In 1618, a quarrel broke out between the Protestants in Bohemia and their Austrian rulers, who were Roman Catholic. This rapidly grew into a religious war that engulfed most of western Europe. Starvation and atrocities were common. Peace came with the Treaty of Westphalia, which recognized the rights of Protestants in Germany.

This region was once the home of Celtic tribes, but by about 550 BC they had mostly been driven out by Germanic peoples from the north and east. The Romans only succeeded in conquering parts of Germany, founding cities such as Cologne. It was Germanic tribes who finally broke the power of Rome in AD 476.

Germany lay within the Frankish empire, which was ruled by Charlemagne (742–814). After it broke up, a new Holy Roman Empire followed. Lasting from 962 to 1806, the empire encompassed a vast area of Central Europe—a patchwork of small kingdoms, principalities, and cities. These fell under the overall rule of the Austrian Habsburg family.

In the 1500s, parts of Germany became Protestant, following the teachings of a monk named Martin Luther. Bitter religious wars followed. The Thirty Years' War (1618–48) devastated most of the country.

During the 1700s power shifted northward, as a state called Prussia built up a large, modern army. By 1871 the king of Prussia, Wilhelm I, was emperor of a united Germany.

○ **OTTO VON BISMARCK**
Bismarck was a powerful Prussian statesman who engineered the Franco–Prussian War and created a united Germany in 1871.

During World War I (1914–18) Germany and Austria suffered disastrous defeat. Germany became a republic, but Communists and national socialists ("Nazis") fought each other on the streets. By the 1930s the Nazis were in power.

NAZI LEADER ⟳
Adolf Hitler was born in Austria. Embittered by World War I, he preached violent and racist right-wing politics. He became leader of the Nazi Party and dictator of Germany, taking it to war in 1939.

⟳ **RIOTS IN BERLIN**
1848 was the "Year of Revolutions" across Europe, and Berlin was one of the main centers of unrest. Women and children were attacked by Prussian soldiers as demands for reform and a united Germany were crushed.

TIMELINE

AD

1282	Rise of Habsburg dynasty in Austria
1517	Luther starts the Protestant Reformation
1618	Thirty Years' War (until 1648)
1740	War of the Austrian Succession (until 1748)
1806	France defeats Prussia at Jena
1834	Prussia unites with small German states
1848	Revolution in Germany; failed
1870	Prussia defeats France
1871	Wilhelm I of Prussia, emperor of united Germany
1914	World War I (until 1918): Central powers (Germany, Austria–Hungary) defeated
1919	Weimar republic set up after emperor abdicates
1933	Hitler becomes German Chancellor
1938	Germany annexes Austria
1939	World War II (until 1945): Axis powers (Germany, Italy, and allies) invade much of Europe; defeated by Allies
1949	Germany is split into Federal Republic (West, capitalist) and Democratic Republic (East, Communist)
1957	German Federal Republic founder member of EEC (later EU)
1961	East and West Berlin divided by fortified wall (until 1989)
1990	Germany reunited after collapse of Communist rule in East Germany; Berlin is national capital again

⊙ GERMAN FOKKER E1 MONOPLANE

⊙ **DRESDEN BOMBED**
As World War II drew to a close, German cities were relentlessly bombed by Allied aircraft. The city of Dresden, with its fine old buildings and priceless works of art, was destroyed in a great firestorm. Up to 130,000 people were killed in the air-raids.

↻ **END OF THE WALL**
Germany was divided after World War II. East Germans built a wall across Berlin in 1961 and shot anyone trying to escape. It was finally knocked down in 1989.

The Nazis annexed Austria, and German troops invaded much of Europe during World War II (1939–45). Their leader, a racist dictator named Adolf Hitler (1889–1945), ordered the murder of millions of Jews. Nazi Germany was defeated by the Allies.

It was next divided into two countries, a Federal Republic in the west, supported by the United States and Western Europe, and a Communist Democratic Republic in the east, supported by the Russians. Germany was not reunited until 1990.

IBERIAN
PENINSULA

The Iberian peninsula is a great block of mainland Europe that juts out into the Atlantic Ocean. It is narrowly separated from North Africa by the Strait of Gibraltar, and its southern shores border the Mediterranean Sea.

The peninsula is largely mountainous. The snow-capped Pyrenees run along the border with France. The Cantabrian ranges, which include the Picos de Europa, run parallel with the north coast, while southern ranges include the Sierra Nevada. Much of the central region is a sun-baked plateau called the Meseta. Major European rivers rise in the mountains. They include the Ebro, Guadalquivir, Duero, Tagus, and Guadiana.

◑ IN THE PYRENEES
The Pyrenees Mountains run from the Bay of Biscay to the Mediterranean coast, a distance of more than 270 miles. Rushing streams descend from high peaks, which rise to 11,170 feet above sea level.

◐ OLIVE GROVES
Olive trees thrive in the arid climate and dusty soil of southwest Spain and Portugal. The fruit are pressed to make oil or eaten whole.

Most of the Iberian peninsula is taken up by Spain. Portugal occupies the southwestern part, facing the Atlantic Ocean. Andorra is a little state high in the Pyrenees, while Gibraltar, a sheer rock guarding the entrance to the Mediterranean, is a British colony. Spain also takes in the Balearic island chain in the Mediterranean, the Canary Islands (geographically a part of Africa), and two ports on the coast of Morocco. Portugal governs Madeira and the Azores.

Although the northern Iberian coast is green and moist, most of the central region is hot and dry, with parts turning to desert.

ANDORRA
Principat d'Andorra
AREA: 175 sq mi.
POPULATION: 0.1 million
CAPITAL: Andorra la Vella
HIGHEST POINT: Coma Pedrosa (9,665 ft)
OFFICIAL LANGUAGE: Catalan
CURRENCY: Euro

PORTUGAL
República Portuguesa
AREA: 31,515 sq mi.
POPULATION: 10.3 million
CAPITAL: Lisbon
OTHER CITIES: Porto, Setúbal
HIGHEST POINT: Estrela (9,721 ft)
OFFICIAL LANGUAGE: Portuguese
CURRENCY: Euro

SPAIN
Reino de España
AREA: 195,365 sq mi.
POPULATION: 40 million
CAPITAL: Madrid
HIGHEST POINT: Pico de Teide (Canary Islands, 12,198 ft)
OFFICIAL LANGUAGE: Spanish
CURRENCY: Euro

DEPENDENCIES
Gibraltar (UK)

◑ BARBARY APE
A legend says that when the apes leave Gibraltar, so will the British.

⟳ CITRUS HARVEST
In spring, Seville is filled with the sweet scent of orange blossom. Seville's bitter oranges are used for making marmalade.

⟳ SPLIT TOWN
The old town of Ronda in Spain's Andalucia region is divided by a river gorge, El Tajo. Sheer rock faces drop for 426 feet. The two halves are linked by a stunning bridge.

ANDORRA

PORTUGAL

SPAIN

GIBRALTAR

BURROS ⟳

⟳ WHITE STORKS

⟳ PARDEL LYNX

⟳ THE ROCK
You can see the African coast from the 1,394-feet-high Rock of Gibraltar.

69

○ FISH AND FISHING

Fishing is a traditional part of the economy along the coasts of Spain and Portugal. In recent years there have been clashes with the fishing fleets of other EU countries over catch quotas.

○ CITY VISIONS

A sculpture of gold dazzles the eye in Barcelona, the chief city of the Catalonia region, Spain. Barcelona is famous as a center of culture and the arts.

The three independent Iberian nations are all democracies, although Portugal and Spain were dictatorships until the 1970s and Andorra was not fully democratic until 1993. Spain is now ruled by a king, while Portugal is a republic. Both have been members of the European Union (EU) since 1986. This has improved the standard of living, which in the past was generally very poor.

The warm climate means that a wide variety of crops can be grown, including oranges, lemons, olives, melons, and sunflowers. Portugal obtains cork from a kind of oak tree. Both Portugal and Spain have vineyards, and wines, sherries, and ports are produced. There are large fishing fleets. The catch includes sardines, tuna, anchovies, and cod. The food of the region includes spicy sausages, paella (a dish of rice mixed with seafood, chicken, or ham, vegetables and garlic) and all sorts of delicious snacks, or tapas.

There are reserves of iron, coal, and copper, and factories produce cars and textiles.

○ CASKS OF PORT

Port takes its name from Porto, a town in Portugal. It is a strong, dark, sweet wine that is aged in oak barrels, and is traditionally drunk after dinner.

○ SPANISH POLICE

Spanish mounted police exercise their horses. There are three police forces in Spain—the Guardia Civil, the Municipal Police, and the National Police. Each has different responsibilities.

70

⟳ ROPE-MAKING

Spain produces a large number of fiber crops, including cotton, flax, hemp, and esparto grass. These are used in the manufacture of rope, yarn, fabrics, textiles, and paper.

⊃ FORESTS OF CORK

Portuguese trees called cork oaks have a thick bark which can be harvested repeatedly to provide cork. This traditional industry is being threatened by the introduction of plastic stoppers for wine bottles.

A major industry throughout the region is tourism, with northern Europeans flocking to the sunny beaches of Spain's Costa del Sol, Portugal's Algarve, the Canary Islands, and Majorca (the largest of the Balearic Islands).

About two-thirds of Portuguese are country-dwellers, but over three-fourths of the Spanish population now live in towns and cities. Many of the towns have historic centers with impressive castles, palaces, and cathedrals, and industrial suburbs. The Spanish capital is Madrid, which is located in the middle of the country, on the hot Meseta. Spain's second city is Barcelona, a lively cultural and commercial center on the Mediterranean coast. Lisbon, the Portuguese capital, is a seaport at the mouth of the River Tagus.

⟳ ON THE BEACH

Tourism has brought wealth to Spain, but has had a major impact on the Spanish environment. Hotels line the southern coasts and many remote regions are dotted with campsites.

⟳ PAELLA

⟳ INTREPID SAILOR

This statue celebrates the pioneering Portuguese navigator, Vasco de Gama (c. 1460–1524). He discovered a new route to the East around the southern tip of Africa.

⊃ INDUSTRIAL SPAIN

Spain is one of Europe's major producers of cars and other vehicles, with factories in Madrid, Barcelona, Valencia, and Saragossa. Vehicles are the country's most important export.

Spanish, officially based on Castilian, the form of the language spoken in the old kingdom of Castile, is spoken throughout Spain. Portuguese is spoken throughout Portugal. Both languages have spread around the world and are spoken in Central and South America. Many other languages and dialects may also be heard in the Iberian peninsula and its islands.

☉ RED RAG TO A BULL
Bullfighting is a very ancient tradition in Spain and tens of thousands of bulls are still killed each year. It has many fans and many opponents.

The Basques, who live in the northeast and in France, speak Euskara, which is not related to any other known language. They are a very ancient European people, with a history of seafaring. The Galicians of the northwest claim Celtic ancestry: their language, Galician, is related to Portuguese. The region of Catalonia is centered on Barcelona, and extends into Andorra and France. It also has its own language, Catalan. Roma (gypsies) have influenced the dance and music of Spain's Andalucia region. The Canary Islanders include descendants of the Guanche, a people related to the Berbers of North Africa.

☉ CERAMIC TILES
The Iberian peninsula is famed for its fine ceramics. These tiles grace the Plaza de España in Seville, which was built in 1929 for a large exhibition.

The modern national borders of the Iberian peninsula do not match those of the peoples and cultures. The Basques continue to call for independence. This has led to some power being devolved from central government, but a violent separatist campaign continues in the Basque country.

The Iberian peninsula has a rich cultural history. Its writers have included Portugal's greatest poet, Luis de Camões (1524–80), Miguel de Cervantes (1547–1616), who wrote the Spanish classic *Don Quixote*, the Spanish painter Francisco de Goya (1746–1828), and the Catalan architect Antonio Gaudí (1852–1926).

↻ FAIRYTALE ARCHITECTURE
The best-known example of Antonio Gaudi's surreal style of architecture is the Sagrada Familia church in Barcelona. He worked on this building from 1884 until his death in 1926.

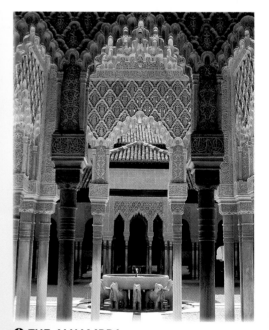

☉ THE ALHAMBRA
This royal palace and fortress was built by the Moorish rulers of Granada, Spain, between the 1000s and the 1400s. It is one of the world's most beautiful buildings.

⟳ SQUASHED TOMATOES

The town of Buñol in the eastern province of Valencia, Spain, holds an unusual festival every August. During the Tomatina, people pelt each other with tomatoes!

The region is strongly Roman Catholic, and everyday life is marked by colorful festivals in which statues of the Virgin Mary and saints are carried through the streets. Other festivals celebrate historical battles, trading fairs, horse-riding, and bullfighting. Traditional costume is worn for many of these events. Popular folk music includes the fiery flamenco music of Andalucia and soulful Portuguese songs known as fado.

⟳ ART IN BILBÃO

The new Guggenheim Museum of Modern Art is in Bilbão, in the Basque country. The gallery's titanium exterior is designed to look like rolling waves. The collection inside includes works by Spanish-born Pablo Picasso (1881–1973).

⟳ SWIRLING SKIRTS

The passionate flamenco is danced to the music of guitars, sometimes with castanets. It comes from around Seville and Cádiz.

⟳ LIVING FAITH

The Iberian peninsula is strongly Roman Catholic. Almost every town or village honors its patron saint. Holy Week, the week before Easter, is marked with festivals (fiestas) and processions.

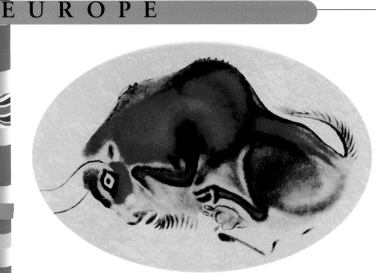

Spain was united in 1512, and ruled Portugal, too, from 1586 to 1646. Seafarers from both countries led European exploration and colonization of the Americas, and traded with Africa and the Far East. They looted, fought, and traded around the world, and became very wealthy and powerful.

Prehistoric cave paintings at Altamira, in northern Spain, date back to 12,000 BC. Many different peoples settled in the region in ancient times, including Iberians from North Africa and Celts from Europe. They were followed in ancient times by Phoenicians, Greeks, Romans, and Jews. From about 200 BC until AD 475, Spain was a very important part of the Roman empire. Modern Spanish and Portuguese both developed from Latin, the language of ancient Rome.

Ↄ CAVE PAINTINGS
The prehistoric artists of Altamira painted the bulls, boars, and buffalo that they hunted. For color, they used red ochre from the soil and black soot.

However, wars with other European nations weakened both countries. In the 1800s their American colonies mostly broke away from European rule.

Spain was torn apart by a bitter civil war between 1936 and 1939. A fascist dictator, General Franco (1892–1975), ruled Spain until 1975, when it became a kingdom once again.

Portugal, too, was ruled by dictators for 50 years, from 1926. It gave up its remaining colonies in Africa, and the region as a whole became seen once again as being central to the development of Western Europe, rather than as a backwater.

Ↄ PHILIP II
Born in 1527, Philip II became one of the most powerful and ruthless Spanish kings.

Ↄ THE REBEL
Spain lost its huge South American empire in the 1800s. Argentinean-born José de San Martín (1778–1850) helped to liberate his native country, as well as Chile and Peru.

The next invaders were Germanic peoples, including Franks and Visigoths. From AD 711, they were pushed back to the far north by armies of Moors—Berbers and Arabs—invading from North Africa. The lands ruled by these Muslims became known as al-Andalus. Great cities with fine palaces and mosques were built. From the north, Christian armies began to fight to regain control—not completed until 1492.

The patchwork of small Catholic kingdoms gradually joined together during the Middle Ages.

Ↄ THE HEROIC KNIGHT
Rodrigo Díaz was born at Burgos in about 1043. He was a Christian knight who mostly fought against the Moors, although sometimes he fought for them. He captured Valencia in 1094, and became known as El Cid (from the Moorish Sidi, or "lord").

◑ DEMOCRATIC PORTUGAL

After long years of dictatorship, Portugal celebrated its return to democracy in 1976.

◑ LISBON, 1755

In the early 1700s, the Portuguese capital was a wealthy city with many fine buildings. In November 1755 it was destroyed by a terrible earthquake just out to sea, which caused floods and fires. Ten thousand people died.

◑ FERDINAND MAGELLAN

This Portuguese seafarer, in Spanish service, set sail for the Americas in 1519. He sailed on to the Pacific, but was killed in the Philippines in 1521. His ship returned to Spain, becoming the first to sail around the world.

◑ THE GENERAL

In 1936 Francisco Franco launched an attack on Spain's government. After three years of civil war, assisted by Nazi Germany, he came to power in 1939.

TIMELINE

AD
264 Germanic invasions
711 First Moorish invasion
1085 Christians capture Toledo
1086 Second Moorish (Almoravid) invasion
1143 Portugal an independent kingdom
1147 Third Moorish (Almohad) invasion
1212 Moors defeated at Las Navas de Tolosa
1278 Status of Andorra confirmed
1440s Portugal expands overseas
1479 Kingdoms of Castile and Aragon unite
1492 Fall of Granada, last Moorish kingdom; Columbus sails to the Americas
1516 Carlos I, of the Austrian Habsburg dynasty, becomes king of Spain
1586 Portugal under Spanish rule (until 1646)
1701 War of Spanish Succession (until 1713)
1713 Gibraltar becomes British
1807 French begin occupation of Iberia (until 1814)
1919 Conflict with anarchists in Barcelona
1926 Dictatorship in Portugal (until 1976)
1936 Spanish Civil War (until 1939, when Franco becomes Spanish dictator)
1975 Spain becomes democratic monarchy
1982 Basque demands for independence
1986 Spain and Portugal join EEC (later EU)

75

ITALY

AND ITS NEIGHBORS

The Alps form the highest mountain chain in western Europe. Switzerland, at the western end of this range, is a land of lakes, forests, high meadows, and icy summits. To the east lies the tiny state of Liechtenstein. The great Alpine peaks of Austria descend to fertile plains around the river Danube. Stretching southward is the Italian peninsula—a long, narrow strip of land jutting far out into the Mediterranean Sea.

In northern Italy, the mountains drop to a low-lying plain around the river Po, a patchwork of fields and towns fringed by coastal marshes and lagoons around the city of Venice. Flat lands also border Slovenia, to the east of the Dolomite range. The Apennine Mountains run down the spine of the peninsula, with fertile, vine-covered slopes descending to the coast. In the far south are dusty plains and scrub-covered hills. Earthquakes and volcanic eruptions are a danger.

Offshore lie a number of small islands, such as Elba, Ischia, Capri, and the Lipari Islands. There are two large islands as well, Sardinia and Sicily. Far to the south, between Sicily and the North African coast, are the islands which make up the small independent nation of Malta.

○ VENETIAN ROOFTOPS
Venice is built on a lagoon and is criss-crossed by canals. The only way to cross the city is on foot or by gondola, water taxi, or water bus.

○ TUSCAN LANDSCAPE
In Tuscany, a region in central Italy, medieval hilltop towns overlook fertile plains and rolling hills covered in vineyards and olive groves.

FACTS

ITALY
Repubblica Italiana
AREA: 116,324 sq mi.
POPULATION: 57.4 million
CAPITAL: Rome
OTHER CITIES: Milan, Naples, Turin
HIGHEST POINT: Monte Bianco (Mont Blanc) (15,771 ft)
OFFICIAL LANGUAGE: Italian
CURRENCY: Euro

MALTA
Repubblika ta' Malta
AREA: 122 sq mi.
POPULATION: 0.4 million
CAPITAL: Valletta
OFFICIAL LANGUAGES: Maltese, English
CURRENCY: Maltese lira

SAN MARINO
Repubblica di San Marino
AREA: 24 sq mi.
POPULATION: 0.03 million
CAPITAL: San Marino
OFFICIAL LANGUAGE: Italian
CURRENCY: Euro

VATICAN CITY
Stato della Città del Vaticano
AREA: 0.17 sq mi.
POPULATION: 1,000
CAPITAL: Vatican City
OFFICIAL LANGUAGES: Latin, Italian
CURRENCY: Euro

AUSTRIA
Republik Österreich
AREA: 32,377 sq mi.
POPULATION: 8.1 million
CAPITAL: Vienna
OTHER CITIES: Graz, Linz, Salzburg
HIGHEST POINT: Gross Glockner (12,461 ft)
OFFICIAL LANGUAGE: German
CURRENCY: Euro

LIECHTENSTEIN
Fürstentum Liechtenstein
AREA: 61.78 sq mi.
POPULATION: 0.03 million
CAPITAL: Vaduz
HIGHEST POINT: Vorder-Grauspitz (8,395 ft)
OFFICIAL LANGUAGE: German
CURRENCY: Swiss franc

LIECHTENSTEIN

AUSTRIA

SWITZERLAND

VATICAN CITY

MALTA

SAN MARINO

ITALY

⟳ BY THE SEASIDE
The fishing town of Positano lies on Italy's stunning Amalfi coast. Its buildings cling to the steep slopes.

⟲ A ROYAL RESIDENCE
This castle is home to the prince of Liechtenstein. It overlooks the capital, Vaduz. Parts of the castle date back to 1500s.

⟳ THE MALTESE CAPITAL
Since the 1500s, sailors entering the natural harbor of Valletta have been greeted by the dome of its cathedral.

⟳ AUSTRIAN TIROL
The province of Tirol in western Austria is a region of lush mountain pastures. In winter, these are buried under a thick blanket of snow.

MOUNTAIN HOMES
Timber-built houses, called chalets, may be seen all over the Alps. They have broad roofs to protect against winter snowfall.

CITY OF STYLE
Milan is the fashion capital of Italy. Famous fashion houses include Gucci, Prada, Armani, and Valentino.

Switzerland is a neutral country. Both the Red Cross and the World Health Organization have their headquarters there. Its wealth comes from international banking, tourism, and making tools, instruments, chemicals, and cheese. Neighboring Liechtenstein is a democratic principality. It shares the same currency as Switzerland, and is also a center of banking and winter sports. Austria is a democratic republic. The mountain slopes provide timber for the mills and water for hydroelectric power. Vienna, the capital, is one of Europe's great historical cities.

The Republic of Italy occupies almost all the Italian peninsula, as well as Sardinia and Sicily. Its capital is the ancient city of Rome, on the River Tiber. Italy is a democratic country. It was the Treaty of Rome, signed in 1957, which set up the European Economic Community (today's European Union, or EU).

The wealthiest and most industrialized part of the country is the north, which is linked to the rest of western Europe by road and rail tunnels through the Alps. The south of the country remains poor. Over the years, many of Italy's workers have emigrated to northern Europe, the United States, Argentina, and Australia.

Nearly 70 percent of Italians are now city-dwellers, but agriculture is still very important.

VENICE REGATTA
Every year in September, Venice celebrates its history with a series of costumed regattas. Gondolas, gilded barges, and oared racing boats fill the Grand Canal.

SWITZERLAND
Eidgenossenschaft Schweiz –
Confédération Suisse –
Confederazione Svizzera
AREA: 15,943 sq mi.
POPULATION: 7.1 million
CAPITAL: Bern
OTHER CITIES: Zurich,
Geneva
HIGHEST POINT: Monte Rosa
(15,203 ft)
OFFICIAL LANGUAGES:
German, French, Italian
CURRENCY: Swiss franc

↻ SWISS GOLD
Bars of gold are stacked up in the vaults of a Zurich bank.

⊃ DOCK WORK
Malta's docks once serviced ships of the British navy, but now repair all kinds of merchant shipping.

Farms grow wheat, rice, corn, olives, and tomatoes. The vineyards of the Tuscany region produce world-famous wines. Indeed, Italy as a whole is the world's largest wine producer. Italian food, much of it based on pasta, risotto, polenta, or pizza dishes, has become a worldwide favorite.

Italy has few mineral resources, but has developed many successful industries, including plastics, textiles, leather goods, fashion, cars, computers, and household goods. Tourism in Italy dates back over 500 years. The country offers visitors winter sports, sunny beaches, ancient Roman and Etruscan sites, beautiful medieval cities, and stunning art treasures.

Set within Italy are two small patches of independent territory. The republic of San Marino, in the Apennines, was recognized as independent in 1631. It attracts many tourists. Vatican City, the world's smallest state, is part of the city of Rome. It serves as the world headquarters of the Roman Catholic Church.

Malta lies far to the south of Italy, on the ancient shipping lanes that cross the Mediterranean. It is a democratic republic and depends on tourism and ship repairs.

◑ PERFECT PIZZA
Pizza has a delicious topping of tomato sauce, cheese, and chopped vegetables, meats, or fish.

⊃ BIRTH OF THE WEB
At the European Laboratory for Particle Physics (CERN), in Switzerland, a scientist tests magnets for a new accelerator. One spin-off of the research here was the development of the World Wide Web.

↻ THE POLISH POPE
John Paul II became pope in 1978. He was the first non-Italian to hold the office in 450 years.

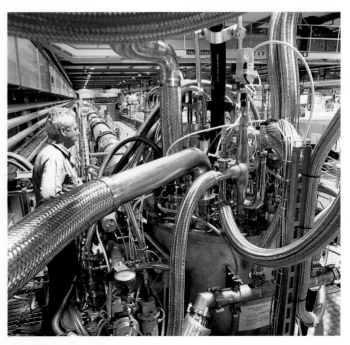

☉ ST NICHOLAS
December 5th is the Christian festival of St Nicholas. In the Lucerne region of Switzerland, this day is marked by a lantern procession and giving gifts.

About 65 percent of the Swiss people speak a regional dialect of German, 18 percent speak French, and you may hear Italian or a language called Romansch in the south. Switzerland is a conservative country, proud of its traditions. Geneva was one of the birthplaces of the Protestant faith.

Liechtenstein is largely Roman Catholic and German-speaking, with most people living in the capital city, Vaduz. Austria, too, is German-speaking. Its countryside is dotted with fine old castles, Catholic churches, and monasteries. Austria's cities have a long tradition of art, theater, and music.

Wolfgang Amadeus Mozart (1756–91) and Johann Strauss the Younger (1825–99) were both Austrian.

Italian, directly descended from the Latin language of the ancient Roman empire, is spoken all over Italy. The dialect spoken on the island of Sardinia is said to be the closest to the original Latin. In the far north there are a few speakers of French, German, and Slovenian. In the high Dolomites, a language called Ladin (related to Romansch) can also be heard.

☉ CLEVER HORSES
The days of the Habsburg emperors are recalled at Vienna's Spanish Riding School, where white Lippizaner horses perform elegant exercises to music.

☉ CATHOLIC AUSTRIA
About 300 years ago, the devout Roman Catholic faith of Austria inspired architects to erect beautiful churches and monasteries. This ornate building style is known as baroque.

Today's Italians are descended from all sorts of native peoples, settlers, and invaders. These included ancient Italian tribes, Etruscans, Romans, Greeks, Celts, Goths, Vandals, Lombards, Sards, and Normans. Today, the Italians' sense of identity depends more on the city or region in which they live than on their ancestry.

☉ PAVAROTTI
Italian is the language of opera. Luciano Pavarotti brought classical music to a wider audience when he formed the "Three Tenors," with Placido Domingo and José Carreras.

○ ST FRANCIS OF ASSISSI

In 1205, Giovanni Bernadone (c.1181–1226)—Francesco—gave up his riches to become a monk, working with the poor and sick. He preached simplicity and a love for all creatures. Thousands followed his teachings and joined the Franciscan order of monks.

The traditional way of life in Italy is still strongly influenced by the Roman Catholic Church and the family. Many colorful festivals mark Christian saints' days and Holy Week.

Italy has probably contributed more to European civilization than any other country. Ancient Rome, heavily influenced by ancient Greece, was a center of literature and the arts, of philosophy and law-making, of engineering and technology. In later phases, the Italian city-states produced great poets such as Dante (1265–1321), artists such as Michelangelo (1475–1564) and Leonardo da Vinci (1452–1519), and composers such as Monteverdi (1567–1643). Opera is still very popular today, arousing as much passion as football.

The Maltese way of life has been strongly influenced by Italian traditions and sea-faring. The Maltese themselves are descended from the various peoples who, at one time or another in history, passed through their islands—including Greeks, Phoenicians, Arabs, Normans, and English, as well as Italians.

○ DANTE ALIGHIERI

Born in 1265, Italy's greatest medieval poet wrote the Divine Comedy, a vision of heaven and hell.

○ MALTESE CROSS

The Maltese cross is the badge of the Knights of St John, a religious fighting order based in Malta from 1530 to 1798.

○ SOCCER MAGIC

Italian soccer clubs attract players from all over the world. Here, the Brazilian Ronaldo takes the field for Inter Milan.

○ CARNIVAL TIME

Of all the world's carnivals, the one staged in Venice before the Christian period of Lent is the most elegant. People dress up (many in 18th century costume) and parade the city. Originally, carnival went on for two months!

81

Austria, during the Middle Ages, was ruled as part of the Holy Roman Empire. Under the rule of the Habsburg family from 1282, it became one of Europe's strongest powers, its influence extending across central Europe. By the 1800s, following the Napoleonic Wars, Austrian power had weakened. It became a republic in 1918, after World War I.

Switzerland was created in the 13th and 14th centuries by cantons (provinces) uniting to throw off Austrian rule. It has been neutral in all wars since 1815. Liechtenstein was formed in 1719, when an Austrian prince bought two tiny states (Vaduz and Schellenberg) belonging to the Holy Roman Empire. It became an independent principality in 1866.

◯ MARIA THERESA
Born in 1717, Maria Theresa became empress and one of the wisest rulers of Austria. She died in 1780.

In Italy, legend tells, the city of Rome was founded in 753 BC. At this time the Etruscans ruled over central Italy, and Greek colonies were being founded in the south. Rome overthrew Etruscan rule in 509 BC. In the following centuries, the Romans conquered the rest of Italy and defeated a powerful rival, the city of Carthage, on the North African coast. They founded a great empire that stretched from Spain to Syria. By AD 476, the western half of this empire, including Italy, had been overthrown by Germanic invaders.

For the next 1,400 years Italy remained divided. There were invasions by Lombards and Byzantines. Normans carved out kingdoms for themselves in the south. The north fell under the rule of the Holy Roman Emperors, from across the Alps. The city of Rome, headquarters of the Roman Catholic Church, however, was still powerful as the center of the Christian world.

◯ CELTIC ART
This Celtic figurine with a wheel symbol was found at Hochdorf in Austria. It dates to the 500s BC.

◯ IN THE ARENA
The Romans loved cruel spectacle. In arenas such as Rome's Colosseum amphitheater—the ruins of which still stand—huge crowds of up to 45,000 spectators watched fights to the death between gladiators (trained slaves or prisoners of war). Slaves were set against wild animals, too—roars of approval went up if a slave was torn apart.

◯ ROMAN COINS
Long before a single European currency was launched in 1999, most of Europe used the same coins—those of the Roman empire.

◯ TRAJAN'S COLUMN
Completed in AD 113, this marble monument records the triumphs of the Roman Emperor Trajan (AD 53–117).

◯ SALZBURG
The Austrian city of Salzburg is dominated by its fine medieval castle and the slightly later cathedral, built between 1614 and 1688.

A number of republics and cities grew up in the north during the Middle Ages. These became centers of commerce, and in Florence, in particular, learning and the arts flourished during the Renaissance.

Italy experienced periods of rule by the French, Spanish, and Austrians. During the 1800s, a movement grew up, under the leadership of Giuseppe Garibaldi (1807–82), to reunite the country. By 1871 Italy was a united kingdom.

Italy supported the Allies in World War I, but soon came under the rule of a fascist dictator, Benito Mussolini. It allied with Germany during World War II and in 1945 Mussolini was shot dead by rebel fighters.

In the years after the war, Italy was rebuilt. It enjoys democratic government, despite continuing problems with organized crime.

◑ CATHERINE DE' MEDICI
The powerful and ruthless Medici family ruled Florence and, later, Tuscany, from the 1400s to the 1700s. Catherine de' Medici (1519–89) married Henry II, king of France.

◑ MAFIA ON TRIAL
The Mafia is a criminal organization based in Sicily. Its leaders have been protected by corrupt police and politicians.

◑ GARIBALDI
In 1860, Giuseppe Garibaldi and his 1,000 "Red Shirts" began a military campaign to reunite Italy. He handed over the Kingdom of the Two Sicilies to Victor Emmanuel, who soon became king of a unified Italy.

TIMELINE

AD

117	Roman empire at greatest extent
568	Lombards invade northern Italy
917	Arabs capture Sicily
1090s	Normans invade Malta, Sicily
1291	Three cantons combine for defence to found the Swiss Confederation
1450	Height of the Renaissance
1494	France invades Italy
1530	Knights of St John (Malta) fight Turks
1631	San Marino independent
1719	Liechtenstein becomes independent
1798	France takes Malta
1800	French kingdom of Italy (until 1815); Britain takes Malta
1848	Revolution fails to end Austrian rule
1859	Austria loses most of its Italian possessions
1860	Garibaldi's patriots liberate Sicily
1861	Unification of Italy
1915	Italy joins Allies in World War I (until 1918)
1922	Fascist leader Mussolini seizes power in Italy
1938	Austria is annexed by Germany
1940	Italy joins World War II on German side; changes sides 1943; Mussolini is shot dead in 1945
1957	Italy founder member of EEC (later EU)
1964	Malta independent from British rule
1971	Women in Switzerland gain the right to vote
1995	Austria joins EU

CENTRAL EUROPE AND THE BALTIC

The northern part of Central Europe borders the Baltic Sea. Its eastern coast is low-lying, bordering sand dunes, bogs, heaths, and forests. Estonia and Latvia lie on the Gulfs of Finland and Riga, with Lithuania's short coastline stretching south to Kaliningrad, a small corner of Russian territory. Below the Gulf of Gdansk, the Baltic coast continues westward to Germany.

Most of Central Europe is far from the sea. The climate may be warm and sunny in summer, but the winters are long and cold. Much of Poland is a great plain, which stretches eastward into Belarus and Russia. Some parts are heavily forested or dotted with lakes; other parts are farmed or industrialized. In southern Poland the land rises to mountains along the borders of the Czech Republic and the Slovak Republic.

The Sudetes mountain range runs along the northern Czech border, while to the southeast the Bohemian Forest stretches into Germany. The Czech lands include wooded hills and rolling farmland, drained by the rivers Vltava, Elbe, and Morava. The Slovak Republic is more mountainous, with the Tatra range descending to fertile lowlands along the River Danube. Northern Hungary is a land of hills and low mountains, while the southeast forms a wide plain, with a rich, black soil that is ideal for farming.

◊ PRIENAI, LITHUANIA
Only one-in-three Lithuanians are now country-dwellers. Farmers grow potatoes, beet, and rye and raise pigs and chickens.

◊ BUDAPEST
Hungary's splendid Houses of Parliament lie at the center of the capital, Budapest, on the banks of the River Danube.

CZECH REPUBLIC
Ceská Republika
AREA: 30,450 sq mi.
POPULATION: 10.3 million
CAPITAL: Prague
OTHER CITIES: Brno, Ostrava
HIGHEST POINT: Snezka (5,259 ft)
OFFICIAL LANGUAGE: Czech
CURRENCY: Koruna

ESTONIA
Eesti Vabariik
AREA: 17,400 sq mi.
POPULATION: 1.5 million
CAPITAL: Tallinn
OTHER CITIES: Tartu, Kohtla-Järve
HIGHEST POINT: Munamagi (1,042 ft)
OFFICIAL LANGUAGE: Estonian
CURRENCY: Kroon

HUNGARY
Magyar Köztársaság
AREA: 35,919 sq mi.
POPULATION: 10.2 million
CAPITAL: Budapest
OTHER CITIES: Debrecen, Miskolc
HIGHEST POINT: Kekes (3,330 ft)
OFFICIAL LANGUAGE: Magyar
CURRENCY: Forint

LATVIA
Latvija – Latvijas Republika
AREA: 24,900 sq mi.
POPULATION: 2.5 million
CAPITAL: Riga
OTHER CITIES: Jelgava, Daugavpils
HIGHEST POINT: Jaizina (1,020 ft)
OFFICIAL LANGUAGE: Latvian
CURRENCY: Lats

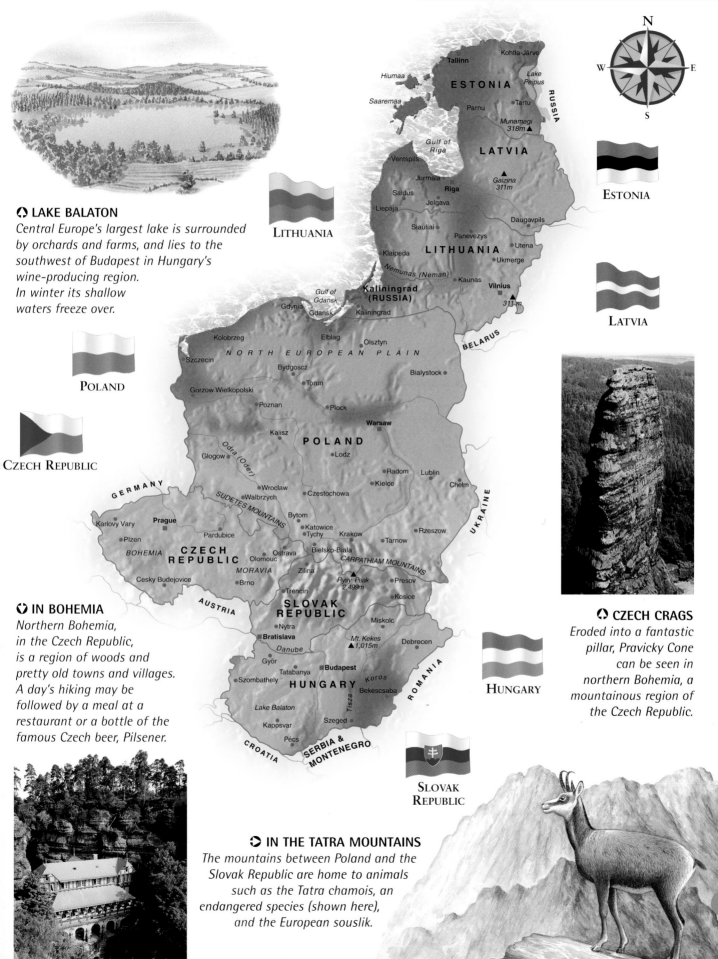

◑ LAKE BALATON
Central Europe's largest lake is surrounded by orchards and farms, and lies to the southwest of Budapest in Hungary's wine-producing region. In winter its shallow waters freeze over.

LITHUANIA

POLAND

CZECH REPUBLIC

ESTONIA

LATVIA

◑ IN BOHEMIA
Northern Bohemia, in the Czech Republic, is a region of woods and pretty old towns and villages. A day's hiking may be followed by a meal at a restaurant or a bottle of the famous Czech beer, Pilsener.

◑ CZECH CRAGS
Eroded into a fantastic pillar, Pravicky Cone can be seen in northern Bohemia, a mountainous region of the Czech Republic.

HUNGARY

SLOVAK REPUBLIC

◑ IN THE TATRA MOUNTAINS
The mountains between Poland and the Slovak Republic are home to animals such as the Tatra chamois, an endangered species (shown here), and the European souslik.

85

From the 1940s until the years 1989–91, the Baltic states formed part of the Soviet Union (as Russia was then known), while Central Europe was ruled by Communist governments that supported the Soviet Union. Today, the entire region has broken free from Russian influence. Multi-party elections are held and the countries' economies are linked to the European Union (from 2004). All the countries of the region are republics. Before 1993, the Czech and Slovak republics formed a single state, Czechoslovakia.

◐ STAPLE CROPS

In Central Europe, staple crops —those that provide the basis of people's everyday diet— include wheat and rye, for making bread, and potatoes.

The Baltic states lack mineral resources and need imports to support their industries. They produce chemicals, textiles, and heavy machinery. The forests provide timber for making paper and matches. Many factories and mills are old-fashioned. Farms grow staple crops and raise cattle and pigs.

Poland has reserves of coal, sulfur, copper, silver, lead, salt, and natural gas. Shipbuilding and repair make up a major industry on the Baltic coast, and factories produce vehicles, heavy machinery, and footwear. Wheat and rye are grown and potatoes are a major crop.

When Czechoslovakia split in two, much of the industry lay on the Czech side of the border. It includes glass-making, iron, and steel. Slovakia depends more on farming. Hungary has reserves of bauxite, coal, and gas, and produces chemicals, plastics, aluminium, vehicles, and electrical goods. Its orchards grow cherries and other fruits for making jams.

◐ VISITING CENTRAL EUROPE

The tourist industry is growing rapidly in Poland, Hungary, and the Czech Republic. Here, visitors admire a waterfall at Souteska, northern Bohemia.

◐ THE TASTE OF PAPRIKA

The red fruit of a type of capsicum plant is dried and ground to make paprika. This peppery spice is used in dishes such as Hungarian goulash.

◐ ON THE MARCH

These Lithuanian soldiers are on parade to mark Independence Day. The country became an independent state in 1991.

PIG-FARMING
Many farms in the Baltic states raise pigs. Bacon and dairy products are major exports in Lithuania and Estonia.

CHERRY RIPE
The orchards of Hungary produce delicious cherries, for canning and jam-making.

FRESH EGGS
In villages across the region, many people keep chickens and enjoy free-range eggs.

OLD PRAGUE
The Czech capital has many fine old buildings dating from the 1300s and 1400s, when the city was the center of the Bohemian kingdom.

FACTS

LITHUANIA
Lietuva, Lietuvos Respublika
Area: 25,200 sq mi.
Population: 3.7 million
Capital: Vilnius
Other cities: Kaunas, Klaipeda
Highest point: Juozapines (964 ft)
Official language: Lithuanian
Currency: Litas

POLAND
Rzeczpospolita Polska
Area: 124,808 sq mi.
Population: 38.6 million
Capital: Warsaw
Other cities: Lodz, Krakow, Wroclaw
Highest point: Gerlachovsky Stit (8,714 ft)
Official language: Polish
Currency: Zloty

SLOVAK REPUBLIC
Slovenská Republika
Area: 18,924 sq mi
Population: 5.4 million
Capital: Bratislava
Other cities: Kosice,
Highest point: Rysy Peak (8,187 ft)
Official language: Slovak
Currency: Koruna

Central Europe is famous for its delicious food, such as Hungarian goulash (a stew made of meat cooked with sour cream and paprika) and Polish *pierogi* (dumplings stuffed with mushrooms and meat). Alcoholic drinks include Polish vodkas, Czech beers, and strong red wines from Hungary.

Tourism is a growing industry in Central Europe. Major attractions include the old cities of Krakow, Prague, and Budapest, the Tatra Mountains, and the hot springs and health resorts of the Czech Republic.

SHIPBUILDING
Ship repair and construction is a traditional heavy industry around the Baltic coast, especially in the Polish port of Gdansk.

HUNGARIAN SPAS
Warm springs near Miskolc, in the north of Hungary, offer a chance to relax with friends. The water can be as hot as 86°F. Rich in minerals, it is said to cure many illnesses.

⟲ DRESSED FOR A FEAST

In Poland, traditional dress is still worn for folk dances and festivals. Bright colors and intricate embroidery are a feature of all the national costumes of Central Europe.

⟳ STILL ON THE ROAD?

The traditional painted caravans of the Roma (gypsies) are a rare sight. In Central Europe, only ten percent of the Roma are still travelers.

Peoples living on the east coast of the Baltic Sea include the Estonians, Latvians, and Lithuanians, each of whom have their own language. The Estonian language is related to Finnish and Hungarian. During the years that this region formed part of the Soviet Union, many Russians, Ukrainians, and Belarussians also settled there.

The Poles, Czechs, and Slovaks are all Slavic peoples, speaking languages that are separate but related to each other. The Magyar people, who invaded southern Central Europe about 1,200 years ago, make up 90 percent of the Hungarian population. Hungary is also home to small numbers of Germans and neighboring peoples such as Czechs, Serbs, Croats, and Romanians.

⟳ PLUCKED STRINGS

The zither is an instrument used in Central European folk music. It has a flat soundbox and its jangling strings may be plucked with the fingers or a plectrum.

⟳ MARIE CURIE

Born Marie Sklodowska (1867–1934), this great Polish physicist (on the left) researched into radioactivity and isolated the elements polonium and radium.

PLANISPHÆRIVM
Sive
VNIVERSI TO
EX HYPO
COPERNI
PLANO

COPERNICANVM
Systema
TIVS CREATI
THESI
CANA IN
EXHIBITVM

⟳ A NEW THEORY

Nicolaus Copernicus (died 1543) was a Polish astronomer who proposed a revolutionary theory: that the Sun, and not the Earth, was at the center of the Universe.

⟳ HORSEMANSHIP

A love of horses and riding was part of the Magyar way of life long before they settled in Hungary, and remains a tradition today.

Central Europe as a whole has a large Roma (gypsy) population, which has suffered from racism in many areas over the years. The region's large Jewish populations were scattered or murdered in terrible death camps during the occupation of the region by Nazi Germany during World War II (1939–45).

Central Europe is mostly Christian, with the Roman Catholic Church especially strong in Poland. The monastery of Jasna Góra at Czestochowa attracts many Catholic pilgrims, who come to see an icon (holy picture) known as the Black Madonna.

The region has contributed greatly to European culture. The musical composer Frédéric Chopin (1810–49) was Polish, and composer Antonín Dvorák (1841–1904) was Czech. Classical music has been much influenced by regional folk music and dances.

⟳ A LONG HISTORY

The Hungarian National Museum in Budapest celebrates a history that goes back to the 800s, when a legendary Magyar chief named Arpad conquered the region and set up a powerful kingdom.

⟳ CATHOLIC POLAND

Churches have been an integral part of the Polish landscape since AD 966, when the country became Christian. Ninety-five percent of Poles are Roman Catholic.

⟳ EGGSHELL PAINT

Hand-painted eggshells go on display in Budapest. Egg painting is an Easter tradition in Central and Eastern Europe, where it has become an art form.

⟳ MIXED NATIONALITY

Ceramic tiles adorn this chemist's shop in the old border town of Sopron. Allotted to Austria after World War I, Sopron voted to join Hungary in 1924.

The flat lands lying between western and eastern Europe are hard to defend. Throughout history, they have been invaded from both the east and the west. Poland has probably changed its position on the map more times than any other country in Europe.

◑ A STRONGHOLD
The medieval city of Kaunas in Lithuania built up strong defences during its long history of warfare.

◑ PRAGUE, 1968
Soviet tanks rolled into Czechoslovakia in 1964 after the Czech government tried to introduce political reforms.

◑ OUT OF THE WINDOW
An incident in Prague, in 1618, marked the start of the Thirty Years' War. The envoys of the Catholic Holy Roman Emperor were thrown out of a window by the Bohemian nobles, who were Protestant. They chose instead to be ruled by a German Protestant prince. Two years later, Catholic forces completely destroyed the Bohemian forces at the Battle of the White Mountain.

About 2,700 years ago, the Celts flourished in the Czech and Slovak region and part of Hungary. They were displaced by Germanic tribes, but in the end it was Slavic peoples who controlled most of Central Europe, from the Baltic Sea to the River Danube. In about AD 800, the plains of Hungary were invaded by the Magyars—fierce horseback warriors from the East.

During the Middle Ages, powerful kingdoms grew up in the region. These included Poland (which united with Lithuania in 1382), Bohemia (capital at Prague), and Hungary. Central Europe came under attack from the east by Tartars and Turks; from the west, Germany's Teutonic Knights rode into Poland and the Baltic.

⟳ THE MAGYARS

In about AD 800, hordes of nomadic warriors, the Magyars, poured across the Ural Mountains from Russia and conquered the plains of Hungary.

The Austrian empire spread eastward and had taken Bohemia by the 1500s. Hungary by the 1700s. Poland and the Baltic states were torn apart and invaded by the great powers of the day—Sweden, Russia, Austria, and the north German state of Prussia.

After World War I (1914–18), the nations of Central Europe were independent once again. However, German invasion during World War II (1939–45) brought terror and devastation to the region. Central Europe was liberated by local freedom fighters and by the army of the Soviet Union.

Post-war Communist governments in Central Europe were effectively controlled by the Soviet Union. There were uprisings against them, but in the end it was the collapse of the Soviet Union in 1991 that spelt the start of a new, post-Communist age for Central Europe and the Baltic states.

⟳ WORKERS UNITED

In 1980 a trade union, Solidarity, was formed in Poland. It challenged the authority of the Communist government with a series of strikes in the Gdansk shipyards. Solidarity's leader, Lech Walesa, became Polish president in 1990.

⟳ INDEPENDENT SLOVAKIA

This monument at Bankska Bystrica celebrates Slovak independence, gained when the country was part of Czechoslovakia. Today, it is independent in its own right.

⟳ ON GUARD

A soldier stands on guard outside Prague Castle, once the capital of the powerful medieval kingdom of Bohemia.

TIMELINE

AD

500s	Slavs settle Central Europe
800s	Magyars seize Hungary
1237	Tartar invasions (until 1242)
1569	Poland, Prussia, Lithuania, and Livonia (Latvia) form a commonwealth
1618	Thirty Years' War
1648	Russia and Sweden seize Polish land
1699	Hungary under Austrian rule
1772	Poland partitioned between Russia, Austria, Prussia
1848	Hungary revolts against Austrian rule
1914	World War I (until 1918): Germany and Austria invade Poland
1918	Lithuania, Poland, Hungary, Czechoslovakia independent
1920	Latvia independent
1921	Estonia independent
1939	World War II (until 1945): Soviet Union annexes Baltic states 1940; Germany invades Central Europe and Baltic; massacre of Jews; Soviet Union pushes back German forces
1948	Communists take power in Central Europe
1956	Anti-Soviet uprising in Hungary
1968	Czech reforms crushed by Soviet Union
1990	Democratic elections in Central Europe
1991	Baltic states recognized as independent
1993	Czech and Slovak states separate

THE BALKANS

The Balkan peninsula extends southward into the Mediterranean Sea from Central and Eastern Europe. It is at its broadest in the north, where it stretches all the way from the islands of the northern Adriatic to the marshy delta of the River Danube, on the Black Sea. It narrows rapidly between the Ionian and Aegean Seas, where it breaks into the ragged headlands and island chains of Greece.

◐ **HERMANN'S TORTOISE**

The only large plains lie in the north. The region as a whole is very mountainous, taking in the Carpathian ranges, the Transylvanian Alps, the Dinaric Alps, and the Balkan, Rhodope, and Pindus ranges. Even the largest of the Greek islands, Crete, is topped by a 8,060-foot-high peak named Mount Ida.

Winters can be cold and snowy in the northern Balkans, but are normally milder in the south. Summers are dry and hot, often fiercely so in Greece. Northern forests give way to scrub-covered rock and olive groves in the south. The Balkans lie in an extremely active earthquake zone.

The Balkans still include large areas of remote forest and mountain habitat, where wolves, brown bears, and wild boar live. The warmer regions have a wide variety of snakes and lizards. Many of the region's rare species are threatened by loss of habitat as forests are cleared and tourist resorts are built.

◐ **MT TRIGLAV**

The Slovenian peak of Triglav rises dramatically to 9,393 feet. It is part of the Julian Alps range, on the border with Austria, and is 40 miles northwest of the capital, Ljubljana.

ALBANIA
Republika e Shqipërisë
AREA: 11,100 sq mi.
POPULATION: 3 million
CAPITAL: Tiranë
OTHER CITIES: Durrës, Shköder, Elbasan
HIGHEST POINT: Korabit (9,026 ft)
OFFICIAL LANGUAGE: Albanian
CURRENCY: Lek

BOSNIA-HERZEGOVINA
Republika Bosnia i Hercegovina
AREA: 19,741 sq mi.
POPULATION: 4.0 million
CAPITAL: Sarajevo
OTHER CITIES: Banja Luka, Mostar
HIGHEST POINT: Maglic (7,831 ft)
OFFICIAL LANGUAGE: Serbo-Croat
CURRENCY: Marka

BULGARIA
Republika Bulgaria
AREA: 42,855 sq mi.
POPULATION: 8 million
CAPITAL: Sofia
OTHER CITIES: Plovdiv, Varna, Burgas
HIGHEST POINT: Musala (9,594 ft)
OFFICIAL LANGUAGE: Bulgarian
CURRENCY: Lev

CROATIA
Republika Hrvatska
AREA: 34,022 sq ft
POPULATION: 4.4 million
CAPITAL: Zagreb
OTHER CITIES: Split, Rijeka
HIGHEST POINT: Troglav (6,005 ft)
OFFICIAL LANGUAGE: Serbo-Croat
CURRENCY: Kuna

GREECE
Elliniki Dimokratia
AREA: 50,949 sq mi.
POPULATION: 10.9 million
CAPITAL: Athens
OTHER CITIES: Thessaloníki, Lárisa
HIGHEST POINT: Olympus (9,570 ft)
OFFICIAL LANGUAGE: Greek
CURRENCY: Euro

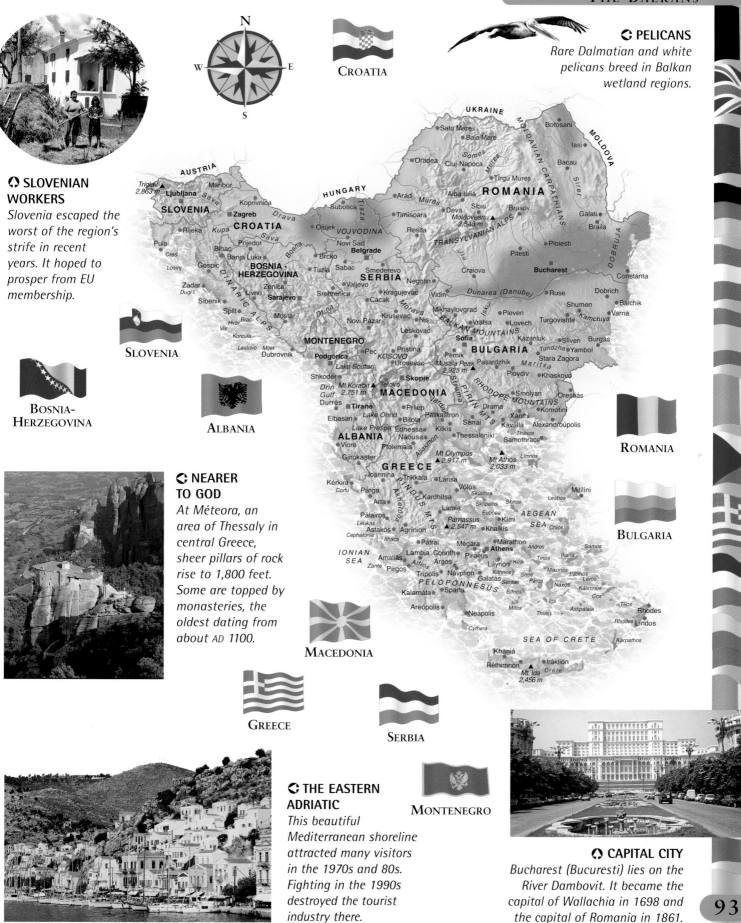

◔ PELICANS
Rare Dalmatian and white pelicans breed in Balkan wetland regions.

CROATIA

◔ SLOVENIAN WORKERS
Slovenia escaped the worst of the region's strife in recent years. It hoped to prosper from EU membership.

SLOVENIA

BOSNIA-HERZEGOVINA

ALBANIA

ROMANIA

◔ NEARER TO GOD
At Méteora, an area of Thessaly in central Greece, sheer pillars of rock rise to 1,800 feet. Some are topped by monasteries, the oldest dating from about AD 1100.

BULGARIA

MACEDONIA

GREECE

SERBIA

MONTENEGRO

◔ THE EASTERN ADRIATIC
This beautiful Mediterranean shoreline attracted many visitors in the 1970s and 80s. Fighting in the 1990s destroyed the tourist industry there.

◔ CAPITAL CITY
Bucharest (Bucuresti) lies on the River Dambovit. It became the capital of Wallachia in 1698 and the capital of Romania in 1861.

93

During the 1990s there was civil war in the northwest as the Communist federation of Yugoslavia split up into separate countries. This were the new, smaller republics of Slovenia, Croatia, Bosnia-Herzegovina, Serbia & Montenegro, and Macedonia. Slovenia was later accepted as an EU member (from 2004), and in 2006 Serbia & Montenegro split into two separate countries.

In Romania, the people overthrew a self-styled Communist dictator, Nicolae Ceausescu (1918–89), in 1989. Communist rule collapsed in Bulgaria in 1990 and in Albania in 1992.

✪ CROATS AND CONFLICT

An elderly Croatian man weaves canes into a basket. Between 1991 and 1995 Croatia fought the Serbs in both Yugoslavia and Bosnia. Many Serbs living in Croatia fled the country.

The Balkans are home to very many different peoples, including Serbs, Croatians, Slovenians, Montenegrins, Romanians, Bulgars, Turks, Roma (gypsies), Albanians, and Greeks. The region has had a very troubled political history, largely as a result of the neglect and division it experienced during the hundreds of years it was ruled by the Austrian and Ottoman (Turkish) empires.

✪ THE WELDER

Serbian metal industries are based in Pancevo, Kragujeva, and Nis. The capital, Belgrade, is a center of both heavy and light engineering. Output has continued despite the political strife and warfare of the 1990s.

✪ OCEAN HARVEST

Squid and octopus are an important ingredient in many Greek meals and snacks. They are served at coastal restaurants and bars during the summer months.

MACEDONIAN REPUBLIC
(Former Yugoslav Republic)
Republika Makedonija
AREA: 9,928 sq mi.
POPULATION: 2.0 million
CAPITAL: Skopje
OTHER CITIES: Bitola, Prilep
HIGHEST POINT: Korabit (9,066 ft)
OFFICIAL LANGUAGE: Macedonian
CURRENCY: Dinar

ROMANIA
România
AREA: 91,699 sq mi.
POPULATION: 22.4 million
CAPITAL: Bucharest
OTHER CITIES: Brasov, Constanta
HIGHEST POINT: Moldoveanu (8,360 ft)
OFFICIAL LANGUAGE: Romanian
CURRENCY: Leu

SLOVENIA
Republika Slovenija
AREA: 7,819 sq mi.
POPULATION: 2.0 million
CAPITAL: Ljubljana
OTHER CITIES: Maribor, Jesenice
HIGHEST POINT: Triglav (9,393 ft)
OFFICIAL LANGUAGE: Slovenian
CURRENCY: Tolar

SERBIA
Republika Srbija
AREA: 34,116 SQ MI
POPULATION: 9.5 MILLION
CAPITAL: BELGRADE
OTHER CITIES: NOVI SAD, NIS
HIGHEST POINT: DERAVICA (8,714 ft)
OFFICIAL LANGUAGE: SERBIAN
CURRENCY: DINAR

MONTENEGRO
Republika Crna Gora
AREA: 5,333 SQ MI
POPULATION: 650,000
CAPITAL: PODGORICA
OTHER CITIES: NIKSIC, ULCINJ
HIGHEST POINT: DURMITOR (8,274 ft)
OFFICIAL LANGUAGE: SERBIAN
CURRENCY: EURO

Greece has faced many problems, including a period of right-wing military rule from 1967 until 1973. It has also had long-running disputes with its eastern neighbor, Turkey, and with the new Slavic republic of Macedonia across its northern border.

The political troubles of the 1990s disrupted the Balkan economy. Greece, as a member state of the European Union (EU) since 1981, was one of the few countries in the region that was able develop peacefully.

The climate of the region is suitable for growing fruits, such as plums in the north and lemons and olives in the south, watermelons, corn, tobacco, and sunflowers. Bulgaria grows roses for the perfume industry. The Balkan lands produce iron and steel, chemicals, machinery, textiles, clothing, and footwear. Tourism is a major industry in Greece, which offers blue seas, island beaches, and pretty, whitewashed villages. Recent political troubles disrupted what had also been a thriving tourist industry on the coast and islands of Croatia.

◑ MELONS
The juicy red flesh of a Greek watermelon, or karpouzi, makes an ideal refreshment on a hot day.

◑ DEFENDING GREECE
The ceremonial uniform of the Greek national guard, the Evzones, includes a tasseled cap, a kilt, and white leggings. It is based on the dress of the mountain troops who fought against Turkey in the 1820s.

◑ THRESHING CORN
Slovenian women thresh a harvest of wheat. Many people still work on farms in rural areas of the Balkans. Hi-tech machinery is rare on these small, family-run farms.

◐ A VOLCANIC ISLAND
The Greek island of Santorini, or Thira, lies just to the north of Crete. Today, it attracts thousands of tourists each year, but about 3,500 years ago it was the scene of one of the biggest volcanic explosions in recorded history.

The early history of the Balkans is marked by the amazing civilizations that developed on the island of Crete from about 2500 BC until 1400 BC, and on the Greek mainland and islands from 1000 BC onward. The city-states of ancient Greece produced great playwrights and poets, sculptors, athletes, soldiers, traders, mathematicians, and thinkers. The idea of democracy—rule by a public assembly instead of by kings or dictators—was first tried out in Athens. Greek culture and ideas spread around the Mediterranean region as seafarers set up new colonies.

In 338 BC the northern kingdom of Macedonia conquered the rest of Greece, and a young ruler named Alexander the Great went on to found a vast empire which stretched southward to Egypt and eastward to India. This broke up after he died. In 146 BC Greece became part of the Roman empire, which soon swallowed up the whole Balkan region.

○ MASK OF MYCENAE
This gold death mask comes from Mycenae, the citadel town in southern Greece that was the center of the Mycenean civilization between 1900 BC and 1100 BC.

The eastern part of the Roman empire survived after the western part collapsed, and this developed into the Byzantine empire, with its capital at Constantinople (modern Istanbul, in Turkey). The Byzantine empire became a center of Eastern Orthodox Christianity and of the Greek language and way of life.

○ DRACULA'S CASTLE
The legend of Dracula, the vampire, is based upon Vlad IV, who ruled part of Romania in a reign of terror (AD 1455–62). He impaled his victims on pointed stakes.

◐ ALEXANDER THE GREAT
Alexander (356–323 BC) conquered all the lands between Greece and India, and founded the Egyptian city of Alexandria.

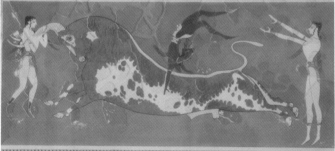

○ THE BULL-LEAPERS
A wall painting from Knossos, on Crete, shows acrobats vaulting over the backs of bulls. About 3,500 years ago, Knossos was the capital of the Minoan civilization.

◐ GREEK ARMIES
Ancient Greece was not a united state until 338 BC. When its armies did join forces, they defeated the mighty Persian empire. In the Greek state of Sparta, military training was strict and started from boyhood.

A GREAT THINKER
Socrates was one of the greatest philosophers of ancient Greece. He was forced to commit suicide in 399 BC, as a punishment for encouraging people to think about good and evil, and disrespect the gods.

A FATEFUL DAY
On June 28, 1914, the Archduke Franz Ferdinand of Austria and his wife were assassinated in Sarajevo, Bosnia. This incident triggered World War I.

The Byzantine empire fell to the invading Turks in AD 1453. Most of the Balkans remained under Turkish rule for over 400 years, with Austria–Hungary controlling parts of the northwest. World War I (1914–18) was started when a Serbian nationalist assassinated the heir to the Austrian throne in Sarajevo.

World War II (1939–45) brought Italian and German invasions of the Balkans and long years of guerrilla warfare, which continued after the war in battles between Communists and monarchists. Communists failed to gain control of Greece, but succeeded in the northern Balkans. All the Communist governments collapsed in the 1980s and 90s, and war followed.

SOPHIA CATHEDRAL
Many Bulgarians belong to the Eastern Orthodox Church. The domed cathedral in Sophia shows the influence of the Byzantine empire.

SLOBODAN MILOSEVIC
Serbian nationalist Milosevic rose to power in the 1980s. In the 1990s, he led ruthless campaigns against Bosnian Muslims and the ethnic Albanians of Kosovo.

THE PARTHENON
The Acropolis in Athens is crowned by the Parthenon—a splendid temple to Athena, the goddess of the city. It was completed in 438 BC.

TIMELINE

AD

330	Roman empire split: the eastern capital, Constantinople, goes on to become center of Byzantine empire
500s	Slavs invade Balkans (through 600s)
680	Bulgars invade Bulgaria
1396	Turks invade Bulgaria
1453	Turks capture Constantinople, then invade Balkans
1821	Greek War of Independence (until 1830)
1908	Bulgaria declares independence
1912	Balkan Wars (until 1913) drive Turks from most of Europe; Albanian independence
1914	World War I starts in Sarajevo: Turkey joins Germany and Austria; Greeks join Allies 1917
1918	Formation of Yugoslavia
1939	World War II (until 1945): 1940, Italy invades Albania; Greece invaded by Italy, Germany, Bulgaria
1946	Communist governments take power in Balkans; Greek Communists defeated in civil war (until 1949)
1967	Military coup in Greece
1975	Greece becomes a democratic republic
1981	Greece joins EEC (later EU)
1989	Revolution in Romania
1990s	Collapse of Communist governments in Balkans (through 1991); break-up of Yugoslavia; ethnic persecution
2001	Yugoslav leader Slobodan Milosevic tried for war crimes

ALASKA
(U.S.A.)

C A N A D A

U．S．A．

MEXICO

BAHAMAS

CUBA

DOMINICAN REP.

HAITI

PUERTO
RICO

BELIZE

GUATEMALA HONDURAS JAMAICA

EL SALVADOR

NICARAGUA

COSTA RICA

PANAMA

VENEZUELA

GUYANA

SURINAM

FRENCH GUIANA

COLOMBIA

ECUADOR

B R A Z I L

P E R U

BOLIVIA

PARAGUAY

CHILE

URUGUAY

ARGENTINA

N
W   E
S

HARLEY DAVIDSON
ELECTRA GLIDE

The AMERICAS

⟡ Disneyworld,
UNITED STATES OF AMERICA

⟡ Lake Moraine,
CANADA

⟡ Amazon rainforest,
BRAZIL

⟡ Toltec temple,
MEXICO

North and South America are two great continents, lying between the Atlantic and Pacific Oceans. They are linked by Central America, which narrows to a strip of land called the Isthmus of Panama. This is cut in two by the Panama Canal, which links the two oceans. Tropical Central America is bordered to the east by the Caribbean Sea, which is encircled by the islands of the Greater and Lesser Antilles.

North America is dominated by the mountain system called the Rockies, which runs from north to south. In the far north, frozen tundra yields to forest. To the south of the forest belt lie the prairies—rolling grasslands that are now used for grazing or are cultivated, part of a great plain drained by the Mississippi–Missouri river system. In the southern United States and Central America are rocky canyons, steamy wetlands, volcanoes, and deserts.

In South America, the Rockies are matched by the mighty Andes mountain chain. To the east, a maze of waterways flows into the River Amazon, which is surrounded by the world's largest tropical rainforest. South American grasslands include the llanos of Venezuela and the Argentinean pampas. There are windy plateaus and coastal deserts. The continent ends in the bleak island of Tierra del Fuego, which reaches out like a claw toward Antarctica.

⟡ SAILFISH

CANADA

○ MUSK OX

C anada is the world's second largest nation in area. Its islands are scattered like pieces of a giant jigsaw puzzle across the Arctic, between the Beaufort and Labrador Seas. A wide expanse of northern Canada is covered by tundra, which has permanently frozen ground. During the brief summer, the snow on the tundra melts and lies in pools that attract insects and migrating birds.

Most of the Canadian mainland is covered by a broad belt of forests and glacial lakes. A vast slab of ancient rock, the Canadian Shield, borders Hudson Bay. In the west are the high peaks of the Mackenzie, Rocky, and Coast ranges, which descend to the moist green coast of British Columbia.

The southern border with the United States crosses the prairies and the Great Lakes. The St Lawrence River and Seaway link Lake Ontario with the Atlantic Ocean. Here, the warm Gulf Stream meets the cold Labrador Current, bringing fog to the waters off Newfoundland, Canada's Maritime provinces, and the little French islands of St Pierre and Miquelon.

○ BATH TIME!
The moose can stand 7.5 feet at the shoulder. This one is pictured at Pukaskawa National Park, Ontario, on the north shore of Lake Superior.

FACTS

CANADA
AREA: 3,558,096 sq mi.
POPULATION: 31 million
CAPITAL: Ottawa
OTHER CITIES: Toronto, Montréal, Vancouver
HIGHEST POINT: Mount Logan (19,524 ft)
OFFICIAL LANGUAGES: English, French
CURRENCY: Canadian dollar

ST PIERRE AND MIQUELON TERRITORIAL COLLECTIVITY OF FRANCE
AREA: 93 sq mi.
POPULATION: 6,500
CAPITAL: Saint-Pierre
OFFICIAL LANGUAGE: French
CURRENCY: Euro

○ TAKKAKAW FALLS
Takkakaw means "wonderful" in the language of the Cree people. These mighty falls tumble over a drop of 833 feet in the Yoho National Park, British Columbia.

○ TUNDRA LIFE

The Arctic tundra supports a wide range of wildlife, including birds such as ptarmigan and mammals such as caribou.

○ IN THE ROCKIES

Moraine Lake may be visited in the Banff National Park, in Alberta. Its vivid blue color is caused by a silt known as "rock flour."

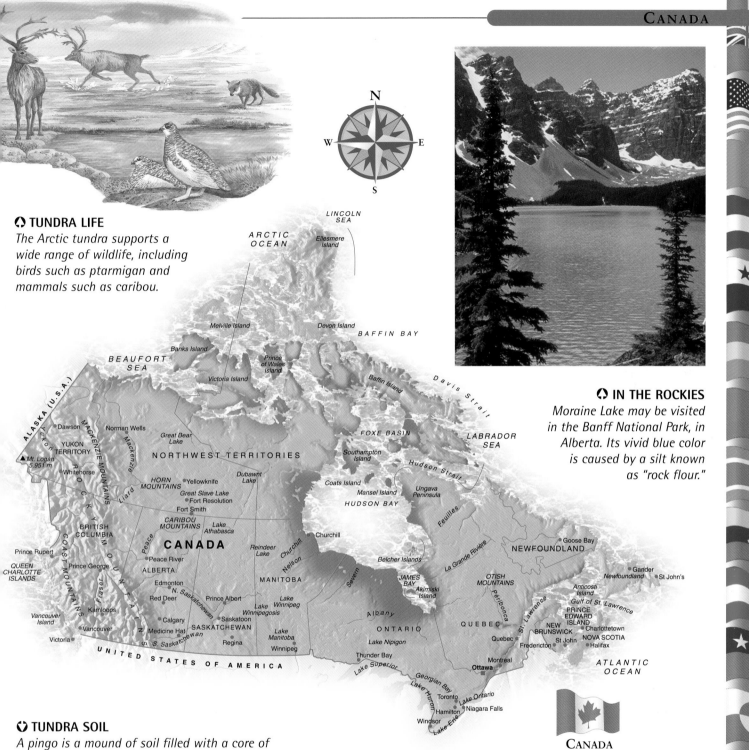

ARCTIC OCEAN
LINCOLN SEA
Ellesmere Island
Melville Island
Devon Island
BAFFIN BAY
Banks Island
BEAUFORT SEA
Prince of Wales Island
Victoria Island
Baffin Island
Davis Strait
Dawson
Norman Wells
Great Bear Lake
FOXE BASIN
LABRADOR SEA
YUKON TERRITORY
Mt. Logan 5,951 m
Whitehorse
NORTHWEST TERRITORIES
Southampton Island
Hudson Strait
ALASKA (U.S.A.)
MACKENZIE MOUNTAINS
Mackenzie
Liard
HORN MOUNTAINS
Yellowknife
Dubawnt Lake
Coats Island
Mansel Island
Ungava Peninsula
Great Slave Lake
Fort Resolution
Fort Smith
HUDSON BAY
Feuilles
BRITISH COLUMBIA
CARIBOU MOUNTAINS
Lake Athabasca
Churchill
NEWFOUNDLAND
Goose Bay
ROCKY MOUNTAINS
Peace
CANADA
Reindeer Lake
Belcher Islands
La Grande Rivière
Prince Rupert
Peace River
Churchill
Nelson
JAMES BAY
OTISH MOUNTAINS
Gander
QUEEN CHARLOTTE ISLANDS
Prince George
ALBERTA
Akimiski Island
Newfoundland
St John's
COAST MOUNTAINS
Edmonton
MANITOBA
Severn
Anticosti Island
Gulf of St. Lawrence
Fraser
Kamloops
Red Deer
N. Saskatchewan
Prince Albert
Lake Winnipeg
Pelibonca
PRINCE EDWARD ISLAND
Vancouver Island
Calgary
Saskatoon
Lake Winnipegosis
Albany
ONTARIO
QUEBEC
NEW BRUNSWICK
Charlottetown
NOVA SCOTIA
Vancouver
Medicine Hat
SASKATCHEWAN
S. Saskatchewan
Lake Manitoba
Lake Nipigon
St Lawrence
Quebec
Fredericton
St John
Halifax
Victoria
Regina
Winnipeg
Thunder Bay
Montreal
ATLANTIC OCEAN
UNITED STATES OF AMERICA
Lake Superior
Georgian Bay
Ottawa
Lake Huron
Toronto
Lake Ontario
Hamilton
Niagara Falls
Windsor
Lake Erie

CANADA

○ TUNDRA SOIL

A pingo is a mound of soil filled with a core of expanding ice. When the ice melts, the pingo collapses.

○ THE BEAVER

Beavers live on many Canadian lakes. They use their powerful gnawing teeth to fell trees and shred wood.

◐ FIGHTING THE BLAZE
A helicopter moves in to fight a forest fire. Canada's vast conifer forests stretch in a broad belt across central and northern regions, from British Columbia to the Laurentian Plateau.

◑ LUMBERJACK YEARS
The loggers who felled the Canadian forests a century ago had few mechanical aids. They lived hard lives in remote camps.

The severe climate in the north of Canada has restricted settlement there. Seventy-seven percent of Canadians are town-dwellers, and the big cities are all in the south, where the climate is milder and transportation easier. The capital is Ottawa, a city in southeastern Ontario. The commercial centers are the much larger cities of Toronto and Montréal.

Canada is an independent nation, whose head of state is the British monarch. The country is organized on federal lines, with provinces and territories. Canada was a founder member in 1994 of the North American Free Trade Agreement (NAFTA), which strengthened economic ties with the United States and Mexico to the south.

◑ IN SEARCH OF COD
The Grand Banks are shallow waters off the coast of Newfoundland. They have attracted international fishing fleets for about 500 years, but stocks of cod have declined in recent years.

The Canadian prairies supply wheat to the world and provide pasture for cattle. The great forests send timber to the sawmills. There are reserves of oil, natural gas, copper, gold, iron ore, and nickel, and there are plenty of rivers and lakes to provide hydroelectric power. Factories manufacture cars, paper, steel, and chemicals.

Food products include maple syrup, apples, cheese, and beer. Until recently Newfoundland on the east coast lay off one of the richest fishing grounds in the world.

◐ SKY LEVEL
Toronto's CN Tower, at about 1,814 feet high, is one of the world's tallest structures. Its viewing platform is a dizzying 1,444 feet above the ground.

◐ LOGGING TODAY
Canada has over 1,120 million acres of forest and is the world's leading exporter of forest products. These include timber in various forms, wood pulp, and paper.

However, overfishing has led to dwindling stocks and a ban on trawling until numbers recover.

Like the United States, Canada is a melting pot of peoples and cultures. For the last 30 years Canadian politics have been dominated by the future of Québec province, where a large number of French-speakers wish to break away from the rest of Canada altogether. English-speaking Canadians share many of the interests of their American neighbors—but are always keen to emphasize their own independent way of life.

◯ IN MONTRÉAL
Montréal, capital of Québec province, is the chief city of French-speaking Canada and a center of commerce and the arts. Shop signs are often in French.

◯ OIL RIG, ALBERTA
Over 90 percent of Canada's reserves of oil and natural gas are found in Alberta province. Major production regions are at Lloydminster, Fort McMurray, and here, at Cold Lake.

◯ TORONTO SKYLINE
With a population of nearly five million, Toronto is Canada's biggest city. It is a national center of business and communications.

◯ SPACE TECH
Canada has an important aerospace industry. It built this robotic lifting device, called the Canadarm, for use on American Space Shuttles.

◯ SUGAR MAPLE
Maple syrup is boiled up from a sweet sap, collected from the maple tree. It was invented long ago by native peoples of the St Lawrence valley. Today it is popular in Canada and the United States, where it is poured over pancakes and waffles.

103

↻ CHUCK WAGON RACE

These are a feature of North America's toughest rodeo, the Calgary Stampede. Held each year in mid-July, this celebration of cowboy skills dates to 1912.

↻ DOGSLED, QUÉBEC

Teams of dogs still pull sleds in the Arctic as a means of transportation. Dogsled racing is a popular sport.

The first people to settle Canada were prehistoric peoples, who came via the Bering Strait "land bridge" from Siberia in Asia during the last Ice Age. Their descendants include the First Peoples, who live in Canada today—groups such as the Mohawk, Micmac, Innu, Cree, Dene, and Kwakiutl.

They were followed by waves of hunters—the ancestors of today's Inuit—who set up scattered settlements across the Canadian Arctic and Greenland. Except in Greenland, the descendants of all these native peoples are today greatly outnumbered by later immigrants. They have faced a long struggle to gain rights to their own land. A huge but very sparsely-populated area of Canada became the Inuit territory of Nunavut in 1999.

Vikings from Scandinavia were the first Europeans to arrive, about 1,000 years ago, but they did not stay— perhaps because of hostility from native peoples.

↻ QUÉBEC INUITS, 1904

A hundred years ago, hunting met all the needs of the Inuit, providing meat, hides, and fur for clothing, bones for needles, and tools and gut for thread.

↻ CANADIAN PACIFIC

This railroad was Canada's first continental crossing. It was completed in 1885 and ran between Montréal and Port Moody, Vancouver.

↻ THE "MOUNTIES"

The Northwest Mounted Police, with their red coats and distinctive hats, were founded in 1873 to tame the "Wild West." In 1920 they became a national force, the Royal Canadian Mounted Police.

○ MONSTER MASH
In a different kind of stampede, heavy-metal racers with big tyres show off in Calgary, Alberta.

In the 1500s, English and French explorers arrived. The French colonized the lands around the St Lawrence River, while the British traded around Hudson Bay. Rivalry over trade brought the two nations into conflict with each other, and in the 1700s they fought for control of Canada. The British won. After the 1770s, families loyal to Britain poured into Canada from the newly independent United States.

Despite British control, the French retained their language and Roman Catholic faith. In 1867, Québec, Ontario, Nova Scotia, and New Brunswick were united as the Dominion of Canada—a part of the British empire. Many more peoples settled in Canada as the nation expanded across the prairies toward British Columbia.

People of British (especially Scots) and French descent make up a large percentage of the population. This also now includes Ukrainians, Dutch, Russians, Poles, Germans, Italians, Chinese, Indians, Vietnamese, and Afro-Caribbeans.

○ THE CHAMPIONS
Ice hockey was first played in Canada in the 1850s, and today is the country's most popular sport.

○ WINTERLUDE
The Winterlude festival is held each February in Ottawa. Events include sculpture in ice and snow, and skating on the Rideau Canal.

○ ACROSS THE ARCTIC
Vehicles fitted with skis, such as skidoos, have become the most popular method of travel for the Inuit and other peoples of the north.

○ TOTEM POLES
Tall poles carved from cedarwood were erected in villages along Canada's Pacific coast by native chiefs. They represented guardian spirits and histories of the family or tribe.

TIMELINE

AD

1497	John Cabot discovers Newfoundland
1534	Jacques Cartier explores the St Lawrence River
1608	Samuel de Champlain founds Québec
1642	Montréal founded
1670	Hudson's Bay Company established
1713	British gain Newfoundland
1759	British defeat French at Québec
1763	Canada becomes a British colony
1840	Act of Union joins Upper and Lower Canada
1867	Dominion of Canada: Ontario, Québec, Nova Scotia, New Brunswick
1870s	Manitoba, British Columbia, Prince Edward Island join Canada
1896	Klondike gold rush (until 1898)
1905	Alberta, Saskatchewan join Canada
1914	World War I (until 1918): Canada joins Allies
1939	World War II (until 1945): Canada joins Allies
1949	Newfoundland joins Canada
1959	St Lawrence Seaway opened
1968	Separatists demand free Québec
1994	Canada in North American Free Trade Agreement (NAFTA)
1995	Québec referendum rejects separatism
1999	Self-governing homeland for Inuit (Nunavut)

105

MAIZE

UNITED STATES OF AMERICA

UNITED STATES OF AMERICA
AREA: 3,615,283 sq mi.
POPULATION: 286 million
CAPITAL: Washington DC
OTHER CITIES: New York City, Los Angeles, Chicago
HIGHEST POINT: Mt McKinley (20,320 ft)
OFFICIAL LANGUAGE: English
CURRENCY: US Dollar

BERMUDA
British Overseas Territory
AREA: 20 sq mi.
POPULATION: 0.06 million
CAPITAL: Hamilton
OFFICIAL LANGUAGE: English
CURRENCY: Bermuda Dollar

BALD EAGLE

The United States of America spans the whole of central North America. The only other territory in the region is a group of 150 small islands, lying 700 miles to the southeast of the state of New York, in the North Atlantic Ocean. These make up the British colony of Bermuda.

Forty-eight of the United States lie between the Canadian and Mexican borders. This is the American heartland. It has both North Atlantic and North Pacific coastlines. The land is amazingly varied, with long, straight highways cutting through deserts and mountains, farmland and forest, linking together the big cities of the east and west.

To the far northwest, separated from the US heartland by Canada, lies Alaska. This is covered by great areas of Arctic wilderness, and is the largest state of all. Its islands are inhabited by grizzly bears and its waters by schools of whales.

Far out to the west of the US mainland, in the Pacific Ocean, are the volcanic Hawaiian islands—an outlying state of the USA. Tourists come here to enjoy the warm climate and to see the island's spectacular volcanoes.

The United States is the fourth-largest country in area in the world, after the Russian Federation, Canada, and China.

CHIPMUNK

THE STATUE OF LIBERTY
This 302-foot-high statue overlooks the New York City harbor. A gift from the French, it was dedicated in 1886.

ORGAN PIPE CACTUS NATIONAL MONUMENT
Summer temperatures can soar to 106°F in this part of Arizona. Spiny cacti, bearing pink flowers in summer, line the Ajo Mountain drive.

ALASKA

Pt. Barrow
Barrow
ARCTIC COASTAL PLAIN
Colville
Noatak
BROOK RANGE
Kobuk
Kobuk
Fort Yukon
CANADA
Bering Strait
Tanana
Fairbanks
Nome
ALASKA (U.S.A.)
Tanana
Yukon
St. Lawrence
Island
Mt. McKinley
Holy Cross
Anchorage
Cordova
Nunivak
Island
Bethel
Kenai
Seward
Sitka
Juneau
Homer
GULF
OF
ALASKA
Ketchikan
Kodiak
BRISTOL
BAY
Kodiak Island
Alaska Peninsula
ALEUTIAN ISLANDS
Rat Is.
Fox Is.
Andreanof Is.

N
W   E
S

◑ SEA COW
The rare manatee lives along the Florida coast.

◑ THE LARGEST STATE
Alaska is a land of misty shores, islands, towering mountains, glaciers, and remote, snowy wilderness.

Main map (contiguous USA)

CANADA

Seattle
Olympia
WASHINGTON
Mt Rainier
4,392 m
Portland
Salem
Eugene
OREGON
Spokane
Kalispell
Missoula
Helena
MONTANA
Lewiston
Pendleton
Butte
Billings
IDAHO
Boise
Idaho Falls
Twin Falls
Pocatello
Klamath Falls
Redding
Eureka
Reno
Carson City
Sacramento
Oakland
San Francisco
San Jose
Salinas
Fresno
Mt. Whitney
4,418 m
NEVADA
GREAT BASIN
Great
Salt
Lake
Ogden
Salt Lake City
Provo
UTAH
Monument
Valley
CALIFORNIA
Death
Valley
Las Vegas
Bakersfield
Los Angelas
San Bernardino
Long Beach
San Diego
CHANNEL ISLANDS
Flagstaff
ARIZONA
Phoenix
Mesa
Yuma
Tucson
Douglas
MEXICO
Havre
Grand Falls
Williston
Minot
NORTH
DAKOTA
Jamestown
Bismarck
Fargo
Sheridan
WYOMING
Casper
Rock Springs
Laramie
Cheyenne
Rapid City
Black
Hills
Fort Collins
Boulder
Denver
Grand
Junction
Mt. Elbert
4,399 m
COLORADO
Colorado
Springs
Pueblo
Durango
Trinidad
Grand
Canyon
NEW MEXICO
Gallup
Santa Fe
Albuquerque
Las Cruces
El Paso
Aberdeen
Pierre
SOUTH
DAKOTA
Sioux
Falls
NEBRASKA
Grand Island
Lincoln
Abilene
Salina
Topeka
KANSAS
Hutchinson
Wichita
Amarillo
Lubbock
Wichita Falls
Abilene
TEXAS
Midland
Odessa
San Angelo
Austin
San Antonio
Laredo
Brownsville
Corpus Christi
Grand Forks
MINNESOTA
Duluth
St. Cloud
Minneapolis
St Paul
WISCONSIN
La Croase
Sioux City
Des Moines
IOWA
Cedar Rapids
Davenport
Omaha
Kansas
City
Jefferson
City
MISSOURI
St. Louis
Joplin
Springfield
Tulsa
OKLAHOMA
Oklahoma
City
Dallas
Fort Worth
Waco
Houston
Galveston
Port Arthur
Beaumont
Shreveport
Alexandria
LOUISIANA
Baton Rouge
New Orleans
Marquette
Green Bay
Milwaukee
Madison
Rockford
Chicago
Peoria
ILLINOIS
Springfield
INDIANA
Indianapolis
Evansville
Paducah
MICHIGAN
Grand
Rapids
Lansing
Detroit
Gary
Toledo
OHIO
Columbus
Dayton
Cincinnati
Louisville
Frankfort
Lexington
KENTUCKY
Nashville
Knoxville
Chattanooga
TENNESSEE
Memphis
ARKANSAS
Fort Smith
Little Rock
Greenville
Tupelo
Birmingham
MISSISSIPPI
Jackson
Meridian
Montgomery
Mobile
Biloxi
Pensacola
ALABAMA
Columbus
Macon
Atlanta
GEORGIA
Albany
Tallahassee
Lake Superior
Lake Huron
Lake Michigan
Lake Erie
Rochester
Syracuse
Buffalo
Albany
Erie
Windsor
Cleveland
Akron
Pittsburgh
PENNSYLVANIA
Scranton
Harrisburg
WASHINGTON D.C.
WEST
VIRGINIA
Charleston
VIRGINIA
Richmond
Roanoke
Greensboro
Raleigh
Winston-
Salem
NORTH CAROLINA
Charlotte
Greenville
SOUTH CAROLINA
Columbia
Augusta
Charleston
Savannah
Jacksonville
St. Augustine
Daytona Beach
Orlando
Tampa
St. Petersburg
FLORIDA
Fort Myers
Lake
Okeechobee
West Palm Beach
Miami
Key West
Florida Keys
Straits of Florida
MAINE
Bangor
Augusta
Burlington
VERMONT
Montpelier
NEW
HAMPSHIRE
Portland
NEW
YORK
Concord
MASSACHUSETTS
Cape Cod
Boston
Providence
RHODE ISLAND
Hartford
CONNECTICUT
New York City
NEW JERSEY
Philadelphia
Trenton
Baltimore
Dover
DELAWARE
MARYLAND
Annapolis
Chesapeake Bay
Norfolk
Cape Hatteras
Cape Fear
Wilmington
Greenville
GULF OF MEXICO
Mississippi Delta
Cape Canaveral

**UNITED
STATES OF
AMERICA**

❤ BRYCE CANYON
Pink, orange, and buff-colored rocks have been eroded by wind, water, and ice into extraordinary pinnacles at this national park in Utah.

BERMUDA

HAWAIIAN ISLANDS

KAUAI
Lihue
NIIHAU
Kauai Channel
OAHU
Honolulu
MOLOKAI
LANAI
Lanai City
Wailuku
MAUI
KAHOOLAWE
Alenuihaha Channel
Mauna Kea 4,205m
HAWAII
Mauna Loa 4,169m
Hilo

◑ NIAGARA FALLS
These spectacular waterfalls are on the United States–Canada border. They are not only a tourist attraction, but also a source of hydroelectric power.

↻ THE EVERGLADES

The Everglades is a vast system of wetlands that drains southern Florida. Its wildlife includes alligators, tree snails, and egrets.

The northeastern United States is a temperate land of green river valleys, woodland, and rocky shores. The coastal plain is narrow in the north, but widens to the south of Chesapeake Bay, where it is fringed by long, sandy beaches. The flat lands rise to the Appalachian system, which includes the Green, White, Allegheny, and Blue mountain ranges. In the far southeast, the sunny peninsula of Florida ends in a string of small sandy islands, known as keys. Here, the calm can be shattered by violent hurricanes.

↻ FIRE WARNING

A notice in Bryce Canyon, Utah, warns of the danger of forest fires. America's vast forests are often devastated by blazes.

To the south of the Great Lakes lies a broad plain, drained by the Missouri and Mississippi rivers. The latter forms a muddy delta where it enters the steamy Gulf of Mexico. Flat, dusty farmland stretches westward, a danger zone for sudden and devastating tornadoes. The American prairies, once a great sea of grass stretching to the badlands at the foot of the Rocky Mountains, are now patchworked with fields of crops, farm buildings, and ranches.

Beyond the massive peaks of the Rockies lie dazzling salt flats and rocks worn into bizarre shapes by the wind and weather. The Colorado River has cut the world's most impressive gorge, the Grand Canyon. The deserts of the southwest shimmer in the heat.

↻ LAVA FLOW

This slow-moving lava from a Hawaiian volcano is known as pahoehoe.

↻ NIGHT-RAIDER

The raccoon, with its banded eyes and tail, often raids garbage cans by night.

↻ CLIFF CASCADE

Beautiful waterfalls roar down the cliffs of California's Yosemite Valley. This is the upper part of the Yosemite Falls, the world's second-highest, with a drop of 2,424 feet.

↻ TORNADO TWISTERS

Raging tornadoes, also called twisters, are common in the Prairie states. They can spin at more than 300 miles per hour, sucking up anything in their path.

The Coast, Cascade, and Sierra Nevada ranges of the far west act as a barrier to rain-bearing winds from the ocean. However, the western slopes catch the rain, making the forests of the northwest cool, moist, and green. The north of California has a pleasant climate when not shrouded in fog from off the ocean. The south is hotter and drier.

Alaska stretches high into the deep-frozen Arctic and includes empty wilderness, icy shores, and some of the highest peaks in the Americas.

The 126-or-so Hawaiian islands are the tops of a broad chain of very high submarine volcanoes.

◑ GRAND CANYON
In Arizona, the Colorado River has carved out the world's biggest gorge. In parts, it is nearly a mile deep.

◑ GOLDEN GATE BRIDGE
This is California's most famous landmark. Opened in 1937, the bridge crosses a strait that connects San Francisco Bay with the open Pacific Ocean.

◑ OKEFENOKEE SWAMP
This wildlife refuge lies on the Georgia–Florida border. It is a maze of waterways, marshes, and floating islands. Its bald cypress trees are draped with Spanish moss.

◑ THE COLORS OF THE FALL
In New England—the far northeastern region of the United States—the leaves of the temperate woodland trees turn to beautiful reds, oranges, and browns before they drop off in the fall.

◑ THE COLORADO ROCKIES
The Rocky Mountains National Park is entered from the town of Estes Park, Colorado, on the Big Thompson River. The massive ranges of the Rockies form the backbone of the North American continent.

◑ SEA LIONS
Graceful in the water, comical on land, sea lions live on many of the islands off the coast of California. The males can be much bigger than a grown man—nearly 10 feet long.

109

EARLY SKYSCRAPERS
The world's first high-rise buildings were built in Chicago and New York City. Better known as the "Flat Iron," because of its shape, New York's 20-storey Fuller Building was erected in 1901.

During the last 75 years the United States has become the world's most powerful nation, and one of the richest.

It is a democratic republic, which works on a federal system; its states have powers to make their own laws. The head of state is the president, who is elected for a term of four years.

In addition to its 50 states, the USA also governs various island territories in the Pacific Ocean and the Caribbean Sea.

The United States is one of the world's great food producers, growing wheat, soya beans, corn, citrus fruits, and vegetables. Coasts and rivers produce large catches of fish. Milwaukee is famous for its beers, Kentucky for its bourbon, and California for its wines.

The United States has great mineral wealth. It drills for oil and natural gas in Texas, the Gulf of Mexico, and Alaska. It is the world's largest producer of coal. It has gold, uranium, copper, and iron ore. Dammed rivers and lakes are used to produce hydroelectric power. Managed forests provide timber, with the far northwest a major center of logging.

ALL-AMERICAN FOOD
As well as fast food such as hamburgers and hot dogs, the United States has given the world cola drinks, breakfast cereals, and orange juice from Florida.

A HOLLYWOOD STAR
Stars are inset in the pavement in Hollywood, California, as a tribute to the big names of movies. Walt Disney (1901–66) is honored as the creator of Mickey Mouse.

BEFORE SEPTEMBER 11, 2001
This photo shows the New York City skyline before September 11, 2001. On that day, the twin towers of the World Trade Center (right of picture) were destroyed by terrorists.

HARLEY DAVIDSON ELECTRA GLIDE, 1988

DISNEYWORLD
This famous Florida theme park opened in 1971—the second one to be dreamt up by the pioneerof animated film, Walt Disney. It attracts many thousands of visitors each year from all over the world.

TEXAS OIL
Texas built its wealth on cattle, cotton, and oil. Today, the United States ranks as the world's second-largest oil producer.

American factories make a wide range of household goods, textiles, and garments. California is the world center of computer technology and software, and also the center of the movie and television industry. The United States is the leading manufacturer of airplanes and spacecraft. The city of Detroit makes cars.

Services such as banking, finance, and insurance are now more important to the American economy than manufacturing. New York City's Wall Street is the center of the American financial world. The United States, with neighboring Canada and Mexico, set up the North American Free Trade Agreement (NAFTA) in 1994.

Although the United States has such great economic power, it too has its problems. Its industries face competition from other countries, where costs are lower.

SHOP TILL YOU DROP!
American ways of buying and selling have spread around the world. Shopping malls are an American invention.

KENNEDY SPACE CENTER
Cape Canaveral, Florida, is the launch site for many US space missions. Space shuttle flights began in 1981. Two shuttles have been lost in accidents, in 1986 and 2003.

CYBER SUCCESS
The world computer revolution of the 1980s and 90s was spearheaded in "Silicon Valley," California.

BIOSPHERE 2
This experimental base was set up in the Arizona Desert. Inside, all of the Earth's habitats are recreated in miniature. It is a practice-run for future space bases on other planets or on the Moon.

MOUNT RUSHMORE
Completed in 1941, these giant heads show the four former US presidents Washington, Jefferson, Roosevelt, and Lincoln.

✪ HOME RUN
Baseball is one of America's most popular sports. It has been played since the 1840s.

✪ IN CHINATOWN
Since the 1800s, the United States has had a large population of Chinese descent. In the Chinatown district of New York's Lower East Side, signs are in Chinese and shops sell Chinese food.

Three-fourths of all Americans live in towns and cities. Hispanic and African-Americans make up the two largest minority groups.

The nation's first peoples (Native Americans, Inuit, and Aleuts) now make up only one percent of the population. There has been a strong revival of interest in their traditional cultures.

The USA has no official religion, but religion plays an important part in everyday life. Eighty-five percent of the population is Christian, with Protestants outnumbering Roman Catholics two-to-one. Two percent of Americans are Jewish, and two percent are Muslim. English is the official language, but Spanish is also widely spoken.

✪ HOT GOSPEL
Christian churches from the African tradition developed the choral sound known as gospel music, which has also influenced popular music. This singer is a New York City policewoman.

✪ RIDING SCHOOL, NEW MEXICO
Horse-riding has been part of the American way of life since the days of the Wild West.

✪ HAWAIIAN DANCE
The Hawaiian islands became a state of the Union in 1959. The islanders' dances and traditional costume of grass skirts and flower garlands belong to the Polynesian culture of the Pacific.

✪ AFRICAN–AMERICANS
America's large black population is of African descent. Afro-Americans have played an important part in the advancement of civil rights and in American culture. They invented many popular musical forms, including jazz and the blues.

⟳ NATIVE AMERICAN TRADITIONS

The first peoples still face many social and economic problems, but they have retained a fierce pride in their traditions and customs.

⟳ SKATING IN CENTRAL PARK

A haven for relaxation, Central Park lies at the heart of New York City's busy Manhattan district. It is a place to walk, jog, rollerblade, or picnic.

The majority of the population is white, of European descent. These include English, Scots, Welsh, Irish, French, Italians, Germans, Dutch, Swedes, and Poles. About nine percent are Hispanics, Spanish-speaking people originally from Mexico, Central America, or the Caribbean. There are Jews, Chinese, Japanese, Koreans, and Vietnamese. There are Polynesians from Hawaii and Samoa. About 12 percent of Americans are blacks, of African and Caribbean descent, whose ancestors were enslaved by the European settlers during the first 300 years of settlement.

The minority peoples of the United States, from the Native Americans to the Afro-Americans, have all experienced racism and poverty. And yet the real wealth of the nation lies in its rich mixture of cultures, and the broad spectrum of styles found in music and dance, writing, art, customs, beliefs, food, and festivals. American writers, artists, musicians, and movie-makers have had a great influence on the world during the last 100 years. The most popular sports—baseball, basketball and American football—are supported by millions of fans across the country.

⟳ 4TH OF JULY

The United States marks its independence, won from Great Britain in 1776, each July 4. This parade is taking place in the New England state of Maine.

⟳ FREE PRESS

The United States has many famous city-based newspapers, including the Washington Post and the New York Times.

⟳ AMERICAN FOOTBALL

Fast and exciting, American football is popular both at college and at professional level. Superbowl contests have been known to attract world television audiences of over 138 million.

○ WARRING STATES
Flags of the Confederacy and the Union, the two conflicting sides in the American Civil War (1861–65).

The Native Americans are descended from prehistoric peoples who crossed into North America from the Asian region of Siberia sometime after 30,000 BC. They developed many different cultures in different parts of the Americas.

In the 1500s, English, Dutch, Spanish, and French colonists began to explore and settle the east and south. At first they made alliances with the Native Americans (whom they called "Indians"), but they soon fought bitter wars with them and with each other. Many Europeans bought African slaves to plant tobacco and cotton on the lands they had seized.

○ FORT PITT
Nineteenth-century traders meet Native Americans at Fort Pitt. The Native Americans lost their lands and their way of life as European settlers moved West.

○ A BITTER CONFLICT
Over 360,000 Union (Northern) troops were killed during the Civil War, and 260,000 Confederate (Southern) troops. Thousands of civilians also died.

The British colonists revolted against rule from London, declaring their independence in 1776. They defeated the British troops and founded a new republic. This survived a bitter civil war between the northern and southern states, which lasted from 1861–65 and brought an end to slavery.

Pioneers pushed west into "Indian Territory," seizing land and killing the Native Americans. Vast areas of land were purchased from the French, Spanish, and Russians (who governed Alaska until 1867).

○ PILGRIMS
The most famous European settlers were a group of Puritans, religious refugees from England, who founded a colony at Plymouth Rock, Massachusetts, in 1620.

⟳ THE RUSH FOR GOLD
In 1848 gold was discovered on the American River, in California. Soon prospectors were arriving from all over the world in the hope of making their fortunes.

⟳ AMERICA MOURNS
John F Kennedy, a young and dynamic president, was assassinated in 1963. Here he is mourned by his wife Jackie and his brother, Robert.

The east became industrialized, railroads crossed the continent, gold was found in California. Thousands of poor people left Europe in search of fame and fortune in this new land.

The United States fought alongside the Allies in World War I (from 1917 to 1918). After the boom years of the 1920s came an economic crash in 1929 and years of hardship. The United States entered World War II in 1941, when Japan bombed the naval base at Pearl Harbor, Hawaii. After the end of the war in 1945, relations with one former ally, the Communist Soviet Union, went from bad to worse. During the "Cold War" that followed, the two rival superpowers remained on the brink of hostilities until the late 1980s.

⟳ MARTIN LUTHER KING
This great campaigner for civil rights won the Nobel Peace Prize in 1964. He was murdered in 1968.

⟳ POLITICAL PARTIES
The two most powerful political parties are the Democrats and Republicans. Here, Democrats hold their convention in Chicago.

⟲ WESTWARD BY WAGON
In the 1840s, thousands of pioneers headed west along routes such as the Oregon Trail, which stretched for 2,000 miles.

TIMELINE

AD	
1565	Spanish found St Augustine, Florida
1607	English found Jamestown, Virginia
1620	Pilgrims found Plymouth colony
1700s	Height of slave trade
1773	"Boston Tea Party"
1775	American Revolution
1776	Declaration of Independence
1783	Britain loses colonies
1789	George Washington first president
1791	Bill of Rights
1803	Louisiana Purchase
1812	War with Britain (until 1814)
1819	Florida bought from Spain
1846	War with Mexico (until 1848): California and New Mexico gained
1861	Civil War (until 1865)
1865	President Lincoln assassinated
1867	Alaska bought from Russia
1876	Battle of Little Big Horn
1898	Spanish–American War
1917	USA joins Allies in World War I (until 1918)
1929	Wall Street Crash
1941	Japan bombs Pearl Harbor; USA enters World War II (until 1945)
1950s	Cold War (until 1990)
1961	Vietnam War (until 1973)
1969	US astronauts land on the Moon
1963	President Kennedy assassinated
1994	USA enters North American Free Trade Agreement (NAFTA)
2001	Terrorist attacks on World Trade Center and Pentagon

115

MEXICO
AND CENTRAL AMERICA

◊ MONARCH
BUTTERFLY

Mexico's northern border runs along the banks of a long river known in the United States as the Rio Grande and in Mexico as the Rio Bravo del Norte. It passes through hot, dusty desert.

A long, thin peninsula, Baja (Lower) California, extends southward from Tijuana into the warm, blue Pacific Ocean. The Western and Eastern Sierra Madre ranges enclose a high central plateau, which includes deserts, lakes, swamps, and smoking volcanoes. Violent earthquakes are common. Southern ranges include the Southern Sierra Madre and the Chiapas Highlands. In the far southeast, the Yucatán Peninsula forms a broad hook around the Bay of Campeche. In the south of the country, the vegetation includes lush tropical forest.

The seven small countries of Central America lie to the south of the Isthmus of Tehuantapec. The landmass snakes from northwest to southeast, reaching its narrowest point at the Isthmus of Panama. Its backbone is a series of peaks, including many active volcanoes, and high plateaus or mesas. This highland chain is broken only by the expanse of Lake Nicaragua, which covers an area of 3,250 square miles. The Caribbean coastal strip is low-lying and flat, with swamps and lagoons. The Central American climate is tropical and often hot and humid.

FACTS

BELIZE
Republic of Belize
AREA: 8,867 sq mi.
POPULATION: 0.2 million
CAPITAL: Belmopan
OTHER CITIES: Belize City,
Dangriga
HIGHEST POINT: Victoria Peak
(3,681 ft)
OFFICIAL LANGUAGE: English
CURRENCY: Belize dollar

COSTA RICA
República de Costa Rica
AREA: 19,730 sq mi.
POPULATION: 3.9 million
CAPITAL: San José
OTHER CITIES: Limón,
Alajuela
HIGHEST POINT: Chirripo
Grande (12,533 ft)
OFFICIAL LANGUAGE: Spanish
CURRENCY: Costa Rican
colon

EL SALVADOR
República de El Salvador
AREA: 8,124 sq mi.
POPULATION: 6.2 million
CAPITAL: San Salvador
OTHER CITIES: Santa Ana,
San Miguel
HIGHEST POINT: Monte Cristo
(7,933 ft)
OFFICIAL LANGUAGE: Spanish
CURRENCY: Salvadorean
colon

GUATEMALA
República de Guatemala
AREA: 42,042 sq mi.
POPULATION: 11.6 million
CAPITAL: Guatemala City
OTHER CITIES: Puerto Barrios,
Quezaltenango
HIGHEST POINT: Tajumulco
(13,845 ft)
OFFICIAL LANGUAGE: Spanish
CURRENCY: quetzal

◔ TEMPLE OF THE WARRIORS
This imposing temple, now ruined, was built by the fierce Toltec warriors who conquered the Maya of Chichén Itzá in AD 987.

☼ HOWLER MONKEY
Some species of these large, noisy monkeys are threatened by the loss of tropical forests in Central American rainforests.

MEXICO

☼ PANAMA CANAL
This vital shipping link was opened in 1914. It cuts through the Isthmus of Panama to link the Atlantic and Pacific Oceans.

BELIZE

☼ TOUCAN
This bird uses its huge bill to eat tropical fruits.

☼ CHICHÉN ITZÁ
The ruined city of Chichén Itzá in Mexico's Yucatán peninsula was a center of the Mayan and Toltec civilizations between AD 800 and 1180.

HONDURAS

GUATEMALA

☼ IN BELIZE
The low-lying, swampy coast of Belize is fringed by coastal shallows and islands called cays. Hurricanes are common in August and September.

NICARAGUA

☼ UNDER THE VOLCANO
Costa Rica is a mountainous country. The Arenal volcano, in the Cordillera de Guanacaste, last erupted in 1968.

EL SALVADOR

COSTA RICA

PANAMA

Map labels
Tijuana, Mexicali, Ensenada, Ciudad Juárez, Hermosillo, Chihuahua, Cedros I., La Paz, Torreón, Culiacán, Saltillo, Monterrey, Durango, San Luis Potosí, Matamoros, Aguascalientes, Guadalajara, León, Tampico, Cape Corrientes, L. de Chapala, Manzanillo, Mexico City, Puebla, Veracruz, Orizaba 5,700m, Acapulco, Balsas, Coatzacoalcos, Oaxaca, Gulf of Tehuantepec, Bay of Campeche, Campeche, Terminos Lagoon, Villahermosa, Mérida, Cancún, Yucatán Peninsula, Yucatán Channel, Belize City, Belmopan, GUATEMALA, Guatemala City, San Salvador, EL SALVADOR, HONDURAS, Tegucigalpa, NICARAGUA, Managua, Lake Nicaragua, Mosquitos Gulf, San José, COSTA RICA, PANAMA, Panama City, Gulf of Panama, COLOMBIA

UNITED STATES OF AMERICA, SIERRA MADRE, Gulf of California, Baja California, Rio Grande, Rio Bravo del Norte, PACIFIC OCEAN, MEXICO, BELIZE

N W E S

☼ SAGUARO CACTUS
The saguaro of Mexico's northwestern deserts is the world's biggest cactus, growing to 50 feet or more.

☼ AFTER THE HURRICANE
Much of Central America, including the Honduran capital, Tegucigalpa, was devastated by Hurricane Mitch in 1998.

117

⟳ DOWN IN ACAPULCO

Tourists flock to Acapulco in southwestern Mexico for the beaches and fishing. The city has one of the best natural harbors in the Pacific.

⟳ MARKET TRADITIONS

Bargain-hunters throng an outdoor market in Mexico City. The modern city is built on the site of the ancient Aztec capital, Tenochtitlán, which held vast, open-air markets.

⟳ COFFEE BEANS

Coffee is a major export of Central American countries such as Nicaragua and Costa Rica.

Mexico is normally considered as part of North America, although its southern regions have more in common with the Central American countries to the south. It is a federal democratic republic, and in 1994 signed up to the North American Free Trade Agreement (NAFTA) with Canada and the USA.

Mexico has large oilfields in the Gulf of Mexico, as well as silver, lead, gold, and uranium. Ninety-five percent of its mineral resources are still to be mined. It manufactures fertilizers, petrochemicals, vehicles, and machines. Mexican farmers grow cotton, coffee, tropical fruits, and vegetables. There is a large fishing industry.

Mexico has the highest foreign debt of any developing country. Many of its people are very poor; over the years, large numbers have crossed illegally into the United States in search of work. Mexico City has more than 20 million people, and is probably the most polluted capital city in the world.

⟳ TACOS, GUACAMOLE DIP, AND CHILLI PEPPERS

Mexico's problems are mirrored in the Central American republics of Guatemala, Belize, Honduras, El Salvador, Nicaragua, Costa Rica, and Panama. Over the last 50 years, extreme right-wing dictators in Central America have used death squads to silence any opposition. The United States—eager to prevent Communism in the region—sometimes backed their governments, who faced prolonged attack from left-wing revolutionaries. Central America also saw bitter border disputes. The root of all these conflicts has been poverty. The warfare has now mostly ended, but the rebuilding process is slow. Poverty and foreign debt remain the chief problems. The regional economy depends on coffee, bananas, cotton, sugarcane, corn, fish products, and seafood. Exports include textiles and handicrafts.

⟳ SEA HARVEST

A Mexican fisherman casts his net. Sardines are by far the largest catch in these waters, followed by anchovies, tuna, and prawns.

⟳ BLUE WATERS

Off Cajún, in northeast Yucatán, tourists can see the wonders of a tropical coral reef through glass-bottomed boats.

○ BANANA TRADE

Bananas are packed for export before they ripen. The Central American countries compete fiercely with their Caribbean neighbors for their share of the world market.

○ MINING FOR TIN

Mexico has rich mineral reserves, including tin, silver, antimony, mercury, and fluorite. Its most valuable reserves are of oil and natural gas.

○ WOVEN BY HAND

The region is famous for its brightly colored, patterned textiles. Traditionally, these are woven on simple backstrap looms, tensioned around a fixed post.

○ MEXICO CITY

The Mexican capital and its sprawling suburbs are home to nearly 25 million people. It is the most populous city in all the Americas and is a center of business, finance, industry, and communications.

FACTS

HONDURAS
República de Honduras
AREA: 43,277 sq mi.
POPULATION: 6.5 million
CAPITAL: Tegucigalpa
OTHER CITIES: San Pedro Sula, Choluteca
HIGHEST POINT: Cerro Las Minas (9,275 ft)
OFFICIAL LANGUAGE: Spanish
CURRENCY: Lempira

MEXICO
Estados Unidos Mexicanos
AREA: 756,066 sq mi.
POPULATION: 100 million
CAPITAL: Mexico City
OTHER CITIES: Guadalajara, Monterrey, Puebla de Zaragoza
HIGHEST POINT: Citlatépetl (18,700 ft)
OFFICIAL LANGUAGE: Spanish
CURRENCY: Mexican peso

NICARAGUA
República de Nicaragua
AREA: 50,193 sq mi.
POPULATION: 4.9 million
CAPITAL: Managua
OTHER CITIES: León, Granada
HIGHEST POINT: Cordillera Isabella (7,998 ft)
OFFICIAL LANGUAGE: Spanish
CURRENCY: córdoba

PANAMA
República de Panamá
AREA: 29,157 sq mi.
POPULATION: 2.9 million
CAPITAL: Panama City
OTHER CITIES: San Miguelito, Colón, David
HIGHEST POINT: Volcán Baru (11,400 ft)
OFFICIAL LANGUAGE: Spanish
CURRENCY: Balboa

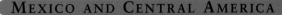

◯ AN OLMEC HEAD

This colossal stone head was carved about 3,000 years ago by the Olmec people of ancient Mexico.

From about 1200 BC onward, Mexico and Central America saw the rise of some great civilizations founded by indigenous (native) peoples—the Olmecs, Maya, Toltecs, and Aztecs. Ruined cities, stepped pyramids, and large temples may still be seen. When the Spanish invaded the region in AD 1519, they were awestruck by the wonders of the Aztec capital, Tenochtitlán (today's Mexico City).

The indigenous peoples, whom the Spanish called "Indians," were skilled astronomers, mathematicians, writers, musicians, and craftspeople. But lacking firearms, they were soon defeated by Spanish guns. The region became part of Spain's overseas empire for the next 300 years or so.

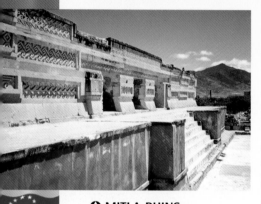

◯ MITLA RUINS

Mitla, in southern Mexico, was an ancient holy site. It was occupied by the Mixtecs about 1,000 years ago. The ruins still bear traces of the original paint, made from berries.

◯ TEXTILE WEAVING

Skeins of brilliant colored wools for hand weaving are piled high ready for sale in this Guatemalan market.

After independence in 1823, power in Mexico remained in the hands of a few wealthy landowners. The country lost large areas of territory to the United States in the 1840s, and from 1910 until 1917 it was torn apart by revolution and civil war.

After the Central American nations gained independence, they at first tried to unite in a federation, but went their separate ways in 1838. Here, too, the people remained poor, while a few landowners grew very rich. Belize was a British colony—British Honduras—from 1862 to 1981.

◯ AN AZTEC HEADDRESS

The Aztecs were fine craftworkers, producing beautiful feather cloaks and headdresses, intricate jewelry, and patterned textiles.

◯ THE MAYA

The classic period of Mayan civilization lasted from about AD 250 to 900. It was marked by the building of cities with great stone temples and pyramids. The homeland of the Maya stretched from Mexico's Yucatán peninsula southward into Guatemala and Belize. Their descendants still live in these regions today.

The peoples of the region enjoy a rich culture. Some are of European descent, and many more are mestizos, people of mixed native and Spanish descent. Indigenous peoples living in the region include large groups of Maya, as well as Otomi, Tarascan, Zapotec, Mixtec, Tarahumara, Nahua, Miskito, Guaymi, and Cuna. The Garifuna, who live in Belize, Honduras, and Nicaragua, are descended from Africans and from an indigenous people—the Caribs. The whole region is Spanish-speaking. Indigenous languages are also spoken and English is heard in Belize and on Nicaragua's east coast.

Mexico and Central America are strongly Roman Catholic, although indigenous traditions have influenced many colorful religious festivals and processions.

◆ COLONIAL ARCHITECTURE
Spanish-built churches may be seen in Taxco de Alarcón, Mexico. The region was a center of mining before the Spanish arrived in 1528.

◆ MIXED TRADITIONS
Ancient Mayan rituals have influenced the Christian worship of the Quiché Maya of Guatemala.

◆ DAY OF THE DEAD
Mexicans commemorate their dead each year on November 1st. Altars are laden with food offerings, papier-mâché skeletons, photographs, and flowers.

TIMELINE

BC	
c.2600	Origins of Maya civilization in Yucatán
c.1000	Origins of Zapotec civilization
AD	
300s	Mayan empire (until 900s)
c.1325	Aztecs build great city of Tenochtitlán
1400s	Height of Aztec empire
1519	Spain invades Aztec empire (conquers by 1521)
1600s	Pirate attacks on Atlantic coast
1810	Revolt against Spanish rule in Mexico
1821	Collapse of Spanish rule in Central America
1823	United provinces of Central America (by 1838): Honduras, Costa Rica, El Salvador, Guatemala, Nicaragua
1846	Mexican War with USA (until 1848): loss of California and New Mexico
1862	British Honduras (Belize) a British colony
1911	Mexican Revolution: political reform
1914	Panama Canal opens
1970s	Political violence in Guatemala
1978	Nicaraguan Revolution
1981	Belize independent
1985	Earthquake, Mexico City
1994	Uprising in Chiapas, Mexico
	Mexico enters North American Free Trade Agreement (NAFTA)
2001	Third Summit of the Americas discusses a wider Free Trade Area

121

THE CARIBBEAN

○ SCARLET IBIS

FACTS

DOMINICA
Commonwealth of Dominica
AREA: 290 sq mi.
POPULATION: 0.07 million
CAPITAL: Roseau
HIGHEST POINT: Morne Diablotin (4,747 ft)
OFFICIAL LANGUAGE: English
CURRENCY: East Caribbean dollar

DOMINICAN REPUBLIC
República Dominicana
AREA: 18,804 sq mi.
POPULATION: 8.6 million
CAPITAL: Santo Domingo
OTHER CITIES: Santiago de los Caballeros, La Romana
HIGHEST POINT: Pico Duarte (10,417 ft)
OFFICIAL LANGUAGE: Spanish
CURRENCY: Dominican Republic peso

GRENADA
AREA: 133 sq mi.
POPULATION: 0.1 million
CAPITAL: St George's
HIGHEST POINT: Mt St Catherine (2,756 ft)
OFFICIAL LANGUAGE: English
CURRENCY: East Caribbean dollar

HAITI
République d'Haïti
AREA: 10,714 sq mi.
POPULATION: 7.7 million
CAPITAL: Port-au-Prince
OTHER CITIES: Jacmel, Les Cayes
HIGHEST POINT: La Selle (8,783 ft)
OFFICIAL LANGUAGES: French, Creole
CURRENCY: Gourde

Many beautiful islands lie between the Straits of Florida and the Venezuelan coast of South America. To the west is the Gulf of Mexico and to the east lies the open Atlantic Ocean. Many of the islands are formed from coral; others are the tops of undersea volcanoes, some of which are still active. Offshore reefs form underwater worlds of corals, seaweeds, and brilliantly colored fish.

The climate is generally tropical and warm, with the humidity relieved by ocean breezes on the smaller islands. Hurricanes bring high winds and rains in late summer and the fall.

The Bahamas and the Turks and Caicos islands form the northern, outer ring of islands. The Greater Antilles chain includes Cuba, the largest island of the region. It has fertile plains, rolling hills, forests, and mountains. Its neighbors are the Cayman Islands, Jamaica, Hispaniola (divided between Haiti and the Dominican Republic), and Puerto Rico.

The islands of the Lesser Antilles are smaller, scattered around a great arc between the Virgin Islands and Aruba. The northern ones are known as the Leeward Islands and the southern ones as the Windward Islands. The area enclosed by the Antilles is the Caribbean Sea.

♡ CORAL REEF
Among the brightly colored corals of a reef live anemones, sponges, seahorses, and all kinds of fish.

ANTIGUA AND BARBUDA
AREA: 171 sq mi.
POPULATION: 71,000
CAPITAL: St Johns
HIGHEST POINT: Boggy Peak (1,329 ft)
OFFICIAL LANGUAGE: English
CURRENCY: East Caribbean dollar

BAHAMAS
Commonwealth of the Bahamas
AREA: 5,382 sq mi.
POPULATION: 0.3 million
CAPITAL: Nassau
HIGHEST POINT: Cat Island (207 ft)
OFFICIAL LANGUAGE: English
CURRENCY: Bahamian dollar

BARBADOS
AREA: 166 sq mi.
POPULATION: 0.26 million
CAPITAL: Bridgetown
HIGHEST POINT: Mt Hillaby (1,115 ft)
OFFICIAL LANGUAGE: English
CURRENCY: Barbados dollar

CUBA
República de Cuba
AREA: 42,803 sq mi.
POPULATION: 11.0 million
CAPITAL: Havana
OTHER CITIES: Santiago de Cuba, Camagüey
HIGHEST POINT: Turquino (6,578 ft)
OFFICIAL LANGUAGE: Spanish
CURRENCY: Cuban peso

⟳ PALM TREES
Everyone's image of the Caribbean is of beautiful palm trees swaying in the breeze. Here, on the sunny island of Jamaica, coconuts are growing in trees that can be as tall as 80 feet.

⟳ STORMY WEATHER
Satellites in space track the progress of a hurricane. These devastating, whirling storms sweep across the Caribbean between August and October each year.

BAHAMAS

CUBA

PUERTO RICO

ST KITTS AND NEVIS

ANTIGUA AND BARBUDA

DOMINICA

ST LUCIA

JAMAICA

HAITI

DOMINICAN REPUBLIC

TRINIDAD AND TOBAGO

BARBADOS

ST VINCENT AND THE GRENADINES

GRENADA

⟳ DONKEY TRAFFIC
Donkeys are a traditional way of getting around in the mountainous countryside of the Dominican Republic.

⟳ TROPICAL BEACH, ST LUCIA
St Lucia is a volcanic island lying in the Windward Islands. Its white sand beaches and spectacular scenery attract many tourists.

CHE GUEVARA
Argentinian-born Ernesto "Che" Guevara played an important part in the Cuban revolution (1956–59). He was killed in Bolivia in 1967.

BOAT BUILDING
A wooden hull is constructed in Barbados. Boats are still built by traditional methods on many Caribbean islands.

There are 13 independent nations in the Caribbean region. Some are democratic republics, some still have European monarchs as their heads of state. Economic links are strengthened by the Caribbean Community and Common Market (Caricom, founded in 1973). Most of the Caribbean's 11 other territories remain dependencies of other countries by choice, because it brings them wealth and security. Some are governed as if they were part of mainland France.

Cuba, the largest Caribbean island, has had a Communist government since 1959, and until 1991 had vital trading links with the Communist countries of Central and Eastern Europe. Since the collapse of Communism in Europe, Cuba has had to struggle against a strict United States ban on trade.

Political violence and corruption have a long history on some islands, such as Haiti. On other islands, the problem has been one of alliances. For example, Anguilla refused to join the federation of St Kitts–Nevis when it became independent, and Aruba pulled out of the Netherlands Antilles. Other islands have been hard hit by natural disasters, such as hurricanes or volcanic eruptions.

Many of the Caribbean islanders are poor. Cash crops produced for export include spices, tropical fruits such as bananas, mangoes, and limes, sugarcane and cotton. Cuba is famous for its rum and tobacco. Many islanders fish and grow their own food. Popular local dishes are made from saltfish, pigeon peas, coconut, chilli peppers, and cornmeal.

RADIO TELESCOPE
The world's biggest single-unit radio telescope is located near Arecibo, on the island of Puerto Rico.

FACTS

JAMAICA
AREA: 4,244 sq mi.
POPULATION: 2.5 million
CAPITAL: Kingston
OTHER CITIES: Spanish Town, Montego Bay
HIGHEST POINT: Blue Mountain Peak (7,402 ft)
OFFICIAL LANGUAGE: English
CURRENCY: Jamaican dollar

ST KITTS – NEVIS
Federation of St Christopher and Nevis
AREA: 104 sq mi.
POPULATION: 0.04 million
CAPITAL: Basseterre
HIGHEST POINT: Liamuiga (3,793 ft)
OFFICIAL LANGUAGE: English
CURRENCY: East Caribbean dollar

ST LUCIA
AREA: 617 sq mi.
POPULATION: 0.16 million
CAPITAL: Castries
HIGHEST POINT: Mt Gimie (3,145 ft)
OFFICIAL LANGUAGE: English
CURRENCY: East Caribbean dollar

ST VINCENT AND THE GRENADINES
AREA: 150 sq mi.
POPULATION: 0.11 million
CAPITAL: Kingstown
HIGHEST POINT: La Soufrière (4,173 ft)
OFFICIAL LANGUAGE: English
CURRENCY: East Caribbean dollar

TRINIDAD AND TOBAGO
Republic of Trinidad and Tobago
AREA: 1,980 sq mi.
POPULATION: 1.3 million
CAPITAL: Port-of-Spain
OTHER CITIES: San Fernando, Arima
HIGHEST POINT: Aripo (3,084 ft)
OFFICIAL LANGUAGE: English
CURRENCY: Trinidad and Tobago dollar

CHANGING TIMES
St Lucia's Rodney Bay was once a swampy coastline with a couple of fishing villages. In the 1940s it was transformed into a US naval airbase. Today it is a tourist center, with a yachting marina and many hotels.

MARKET DAY
What's on sale in a Caribbean market? Lush tropical fruits, coconuts, saltfish, seafood, and vegetables. Snacks on offer are sure to include rotis—pancakes wrapped around curried chicken and vegetables.

◑ Fidel Castro
The leader of Cuba's revolution was Fidel Castro. He overthrew the regime of Fulgencio Batista in 1959.

Manufacturing is limited, but Trinidad produces oil and natural gas. The region's blue seas and beaches of white sand fringed with palms have made tourism a major industry in many islands. Other islands, such as the Caymans, have passed tax laws that allow international finance companies and banks to set up their headquarters there. The wealth made from tourism and offshore banking often fails to benefit the local people.

◐ CARIBBEAN VILLAGE
Most Caribbeans live in simple, one-storey homes. White walls reflect the sun and keep the interiors cool despite the fierce heat outside. Up to four generations of the same family may live together in one or these small houses.

◑ WORLD-CLASS CIGARS
Cuba has long been famous for the finest quality cigars and for rum, made from sugarcane.

FACTS

Caribbean dependencies

ANGUILLA
British Overseas Territory
AREA: 35 sq mi.
POPULATION: 9,000
CAPITAL: The Valley
OFFICIAL LANGUAGE: English
CURRENCY: East Caribbean dollar

ARUBA
Self-governing island of the Netherlands
AREA: 75 sq mi.
POPULATION: 0.08 million
CAPITAL: Oranjestad
OFFICIAL LANGUAGE: Dutch
CURRENCY: Florin

CAYMAN ISLANDS
British Overseas Territory
AREA: 102 sq mi.
POPULATION: 0.03 million
CAPITAL: George Town
OFFICIAL LANGUAGE: English
CURRENCY: Cayman Islands dollar

GUADELOUPE
Overseas region of France
AREA: 658 sq mi.
POPULATION: 0.4 million
CAPITAL: Basse-Terre
OFFICIAL LANGUAGE: French
CURRENCY: Euro

MARTINIQUE
Overseas region of France
AREA: 425 sq mi.
POPULATION: 0.4 million
CAPITAL: Fort-de-France
OFFICIAL LANGUAGE: French
CURRENCY: Euro

125

○ THE SLAVE TRADE

From the 1500s to the 1800s, slaves were brought to the Caribbean from Africa and were sold at markets. Families were separated, and punishments were harsh, often fatal.

○ SUGAR PLANTATIONS

Sugarcane was the mainstay of the Caribbean economy from the 1600s until recent times. Sugar was shipped to Europe and North America. Slaves imported from West Africa worked the European-owned plantations.

FACTS

Caribbean dependencies

MONTSERRAT
British Overseas Territory
AREA: 39 sq mi.
POPULATION: 6,000
CAPITAL: Plymouth
OFFICIAL LANGUAGE: English
CURRENCY: East Caribbean dollar

NETHERLANDS ANTILLES
Self-governing islands of the Netherlands
AREA: 308 sq mi.
POPULATION: 0.2 million
CAPITAL: Willemstad
OFFICIAL LANGUAGE: Dutch
CURRENCY: Netherlands Antilles guilder

PUERTO RICO
Commonwealth territory of the USA
AREA: 3,427 sq mi.
POPULATION: 3.8 million
CAPITAL: San Juan
OFFICIAL LANGUAGES: English, Spanish
CURRENCY: US dollar

TURKS AND CAICOS ISLANDS
British Overseas Territory
AREA: 166 sq mi.
POPULATION: 0.01 million
CAPITAL: Cockburn Town
OFFICIAL LANGUAGE: English
CURRENCY: US dollar

VIRGIN ISLANDS (BRITISH)
British Overseas Territory
AREA: 58 sq mi.
POPULATION: 0.02 million
CAPITAL: Road Town
OFFICIAL LANGUAGE: English
CURRENCY: US dollar

VIRGIN ISLANDS (USA)
Unincorporated Territory of the USA
AREA: 134 sq mi.
POPULATION: 0.1 million
CAPITAL: Charlotte Amalie
OFFICIAL LANGUAGE: English
CURRENCY: US dollar

In prehistoric times the Caribbean islands were settled by indigenous people from the American mainland. By the time Columbus sailed to the islands in 1492, there were two main groups of peoples on the islands—the Arawaks and Caribs. The Arawaks were savagely treated by the Spanish. They were enslaved, murdered, or infected with diseases. The Caribs, who had a fearsome reputation among the Europeans, resisted longer. In the end, however, few communities survived.

The Spanish took over many islands. As their fleets shipped back plundered treasures from the mainland (the "Spanish Main"), they were preyed on by British, French, and Dutch pirates. Soon these countries too seized islands and planted them with tobacco and sugarcane. They imported slaves from Africa to work the land. Cruelly treated, some slaves escaped and there were violent revolts in Jamaica and Haiti in the 1700s. In the 1800s, Haiti became the first independent Afro-Caribbean republic.

○ CARNIVAL

Carnival in Trinidad is a time for dressing up in costumes, dancing, steel-band music, and verses called calypsos.

○ THE SANTA MARIA

Christopher Columbus' ship reached San Salvador, in the Bahamas, in 1492—a turning point in American history.

○ PIRATE WOMEN

Two notorious women pirates, Anne Bonny and Mary Read, went on trial in Jamaica in 1720. Caribbean coasts had long been terrorized by pirates and buccaneers.

⟳ BACK TO AFRICA

Rastafarians look back to their African roots and honor Haile Selassie (1891–1975), former emperor of Ethiopia.

After the abolition of slavery (mostly in the 1830s) many European settlers left the region they called the West Indies. People from India and Southeast Asia were hired to work on some islands, such as Trinidad. Most Caribbean islands remained colonies until the 1960s.

Today's Caribbeans are descended from many peoples—Native Americans, Africans, Spanish, English, Irish, French, Dutch, and Asians. The two largest ethnic groups are of Afro-Caribbean and Hispanic descent. Spanish, English, and French are widely spoken, often in Creole dialects influenced by African languages.

Christianity is strong. On Haiti, some people practice Voodoo, an African spirit religion. The Rastafarians of Jamaica are inspired by African spirituality.

Caribbean music and dance styles—from salsa to reggae—have become popular all over the world. Music comes to the fore in the region's famous carnivals. Popular sports include cricket, soccer, and baseball.

⟳ STEEL BAND

Steel drums called pans make the typical sound of Trinidad.

⟳ HAITIAN VOODOO

Drums and dancing send people into a trance at Cap Haitien. Voodoo, known as Vodun in the Creole dialect of Haiti, is based on an African belief in spirits called loas. It inspired the slave revolts on Haiti and is still popular today.

⟳ THE MUCH-LOVED GAME OF CRICKET

West Indian cricket teams have been world-beaters since the 1960s. It is a hugely popular sport in the Caribbean islands.

TIMELINE

AD

c.200	Native American settlement: Ciboney people expelled from Cuba by the Taíno
c.1000	Arawak and Carib migrations and wars
1492	Christopher Columbus lands in the Bahamas
1496	First Spanish settlement, Santo Domingo (Hispaniola)
1511	Spanish settle Cuba
1523	Slave trade with Africa
1655	British capture Jamaica
1660s	Piracy widespread (until 1720s)
1697	French gain control of Haiti (Hispaniola)
1804	Haiti independent republic under black rule
1838	Abolition of slave trade in some parts of the region
1868	Independence movement defeated in Cuba (by 1878)
1895	Uprising in Cuba (until 1898)
1898	Puerto Rico ceded to USA
1952	Fulgencio Batista seizes power in Cuba
1959	Fidel Castro overthrows Batista in Cuba
1961	Barbados independent
1962	Cuban Missile Crisis: clash with USA over siting of Soviet missile base. Jamaica, Trinidad independent
1973	Bahamas independent
1983	USA invades Grenada
1995	Series of volcanic eruptions on Montserrat

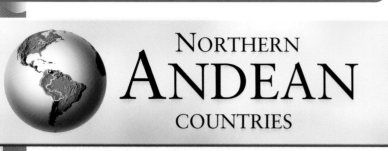

NORTHERN ANDEAN COUNTRIES

○ BIRD WITH SNAKE
Beautiful stone carvings were made at San Augustín, Colombia, about 2,000 years ago.

FACTS

BOLIVIA
República de Bolivia
AREA: 424,164 sq mi.
POPULATION: 8.5 million
CAPITALS: La Paz, Sucre
OTHER CITIES: Santa Cruz, Cochabamba
HIGHEST POINT: Nevado Sajama (21,463 ft)
OFFICIAL LANGUAGE: Spanish
CURRENCY: Peso boliviano

COLOMBIA
República de Colombia
AREA: 440,831 sq mi.
POPULATION: 43 million
CAPITAL: Bogotá
OTHER CITIES: Medellín, Cali, Barranquilla
HIGHEST POINT: Cristobal Colón (19,029 ft)
OFFICIAL LANGUAGE: Spanish
CURRENCY: Colombian peso

ECUADOR
República del Ecuador
AREA: 178,176 sq mi. (including Galapágos Islands)
POPULATION: 12.8 million
CAPITAL: Quito
OTHER CITIES: Guayaquil, Cuenca
HIGHEST POINT: Chimborazo (20,702 ft)
OFFICIAL LANGUAGE: Spanish
CURRENCY: Dollar

PERU
República de Peru
AREA: 496,225 sq mi.
POPULATION: 26 million
CAPITAL: Lima
OTHER CITIES: Callao, Arequipa, Chiclayo
HIGHEST POINT: Nevado Huascarán (22,205 ft)
OFFICIAL LANGUAGES: Spanish, Quechua, Aymará
CURRENCY: Nuevo sol

The Andes mountains run the length of South America, from Colombia in the north to Tierra del Fuego in the south—nearly 4,000 miles. The mountains are very high, very beautiful, and very valuable, for they contain precious silver, tin, and other minerals.

The Andes range includes massive snow-capped volcanoes, gleaming glaciers, and wide, cool plateaus. Titicaca, the world's highest navigable lake, occupies 3,200 square miles of the plateau on the border between Peru and Bolivia. To the north, the Andes drop to low-lying plains around the humid Caribbean coast. To the west, they are bordered by a coastal strip along the Pacific Ocean. In parts this is humid and fertile, but in Peru much of it is dusty desert, made dry because cold ocean currents make it more difficult for the air to fill with moisture and form rain.

Far out west in the Pacific is the Galápagos island chain, which belongs to Ecuador. In eastern Ecuador, the peaks and sunlit plateaus of the Andes descend through misty foothills and sheer-sided valleys into the vast rainforests of central South America. Streams rising on the eastern slopes drain into the great Orinoco and Amazon river systems.

⚫ BAÑOS, ECUADOR
This small town lies in the eastern Andes, on the route to El Oriente, Ecuador's province in the Amazon River basin.

COLOMBIA

⚘ ANDES WATERSHED
South America is divided into two by the Andes range. Some rainfall drains into the Pacific Ocean, but the rest flows eastward into the distant Atlantic.

⚘ LAKE TITICACA
This is the largest lake in South America. It is really made up of two smaller lakes, Chucuito and Uinamarca, which are linked by a narrow strait.

ECUADOR

⚘ ONE MORE RIVER TO CROSS
The Urubamba rises in the Andes and flows through deep gorges. It eventually joins up with the Apurímac to form the Ucayali, which in turn drains into the mighty Amazon.

PERU

⚘ EASTERN BOLIVIA
These village huts are in the Las Yungas region of eastern Bolivia, where the Altiplano (high plateau) drops to the humid, forested lowlands of the Amazon basin.

BOLIVIA

⚘ CONDOR

⚘ HIGH ALTITUDE
The Chacaltuya ski lodge near La Paz, Bolivia, is the world's highest. It overlooks the tablelands of the Altiplano.

⚘ RIVER OF ICE
In Peru, the Andes divide into three main sections. The highest peaks rise in the Cordillera Blanca. Here, snow-capped peaks tower above glaciers such as Pastoruri, at 17,390 feet above sea level.

Map labels

Point. Gallinas
Barranquilla
Cartagena
Cristobal Colón 5,775 m
PANAMA
VENEZUELA
Cauca
Magdalena
Meta
Medellin
Cape Corrientes
Pereira · Manizales
Ibagué · Bogotá
COLOMBIA
Buenaventura
Cali · Neiva
Nevado del Huila 5,750 m
Pasto
Guaviare
Point Galera
Quito
ECUADOR
Caquetá
Chimborazo 6,267 m
Guayaquil
Gulf of Guayaquil
Putumayo
Amazon
Marañón
Iquitos
Point Aguja
Piura
Chiclayo
BRAZIL
Trujillo
Ucayali
Chimbote · Nevado Huascarán 6,768 m
PERU
Callao
Lima · Huancayo
Paracas Pen.
Cuzco
Nazca
Volcán El Misti 5,842 m
Arequipa
Lake Titicaca
PACIFIC OCEAN
Mamoré
Guaporé
Nevado Ancohume 6,550 m
BOLIVIA
La Paz
Cochabamba
Santa Cruz
Oruro
Lake Poopó
Sucre
Potosí
Pilcomayo
CHILE
ALTIPLANO
PARAGUAY

N / W E / S

◑ FISHING
The Aymara and Uru peoples of Lake Titicaca fish in the deep lake for catfish, trout, and killifish.

◑ COCAINE PATROL
A plane hunts for secret plantations of coca. The coca plant is processed to make the drug called cocaine.

The four countries of the northern Andes are all republics. The army has often seized power in this region, or controlled governments behind the scenes. There have been long years of guerrilla warfare, fueled by widespread poverty and social injustice. There have been murderous activities by the criminal gangs who export cocaine. This illegal drug is made from the coca plant, which has been grown by poor peasants in the region for thousands of years.

The northern Andes region has great mineral wealth in the form of oil, copper, emeralds, silver, tin, zinc, lead,

◑ GATHERING REEDS
Tall, tough reeds called totora grow on the shores and islands of Lake Titicaca, and on floating platforms of vegetation. The reeds are harvested and bound together in bundles to make houses and fishing boats, called balsas.

◑ ANDEAN STATION
Alausí, in Ecuador's Chimborazo province, is built on the Guayaquil–Quito railroad. The world's highest railroads are in the Andes, in Peru.

silver and gold. However, many people, both in the cities and in the country, remain very poor. In the hot lowlands, farmers grow cotton, sugarcane, and bananas. Colombian coffee beans, grown on tropical slopes, are among the best in the world. On the cool plateaus, potatoes, corn, wheat, and a grain called quinoa are grown.

The forests produce valuable timber. Sardines, anchovies, and tuna are caught by the large Pacific fishing fleets. Shrimps are farmed along the coast. Fish are also processed to make fertilizers.

◑ REED PIPES
Known as antaras or zampoñas, panpipes have been played since the days of the Incas.

◑ LOCAL TRANSPORT
A motorized rickshaw provides transportation in Chiclayo, the chief town of Peru's Lambayeque region. It lies on the Pan-American Highway, the road network that links North and South America.

◑ LIMA STADIUM

Peru's National Stadium is sited in Lima, the capital. Lima is home to nearly six million people.

◑ SILVER MOUNTAIN

When the Spanish conquered Bolivia, Cerro Rico, in Potosí, became the world's biggest silver mine. The riches were shipped back to Europe.

◑ COLOMBIAN CAPITAL

Mountains rise behind Bogotá's modern high-rise skyline. Colombia's chief city is home to some five million people.

The region is strongly Roman Catholic and there are many religious festivals and pilgrimages. Spanish is spoken in all four countries. There are many people of mestizo (mixed European and Indian) descent, as well as some of European, African, or Asian descent. Indigenous (native) peoples make up just one percent of the population in Colombia, but 25 percent in Ecuador, 45 percent in Peru, and 55 percent in Bolivia.

The two largest indigenous groups are the Aymara and Quechua. Most of these "Indians" are poor peasants and are largely ignored by those who hold power in the cities. In the mountains, life carries on as it has for centuries, with the local people weaving, going to market, and herding llamas. The haunting folk music of the Andes is played on guitars, panpipes, flutes, and drums.

◑ FARMING THE SLOPES

Farmers were already terracing the steep Andean slopes in ancient times, in order to conserve soil. The Incas were masters of irrigation techniques.

◑ MULE TRAIN

Surefooted but stubborn, mules have been used to transport goods in the Andes since the 1500s.

131

In prehistoric times, the northern Andes region was settled by waves of different tribes, and many advanced ancient civilizations developed there.

From about 1200 BC to 200 BC, the Chavín civilization produced stone carvings, pottery, and painted textiles. Strange lines and complex designs cut deep into the desert near Nazca in southern Peru may have been made to honor the gods. Farther north, the Moche valley was the center of a civilization that built pyramids in honor of the Sun, and engineered an irrigation system for crops in dry regions.

⟁ TEMPLE OF THE SUN
This pyramid dominated the Moche capital. Standing 131 feet high, it is believed to have been made of about 140 million mud bricks.

⟁ INCA STONES
The Incas were master stone masons. Their stone buildings have withstood the strongest earthquakes.

Over 1,000 years ago, the Chimú people of northern Peru were masters at working gold. They also produced pottery on a large scale.

Perhaps the most amazing civilization was that of the Incas, who defeated the Chimú in AD 1476. The Inca empire, with its capital at Cuzco in Peru, stretched from Ecuador to Chile, and ruled some 12 million people. The Incas built cities and towns with great temples, and they studied the stars.

Spain invaded Colombia in 1499. By 1532 a small force of Spanish soldiers, the conquistadors,

⟁ LA PAZ, BOLIVIA
A street vendor sells vegetables in La Paz, one of Bolivia's twin capitals. La Paz, at 11,913 feet above sea level, is the world's highest capital.

had used treachery to overthrow the powerful Inca empire to the south. They were greedy for gold and silver, and the northern Andes offered wealth beyond their dreams.

⟁ LURE OF GOLD
The Spanish were first attracted to South America by rumors of a wealth of gold.

⟁ INCA TRAIL
Across the empire, the Incas built mountain strongholds, towns, canals, forts, resthouses, and irrigation schemes, so more land could be farmed. Goods were carried by llama and messages by relays of runners.

◯ MACHU PICCHU
The best-known of Peru's Inca cities was built high above the gorges of the Urubamba valley, probably in the 15th century. It was surrounded by terraced field strips for farming.

Spain's rule over the region lasted nearly 300 years. The Spanish built churches and cities, mined for silver, and used the indigenous people to work the land. In the 1820s a revolutionary named Simón Bolívar (1783–1830) led the struggle against continuing rule by Spain. His name was given to one of the territories he freed—Bolivia.

Liberated from Spanish rule, the newly independent countries soon fought each other. A few families of the ruling class became very wealthy, but most people remained poor into modern times.

◯ QUITO, ECUADOR
The capital of Ecuador has old colonial buildings alongside modern offices and factories. The city is built at 9,350 feet above sea level, beneath the Pichincha volcano.

◯ PILGRIMAGE
The Spanish conquerors brought Roman Catholicism to the Andes. This is the Sanctuary of Nuestra Señora de Acua Santa, in Ecuador.

◯ CONQUEST
The Spanish reached Peru in 1532. They captured the emperor, Atahualpa, by treachery and soon conquered all the Inca lands, although resistance continued for 40 years.

TIMELINE

BC

8500	Possible origins of farming in Peru
3000	Pottery made in Colombia and Ecuador
1500	Metalworking in Peru
900	Chavín civilization in Andes
200	Nazca civilization, Peru

AD

1	Moche civilization, Peru
600	Tiahuanaco civilization, Bolivia
1200	Beginnings of Inca empire
1250	Chimu civilization, Peru
1400s	Inca empire at greatest extent
1531	Spanish land in Ecuador
1533	Incas defeated by Spanish
1538	Colombia conquered by Spanish
1545	Silver mining in Bolivia
1780	Indigenous uprising in Peru
1819	Colombia independent from Spain
1822	Ecuador joins Colombia
1824	Peru independent from Spain
1825	Bolivia independent from Spain
1830	Full independence for Colombia; Ecuador independent
1932	Chaco War (until 1935): Bolivia defeated by Paraguay
1941	Peru invades Ecuador
1948	Organization of American States signed, Colombia
1952	Bolivian National Revolution
1989	Drug gang violence in Colombia

133

BRAZIL
AND ITS NEIGHBORS

☉ FLESH-EATERS
Shoals of flesh-eating piranha fish are found in the Amazon basin.

Venezuela ("Little Venice") was given its name because the vast, shallow inlet of Lake Maracaibo reminded early European explorers of the lagoons around Venice in Italy.

Venezuela is dominated by the Orinoco River, which forces its way between a northern spur of the Andes Mountains and the Guiana Highlands. It flows through the grassy plains of the llanos to form a wide, swampy delta on the Caribbean coast. In the central southeast, the Angel Falls—the world's highest waterfall—drop a spectacular 3,211 feet.

The low-lying Caribbean coast, with its hot, sticky climate, continues eastward through Guyana, Surinam, and French Guiana. In the south of these countries the land rises to the forested slopes of the Guiana Highlands.

Across the Brazilian border, the highlands descend to the great basin of the Amazon River. This mighty river is fed by thousands of waterways that seep through the tropical growth of the world's largest rainforest, which covers an area of over 815 million acres. Broad and muddy, the Amazon flows eastward to the Atlantic Ocean. Southern Brazil rises to the Brazilian Highlands and the tropical plateau of the Matto Grosso. This is drained in the south by the Paraná River.

☉ GIANT SNAKE
The anaconda can grow to 30 feet long. It hunts in rivers and pools, and strangles or drowns its prey.

☉ PALMS IN THE PANTANAL
In southwestern Brazil, the Pantanal wetlands are created by the seasonal flooding of the Paraguay River. The waters cover about 39,000 square miles of the Matto Grosso.

BRAZIL
República Federativa do Brasil
AREA: 3,265,076 sq mi.
POPULATION: 172 million
CAPITAL: Brasília
OTHER CITIES: São Paulo, Rio de Janeiro, Salvador, Belo Horizonte, Pôrto Alegre
HIGHEST POINT: Neblina (9,888 ft)
OFFICIAL LANGUAGE: Portuguese
CURRENCY: Real

GUYANA
Co-operative Republic of Guyana
AREA: 83,000 sq mi.
POPULATION: 0.8 million
CAPITAL: Georgetown
OTHER CITIES: New Amsterdam, Linden
HIGHEST POINT: Roraima (9,094 ft)
OFFICIAL LANGUAGE: English
CURRENCY: Guyana dollar

SURINAM
Republic of Suriname
AREA: 63,251 sq mi.
POPULATION: 0.4 million
CAPITAL: Paramaribo
OTHER CITIES: Groningen, Nieuw Amsterdam
HIGHEST POINT: Juliana Top (4,035 ft)
OFFICIAL LANGUAGE: Dutch
CURRENCY: Surinam guilder

◑ ANTEATER
There are three South American anteater species. All have long, sticky tongues for eating ants and termites.

GUYANA

◑ IGUAÇU FALLS
The Iguaçu River plunges over rocks in hundreds of waterfalls before it joins the Paraná River on the Brazil–Argentina border.

VENEZUELA

SURINAM

FRENCH GUIANA

BRAZIL

◑ IN EASTERN BRAZIL
This sandstone pillar at Vila Velha, in Brazil's Espirito Sánto state, has been weathered by wind and rain from the South Atlantic.

◑ POISON-ARROW FROG

◑ TAPIR
Tapirs live in the dense tropical rainforests and swamps of South America. They use their flexible top lips to gather food.

◑ BIG RIVER
The Amazon, with a total length of about 4,000 miles, is the world's second-longest river after the Nile in North Africa.

135

The northern half of South America is divided up into four independent republics—Brazil, the largest country in the continent; Venezuela; and two small Caribbean countries, Surinam and Guyana. Neighboring French Guiana is still governed directly as a region of France.

This part of the world has huge cities and busy ports, as well as remote forest and mountain areas that have never been explored. The region has great natural wealth in the form of Venezuelan oil, coal, iron ore, bauxite (for making aluminium), chrome, copper, gold, and silver. Brazilian factories make cars and computers.

The rainforests of the Amazon provide timber. Rapid clearance of the forests by farmers, miners, and loggers threatens to be a disaster not just for Brazil but for the planet as a whole. Beef cattle are raised on much of the cleared land.

↻ LAKE OF OIL
The Venezuelan economy depends on Lake Maracaibo's oil reserves.

Cattle are also reared on the wide llanos grasslands of Venezuela.

Brazil is the world's leading producer of coffee and sugarcane. Other crops include rice, corn, soya beans, cassava, and citrus fruits. Cayenne, in French Guiana, is famous for its red hot pepper, while Guyana is known for the sticky brown sugar first produced in the Demerara region.

VENEZUELA
República de Venezuela
AREA: 352,144 sq mi.
POPULATION: 24.6 million
CAPITAL: Caracas
OTHER CITIES: Maracaibo, Valencia
HIGHEST POINT: Pico Bolívar (16,427 ft)
OFFICIAL LANGUAGE: Spanish
CURRENCY: Bolívar

FRENCH GUIANA
Guyane Française
Overseas region of France
AREA: 34,749 sq mi.
POPULATION: 0.2 million
CAPITAL: Cayenne
OFFICIAL LANGUAGE: French
CURRENCY: Euro

◯ BRAZIL NUTS

↻ A VANISHING WORLD
The Amazon basin contains one-third of the world's surviving rainforest. This is one of the planet's most precious resources, but vast areas have already been destroyed.

◯ CASSAVA PLANTATION
The fleshy roots of the cassava plant are used to make flour; its leaves are eaten as a vegetable.

◯ CAYENNE PEPPER
This hot spice takes its name from the capital of French Guiana.

PARROT TRADE
Many wild parrots are collected from the rainforest to be sold as pets.

Despite its wealth of resources, the region has faced huge economic problems. There has been severe inflation, rising debt, and political corruption. Venezuela relies heavily on its oil, for which the price has fallen in recent years.

Although some people are wealthy, many are desperately poor. In big cities, such as Caracas and Rio de Janeiro, families with little chance of finding work crowd into makeshift shanty towns and slums. In remote areas, many of the indigenous peoples, referred to as "Indians," have been killed and had their land stolen. Their rivers have been poisoned and the forests where they hunt have been cut down.

SUGARCANE
Workers harvest the sugarcane crop. Next, the stalks are crushed and soaked in water to produce a sugary liquid. When this is heated, it separates into brown crystals of cane sugar and sticky molasses.

A SAFE ROAD
Cattle are herded along the Transpantaneira, the only route through Brazil's Pantanal wetlands.

SPACE AGE
The rocket launch site at Kourou in French Guiana is operated by the European Space Agency.

PARAMARIBO, SURINAM
Paramaribo, at the mouth of the Surinam River, is Surinam's capital and its biggest port. Nearly 50 percent of the population live there.

☢ SOCCER FANS

Soccer is popular all over South America, and nowhere more so than Brazil, five-times World Cup winners.

The first or indigenous peoples of northern South America now make up only a very small portion of the population—just five percent in Guyana and under two percent in Brazil. They mostly live in scattered communities, many in remote areas of rainforest where they hunt and fish. Groups include the Xingu, Yanomami, Shavanti, Kayapo, coastal Caribs, Warrau, and many others besides. More than 85 indigenous groups are known to have been wiped out over the last 100 years.

Many people of the region are mestizos, of mixed European and indigenous descent.

☢ MIXED DESCENT

Brazil is a multiracial society, with many people of mixed indigenous, European, or African descent.

☢ A RAINFOREST VILLAGE

The round huts of the Yanomami may be seen in Venezuela and Brazil. Yanomami lands have been steadily destroyed by mining since the 1970s.

European settlement of the region has been from Portugal, Spain, Italy, the Netherlands, France, Britain, and Germany. There are also sizeable black populations, of African descent. The Caribbean coast has a large Asian population, with many Javanese living in Surinam.

The region's official languages all date from its period of colonial rule—Portuguese in Brazil, Spanish in Venezuela, English in Guyana, Dutch in Surinam, and French in French Guiana.

☢ RIVER BORDERS

The Paraguay River flows past Corumba, a town on Brazil's border with Bolivia. The river goes on to form the Brazil–Paraguay, and Paraguay–Argentina borders.

◆ ON THE BEACH
Swimmers and sunbathers are attracted to Rio de Janeiro's beaches, on the South Atlantic coast. This one is at a wealthy southern suburb, Barra de Tijuca.

◆ KAYAPO MUSICIAN
The Kayapo people live in northeastern Brazil, between the Araguaia and Xingu rivers.

As in most Latin American regions, soccer is by far the most popular sport. It is practiced on almost every beach, village clearing, or street corner. Brazil has the most successful World Cup record of any nation.

Brazil and Venezuela are largely Roman Catholic, but there are also Protestants, Hindus, and Muslims. Spirit religions such as Candomblé, influenced by both African and Roman Catholic traditions, are popular in Brazil.

The fascinating mixture of cultures in the region has influenced festivals such as the five-day carnival in Rio de Janeiro, with its dazzling costume parades and dancing to Brazil's own rhythm, the samba. Ethnic variety has also contributed to regional cooking, which combines African, Asian, and European influences.

◆ SHANTY TOWN
São Paulo, home to over 15 million people, is Brazil's biggest city. Many desperately poor families live in makeshift housing and slums.

◆ CARACAS
The Venezuelan capital, Caracas, has spread out from its old colonial center to include city parks, high-rise offices and apartments, shopping malls, and factories.

◆ JAVA COMES TO SURINAM
Many workers from Dutch colonies in Southeast Asia found work in Surinam after 1863. They brought their own culture, such as this ritual horse dance.

◆ CARNIVAL IN RIO
For five days each year the Brazilian city of Rio de Janeiro is taken over by carnival, with costumed revelers dancing the samba in the streets.

The early peoples of the rainforest left behind fewer reminders of their way of life than the peoples of the high Andes. They built with wood, creepers, and straw instead of stone—materials that do not survive long in humid, tropical climates. Even so, archeologists are beginning to learn more about the skill with which these peoples managed the forest, planting trees and seeds they could use for food, medicines, and shelter.

⊙ GEORGETOWN, GUYANA
The Caribbean port of Georgetown is Guyana's capital. City Hall, on the Avenue of the Republic, dates from the colonial period (1831–1970).

Cabral vor dem Samorin.

⊙ PEDRO ALVARES CABRAL
This Portuguese navigator discovered Brazil by mistake, in 1500, when his fleet, bound for India, was carried west by ocean currents.

The Spanish arrived in Venezuela In 1498, and the Portuguese in Brazil two years later. Their arrival was a disaster for the indigenous peoples, many of whom died of European diseases. The French and Dutch occupied territory on the Caribbean coast during the 1600s and 1700s, with Britain capturing what is now Guyana in 1796. The Europeans planted sugarcane and other crops, and brought slaves from Africa to work the plantations. Later, many Asian laborers were hired to work along the Caribbean coast.

Venezuela broke away from Spanish rule between 1811 and 1821, after a war of independence led by freedom-fighter Simón Bolívar. Portugal became a kingdom in its own right in 1815, and was declared an independent empire seven years later.

⊙ OPERA HOUSE, MANAUS
Manaus lies in the rainforest, on the Río Negro. Its ornate opera house dates from 1896, when the region was profiting from the rubber trade.

⊙ THE LIBERATOR
Simón Bolívar was born in Venezuela in 1783. In the 1820s, his armies helped to drive the Spanish out of South America.

⊙ FOREST HOME
The first Amazonians used forest products for building materials, foods, and medicines.

However, the rich landowners threw out the Portuguese royal family when it ordered an end to slavery.

In 1889, Brazil became a republic. In the 1960s it moved its capital from Rio de Janeiro, on the Atlantic coast, to Brasília, a new, specially built capital up in the Brazilian Highlands.

In 1946, French Guiana became ruled on an equal status with mainland France. Guyana gained independence from Britain in 1970, and Surinam from the Netherlands in 1975.

◐ BRASÍLIA
This purpose-built city, planned by architect Lucio Costa, became Brazil's capital in 1960. It was more centrally located than the previous capital, Río de Janeiro.

◐ THE OIL PRESIDENT
Carlos Andréas Perez was president of Venezuela 1974–79, during the country's oil boom.

◑ SPANISH CARACAS
Colonial buildings date back to the 1500s and 1600s, when Venezuela was ruled by Spain.

◐ LANDLESS PROTEST
Despite Brazil's vast natural resources, many millions of its citizens live below the poverty line. Here, landless farm laborers join a protest rally in São Paulo.

TIMELINE

AD

400	Marajoara culture, mouth of Amazon
1498	Spanish land in Venezuela
1500	Portuguese claim Brazil
1593	Spanish claim Surinam
1600s	Sugar plantations in Brazil: slave labor imported from Africa
1602	Dutch settle Surinam
1604	French settle Cayenne
1620s	Dutch settle Guyana
1667	Surinam becomes a Dutch colony
1749	Venezuelan revolt against Spain
1815	Brazil united with Portuguese kingdom
1821	Venezuela joins independent Colombia
1822	Brazil declares independence under Spanish prince, Pedro
1825	Pedro I recognized as emperor of Brazil
1829	Venezuela becomes independent state
1831	Guyana becomes colony of British Guiana
1834	Slavery abolished in British Guiana
1888	Slavery abolished in Brazil
1889	Brazil becomes a republic
1910	Oil discovered in Venezuela
1946	French Guiana becomes overseas department of France
1960	Brasília becomes capital of Brazil
1966	Guyana becomes independent
1975	Surinam becomes independent
1992	First Earth Summit (UN world environment conference), Río de Janeiro

ARGENTINA
AND ITS NEIGHBORS

○ BROWN
PELICAN

Paraguay lies at the heart of South America. It is crossed by the Paraguay River, which flows into the Paraná. In the west is the tropical wilderness of the Gran Chaco, and in the east are both forests and grasslands, farms and ranches. Uruguay lies on the mouth of the River Plate, on the South Atlantic coast. It is a land of fertile plains and low hills.

In the northeast of Argentina is the rich farmland of the Mesopotamia region, lying between the Paraná and Uruguay rivers. The central north takes in part of the Gran Chaco, while the central eastern region is made up of open, rolling grassland. Known as the pampas, it is now used for ranching and agriculture. To the south again are the bleak, grassy plateaus and valleys of Patagonia.

The southern Andes form the border between Argentina and Chile, rising to the highest peaks in all the Americas. Chile lies between the western slopes and the South Pacific Ocean. This narrow coastal strip includes cool green regions, warm lands with a mild, Mediterranean climate, and the Atacama Desert—one of the driest spots on Earth, where rain may not fall for years at a time.

Across the Strait of Magellan, the continent breaks up into the islands of Tierra del Fuego and the cold, gray seas off Cape Horn.

○ GUANO ROCKS
This rock near Constitución in central Chile is covered in guanos (the droppings of seabirds). In parts of South America, guano is a valuable resource, collected to make fertilizers.

○ VOLCANO
Volcanic peaks rise above Lake Chungara in Chile.

FACTS

ARGENTINA
República Argentina
AREA: 1,073,399 sq mi.
POPULATION: 37.4 million
CAPITAL: Buenos Aires
OTHER CITIES: Córdoba, La Plata, San Miguel de Tucumán
HIGHEST POINT: Aconcagua (22,834 ft)
OFFICIAL LANGUAGE: Spanish
CURRENCY: Argentinean peso

CHILE
República de Chile
AREA: 292,135 sq mi.
POPULATION: 15.4 million
CAPITAL: Santiago
OTHER CITIES: Vina del Mar, Valparaíso, Concepción
HIGHEST POINT: Ojos del Salado (22,572 ft)
OFFICIAL LANGUAGE: Spanish
CURRENCY: Chilean peso

PARAGUAY
República del Paraguay
AREA: 157,048 sq mi.
POPULATION: 5.6 million
CAPITAL: Asunción
OTHER CITIES: Ciudad del Este, Pedro Juan Caballero
Highest point: Villarrica (2,230 ft)
OFFICIAL LANGUAGE: Spanish
CURRENCY: guaraní

URUGUAY
República Oriental del Uruguay
AREA: 67,574 sq mi.
POPULATION: 3.3 million
CAPITAL: Montevideo
OTHER CITIES: Salto, Rivera
HIGHEST POINT: Mirador Nacional (1,643 ft)
OFFICIAL LANGUAGE: Spanish
CURRENCY: Uruguayan peso

FALKLAND ISLANDS
Islas Malvinas
British Overseas Colony
AREA: 4,700 sq mi.
POPULATION: 2,000
CAPITAL: Stanley
OFFICIAL LANGUAGE: English
CURRENCY: Falkland Islands pound

CURTAIN OF SPRAY
Argentina borders Brazil along the Iguazú (Iguaçu) River. A long stretch of the river is broken by islands, rapids, and waterfalls.

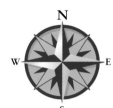

CANYON LANDS
Rivers have carved out canyons from the rocks of Patagonia. The Andes Mountains shield this vast, dry region of Argentina from the Pacific Ocean's rain-bearing winds.

IN PATAGONIA
South of the Río Negro, Argentina is a land of wind-swept plateaus and valleys.

PRICKLY PEAR

TIERRA DEL FUEGO
The southern tip of South America is a bleak peninsula occupied by both Argentina and Chile. The southernmost town in the world, Ushuaia, lies on the Beagle Channel.

PARAGUAY

ELEPHANT SEALS

IN THE SOUTHERN ANDES
The heavy ice of the Moreno Glacier grinds its way down to Lago Argentina, one of the most awesome sights in South America.

URUGUAY

ARGENTINA

SOUTH GEORGIA (U.K.)

CHILE

ARMADILLO

Map labels
Arica
Iquique
Antofagasta
Calama
BOLIVIA
Salta
Ojos del Salado 6,880 m
San Miguel de Tucumán
Copiapó
Santiago del Estero
Catamarca
La Rioja
Coquimbo
Pta. Lengua de Vaca
Mar Chiquito
San Juan
Córdoba
Aconcagua 6,959 m
Mendoza
Valparaiso
Santiago
Rancagua
San Rafael
San Luis
Rio Cuarto
Rosario
Santa Fe
Paraná
Talca
Chillán
Concepción
Pta. Lavapié
PAMPAS
ARGENTINA
Bahía Blanca
CHILE
Temuco
Neuquén
Negro
Colorado
Bahía Blanca
Valdivia
Pta. de la Galera
Osorno
Limay
Puerto Montt
Chiloé I.
Chubut
Rawson
C. Quilán
Viedma
San Matías Gulf
Valdés Peninsula
LOS CHONOS ARCHIPELAGO
Chico
Lake Buenos Aires
Deseado
Comodoro Rivadavia
San Jorge Gulf
C. Tres Puntas
Puerto Deseado
Penas Gulf
PACIFIC OCEAN
Chico
Wellington I.
Santa Cruz
Puerto Santa Cruz
FALKLAND/MALVINAS ISLANDS
Bahía Grande
West Falkland
East Falkland
Stanley
Río Gallegos
REINA ADELAIDA ARCHIPELAGO
Strait of Magellan
Punta Arenas
Tierra del Fuego
C. San Diego
Santa Inés I.
Ushuaia
Cape Horn
PARAGUAY
Verde
Concepción
BRAZIL
Pilcomayo
Bermejo
Asunción
Ciudad del Este
Formosa
Paraguay
Resistencia
Alto Paraná
Corrientes
Posadas
MESOPOTAMIA
Paraná
Salado
Concordia
Salto
Paysandú
URUGUAY
Negro
Buenos Aires
La Plata
Montevideo
Río de La Plata
Pta. Norte
Cape San Antonio
Mar del Plata
Cape Corrientes
ATACAMA DESERT
ANDES MOUNTAINS
SIERRA DE CORDOBA
PATAGONIA
GRAN CHACO
PACIFIC OCEAN

○ JUICY FRUIT
The orchards of central Chile produce fruit for export, including oranges, lemons, apples, grapes, and pears.

The southern mainland of South America is divided into four independent republics—the small northern nations of Uruguay and Paraguay, the wide open spaces of Argentina, and the long, narrow territory of Chile. The region has experienced long years of rule by military regimes and there have also been wars over borders and territory. In 1982 Argentina went to war with the United Kingdom over ownership of the Falkland or Malvinas Islands, a small British colony in the South Atlantic Ocean. Today the region as a whole has moved to democratic systems of government, but faces many economic and political problems.

○ CATTLE MARKET
A Chilean cowboy is called a huaso. Cattle are raised in the the central Chilean regions to the south of Santiago.

In Paraguay, cattle are raised and cotton is grown. The leaves of a plant called the Paraguay holly are used to make a bitter tea called yerba maté, which is also popular in Argentina. Uruguay, too, is a cattle country, with fruit grown on the coastal plains.

Argentina first became wealthy by exporting beef. Great herds of cattle are still raised on the pampas, and in Patagonia sheep are kept.

○ ATLANTIC OUTPOST
Sheep are raised on the remote British colony of the Falkland Islands, or Islas Malvinas.

○ SALT LAKE
The bone-dry air of Chile's Atacama Desert evaporates pools of water, leaving behind salt pans.

○ SANTIAGO
Nine-out-of-ten Chileans live in towns or cities. The capital is the country's largest city. It is home to nearly five million people.

○ COPPER KINGS
Chile is the world's biggest copper producer. The monster Chuquicamata open-cast mine is sited in the far north, in the Atacama Desert.

✪ ARGENTINIAN WINES

The sheltered region around Mendoza has a mild, dry climate. Rivers and irrigation schemes have allowed vines to be grown here since the 1600s.

✪ PLAZA DEL CONGRESO

At the heart of Buenos Aires, capital of Argentina, is the Palace of Congress. Congress is made up of two houses, the Senate and the Chamber of Deputies.

✪ VALDÉS WILDLIFE

Magellan penguins may be seen off Argentina's Valdés peninsula, along with elephant seals and whales.

The foothills of the Andes provide shelter for vineyards in the sunny region around Mendoza. Fisheries, oil, and natural gas are important industries of the far south—Ushuaia is the most southerly town in the world. Industry is centered around the capital of Buenos Aires and is based on food processing, leather goods, textiles, chemicals, and car manufacture.

Chile's industry is based around the port of Valparaiso, where iron, steel, chemicals, and textiles are produced, and the capital city of Santiago. The country has large reserves of copper in the north. The warm regions of central Chile produce wine and citrus fruits for export and the long coastline provides harbors for large fishing fleets.

✪ MILITARY RULE

The army held power in Argentina from 1976 to 1983, in Chile from 1973 to 1989, in Paraguay from 1954 to 1993, and in Uruguay from 1973 to 1984.

✪ CITY MEMORIAL

This obelisk rises above the Plaza de la República in central Buenos Aires. It commemorates the founding of the city in 1536.

✪ ITAIPÚ DAM

This is the world's biggest hydroelectric scheme, jointly run by Argentina and Paraguay. Building the dam created a 520 square mile reservoir, at a cost of US$25 billion.

145

Native American peoples migrated southward through the continent in prehistoric times. They had reached central South America by 14,000 BC and were in Patagonia by 12,000 BC.

While northern Chile came under the influence of the great civilizations of the northern Andes, the peoples of the far south lived by hunting on the grasslands or fishing along the coast in canoes.

○ THE GAUCHOS
The tough, bragging cowboys of the Argentinean pampas were called gauchos. Today's cowboys still honor the gaucho tradition.

The Spanish invaded the region in the 1500s. They were fiercely resisted by indigenous groups such as the Querandí of the pampas and the Mapuche of Chile. The region broke away from Spanish rule in the 1800s, but generals fought out regional and civil wars. Native peoples were wiped out, and vast tracts of the pampas of Argentina were claimed as ranchland by wealthy landowners.

○ ANDEAN CHURCH
A white church stands on the edge of the Andes at Tocanao, in Chile's Antofagasta region. It is built from volcanic stone.

○ VIÑA DEL MAR
South American tourists flock to this resort, near Valparaíso in Chile, for the beaches and casino.

The ranches were worked by gauchos, wild-living cowboys of mixed Spanish–indigenous descent.

Immigrants poured into the region in the 1800s and 1900s: Spanish, Italians, Basques, Welsh, English, Germans, Swiss, Poles, Russians, Jews, and Syrians. More recently there were arrivals from Japan and Korea, and from other parts of South America.

Today the descendants of all these peoples dominate the region. Indigenous peoples now make up a tiny percentage of the population, but their cultures survive in some areas. The native Guaraní language is widely spoken in Paraguay. Spanish is spoken everywhere, but other European languages, from Italian to Welsh, may also be heard.

○ DESERT MUMMY
Dead bodies from early South American civilizations have been preserved as mummies. This woman's skull was found in the Atacama Desert.

○ POLO CHAMPIONS
European influence is evident in Argentina's passion (among the rich) for the game of polo. It has achieved international success in the sport.

◎ EVITA

Eva Perón (1919–52), a former actress, married Argentinean politician Juan Perón in 1945. "Evita" became a popular and powerful figure.

◎ LA BOCA

This district of Buenos Aires, along the polluted Riachuelo waterway, was founded by poor Basque and Italian immigrants. Today it is an artists' quarter, and the buildings are painted in bold, bright colors.

◎ GRAND PRIX

Motor racing has been a passion since the 1950s, when Argentinean Juan Fangio was five times Grand Prix champion.

Far out in the South Atlantic, the Falkland Islanders remain English in their speech and customs. The mainland nations are mostly Roman Catholic, with Protestant and Jewish minorities.

The region has produced sporting champions in motor racing, soccer, and tennis, and the Andes Mountains are increasingly popular for skiing and outdoor pursuits. Both Chile and Argentina have produced great writers and poets in the last century, including the Argentinian Jorge Luis Borges (1899–1986) and the Chilean novelist Isabel Allende (b.1942).

TIMELINE

AD

1516	Río de la Plata discovered by the Spanish
1536	First founding of Buenos Aires by Spanish
1537	Spanish found Asunción
1541	Querandí people attack Buenos Aires; Spanish conquer Chile
1543	Rebuilding Buenos Aires (until 1580)
1726	Spanish build fort at Montevideo
1811	Paraguay becomes independent
1816	Argentina becomes independent
1818	Chile becomes independent
1825	Uruguay declares independence (recognized 1828)
1857	European settlement of the pampas
1865	Paraguay fights Uruguay, Argentina, and Brazil (until 1870)
1878	Wars against Native Americans in Argentina (until 1883)
1879	War of the Pacific (until 1884): Chile defeats Peru and Bolivia
1946	Juan Perón becomes president of Argentina
1954	Military coup in Paraguay
1973	Allende overthrown by General Augusto Pinochet in Chile
1976	Military rule in Argentina: imprisonment and murder of opponents
1982	Argentina invades the Falkland Islands, but is defeated by a British force
1991	Argentina, Brazil, Paraguay, and Uruguay form a trade grouping called Mercosur

147

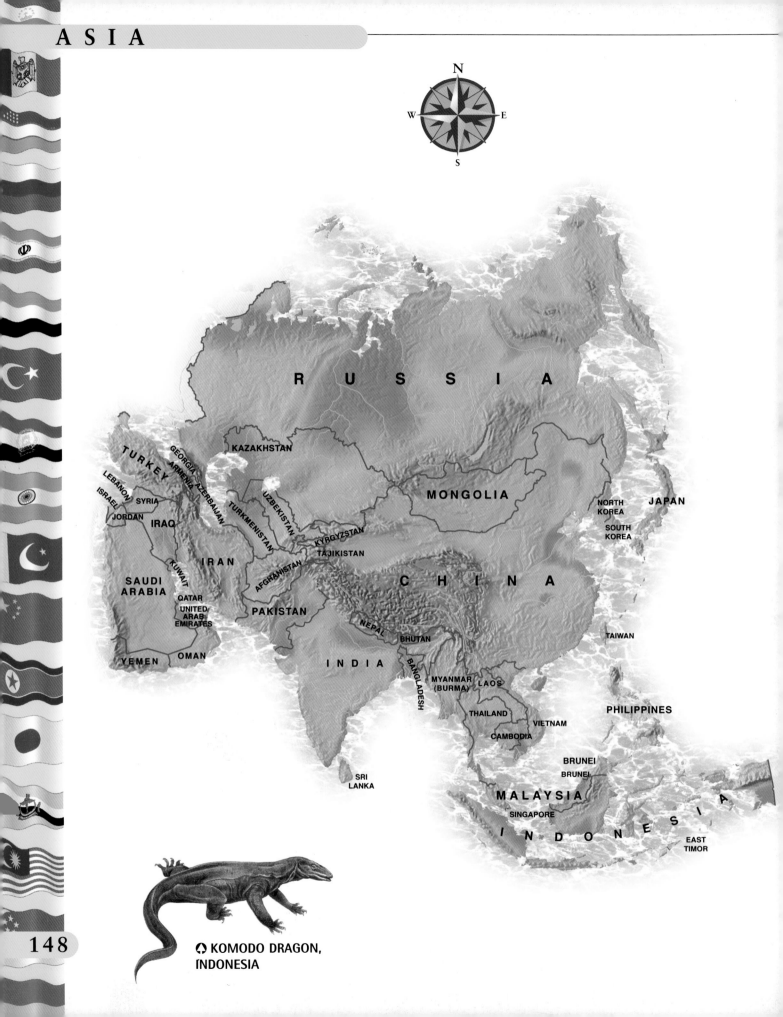

N
W E
S

RUSSIA

KAZAKHSTAN

TURKEY
GEORGIA
ARMENIA
AZERBAIJAN
LEBANON
ISRAEL
SYRIA
JORDAN
IRAQ
KUWAIT
SAUDI
ARABIA
QATAR
UNITED
ARAB
EMIRATES
YEMEN
OMAN
IRAN
TURKMENISTAN
UZBEKISTAN
KYRGYZSTAN
TAJIKISTAN
AFGHANISTAN
PAKISTAN
NEPAL
BHUTAN
INDIA
BANGLADESH
SRI
LANKA
MONGOLIA
CHINA
NORTH
KOREA
SOUTH
KOREA
JAPAN
TAIWAN
MYANMAR
(BURMA)
LAOS
THAILAND
CAMBODIA
VIETNAM
PHILIPPINES
BRUNEI
BRUNEI
MALAYSIA
SINGAPORE
INDONESIA
EAST
TIMOR

⬡ KOMODO DRAGON,
INDONESIA

ASIA

◔ Yangon, MYANMAR

◔ Hong Kong, CHINA

◔ Urgup Cones, TURKEY

◔ Space Monument, RUSSIA

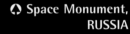

Asia, the world's largest continent, covers about 30 percent of the world's land area. It is bordered by Europe and Africa to the west and by the Pacific Ocean to the east. There are chains of tiny volcanic islands in the east, an area known as "The Ring of Fire," because it is so prone to volcanoes.

Asia's northwestern limits are marked by the Ural and Caucasus mountains. Lands in the far north overlap the Arctic Circle and much of the region is tundra, frozen solid for most of the year. Farther south lies a swathe of evergreen forest and, beyond that, the steppes—open, fertile grasslands. Little rain reaches Central Asia, much of which is desert.

The world's highest mountain ranges, the Himalayas and the Karakorams, form a snowy barrier to the north of the Indian peninsula, and include the world's highest peak, Mount Everest. To the south, two of the world's greatest rivers, the Ganges and Brahmaputra, run toward the warm Indian Ocean. They often flood, depositing rich, alluvial soil over the wide delta.

Asia's southwest coastline is cooled by breezes from the Red Sea and the Mediterranean, but the lands and islands of southern Asia have a tropical climate. There, the winters are hot and dry, while in summer stormy winds called monsoons bring heavy rains.

Asia's many ethnic groups include the Arabs of Southwest Asia, the Hindu people of India, and the Chinese in Eastern Asia. The continent was the home of major early civilizations and the birthplace of all the major world religions.

Many Asians are poor and about 60 percent live by farming. But in the last 50 years, some countries have developed quickly and raised their living standards. In parts of Southwest Asia, wealth has come from oil, while countries in Eastern and Southeast Asia have developed industries. Japan is Asia's most industrialized country, but some other countries in Eastern Asia have also developed quickly. Eastern Asia will dominate the world economy in the 21st century.

149

RUSSIA
AND ITS NEIGHBORS

↻ **GRAY WOLF**

FACTS

ARMENIA
Haikakan Hanrapetoutioun
AREA: 11,500 sq mi.
POPULATION: 3.8 million
CAPITAL: Yerevan
OTHER CITIES: Gyumri,
Ejmiadzin
HIGHEST POINT: Aragats
(13,418 ft)
OFFICIAL LANGUAGE:
Armenian
CURRENCY: Dram

AZERBAIJAN
Azerbaijchan Respublikasy
AREA: 33,400 sq mi.
POPULATION: 8 million
CAPITAL: Baku
OTHER CITIES: Ganka,
Sumgait
HIGHEST POINT: Bazar Dyuzi
(14,652 ft)
OFFICIAL LANGUAGE: Azeri
CURRENCY: Manat

BELARUS
Respublika Belarus
AREA: 80,200 sq mi.
POPULATION: 10 million
CAPITAL: Minsk
OTHER CITIES: Gomel, Pinsk
OFFICIAL LANGUAGE:
Belarussian
CURRENCY: Rouble

GEORGIA
Sakartvelos Respublika
AREA: 26,900 sq mi.
POPULATION: 5 million
CAPITAL: Tbilisi
OTHER CITIES: Kutaisi,
Rustavi
HIGHEST POINT: Shkhara
(17,063 ft)
OFFICIAL LANGUAGE:
Georgian
CURRENCY: Lari

KAZAKHSTAN
Qazaqstan Respublikasï
AREA: 1,049,200 sq mi.
POPULATION: 14.9 million
CAPITAL: Astana
OTHER CITIES: Qaraghandy,
Shymkent
HIGHEST POINT: Tengri
(20,991 ft)
OFFICIAL LANGUAGE: Kazakh
CURRENCY: Tenge

Europe runs into Asia without any obvious borders, apart from mountain ranges and rivers. The Russian Federation and some of its neighbors straddle both continents.

Belarus lies on the great plain that stretches from Germany to Russia. To the south lie the steppes of Ukraine and Moldova, natural grasslands now harvested for wheat. Ukraine borders the Carpathian Mountains to the west and the warm Black Sea to the south. The Caucasus Mountains run southeastward through Georgia, Armenia, and Azerbaijan toward the Caspian Sea, the world's broadest inland sea. To the east of the Caspian Sea lie the Central Asian republics of Kazakhstan, Turkmenistan, Uzbekistan, and Kyrgyzstan. Here, dusty grasslands give way to deserts and soaring mountain peaks.

The Russian Federation is the biggest country in the world. The Ural Mountains are generally taken to be the dividing line between European Russia and Asian Russia, which extends as far as the Pacific Ocean. Russia's northern coast is mostly locked in Arctic ice. A vast, treeless plain—the tundra—gives way in the south to a great belt of forest, or taiga, made up of spruce and birch trees. In the southwest there are steppes (grassland) and in the southeast, deserts and mountains. Russia is drained by a number of great rivers including the Don, the Volga, the Ob, the Irtysh, and the Lena.

↻ **SNOW POWER**
A snowmobile makes it possible to travel across the ice of the Siberian winter.

↻ **TASHKENT MARKET**
The capital of Uzbekistan is an ancient center of trade and of textile manufacture.

⬡ ANANURI CASTLE, GEORGIA

Georgia became a powerful kingdom in the early Middle Ages. It was absorbed into the Russian empire in the 1800s.

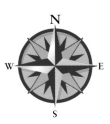

⟳ UKRAINIAN SUNSHINE

River shores on the Dnepr and Dnestr and warm coastlines on the Black Sea attract Eastern European holidaymakers to Ukraine.

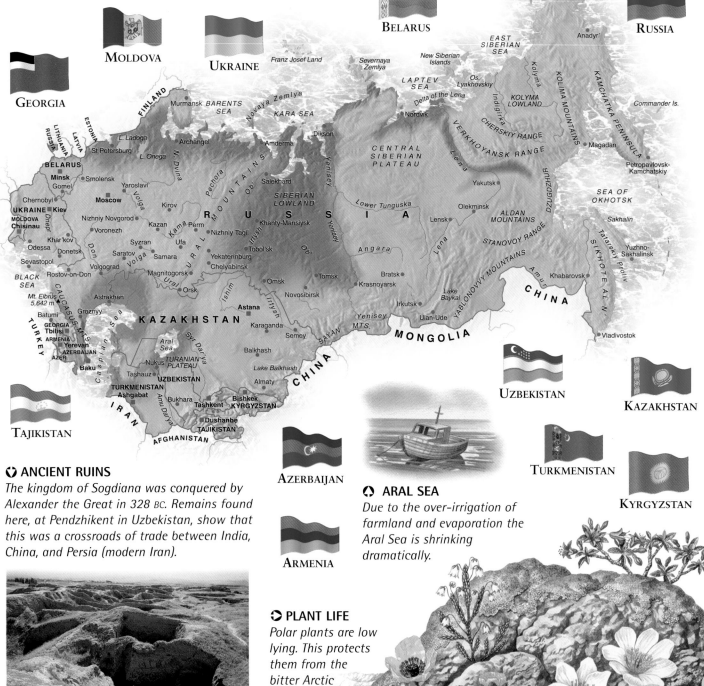

MOLDOVA

UKRAINE

BELARUS

RUSSIA

GEORGIA

Wrangel I.

EAST SIBERIAN SEA

Anadyr'

Franz Josef Land

Novaya Zemlya

Severnaya Zemlya

New Siberian Islands

LAPTEV SEA

Os. Lyakhovskiy

KOLYMA LOWLAND

Kolyma

KOLIMA MOUNTAINS

KAMCHATKA PENINSULA

Commander Is.

FINLAND

Murmansk

BARENTS SEA

KARA SEA

Dikson

Nordvik

Delta of the Lena

CHERSKIY RANGE

Magadan

VERKHOYANSK RANGE

Lena

ESTONIA

LITHUANIA

LATVIA

RUSSIA

St Petersburg

L. Ladoga

L. Onega

Archangel

N. Dvina

Amderma

Salekhard

CENTRAL SIBERIAN PLATEAU

Yakutsk

DZHUGDZHUR

SEA OF OKHOTSK

BELARUS

Minsk

Gomel

Smolensk

Yaroslavl'

Moscow

Pechora

Ob

SIBERIAN LOWLAND

Lower Tunguska

Olekminsk

Petropavlovsk-Kamchatskiy

Chernobyl

UKRAINE Kiev

Nizhniy Novgorod

Kirov

Kazan

Perm

Khanty-Mansiysk

Yenisey

Lensk

ALDAN MOUNTAINS

Sakhalin

MOLDOVA

Chisinau

Volga

Kama

Nizhniy Tagil

Irtysh

Ob

Angara

STANOVOY RANGE

SIKHOTE ALN

Yuzhno-Sakhalinsk

Khar'kov

Voronezh

Ufa

Yekaterinburg

Tobol'sk

Odessa

Donetsk

Syzran

Saratov

Samara

Don

URAL MOUNTAINS

Chelyabinsk

Omsk

Tomsk

Bratsk

Krasnoyarsk

Yablonovvy Mountains

Amu

CHINA

Khabarovsk

Sevastopol

Rostov-on-Don

Volgograd

Magnitogorsk

Orsk

Novosibirsk

Irkutsk

Lake Baykal

Ulan-Ude

Tatarskiy Proliv

BLACK SEA

Mt. Elbrus 5,642 m

Astrakhan

Ural

Ishim

Irtysh

Yenisey

SAYAN MTS.

MONGOLIA

Vladivostok

Batumi

Grozny

CAUCASUS MTS

Caspian Sea

KAZAKHSTAN

Astana

Karaganda

Semey

CHINA

TURKEY

GEORGIA Tbilisi

ARMENIA

Yerevan

AZERBAIJAN

AZER.

Baku

Aral Sea

Syr Darya

TURANIAN PLATEAU

Balkhash

Lake Balkhash

Almaty

CHINA

Nukus

Tashauz

UZBEKISTAN

UZBEKISTAN

KAZAKHSTAN

TAJIKISTAN

TURKMENISTAN

Ashgabat

Bukhara

Amu Darya

Tashkent

Bishkek KYRGYZSTAN

TURKMENISTAN

IRAN

Dushanbe

TAJIKISTAN

AFGHANISTAN

KYRGYZSTAN

AZERBAIJAN

ARMENIA

⬡ ANCIENT RUINS

The kingdom of Sogdiana was conquered by Alexander the Great in 328 BC. Remains found here, at Pendzhikent in Uzbekistan, show that this was a crossroads of trade between India, China, and Persia (modern Iran).

⬡ ARAL SEA

Due to the over-irrigation of farmland and evaporation the Aral Sea is shrinking dramatically.

⟳ PLANT LIFE

Polar plants are low lying. This protects them from the bitter Arctic winds.

151

⟳ NUCLEAR DISASTER
A nuclear power plant at Chernobyl, in Ukraine (then part of the Soviet Union) melted down in 1986. Deadly radiation was blown across northern Europe.

⟳ SHOPPING IN MOSCOW
In the days of the Soviet Union, grand-looking state-owned stores offered little choice for consumers. Economic problems continue today.

Until 1991, all the countries of this region were part of a single country, the Soviet Union. This was formed in 1922, following the revolution in 1917 which brought Communists to power in Russia. Communist rule ended in 1991, and the country was renamed the Russian Federation.

At that time, many of the border regions broke away to become independent nations. Russian armed forces prevented some other bids for independence, as in the Chechenya region. A Commonwealth of Independent States (CIS) was formed to keep up economic links between the new nations.

The region as a whole is immensely rich in resources, including timber, oil, natural gas, gold, and diamonds. Transportation is a major problem in such a vast country, particularly in the remote wilderness of Siberia, where many resources are found. The Trans-Siberian rail network links Moscow, the Russian capital, with the Pacific port of Vladivostok.

⟳ SNOWY WINTERS
Most of the Russian Federation experiences long winters with heavy snowfall. Average January temperatures vary from 16°F in Moscow to 7°F in Vladivostok.

Cereal crops grow well in the fertile west and south, while warm southern lands such as Georgia produce fruits and wine. The Central Asian lands grow cotton. Industries are mostly based in the eastern European part of the region, and include iron and steel, truck manufacture, shipbuilding, and mining.

☾ THE SUMMER PALACE

The Summer Palace, built on one of the islands that make up the great city of St Petersburg, was built for Czar Peter the Great between 1710 and 1714.

☽ TRANS-SIBERIAN EXPRESS

The Trans-Siberian Railway runs between Moscow and Vladivostok. It was opened in 1905 and played an important part in Russian history. It remains the world's longest track, at 5,865 miles. The whole route takes eight days to travel. It now links up with services to Mongolia and China.

During the Communist era, the Soviet Union rapidly transformed from a largely undeveloped country into a great industrial power. By the 1980s, however, Russian industry was old-fashioned, inefficient, and polluting. In the post-Communist Russia of the 1990s, unemployment was high and many businesses were run by corrupt officials. Output fell disastrously and wages went unpaid. Even so, Russia remains powerful, and the poor countries around the Caspian and Aral Seas may soon be transformed by new oil wealth.

☽ JEWELED EGGS

Fabulous "eggs" were made as Easter gifts for the czars by jeweler Carl Fabergé (1846–1920).

☽ UZBEKI COTTON

Uzbekistan is the world's fourth-largest producer of cotton. This crop is being harvested and processed at Urgench.

☽ THE WINTER PALACE

The St Petersburg residence of the czars was built in 1762 and restored in 1839. With the adjoining Hermitage, it now houses one of the world's great art collections.

FACTS

MOLDOVA
Republica Moldova
AREA: 13,000 sq mi.
POPULATION: 4.3 million
CAPITAL: Chisinau
OTHER CITIES: Tiraspol, Beltsy
HIGHEST POINT: Balaneshty (1,409 ft)
OFFICIAL LANGUAGE: Moldovan
CURRENCY: Leu

RUSSIAN FEDERATION
Rossiskaya Federatsiya
AREA: 6,592,863 sq mi.
POPULATION: 144.4 million
CAPITAL: Moscow
OTHER CITIES: St Petersburg, Novosibirsk
HIGHEST POINT: Elbrus (18,510 ft)
OFFICIAL LANGUAGE: Russian
CURRENCY: Rouble

TAJIKISTAN
Repoblika i Tojikiston
AREA: 55,300 sq mi.
POPULATION: 6.2 million
CAPITAL: Dushanbe
OTHER CITIES: Kulyab, Khodzhent
HIGHEST POINT: Mt. Kommunizma (24, 590 ft)
OFFICIAL LANGUAGE: Tajik
CURRENCY: Somoni

153

○ ST BASIL'S CATHEDRAL
Dating back to 1555, the colorful onion-shaped domes of St Basil's rise above Red Square in the center of Moscow, the Russian capital.

The Russians are a Slavic people. They make up 80 percent or so of the population in the Russian Federation. The remaining 20 percent is made up of over 150 minority groups. Some of these peoples, including the Chukchee, Evenks, Nenets, and Saami, live in the sparsely populated Russian Arctic. Some of the Arctic peoples live by herding reindeer or by hunting. Among Russia's many other ethnic groups are the Cossacks of the steppes, the Kalmuk, Yakut, Tartars, Chechens, Cherkess, Dagestanis, Bashkir, Kets, Jews, Tuvinians, and Buryats.

To the west of the new Russian borders are the Slavic Belarussians and Ukrainians, and also the Moldovans, who are related to Romanians.

○ RUSSIAN BALLET
St Petersburg has a history of ballet dating back to 1738. Many great works were performed in the 1800s. The most famous company is the Maryinsky (formerly Kirov) Ballet.

South beyond the Caucasus are the Georgians, Osset, Armenians, and Azeris. To the east of the Caspian Sea are the Kazakhs, Turkmen, Uzbek, Kyrgyz, and Tajik.

Despite the Russian Federation's wide-open spaces, most people live to the west of the Urals, 75 percent of them in cities and towns.

○ ICE HOCKEY
Ice hockey is a popular sport in the Russian Federation. National (and earlier Soviet) teams are record-breaking winners of world-class and Olympic championships.

○ ORTHODOX PRIESTS
The Orthodox form of Christianity was brought to the Slavs by the Greek missionary St Cyril (AD 827–69).

○ THE TOMB OF A FAMOUS WARRIOR
The Gur-e Amir mausoleum in Samarkand, Uzbekistan, is decorated with mosaic tiles. It commemorates the Mongol emperor Timur the Lame, or Tamerlane (1336–1405), who conquered most of Central Asia. He died marching eastward to invade China.

○ THE COSSACKS
The Cossacks of the steppes were famed for their riding skills and wild dances. They were later recruited by the czars as soldiers.

◐ LEO TOLSTOY

◑ PETER TCHAIKOVSKY

◑ THE ARTS
Russia has a rich history of writers and musicians. Notable among them were composer Peter Ilyich Tchaikovsky (1840–93) and writer Leo Tolstoy (1828–1910), author of War and Peace *and* Anna Karenina.

Christianity is the main religion in the west and southwest of the region; most people are Eastern Orthodox Christians. Onion-domed churches, some gilded, may be seen glittering in the sunshine in many towns. The Central Asian peoples are mostly Muslim, and there are also Jews and Buddhists. Many religions, including Christianity, were heavily suppressed in the early days of the Communist era.

◔ MUSICAL TRADITION
Traditional folk music is popular throughout Russia. These musicians are performing in St Petersburg. The balalaika has a triangular body and a neck like a guitar.

During the Middle Ages, the Eastern Orthodox Church produced great works of art in the form of icons (holy pictures), and its worship is accompanied by fine choral singing. The arts have always been valued in Russia. St Petersburg and Moscow are centers of ballet. Great Russian composers included Dmitri Shostakovich (1906–75), and writers included the great playwright Anton Chekov (1860–1904).

◔ ARCTIC TRAVEL
Dogs, reindeer, and horses were traditionally used to haul loads in the Russian Arctic. The rivers there freeze so hard that trucks are able to use them as highways.

◔ RUSSIAN DOLLS
Hollow wooden dolls are a Russian tradition and a popular souvenir for any visitor to Russia. Each doll can be opened at the middle to reveal a smaller doll nesting inside.

FACTS

TURKMENISTAN
Turkmenistan
AREA: 188,500 sq mi.
POPULATION: 5.4 million
CAPITAL: Ashgabat
OTHER CITIES: Charjew, Dashkhovuz
HIGHEST POINT: Köpetdeg Range
OFFICIAL LANGUAGE: Oguz Turkic
CURRENCY: Manat

UKRAINE
Ukrayina
AREA: 233,100 sq mi.
POPULATION: 48.7 million
CAPITAL: Kiev
OTHER CITIES: Kharkiv, Odessa
HIGHEST POINT: Goverla (6,726 ft)
OFFICIAL LANGUAGE: Ukrainian
CURRENCY: Hryvnya

UZBEKISTAN
Uzbekiston Respublikasi
AREA: 172,700 sq mi.
POPULATION: 25.1 million
CAPITAL: Tashkent
OTHER CITIES: Samarkand, Bukhara
HIGHEST POINT: Beshtor Peak (14,104 ft)
OFFICIAL LANGUAGE: Uzbek
CURRENCY: Sum

○ HOLY ICONS

Painting an icon was considered to be an act of worship in itself.

The steppes were settled in prehistoric times. About 2,500 years ago they were home to horseback warriors known as Scythians. In about AD 400 Slavs began to settle western Russia. Swedish Vikings known as Rus traded along the Volga and Dniepr rivers and as far east as the Aral Sea. They gave their name to Russia.

The first Russian states were based on trading posts at Kiev (in today's Ukraine) and Novgorod. Moscow was founded in 1147. In the 1200s the Slavs came under fierce attack by Mongol armies from Asia.

Russia was strong enough to resist the Mongols and built up its own empire. Its rulers were called czars. In the 1600s Czar Peter I, the "Great," modernized Russia and built the fine city of St Petersburg. Russian armies soon clashed with Turkey to the south. The empire spread eastward into Siberia and westward into Poland. It was invaded in turn by France in 1812.

A hundred years ago, the Russian people had few political rights. Their ruling class resisted calls for change.

○ CUTTER OF BEARDS

Peter I abolished the special powers of Russia's old aristocratic families. Their long beards, symbols of privilege, were cut off.

○ LENIN AND HIS TOMB

Vladimir Ilyich Ulyanov, known as Lenin (1870–1924), led the Bolsheviks in Russia's October Revolution. His tomb is in Moscow's Red Square (above left).

Revolution broke out in 1905 and again in 1917, when the czar and his family were killed. A socialist group called the Bolsheviks, led by a revolutionary known as Lenin, gained control of Russia and the old Russian empire during a civil war that lasted until 1920.

○ RED ARMY LEADER

Leon Trotsky (1879–1940) was a Marxist revolutionary who led the Communist Red Army in Russia's civil war (1917–20). He was later exiled and murdered on the order of Joseph Stalin.

○ PETER THE GREAT

Born in 1672, Czar Peter I traveled widely in Western Europe. By the time of his death in 1725, Russia had been transformed into a powerful modern state.

○ OCTOBER REVOLUTION

Centuries of injustice under the rule of the czars came to an end in 1917, when revolutionary workers, students, and soldiers seized power in Russia.

↻ SPACE AGE
A monument to space exploration reaches skyward. The Soviet Union was the first nation to launch a satellite into the Earth's orbit.

↻ LAIKA, SPACE DOG

TIMELINE

AD

900s	Vikings found states in Russia and Ukraine
988	Orthodox Christianity introduced
1223	Mongols invade steppes
1462	Ivan the Great frees Russia from Mongols (until 1505)
1547	Ivan the Terrible becomes czar
1881	Russian Czar Alexander I assassinated
1905	Russia defeated by Japan; revolution in Russia, democratic reform
1917	October Revolution in Russia
1922	Soviet Union (USSR) founded
1924	Death of Lenin
1936	Joseph Stalin terrorizes opponents
1939	Soviet pact with Nazi Germany
1940	USSR annexes Baltic states
1941	USSR joins Allies in "Great Patriotic War" against Nazi Germany (until 1945)
1946	USSR controls Eastern Europe; Cold War with West (until 1989)
1979	USSR invades Afghanistan
1985	Mikhail Gorbachev introduces reforms
1989	Central Europe breaks away from Soviet control
1991	Break-up of USSR; Russian Federation founded

Lenin died in 1924. His successor was a ruthless politician named Joseph Stalin (1879–1953). Many thousands of Russians starved or died in labor camps under his rule. In 1941, Germany invaded. The Russian people resisted bravely and by 1945 the Germans had been pushed back into western Europe.

After the war, the Soviet Union controlled Eastern Europe. Its technology was advanced enough by 1961 to send the first person into space. The United States and its allies constantly challenged this power, during a "Cold War," which lasted until the 1980s. Then Soviet Communism collapsed and the Soviet Union broke up into separate states.

↻ IN MEMORY
Beneath the walls of the Kremlin, Moscow's medieval fortress, a flame burns in memory of the "unknown soldier." The Soviets suffered more casualties than any other nation during World War II.

↻ LOCAL WARS
As new states were created from the ruins of the Soviet Union, there were violent clashes over territory and borders. Between 1989 and 1994, Armenia fought with Azerbaijan over the territory of Nagorno-Karabakh.

↻ NEW RUSSIA
In 1990 Boris Yeltsin (on the right) became Russian president. He presided over the break-up of the old Soviet Union. Yeltsin's successor, the younger Vladimir Putin, faced severe problems in modernizing Russia.

SOUTHWEST ASIA

○ **CEDAR TREE, LEBANON**

FACTS

BAHRAIN
Dawlat al Bahrayn –
State of Bahrain
AREA: 267 sq mi.
POPULATION: 700,000
CAPITAL: Al Manamah
OTHER CITIES: Muharraq
HIGHEST POINT: Jabal ad
Dukhan (440 ft)
OFFICIAL LANGUAGE: Arabic
CURRENCY: Bahraini dinar

CYPRUS
Kypriaki Dimokratia –
Republic of Cyprus
AREA: 3,572 sq mi.
POPULATION: 873,000
CAPITAL: Nicosia
OTHER CITIES: Limassol,
Larnaca
HIGHEST POINT: Mount
Olympus (6,403 ft)
OFFICIAL LANGUAGES: Greek,
Turkish
CURRENCY: Cyprus pound

IRAN
Jomhuri-e-Eslami-e-Iran –
Islamic Republic of Iran
AREA: 634,440 sq mi.
POPULATION: 63.4 million
CAPITAL: Tehran
OTHER CITIES: Mashhad,
Esfahan
HIGHEST POINT: Mount
Damavand (18,385 ft)
OFFICIAL LANGUAGE: Farsi
(Persian)
CURRENCY: Rial

IRAQ
Joumhouriya al Iraqia –
Republic of Iraq
AREA: 169,235 sq mi.
POPULATION: 23.3 million
CAPITAL: Baghdad
OTHER CITIES: Mosul, Kirkuk
HIGHEST POINT: Haji Ebrahim
(11,811 ft)
OFFICIAL LANGUAGE: Arabic
CURRENCY: Iraqi dinar

Southwest Asia—also known as the Middle East or the Near East—is a large region bordered by the Mediterranean and Black seas to the northwest and north, by the Red Sea to the southwest, and by the Indian Ocean to the southeast. Thinly populated deserts and dry grassland predominate. The most fertile regions are in the north, and include the Mediterranean island of Cyprus.

The northern part of Southwest Asia is mountainous, with high ranges extending through Turkey into Iran, where they include the Elburz Mountains in the north and the Zagros Mountains, which run southeast through western Iran. Mount Damavand in the Elburz Mountains is the region's highest peak. The Arabian peninsula also has mountain ranges, the longest of which borders the Red Sea and extends into southern Yemen. Inland are large plateau.

Most of Southwest Asia has a hot, desert climate. Part of the dry Arabian peninsula is covered by one of the world's bleakest sandy deserts—the Rub 'al Khali, or "Empty Quarter." Iran also has large deserts, some of which are covered by salt, created by evaporation following the occasional flood. Other dry areas include steppe grasslands, which also support low-growing shrubs.

Turkey has a wetter climate than most of the rest of the region. Its Mediterranean coastline has hot, dry summers and rainy, mild winters. But the dry, grassy interior plateaux have bitterly cold winters and frequent snowstorms.

Water is scarce in much of Southwest Asia. There are few major rivers—the two longest being the Euphrates and Tigris. These rise in the mountains of Turkey and flow across the dry country of Iraq. The fertile area between these two great rivers—the Fertile Crescent—saw the birth of some major early civilizations, including the Assyrians and Babylonians.

○ **PALACE IN YEMEN**
The Wadi Dahr Palace is perched on a steep rock in San'a, capital of Yemen.

○ **JERBOA**

⟳ ESFAHAN, IRAN
The city of Esfahan in Iran is famous for its beautiful mosques.

IRAN

TURKEY

IRAQ

BAHRAIN

⟳ SHIPS OF THE DESERT
Camels can survive for long periods without water. They are still used to carry goods across the deserts of Southwest Asia.

KUWAIT

CYPRUS

LEBANON

ISRAEL

SYRIA

JORDAN

⟳ FORT IN OMAN
Most Omani towns contain an old fort. Oman guards the entrance to The Gulf.

YEMEN

SAUDI ARABIA

OMAN

QATAR

⟳ CITADEL, ALEPPO
This citadel in the ancient city of Aleppo, northern Syria, was built in the Middle Ages.

UNITED ARAB EMIRATES

⟳ URGUP CONES
In the Goreme Valley in central Turkey, strange volcanic rock formations make a spectacular landscape.

Map labels

Istanbul
Gallipoli
Bursa
Eskisehir
Izmir
Ankara
Tuz Lake
Konya
Antalya
TURKEY
TAURUS MTS.
Samsun
BLACK SEA
PONTIC MOUNTAINS
Kizil
Sakarya
Kayseri
Gaziantep
Adana
Diyarbakir
Aleppo
Mosul
Euphrates
Tigris
SYRIA
Homs
Tripoli
Nicosia
CYPRUS
Limassol
LEBANON
Beirut
Damascus
SYRIAN DESERT
Haifa
Tel Aviv
ISRAEL
Jerusalem
Amman
JORDAN
Elat
EGYPT
Mt.Ararat 5,185m
Aras
Tabriz
Lake Van
Lake Urmia
Rasht
CASPIAN SEA
ELBURZ MTS.
Mt. Damavand 5,604m
Tehran
As Sulaymaniyah
Kirkuk
Hamadan
Qom
Bakhtaran
Kashan
Baghdad
IRAQ
Karbala
Dasht-e-Kavir
TURKMENISTAN
Mashhad
AFGHANISTAN
Babol
IRAN
Esfahan
Yazd
Ahvaz
Kerman
Dasht-e-Lut
An Nasiriyah
Basra
Abadan
Shiraz
Zahedan
KUWAIT
Kuwait
Bushehr
Bandar Abbas
Al Jawf
Sakakah
AN NAFUD
Ad Dahna
Ad Damman
Bandar e Lengah
The Gulf
Jask
Strait of Hormuz
Gulf of Oman
Buraydah
Al Manamah
BAHRAIN
QATAR
Doha
Dubai
Abu Dhabi
UNITED ARAB EMIRATES
Muscat
Shaqra
Medina
Riyadh
HIJAZ
SAUDI ARABIA
Jabal Ash Sham 3,035m
OMAN
Sur
RED SEA
Jiddah
Mecca
ASIR
Tihamah
Jabal Sawda 3,133 m
Rub' al Khali (Empty Quarter)
Masirah I.
Salalah
Kuria Muria Is.
Jaza'ir Farasan
Tarim
Hadramaut
San'a
YEMEN
Al Hudaydah
Al Mukalla
Bab al Mandab
Aden
Gulf of Aden
Socotra (YEMEN)
'Abd al kuri
ZAGROS MOUNTAINS

○ ARABIAN SPICES
Many aromatic spices are used in Arab cooking.

FACTS

ISRAEL
Medinat Israel – State of Israel
AREA: 8,130 sq mi.
POPULATION: 6.2 million
CAPITAL: Jerusalem
OTHER CITIES: Tel Aviv-Jaffa, Haifa
HIGHEST POINT: Mount Meron (3,963 ft)
OFFICIAL LANGUAGES: Hebrew, Arabic
CURRENCY: Shekel

JORDAN
Al-Mamlaka Al-Urduniya Al-Hashemiyah – Hashemite Kingdom of Jordan
AREA: 37,737 sq mi.
POPULATION: 5.1 million
CAPITAL: Amman
OTHER CITIES: Zarqa, Irbid
HIGHEST POINT: Jabal Ramm (5,755 ft)
OFFICIAL LANGUAGE: Arabic
CURRENCY: Jordan dinar

KUWAIT
Dowlat al Kuwait – State of Kuwait
AREA: 6,879 sq mi.
POPULATION: 2.2 million
CAPITAL: Kuwait
OTHER CITIES: Al Jahra, Salimiya
HIGHEST POINT: 928 ft
OFFICIAL LANGUAGE: Arabic
CURRENCY: Kuwaiti dinar

LEBANON
Jumhouriya al-Lubnaniya – Republic of Lebanon
AREA: 4,015 sq mi.
POPULATION: 3.6 million
CAPITAL: Beirut
OTHER CITIES: Tripoli, Sidon
HIGHEST POINT: Qurnat as Sawda (10,115 ft)
OFFICIAL LANGUAGE: Arabic
CURRENCY: Lebanese pound

Southwest Asia contains 15 countries. The Arabs are the largest single group of people. Other large groups include the Iranians and the Turks. Smaller groups include the Greek and Turkish Cypriots, and the Jews in Israel.

Seven countries in the region are monarchies: Jordan and Saudi Arabia are headed by kings, while emirs rule Bahrain, Kuwait, Qatar, and United Arab Emirates. The head of state in Oman is the sultan. The other countries are republics. They include Iran, an Islamic republic, whose laws are based on the teachings of Islam.

Since 1974, Cyprus has been divided into the Greek Cypriot Republic in the south and the so-called Turkish Republic of Northern Cyprus, recognized only by Turkey.

○ TURKISH COPPERSMITH
Beautiful metal objects, carpets, and highly decorated dishes and bowls are made by Turkish craftworkers and sold in souks (markets).

○ GRAPEFRUITS, CYPRUS
Citrus fruits, such as grapefruits, oranges, and lemons, grow well in the sunny countries of Cyprus, Iran, and Israel.

○ OIL REFINERY, SAUDI ARABIA
Refineries process Saudi Arabia's valuable oil, producing fuels and chemicals that are used to make many products.

○ KUWAIT CITY
Kuwait City is capital of the oil-rich country of Kuwait. Iraq seized Kuwait in 1990, but Iraqi troops were forced out in 1991.

○ GATEWAY TO A SOUK
Damascus, Syria's capital, has a large souk (market). Inside, the maze of narrow streets is lined with traders.

The division of Cyprus followed fighting between the island's peoples. Conflict has also been a long-term problem between Israelis and their Arab neighbors.

Several Southwest Asian countries are rich in oil, the chief natural resource of the region. Exports of oil have helped several countries to raise their living standards. Saudi Arabia is the chief oil producer and has the world's largest reserves. Crude oil is refined to make many useful exports including petrol and petro-chemicals.

◯ DIAMOND POLISHING
Israeli craftsmen cut and polish diamonds, which are exported to many countries.

Two-thirds of the people of Southwest Asia live in cities. The largest cities include Istanbul and Ankara in Turkey, Tehran in Iran, Baghdad in Iraq, and Damascus in Syria. Many cities contain old quarters, with narrow roads and large, traditional markets—bazaars or souks—alongside modern skyscrapers.

◯ BEACH RESORT, TURKEY
Tourism is changing parts of Turkey, which has sunny beaches and many fascinating historic ruins.

About a third of the people live in villages and work as farmers. Others graze herds of camels, goats, and sheep. Major crops, often grown on irrigated land, include barley and wheat, while dates, olives, nuts, and citrus fruits are also important. The chief manufacturing countries are Iran and Turkey.

◯ YEMENI MARKET
Goods are piled high for sale at a market in San'a, Yemen.

◑ DESERT PATROL
Soldiers in Jordan are fiercely loyal to their king.

◯ OIL WELL IN IRAQ
Southwest Asia has about two-thirds of the world's known oil reserves—a valuable commodity to the West.

FACTS

OMAN
Sultanat 'Uman – Sultanate of Oman
AREA: 82,030 sq mi.
POPULATION: 2.5 million
CAPITAL: Muscat
OTHER CITIES: Salalah, Sur
Highest point: Jabal Ash Sham (9,957 ft)
OFFICIAL LANGUAGE: Arabic
CURRENCY: Omani rial

QATAR
Dawlat Qatar – State of Qatar
AREA: 4,247 sq mi.
POPULATION: 658,000
CAPITAL: Doha
OTHER CITIES: Dukhan, Umm Said
HIGHEST POINT: 338 ft
OFFICIAL LANGUAGE: Arabic
CURRENCY: Qatar riyal

SAUDI ARABIA
Mamlaka al-'Arabiya as Sa'udiya – Kingdom of Saudi Arabia
AREA: 829,996 sq mi.
POPULATION: 22.7 million
CAPITAL: Riyadh
OTHER CITIES: Jiddah, Mecca
HIGHEST POINT: Jabal Sawda (10,278 ft)
OFFICIAL LANGUAGE: Arabic
CURRENCY: Saudi riyal

SYRIA
Jumhuriya al-Arabya as-Suriya – Syrian Arab Republic
AREA: 71,498 sq mi.
POPULATION: 16.7 million
CAPITAL: Damascus
OTHER CITIES: Aleppo, Homs
HIGHEST POINT: Mount Hermon (9,232 ft)
OFFICIAL LANGUAGE: Arabic
CURRENCY: Syrian pound

WHIRLING DERVISHES
Some Muslim mystics, called dervishes, whirl and dance as part of their religious worship. The order of dancing dervishes was founded in 1273.

The most numerous people of Southwest Asia are the Arabs. Their language, Arabic, is the only official language in 11 of the 15 countries. Arabic is also an official language in Israel, together with Hebrew, which is spoken by the largest group of people, the Jews. The other main languages in Southwest Asia are Farsi (also called Persian)in Iran, Greek in Cyprus, and Turkish in Turkey and Cyprus.

Southwest Asia was the birthplace of three great religions: Judaism—the chief religion in Israel; Christianity, which is important in Cyprus and Lebanon; and Islam. About 86 percent of the people of Southwest Asia follow Islam, the religion of the Arabs.

WAILING WALL
Jews visit the Western, or Wailing, Wall of an ancient temple in Jerusalem, Israel, to pray.

Islamic art is highly decorative and adorns buildings and all kinds of artifacts. Arts and crafts practiced include book binding and illustrations, calligraphy (beautiful hand-written lettering), carvings, ceramics, glassware, metalware, rugs, and textiles. Mosques (places of worship) throughout the region follow the elegant lines of Islamic architecture. The decorations use abstract patterns, often intertwining the shapes of leaves or winding plant stems. Unlike Christian churches, mosques do not show pictures of people or animals—such pictures in a religious setting are forbidden by Islamic teaching.

DONKEY RIDE
Donkeys and camels are used to carry people in many country areas in Southwest Asia.

BACKGAMMON BOARD
Backgammon is a board game for two players. It is especially popular in the countries bordering the eastern Mediterranean Sea.

MARSH ARABS
The marshy lower valleys of the Tigris and Euphrates rivers in southern Iraq are home to a people called the Marsh Arabs.

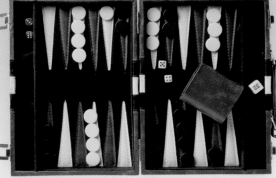

COVERED FACES
In this region, many Muslim women cover most of their bodies when outdoors. Some countries observe Islamic law strictly.

◑ LIVING TOGETHER

A kibbutz *is the name for a type of Jewish community in Israel in which everyone shares the property, work, goods, and services.*

◑ ISLAMIC ART

Abstract patterns and Arabic script are used to decorate mosques and other Islamic buildings. Islam forbids the depiction of people in art.

◑ RING-SHAPED BREAD ROLLS

Israelis enjoy bread rolls, called bagels. Other Israeli foods include chicken soup, chopped liver, and felafel (ground, fried chickpeas flavored with onion and spices).

◑ MOSQUE IN QOM

Qom is a holy city in Iran. Muslim traditions are strictly enforced in Iran. Its mosques are among the most beautiful in the world.

Islam plays a central part in daily life. In Iran, women wear full-length, black body veils, called *chadars*. They cover their ordinary clothes, concealing their head, shoulders, and, usually, the lower part of their faces. In some Muslim countries, women wear western clothes. Muslim women were once confined to their homes, but today many work in business, education, and government.

Basketball, soccer, weight-lifting, and wrestling are popular sports in many areas. Less energetic, but also popular, are the board games backgammon and chess. Skiing takes place in mountain areas, and camel-racing in the Arabian peninsula.

Flat bread and rice are basic foods in Southwest Asia, and dates are important in desert countries. Kebabs—pieces of meat and vegetables cooked on skewers—are popular, as are dairy products, such as cheese and yogurt.

مسجد اعظم

163

ASIA

Southwest Asia played a leading role in the development of world civilization. It was there, about 11,000 years ago, that people first began to farm the land. The first towns and cities also grew up there, and people of the region invented writing and devised systems of laws.

The great civilizations developed in the lands around the Tigris and Euphrates rivers, a region called Mesopotamia, which means "between the rivers." The major civilizations were those of the Sumerians, Babylonians, and Assyrians. The Persians conquered Mesopotamia in 539 BC. Later, the Persian empire fell to the Greek general Alexander the Great in 331 BC.

◑ TROJAN HORSE, TURKEY
According to legend, during the Trojan War in the 12th century BC, Greek soldiers tricked their way into the city of Troy by hiding inside a huge, wooden horse.

◑ ANCIENT SUMERIAN
Sumer, in southeast Iraq, was the world's first major civilization (c. 3000–2000 BC). The Sumerians made fine cloth, jewelry, and pottery.

◑ ROMAN CITY
The ruins of the Roman city of Palmyra stand in the desert in central Syria.

The Romans ruled much of Southwest Asia at the time when Jesus Christ was born. Muhammad, the founder of Islam, was born in Mecca in the Arabian peninsula in about AD 570. His followers later built up a great Arab empire, which extended as far west as Spain. Later, the Turks ruled much of Southwest Asia.

FACTS

TURKEY
Türkiye Cumhuriyeti – Republic of Turkey
AREA: 299,156 sq mi.
POPULATION: 66.2 million
CAPITAL: Ankara
OTHER CITIES: Istanbul, Izmir
HIGHEST POINT: Mount Ararat (17,011 ft)
OFFICIAL LANGUAGE: Turkish
CURRENCY: Turkish lira

UNITED ARAB EMIRATES
Imarat al-Arabiya al-Muttahida – United Arab Emirates
AREA: 32,278 sq mi.
POPULATION: 3.1 million
CAPITAL: Abu Dhabi
OTHER CITIES: Dubai, Sharjah
HIGHEST POINT: Jabal Yibir (5,010 ft)
OFFICIAL LANGUAGE: Arabic
CURRENCY: Dirham

YEMEN
Jamhuriya al Yamaniya – Republic of Yemen
AREA: 203,849 sq mi.
POPULATION: 18 million
CAPITAL: San'a
OTHER CITIES: Aden, Ta'izz
HIGHEST POINT: Mount Hadur Shuayb (12,336 ft)
OFFICIAL LANGUAGE: Arabic
CURRENCY: Riyal

◑ MUSLIM WARRIOR
Saladin (c. 1137–93) led the Muslims against the Crusaders. He captured Jerusalem in 1187.

◑ CRUSADERS' CASTLES
The Krac des Chevaliers (Castle of the Knights) is the greatest medieval castle in Syria. It was an important base for the Christian Crusaders from 1142 to 1271.

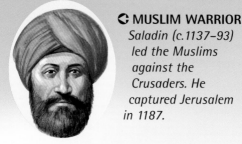

◑ HITTITE SOLDIER
The Hittites of ancient Turkey conquered much of southwest Asia (c. 900–1200 BC).

◆ ARABIAN HERO

T.E. Lawrence (1888–1935), a British soldier, helped to organize an Arab revolt against the Turks during World War I. He became known as Lawrence of Arabia.

◆ GOLDA MEIR

Meir (1898–1978) was Israel's prime minister in 1974 when Israel fought the Yom Kippur War against Arab forces.

However, after years of decline, the Turkish Ottoman empire collapsed at the end of World War I. After the war, several new Arab nations were created, and oil was discovered in some regions.

In the 1930s, many Jewish refugees settled in Palestine. The State of Israel was created in 1948— Israelis defeated Arab forces in a war that ended in 1949. Further Arab–Israeli wars occurred in 1956, 1967, and 1974. During the wars, Israel occupied the Sinai peninsula and the Gaza Strip from Egypt, the West Bank from Jordan, and the Golan Heights from Syria. In 1979, Israel and Egypt signed a peace treaty and Egypt regained the Sinai peninsula.

In the 1990s, Israel and the PLO (Palestine Liberation Organization) led by Yasir Arafat (b.1929) agreed on the creation of a new state for Palestinians, including the Gaza Strip and part of the West Bank.

The Kurds of northern Iraq fought unsuccessfully to found a Kurdish state, and Iran and Iraq fought a border war in the 1980s. In 1990, Iraq invaded Kuwait. But an international force led by the United States forced the Iraqi president Saddam Hussein (b.1937) to withdraw his troops in 1991. In 2003, Saddam's regime in Iraq was toppled from power by a US-led invasion force.

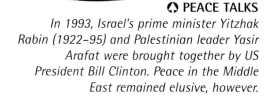

◆ PEACE TALKS

In 1993, Israel's prime minister Yitzhak Rabin (1922–95) and Palestinian leader Yasir Arafat were brought together by US President Bill Clinton. Peace in the Middle East remained elusive, however.

TIMELINE

BC

3500	Civilizations develop in the lower Tigris-Euphrates valleys (Mesopotamia)
539	Persians conquer Mesopotamia
331	Alexander the Great defeats the Persians
30	Most of Southwest Asia under Roman rule

AD

600s	Arabs found an Islamic empire
1095	Christian Crusades begin
1187	Saladin captures Jerusalem
1270	Christian Crusades end
1300s	Ottoman Turks begin to rule
1918	Collapse of the Ottoman empire
1948	State of Israel founded
1967	The Six-Day War: Israel seizes land from neighboring Arab countries
1979	Revolution in Iran: the shah (king) is overthrown and Ayatollah Khomeini heads an Islamic government
1980	Iran-Iraq War begins (until 1990)
1990	Iraq occupies Kuwait (until 1991)
1995	Assassination of Israeli prime minister Yitzhak Rabin
2003	US-led invasion of Iraq; Saddam Hussein is defeated

SOUTHERN ASIA

↻ YAK

The biggest country in Southern Asia is India, which covers an area about one-third the size of Europe. The northern part of the region is mountainous. It includes the great mountain ranges of the Hindu Kush in Afghanistan, the Karakoram Range between Pakistan and China, and the mighty Himalayas. Fertile plains extend from eastern Pakistan across northern India into Bangladesh. Some of the world's greatest rivers—the Indus, Ganges, and Brahmaputra—drain these plains. The lower parts of the Brahmaputra and Ganges in Bangladesh have created the world's largest delta.

Southern India consists mainly of a large plateau, the Deccan, which is bordered by two mountain ranges, the Western and Eastern Ghats. The large island of Sri Lanka, off the southern tip of India, has a mountainous central area surrounded by fertile plains. The Maldives are a chain of low coral islands to the southwest.

The northwest is mostly dry, especially in the Thar Desert on the border between Pakistan and India. The northern mountains have cold winters, but much of Southern Asia is warm and tropical.

The heavy rains that fall in summer are the main feature of the climate. The rains are brought by moist, monsoon winds that blow from the sea between May and October. Farmers eagerly await the rains, but the rains can make the rivers overflow, causing widespread flooding. The rivers in Bangladesh burst their banks in 1998 and flooded two-thirds of the country.

FACTS

AFGHANISTAN
Islamic Emirate of Afghanistan
AREA: 251,772 sq mi.
POPULATION: 26.8 million
CAPITAL: Kabul
OTHER CITIES: Qandahar, Herat, Mazar-e-Sharif
HIGHEST POINT: Nowshak (24,557 ft)
OFFICIAL LANGUAGES: Pashto, Dari (Persian)
CURRENCY: Afghani

BANGLADESH
Gana Prajatantri Bangladesh – People's Republic of Bangladesh
AREA: 55,598 sq mi.
POPULATION: 131.3 million
CAPITAL: Dhaka
OTHER CITIES: Chittagong, Khulna
HIGHEST POINT: Mount Keokradong (4,035 ft)
OFFICIAL LANGUAGE: Bengali
CURRENCY: Taka

BHUTAN
Druk-yul – Kingdom of Bhutan
AREA: 18,147 sq mi.
POPULATION: 715,000
CAPITAL: Thimphu
OTHER CITIES: Phuntsholing
HIGHEST POINT: Kula Kangri (24,783 ft)
OFFICIAL LANGUAGE: Dzonghka
CURRENCY: Ngultrum

INDIA
Bharat – Republic of India
AREA: 1,269,339 sq mi.
POPULATION: 1,030 million
CAPITAL: New Delhi
OTHER CITIES: Mumbai, Calcutta, Chennai
HIGHEST POINT: Kanchenjunga (28,209 ft)
OFFICIAL LANGUAGE: Hindi, English
CURRENCY: Indian rupee

↻ **THE GANGES: A HOLY RIVER**
In India, Hindu pilgrims visit the holy city of Varanasi to bathe in the sacred Ganges River.

◑ THE HIMALAYAS
The Himalayan mountain range is the highest in the world. Its highest peak, Mount Everest, rises to 29,028 feet above sea level.

◑ MOUNTAIN COUNTRY
Leh is capital of the region of Ladakh in northwestern India. It has a large Tibetan Buddhist monastery.

AFGHANISTAN

PAKISTAN

NEPAL

BHUTAN

◑ NEPALESE TEMPLE
Nyatapola temple, in Bhaktapur, is the highest temple in Nepal. The town is to the east of the capital, Katmandu.

SRI LANKA

BANGLADESH

INDIA

◑ TRICKY TERRAIN
Travel is difficult in the mountains of northern Pakistan. Rope bridges span many of the fast-flowing rivers.

MALDIVES

◑ RECLINING BUDDHA
The ancient Sri Lankan capital of Polonnaruwa has huge carvings of the Buddha. Buddhism is the chief religion in Sri Lanka.

◑ HINDU ARCHITECTURE
The Teli-ka-Mandir is an ancient Hindu temple in the city of Gwalior, central India.

Map labels

TURKMENISTAN
TAJIKISTAN
Mazar-e-Sharif
Herat
HINDU
AFGHANISTAN
Kabul
Farah
Khyber Pass
Peshawar
DISPUTED AREA
K2 8,611m
Islamabad
Qandahar
Srinagar
JAMMU & KASHMIR
Rawalpindi
RIGESTAN DESERT
Quetta
Faisalabad Lahore
Amritsar
PAKISTAN
BALUCHISTAN PLATEAU
Sukkur
Multan
Sutlej
PUNJAB
Bahawalpur
Indus
Tibet (CHINA)
Hyderabad
GREAT INDIAN DESERT (THAR DESERT)
Nanda Devi 7,817m
Delhi
NEPAL
Karachi
Gulf of Kachch
New Delhi
Jodhpur
Jaipur
Agra
Bareilly
Annapurna 8,078m
Mt Everest 8,848m
Thimphu
Ajmer
Lucknow
Ghagara
Katmandu
BHUTAN
Udaipur
Kota
Gwalior
Kanpur
Yamuna
Varanasi
Ganges
Patna
Brahmaputra
NAGA HILLS
Gauhati
Jamnagar
Ahmadabad
Indore
Bhopal
Son
Allahabad
Bhavnagar
Vadodara
Narmada
Jabalpur
BANGLADESH
Imphal
Surat
Jamshedpur
Asanol
Dhaka
MYANMAR (BURMA)
Gulf of Khambhat
I N D I A
Aurangabad
Nagpur
Raipur
Khulna
Chittagong
Mumbai (Bombay)
D E C C A N
Mahanadi
Kolkata (Calcutta)
Pune
Godavari
Cuttack
Mouths of the Ganges
Solapur
Hyderabad
Kolhapur
Krishna
Vishakhapatnam
WESTERN GHATS
Hubli-Dharwar
Kurnool
Vijayawada
EASTERN GHATS
Penner
Nellore
Mangalore
Bangalore
Mysore
Chennai (Madras)
Kozhikode
Coimbatore
Tiruchchirappalli
Cochin
Madurai
Palk Strait
Jaffna
Trivandrum
Trincomalee
C. Comorin
Gulf of Mannar
SRI LANKA
Colombo
Kandy
MALDIVES
Pidurutalagala 2,524m
INDIAN OCEAN
Galle

☼ ELEPHANT MAKE-UP
Painted elephants carry visitors up the steep slopes to the Indian fort of Amber, near Jaipur.

There are eight countries in Southern Asia. The largest is India, which makes up nearly two-thirds of the region and contains about three-fourths of the people. Pakistan, the second-largest country, makes up more than 15 percent of the region.

India is a federal state, made up of 25 states, each with its own government, and seven territories. Bangladesh, the Maldives, Pakistan, and Sri Lanka are also republics. So is Afghanistan, after a period of Islamic fundamentalist rule in the 1990s. Southern Asia also numbers two kingdoms: Bhutan and Nepal.

☼ PINK PALACE
The Hawa Mahal, or Palace of the Winds, is in the beautiful "pink" city of Jaipur. Jaipur was founded in 1728.

☼ BASKET-MAKING
Indian basket-makers use natural fibers, such as the leaves of palm trees.

Since 1947, when modern India and Pakistan were born, some of their boundaries have been disputed. The chief problem concerns the region of Jammu and Kashmir in northwest India. India claims the entire area, but Pakistan occupies part of it.

Many people in Southern Asia are poor and live simply, from the land; more than 90 percent of the people in Bhutan and Nepal are poor farmers. Farming is the chief activity throughout the region.

About 63 percent of the people work in farming. The chief crop is rice. India ranks second only to China in world production, while Bangladesh ranks fourth.

Other food crops include barley, millet, sorghum, and wheat, together with vegetables such as beans and peas, coconuts, a variety of fruits, and tea. Cotton, jute, rubber, and tobacco are also grown. Livestock farming is important in some countries, but Hindus do not eat meat—and cows are considered sacred.

☾ INDIAN MARKET
Vegetables are cooked with spices and eaten with rice—the main food in India—or a flat bread called chapati.

☼ SANDAL MAKER
Footwear and clothes are still made by hand in parts of Southern Asia. Huge factories also manufacture items for export.

Calcutta), and Chennai (formerly Madras). Other large cities include Karachi and Lahore in Pakistan. Many cities of Southern Asia contain old areas with slums, alongside modern high-rise buildings. The contrasts between the lives of rich and poor people are very great.

◑ FISHING IN BANGLADESH
Fish are caught in the Bay of Bengal and also in the many waterways that drain the flat parts of Bangladesh.

◑ COMPUTER INDUSTRY
Factories in Bangalore produce computers. High-tech industry is increasing in India, although most people still live by farming.

◑ TEA LEAVES
The leaves of tea plants are so delicate they must be hand-picked. India and Sri Lanka are among the world's leading tea producers.

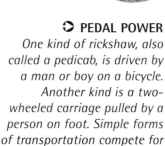

◑ CHILLI PEPPERS

◑ PEDAL POWER
One kind of rickshaw, also called a pedicab, is driven by a man or boy on a bicycle. Another kind is a two-wheeled carriage pulled by a person on foot. Simple forms of transportation compete for passengers with taxis in many towns and cities.

◑ GROWING RICE
Paddy fields, enclosed by low banks of soil, are plowed and flooded before rice shoots are planted.

FACTS

MALDIVES
Divehi Raajjeyge Jumhooriyya –
Republic of the Maldives
AREA: 115 sq mi.
POPULATION: 275,000
CAPITAL: Malé
OTHER CITIES: none
HIGHEST POINT: Wilingili
Island (79 ft)
OFFICIAL LANGUAGE: Divehi
CURRENCY: Rufiyaa

NEPAL
Nepal Adhirajya – Kingdom of
Nepal
AREA: 56,827 sq mi.
POPULATION: 25.2 million
CAPITAL: Katmandu
OTHER CITIES: Lalitpur,
Biratnagar
HIGHEST POINT: Mount
Everest (29,028 ft)
OFFICIAL LANGUAGE: Nepali
CURRENCY: Nepalese rupee

PAKISTAN
Islami Jamhuriya e Pakistan –
Islamic Republic of Pakistan
AREA: 307,373 sq mi.
POPULATION: 144.6 million
CAPITAL: Islamabad
OTHER CITIES: Karachi,
Lahore, Faisalabad
HIGHEST POINT: K2 (28,251 ft)
OFFICIAL LANGUAGE: Urdu
CURRENCY: Pakistan rupee

SRI LANKA
Sri Lanka Prajathanthrika
Samajavadi Janarajaya –
Democratic Socialist
Republic of Sri Lanka
AREA: 25,332 sq mi.
POPULATION: 19.4 million
CAPITAL: Colombo
OTHER CITIES: Dehiwela-Mt
Lavinia, Moratuwa
HIGHEST POINT:
Pidurutalagala (8,280 ft)
OFFICIAL LANGUAGES: Sinhala,
Tamil
CURRENCY: Sri Lanka rupee

169

◯ SHERPAS IN NEPAL
The tough Sherpa people of northeastern Nepal are known for their mountaineering and military skills. Some work as mountain guides.

◯ PAINTED VEHICLES
Long-distance drivers in India and Pakistan often decorate their trucks. Road transportation is important because distances in Southern Asia are so great.

◯ DIWALI
Held each fall, Diwali is the Hindu festival of light. To mark the new year and to honor Lakshmi, the goddess of good fortune, people light oil lamps or candles and exchange cards and gifts.

India's people are divided into two main groups: the lighter-skinned Indo-Aryans in the north and the darker-skinned Dravidians in the south. There are 16 major languages and more than 1,000 minor languages and dialects. The main official language is Hindi. English is an "associate" national language.

The people in the northwestern part of Southern Asia include Afghans, Indo-Aryans, and Persians. The Sinhalese of Sri Lanka and the people in the Maldives are descendants of people from northern India, while the ancestors of Sri Lankan Tamils came from southern India.

Southern Asians excel in the decorative arts and in architecture and sculpture—across the region can be seen superb Hindu temples, Muslim mosques, and huge statues of the Buddha. Traditional music and dance are popular, and movie-making is another Indian art-form.

◯ HINDU WEDDING
Wealthy Indians have elaborate wedding ceremonies. These days, many weddings take place at hotels.

◯ JAIN BUILDING
Jainism is an Indian religion dating back 2,500 years. This Jain temple is in the Great Indian (Thar) Desert region in northwest India.

◑ HOUSEBOATS
In India's troubled region of Jammu and Kashmir, some people live on houseboats on the lakes. Their handicrafts include making beautiful hand-painted papier mâché boxes, which are sold to tourists in Delhi.

Many people in the cities of Southern Asia wear Western clothes, but traditional dhotis—white cloths wrapped around the body and tucked between the legs—are also worn by men. Many Indian women wear brightly colored silk or cotton saris.

◯ BUDDHIST GATEWAY
Buddhism is the chief religion in Bhutan and Sri Lanka. This is the gateway to a Buddhist shrine.

Hinduism, one of the world's oldest religions, dates back about 4,000 years. It is followed by 63 percent of the people of Southern Asia. Hindus worship many gods—Shiva, Krishna, and Vishnu are the most well-known—who are forms of one universal spirit. Hindus believe that the soul never dies. Instead, it is reincarnated (reborn) in the body of a human or animal. One of the many religious festivals celebrated is Diwali, the Hindu festival of light. Another is the spring festival of Holi.

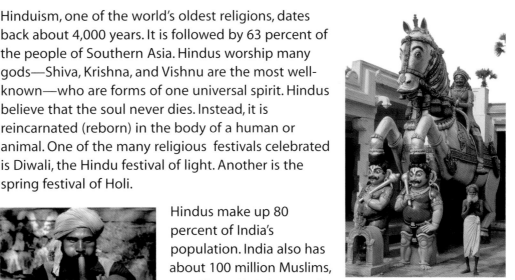

◯ LAMAS
Lamas are monks who practice Lamaism, or Tibetan Buddhism.

◯ SNAKE CHARMER
An Indian snake charmer sways to-and-fro as he plays his music. The cobra rises up, mesmerized by the movement of the instrument.

Hindus make up 80 percent of India's population. India also has about 100 million Muslims, 36 million Christians, and nearly seven million Buddhists. Hinduism is the main religion in Nepal, while Islam is the religion of Afghanistan, Bangladesh, the Maldives, and Pakistan. Buddhism is the leading faith in Bhutan and Sri Lanka.

◯ VILLAGE GODS
Eight-out-of-ten Indians are Hindus. Many villages have their own statues of gods.

◯ TEMPLE AT KHAJURAHO
In the Hindu temple-complex at Khajuraho, in north-central India, there are 22 great temples, each decorated with elaborate carvings.

◯ PRAYER BELLS
Buddhists shake bells during worship to frighten away evil spirits and attract good ones.

◯ SPRING FESTIVAL
Holi is an ancient Hindu spring festival, when people throw colored water and powders over each other. Differences of age, caste, and sex are disregarded on this day.

⊙ INDUS CIVILIZATION
The ancient citadel of Mohenjo-daro had wide streets, large houses, good sewers, grain stores, and a Great Bath, used for religious rituals.

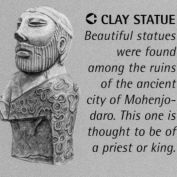

⊙ CLAY STATUE
Beautiful statues were found among the ruins of the ancient city of Mohenjo-daro. This one is thought to be of a priest or king.

⊙ TAJ MAHAL
The white marble Taj Mahal, in Agra, India, was built as a tomb for Mumtaz Mahal, favorite wife of Shah Jahan (1592–1666). It is one of the world's most famous and beautiful buildings.

⊙ DEMOCRATIC ELECTIONS
India is the world's biggest democracy, with more voters than any other country. It has held regular elections since it won independence.

Between 2500 BC and 1700 BC, the Indus Valley civilization flourished in what is now Pakistan and northwestern India. Their two great cities were Harappa and Mohenjo-daro. About 1500 BC, Aryan people from the northwest invaded India and developed the Hindu cultures of the region. After Alexander the Great reached the Indus Valley region about 320 BC, a major Buddhist culture grew up in the north. Following other invasions, Mongol invaders took northern India in the AD1400s. By 1526, India was part of a large Mongol empire.

⊙ INDEPENDENCE DAY PARADE
Soldiers march to celebrate India's independence from Britain. Military service in India is voluntary.

◐ MASS MIGRATION

When India and Pakistan became independent in 1947, millions of Muslims and Hindus moved country. Attacks on refugee columns resulted in many deaths.

◑ EMPEROR ASOKA

Emperor Asoka ruled over the Maurya empire (272–232 BC). He conquered large areas and converted from Hinduism to Buddhism.

From the 16th century, European traders began to visit Southern Asia. As the Mongol empire declined, the British East India Company gradually gained control of large areas. An unsuccessful rebellion against the East India Company took place in 1857 and, in 1858, Britain took control of the region. Britain helped to develop the region with railroads, a telephone system, and irrigation works.

But many Indians wanted independence. From 1920, they were led by a lawyer, Mohandas K. Gandhi (1869–1948), also known as Mahatma Gandhi, who led campaigns of non-violent resistance. After World War II, Britain agreed to make India independent. Following violence between Hindus and Muslims, the country's leaders agreed to partition British India into Muslim Pakistan and a mainly Hindu India. Millions of people became refugees and many were killed.

Fighting also occurred in the northwest, where India and Pakistan fought over Kashmir. Pakistan was divided into two separate areas: West and East Pakistan. In 1971, civil war broke out and East Pakistan became a separate country, Bangladesh. In Afghanistan, Russian troops invaded to prop up the Communist government, but pulled out in 1988, after which Islamic Taliban forces imposed a strict regime. In 2001 a coalition of US and allied forces, backing Afghan rebels, drove out the Taliban, and set up a new government.

In Sri Lanka, some Hindu Tamils supported a guerrilla group, the Tamil Tigers, who want their own country. Relations between India and Pakistan are strained over Kashmir. Both countries have nuclear weapons.

◐ GOLDEN TEMPLE, AMRITSAR

The Golden Temple, the most sacred Sikh temple, is in Amritsar, in northwest India. Sikhs make up two percent of India's population.

TIMELINE

BC

2500	Indus Valley civilization develops
320s	Alexander the Great reaches southern India
272	Buddhist empire unites much of southern India (until 232)

AD

1200s	Mongols capture northern India
1526	Mongol empire established in Southern Asia
1619	Portuguese control most of Ceylon (now Sri Lanka)
1649	Taj Mahal completed
1757	British East India Company wins control of Bengal
1802	Ceylon becomes a British Crown Colony
1858	Britain governs India
1947	British India gains independence and splits into two countries: India and Pakistan. Fighting breaks out in Kashmir
1948	Mahatma Gandhi assassinated by Hindu fanatic
1971	East Pakistan becomes Bangladesh
1972	Ceylon becomes the Republic of Sri Lanka
1988	USSR withdraws from Afghanistan
2001	Afghanistan's Taliban rulers are overthrown by a US-led coalition

◑ NATIONAL LEADERS

In 1947, Muslim Pakistan came into being, led by Muhammad Ali Jinnah (1876–1948, on the right). India's first prime minister was Jawaharlal Nehru (1889–1964, on the left).

173

EASTERN ASIA

↻ BUDDHIST MONK, LHASA
Lhasa is the capital of Tibet—now a region of China. Many Tibetans would like Tibet to become an independent country.

By area, Eastern Asia is dominated by China, the world's third-largest country after Russia and Canada. China claims the island of Taiwan, although Taiwan is a separate territory with its own government. Eastern Asia also includes North Korea, South Korea, and Mongolia. Japan is also part of Eastern Asia, but is covered separately (see page 182).

In the western part of Eastern Asia are high plateaus, mountain ranges, and deserts. On the border between Tibet and Nepal rises Mount Everest, the world's highest mountain. The inland deserts are hot in summer, but are bitterly cold in winter. The Gobi Desert, which lies partly in northern China and partly in Mongolia, is one of the bleakest deserts on Earth.

By contrast, the eastern part of this region has fertile plains, uplands, and densely populated river valleys. Three great rivers cross eastern China—the Huang He (formerly named the Yellow River), the Chang Jiang (Yangtze), and the Xi Jiang in the southeast. North and South Korea occupy a rugged peninsula that juts out from northeastern China. Most Koreans live on the plains and around the coast.

CHINA
Zhonghua Renmin Gonghe Guo
– People's Republic of China
AREA: 3,676,300 sq mi.
POPULATION: 1,275 million
CAPITAL: Beijing
OTHER CITIES: Shanghai, Tianjin, Shenyang, Wuhan
HIGHEST POINT: Mount Everest (29,028 ft)
OFFICIAL LANGUAGE: Mandarin Chinese
CURRENCY: Yuan

MONGOLIA
Mongol Uls – Mongolia
AREA: 604,800 sq mi.
POPULATION: 2.5 million
CAPITAL: Ulan Bator
OTHER CITIES: Darhan, Erdenet
HIGHEST POINT: Altai Mountains (14,350 ft)
OFFICIAL LANGUAGE: Khalka Mongolian
CURRENCY: Tugrik

NORTH KOREA
Chosun Minchu-chui Inmin Konghwa-guk – People's Democratic Republic of Korea
AREA: 46,536 sq mi.
POPULATION: 22 million
CAPITAL: Pyongang
OTHER CITIES: Hamhung, Cho'ngjin
HIGHEST POINT: Paektu-san (Paektu Mountain) 9,003 ft
OFFICIAL LANGUAGE: Korean
CURRENCY: Won

Tibet is a high, windswept plateau, with bitterly cold winters and short, cool summers. The north and northwest is mainly dry, with bare desert or areas of dry grassland, called steppe. Summers in southeast China range from warm to hot, while winters are cool. The northeast, including most of Korea, has cold winters.

↻ FOREST OF STONE
Worn limestone rocks resembling giant tree trunks form the Yunnan stone forest in southern China. The area lies southeast of Kunming.

↻ GIANT PANDA
Giant pandas are rare. They live in the bamboo forests of west and southwest China, and are threatened by loss of their habitat.

NORTH KOREA

MONGOLIA

☉ HONG KONG
Formerly a British colony, Hong Kong was returned to Chinese rule as a Special Administrative Region in 1997.

☉ SEOUL, KOREA
Seoul is the capital of South Korea. It is one of the world's largest cities and has many high-rise buildings and industries.

☉ PEKINESE DOG

CHINA

☉ GREAT WALL OF CHINA
The 4,600-mile-long Great Wall of China was built to keep out invaders from the north.

SOUTH KOREA

TAIWAN

☉ SHANGHAI
Shanghai is China's largest city. It is also the country's chief port and industrial city.

◐ KOWLOON, HONG KONG
Hong Kong consists of 235 islands and an area on the mainland of China. Kowloon is on the mainland. It is a busy place, with many shops and industries.

◐ PICKING TEA
Tea is one of the main crops in southern China. China ranks second only to India in the production of tea.

FACTS

SOUTH KOREA
Daehan Min-Kuk – Republic of Korea
AREA: 38,330 sq mi.
POPULATION: 47.6 million
CAPITAL: Seoul
OTHER CITIES: Pusan, Taegu
HIGHEST POINT: Halla San (Halla Mountain, 6,398 ft)
OFFICIAL LANGUAGE: Korean
CURRENCY: Won

TAIWAN
Chung-hua Min-kuo – Republic of China
AREA: 13,968 sq mi.
POPULATION: 22.3 million
CAPITAL: Taipei
OTHER CITIES: Kao-hsiung, T'ai-chung
HIGHEST POINT: Yü Shan (Mount Morrison, 13,113 ft)
OFFICIAL LANGUAGE: Mandarin Chinese
CURRENCY: New Taiwan dollar

In recent years, Eastern Asia has suffered from many disputes. One issue concerns Taiwan and other offshore islands. Since 1949, when the Chinese Communists took over the mainland, Taiwan has been the home of the Nationalists, who founded a rival "Republic of China." China still claims Taiwan, but the Taiwanese oppose union with Communist China. Some old colonial problems have been solved. First, in 1997, Britain returned Hong Kong to China. Then, in 1999, Portugal returned Macao, a small territory in southwestern China. China and Russia ended long-running border disputes in 1998.

No solution appears in sight concerning Tibet in the southwest. Tibet has been part of China since the early 1950s, but many Tibetans want to regain their independence and see the return of their exiled religious leader, the Dalai Lama.

◐ FISHING WITH BIRDS
Chinese fishermen train birds called cormorants to catch fish for them in inland waters.

◐ STOCK EXCHANGE, HONG KONG
Hong Kong is one of the world's leading financial centers.

The border between North and South Korea is disputed. After World War II, North Korea became a Communist country, while South Korea, aided by the United States, allied itself with Western countries. From 1950 to 1953, the Korean War caused great destruction, and North and South Korea remain divided. South Korea is a multi-party democracy, as is Mongolia, which was a Communist country until 1990. Communist governments still rule North Korea and China.

◑ GOLDEN LION
This golden lion is one of the many statues found in Beijing's Forbidden City, the large palace-complex of the former emperors.

◑ MARKET, BEIJING
Chinese people from the countryside travel to the cities to sell their produce at markets. As well as vegetables, many live birds and other animals are sold, to be cooked and eaten with rice or noodles.

◑ RICE PLANT

◑ JADE CAMEL
Since ancient times, the Chinese have mined jade and used it to make beautiful carvings. This jade camel is more than 1,000 years old.

Nearly 70 percent of the people of Eastern Asia, excluding Japan, work on farms. Only ten percent of the land in China is farmed, but the country is a major producer of farm products, including rice, sweet potatoes, tea, and wheat. China also raises more than a third of the world's pigs.

Only 29 percent of China's people live in cities and towns, yet over 30 Chinese cities have populations of more than a million people. China's resources include coal and oil. Although many people are poor, China is a rapidly developing country.

"Special economic zones" in the east have many industries, which are partly financed by foreign companies.

South Korea and Taiwan are also important manufacturing nations. Communist North Korea also has industries, but living standards are lower there.

◑ PRINTING IN SOUTH KOREA
The printing of books, newspapers, and magazines is important in the drive to educate people. Most Asians believe that education is vital if their countries are to make economic progress.

◑ CHINESE JUNK
Junks are wooden vessels with two or more sails. They were traditionally used by Chinese and other sailors in Eastern Asia. Some people live on junks.

☯ CHINESE FOOD
Rice is eaten in southern China, but most northerners prefer wheat. Vegetables, pork, and poultry are also popular.

China contains more than one-fifth of the world's population. The birth-rate was so high that the government made laws to slow down the rate of population growth. For example, couples are encouraged to have one child only; women may not marry until the age of 20; and men may not marry until they are 22.

About 92 percent of the people of China belong to the Han group. Their language, Chinese, is always written in the same way, but spoken Chinese has many dialects. People from one part of the country often cannot understand people from elsewhere. The dialect called Northern or Mandarin Chinese is the official language.

☯ UNARMED COMBAT
Chinese karate is called kung fu. It employs circular movements that differ from the powerful movements of other forms of karate.

☯ LIFE ON THE WATER
Most Chinese cities have housing shortages. Some people live on boats moored along the coast or rivers. China contains some of the world's most densely populated areas.

Besides the Han, China also has 55 minority groups. Some speak Chinese dialects, others have their own languages. Important minorities include Kazaks and Uigurs in the northwest, Mongols in the north, Koreans in the northeast, and Tibetans in the southeast.

The Communist governments in Eastern Asia have discouraged religious worship. However, many people follow Buddhism, Confucianism, or Taoism, and sometimes a mixture of all three. Some Muslims live in western China and in Mongolia. Christians make up about one-fourth of the population of South Korea.

☯ TALENTED CHILDREN
Chinese children with special talents receive extra schooling at the weekend. Some learn to play the piba, a stringed instrument.

☯ MONGOLIAN YURT
The traditional homes of Mongolian herders are felt tents, called yurts. They can be easily taken down and moved to a new site.

☉ BUDDHIST MONK
Forms of Buddhism are followed in China (including Tibet), South Korea and Mongolia.

Eastern Asia has long artistic traditions. Early Chinese art includes beautiful pottery and carved jade statues. China also has much great literature, delicate watercolor painting, sculpture, embroidery, music, and theater.

People enjoy many kinds of recreation. Many Chinese get up early every morning to engage in an ancient and graceful form of exercise called taijiquan. Sports include baseball, basketball, soccer, table tennis, and volleyball.

Rice is the chief food in the warm, southern parts of the region, while wheat is important in the cooler north. Pork and poultry are the main meats, while bamboo shoots, cabbages, and tofu (soya bean curd) are popular vegetables. Beijing duck is a special treat in China. It consists of slices of crisp roast duck wrapped in thin pancakes. Koreans enjoy kimchi, a spicy mixture of cabbage, radishes, and other vegetables. Tea is the chief drink.

☉ SUMMER FESTIVAL
Every May, dragon boat races are held in Hong Kong. After the races, there are displays of martial arts and street theater to enjoy. The revelers snack on dragon boat dumplings and roasted pinenuts, and firecrackers are let off well into the night.

☉ CHINESE OPERA
Beijing opera combines drama with songs and dances. The actors wear elaborate costumes and make-up.

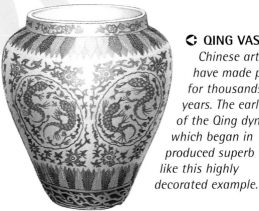

☉ QING VASE
Chinese artists have made pottery for thousands of years. The early part of the Qing dynasty, which began in 1614, produced superb vases like this highly decorated example.

☉ CHINESE WRITING
Chinese writing consists of characters that stand for words or parts of words.

☉ TIANANMEN SQUARE, BEIJING
Firework displays and parades are held in Tiananmen Square in central Beijing. The Forbidden City and parliament buildings border the square.

179

○ BEIJING
In the Ming dynasty, a wall and moat were built around Beijing. In the Qing dynasty, more palaces, temples, and other buildings were added outside the city wall.

Early civilizations developed in the fertile valleys of eastern China about 3,500 years ago. China's history from the 1700s BC until 1912 is divided into dynasties—rule by members of a family or group.

The Qin dynasty (221 BC–206 BC) was the first to set up a strong central government to rule eastern China. The Han dynasty that followed founded a strong empire, ruling an area as large as the Roman empire. China came under foreign rule when the Mongols conquered the country in the 13th century and set up the Yuan dynasty. The Mongols conquered a vast area extending westward from Korea to eastern Europe.

Chinese rule was restored in 1368, but in the 17th century, the Manchu from Manchuria set up the Qin dynasty. Manchu rule was weakened in 1895 when China was defeated by Japan, which occupied Korea in 1910. Dynastic rule came to an end in 1912, when China became a republic. Japan seized Manchuria in 1931 and China fought against Japanese invaders between 1937 and 1945.

At the end of World War II, civil war in China continued between the Communists and the Nationalists. In 1949, the Communists, under Mao Zedong (1893–1976), took over mainland China, while the Nationalists under Chiang Kai-shek (1887–1975) retreated to Taiwan.

Under Communist rule, the governments of China, North Korea, and Mongolia took over all land and industry. Although they improved the lives of many poor peasants, they also suppressed all opponents of Communism.

○ TERRACOTTA ARMY, XI'AN
In the vast burial chamber of Emperor Shi Huangdi, who lived in the 3rd century BC, thousands of lifesized clay soldiers were found.

○ SILK ROAD TRADERS
The Silk Road was the long, arduous trade route between China and Syria, used in Roman and later times. It crossed mountains and deserts.

○ MANCHU EMPEROR
The Manchus set up the Qing dynasty. Only the emperor was allowed to wear a silk gown embroidered with a five-clawed dragon.

○ CANTON HARBOR
Guangzhou (formerly Canton) is a Chinese port to the northwest of Hong Kong. During the 1800s, it was the only Chinese port open to Westerners.

☾ LAST EMPEROR
Pu Yi was China's last emperor. He was two when he became emperor in 1908.

Some Communist policies caused severe economic problems. From the 1980s, China introduced economic reforms, especially in the east, where foreign companies were welcomed. But the Communists kept control of China's government.

In 1990 Mongolia held free elections, which led to the establishment of democratic government. South Korea, Taiwan, and the British territory of Hong Kong set up high-tech and other industries, rapidly developing their economies. In 1997, Hong Kong, which Britain had controlled since 1842, was returned to China. It became a "Special Administrative Region," but retained many of the laws introduced by Britain.

☾ MING TOMB
Many Chinese and foreigners visit the Ming tombs. The Ming dynasty lasted from 1368 until 1644.

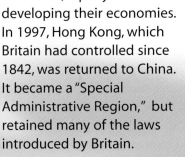

☾ CHAIRMAN MAO
Mao Zedong (or Mao Tse-tung) became China's leader when the Communists took power in 1949. He died in 1976.

☾ DENG XIAOPING
From 1976, Deng Xiaoping made many economic changes in China.

☾ THE LONG MARCH
In the 1930s, under Nationalist attack, the Chinese Communists undertook the Long March to northern China. On the march, Mao Zedong emerged as the Communist leader.

TIMELINE

BC

1700s   Eastern Asia's first major civilization founded in the Huang He valley

214   Under Emperor Shi Huangdi, China is united; Great Wall of China is fortified and sections joined

202 BC–AD 220 Chinese culture flourishes under Han dynasty (until 220 AD)

AD

1279   Mongols begin to rule Mongolia, Korea, and all of China

1368   Chinese culture develops under the Ming dynasty (until 1644)

1644   Manchus rule China, Mongolia, and Korea (until 1910, when Japan occupies the peninsula)

1912   Republic of China founded

1937   China at war with Japan (until 1945)

1949   Communists establish the People's Republic of China

1950   Korean War (until 1953)

1989   Tiananmen Square massacre of student demonstrators, Beijing

1997   Britain hands Hong Kong to China

1999   Portugal hands Macao to China

JAPAN

JAPAN
Nihon, or Nippon Koku –
Land of the Rising Sun
AREA: 145,869 sq mi.
POPULATION: 127 million
CAPITAL: Tokyo
OTHER CITIES: Osaka,
Yokohama, Nagoya
HIGHEST POINT: Mount Fuji
(12,388 ft)
OFFICIAL LANGUAGE:
Japanese
CURRENCY: Yen

◯ SPRING FLOWERS
*Each spring, the cherry trees blossom
first in the warm south, then in the
north. This is marked by spring festivals.*

◯ BUDDHIST STATUE, KYOTO
*Many Japanese follow a
mixture of Shintoism and
Buddhism, the country's two
main religions.*

Japan is part of Eastern Asia. It consists of four main islands and thousands of small ones. The main islands, in order of size, are Honshu, Hokkaido, Kyushu, and Shikoku. These islands make up more than 98 percent of Japan.

South of Shikoku lies the Ryukyu island chain, and south of Tokyo are the Bonin Islands. The land is mainly mountainous, with some small, fertile, and thickly populated plains around the coast. Mount Fuji, a dormant volcano, is Japan's highest peak. Most of the country's rivers are short and fast-flowing.

The climate varies from north to south. Hokkaido in the north has cold, snowy winters, while Kyushu and Shikoku have mild winters and long, hot summers. The rainfall is generally abundant and forests cover about two-thirds of the land. Evergreens, such as fir and spruce, grow in the north, with deciduous trees, such as maple and oak, in the warmer center and south. Wild animals include bears, wild boar, and deer. Japan is the world's northern limit for monkeys, including the Japanese macaque.

Whales, dolphins, and many kinds of fish live in the seas around Japan. The country is rich in waterbirds, including the cormorant, which can be trained to catch fish.

Japan lies on a part of the Earth called "the Pacific ring of fire." Along this zone, the Earth's plates are on the move. Under much of Japan, the Pacific plate is sinking under the Eurasian plate. Every time the Pacific plate moves downward, it makes the ground shake. An earthquake in 1923 struck the Tokyo-Yokohama area, killing 100,000 people. Earthquakes off the coast can trigger huge waves, called tsunamis. When these waves hit the shore, they do tremendous damage. The 1923 earthquake generated a 36-foot-high tsunami.

◯ THE LIGHTS OF TOKYO
*Badly damaged by an earthquake in 1923, and by bombing
in World War II, Tokyo is now a huge, thriving, densely
populated modern city and a major center for industry.*

○ WARM BATHS

Japanese macaques are large monkeys that live on the island of Hokkaido in the far north of Japan. In cold weather, they sometimes bathe in warm springs, known as onsen.

○ EARTHQUAKE DAMAGE

A powerful earthquake struck Kobe in 1995, killing more than 5,000 people.

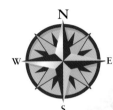

JAPAN

La Pérouse Strait

Rebun I.
Rishiri I.
Wakkanai

Teshio

Kuril Is. (Russia)

Asahigawa

H o k k a i d o

Ishikari Bay

Asahi Mt. 2,290 m

Otaru

Kushiro

Sapporo
Obihiro

Muroran

Uchiura Bay

Erimo Cape

Hakodate

Tsugaru Strait

Mutsa Bay

SEA OF JAPAN

Aomori

Hirosaki
Hachinohe

Akita

Kitakami

Morioka

Kamaishi

Sakata

Yamagata
Sendai

Sado
Niigata

Nagaoka

Fukushima

Koriyama
Iwaki

Toyama

Shinano

J A P A N

Utsunomiya

Hitachi

Kanazawa

Ueda

Takasaki
Mito

Fukui

JAPANESE ALPS

Matsumoto

Oki Is.

Takefu

Kofu

Tokyo

Kawasaki
Chiba

Gifu

Yokohama

Matsue

Biwa Lake

Kyoto

Nagoya

Toyota

Mt. Fuji 3,776 m

Sagami Bay

H o n s h u

Okayama

Kobe

Shizuoka

O-shima

Hiroshima

Osaka

Hamamatsu

Sakai

Matsusaka

Inland Sea

Takamatsu

Wakayama

Miyake I.

Tsushima

Tokushima

Kii Channel

PACIFIC OCEAN

Kitakyushu

Suo Sea

Shikoku

Fukuoka

Matsuyama

Sasebo

Bungo Channel

Kochi

Hachijo I.

Nagasaki

Omuta
Kumamoto

Amakusa Is.

K y u s h u

Koshiki Is.

Sendai

Miyazaki

Kagoshima

Tanega

Yaku

○ BONSAI TREE

 *(note: bonsai tree image above this caption)*

Japanese gardeners have perfected the art of growing miniature trees, known as bonsai.

○ KYUSHU ISLAND

Kyushu is the most southerly of Japan's four main islands. Its climate is much warmer than that of northern Japan.

○ PUFFER FISH

The poisonous puffer fish, or fugu, is found in the Pacific Ocean. Its flesh is a delicacy in Japan. Chefs must train for at least three years to learn how to cut off the poisonous parts of the fish.

○ MOUNT FUJI

Volcanic Mount Fuji, also called Fujiyama or Fuji-san, is Japan's highest peak, at 12,388 feet. It last erupted in 1708.

183

⟳ PAPER LANTERNS

Wood, wood pulp, and paper are made in Japan. Paper products range from lanterns to sliding walls used in homes.

For long periods in the past, Japan was ruled by emperors, who held great power. Before and during World War II, Emperor Hirohito was regarded as a god. After World War II, Japan became a constitutional monarchy and the emperor a symbol of the state confined to ceremonial duties. The country has an elected two-chamber Diet (parliament), whose members choose the prime minister.

By population, Japan ranks eighth among the countries of the world. Although the forested mountains are thinly populated, the coastal plains are among the world's most densely populated areas. About 78 percent of the people live in cities and towns. There are 11 cities with a population of more than a million.

⟳ TEA PLANTATION

Japan is one of the world's top ten producers of tea. Green tea is drunk with every meal.

⟳ ROBOTS AT WORK

Automation has helped Japan become the world's leading car producer. Japan also exports trucks and motorcycles. Using modern technology to make Japanese goods keeps down the prices in world markets.

Japan lacks natural resources and has to import food and many of the materials needed by its industries. But it ranks second only to the United States in its production of goods and services. Only 15 percent of the land is farmed, but Japanese farmers use intensive, scientific methods to achieve some of the world's highest yields, and Japan produces about 70 percent of the food it needs. Rice is the main crop, but eggs, fruit, meat, milk, and vegetables are also important. Japan is the world's fourth-largest fishing nation, judged by the volume of its catch. Fish, rice, and vegetables are the main ingredients for many meals, such as the ever-popular sushi.

⟳ SUSHI

Sushi, a delicious and popular dish, consists of rice "rolls" flavored with vinegar, raw fish, shellfish, and pickles.

⟳ WHALING

Whales are an important source of meat and oil in Japan, and festivals are held to celebrate them. But international laws have forced Japanese fleets to restrict their catches.

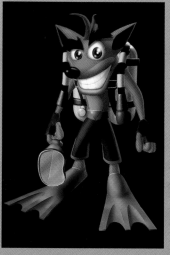

⟳ CRASH BANDICOOT

Japan's top quality electronic goods, including big-name computer games, are sold around the world.

◆ AKASHI KAIKYO ROAD BRIDGE

Completed in 1998, the bridge linking the island of Awaji to Honshu is the world's longest cable suspension bridge.

◆ MAGLEV TRAIN

Maglev (magnetic levitation) trains float above a fixed track without touching it. High-speed maglev trains can reach 311 mph. Japan has an extensive rail system for city commuters.

The country is one of the world's great industrial and trading nations. It leads the world in producing cars, ships, and steel. It is also a major producer of commercial vehicles, computers and other electronic goods, home appliances such as refrigerators, freezers, and washing machines, and radios and television sets. Japan also has a large chemical industry and silk is a traditional product.

◆ DECORATED FAN

The folding fan was probably invented in Japan about 1,300 years ago. Fans are used by entertainers.

Japan imports coal and oil to fuel power plants, and also has nuclear power plants. Many of its rivers are harnessed to produce electricity at hydroelectric plants. The country has one of the world's best transportation services and one of the world's largest merchant fleets.

◆ DIGITAL CAMERAS

Japan produces many of the world's finest cameras, lenses, video cameras and recorders, and precision instruments.

◆ OYSTER BEDS

The Japanese cultivate oyster beds, which provide delicious seafood and precious pearls.

Almost 99 percent of the people of Japan are Japanese. The chief minorities are the Ainu—most of whom live on Hokkaido—Koreans, and Chinese. Some scholars think that the Ainu may have been the first people in Japan. Japanese is the official language, but it has many dialects. The Tokyo dialect is the standard form used on radio and television. Shinto and Buddhism are the chief religions, and many people follow elements from both of these faiths.

◑ TEA CEREMONY
Geisha women conduct traditional tea ceremonies. They learn from childhood how to entertain guests with conversation, music, and dance.

Baseball and sumo (a kind of wrestling) are leading sports, together with martial arts such as judo, karate, and kendo (a type of fencing). The Japanese also enjoy golf, skiing, tennis, and volleyball. Calligraphy (beautiful lettering, often painted with a soft brush), music, and dance are art forms in Japan.

◑ WEALTHY WOMAN
In the Tokugawa period, rich women had very elaborate hair styles held together with giant pins.

◐ JAPANESE SAMURAI
The samurai were professional knights or warriors in the Middle Ages.

Theater is popular. The ancient No plays are performed by actors in masks, while kabuki plays are melodramas, usually with spectacular sets. Since World War II, Japanese movies have become popular around the world. Many films tell stories about samurai (warriors) or the shoguns (generals who ruled in the name of the emperors). Other art forms include architecture, especially Buddhist temples, literature (including poems called haiku), painting, and sculpture.

◑ KOI CARP
Beautiful koi carp are bred to decorate the tranquil ponds in Japanese ornamental gardens.

◐ TEMPLE OF THE GOLDEN PAVILION, KYOTO
Kyoto was the capital of Japan from 794 to 1868. It has many beautiful old buildings, including this magnificent temple, which was rebuilt in 1955 after a devastating fire.

Japan's modern history began when Portuguese sailors reached the islands in 1543. However, the Japanese feared that the introduction of Christianity by missionaries would lead to domination by European powers. During the 1630s, Japan cut itself off from the world and by 1640 Christianity had almost disappeared from Japan.

In 1853, the United States forced the Tokugawa shogunate to open ports to US trade. After the restoration of the emperor's powers in 1867, Japan began to modernize its economy and set up many industries. This gave Japan increasing military power, leading to wars with China and Russia.

Japan supported the Allies in World War I (1914–18). In 1931 it occupied Manchuria. From 1937, it conquered much of China, and during World War II (1939–45), it conquered Southeast Asia and the western Pacific. Japan was finally defeated in 1945. From the 1950s, it rebuilt its industries with great determination and has become one of the world's leading economic powers.

◯ LANTERN MONUMENT
In 1945, the United States dropped atomic bombs on Hiroshima and Nagasaki. The terrible destruction led to Japan's surrender.

◯ ARMORED CAR
Japan began a war with China in 1937. This war became part of World War II (1939–45).

◯ SUMO WRESTLERS
A form of wrestling called sumo is the leading spectator sport in Japan.

◯ WIND-BLOWN WAVES AT SHICHI-RI BY HIROSHIGE
Hiroshige (1797–1858) was one of the greatest Japanese artists of the 19th century.

◯ KABUKI
In traditional Japanese kabuki plays, actors use exaggerated gestures and wear elaborate costumes.

TIMELINE

BC

660	According to legend, Jimmu Tenno becomes Japan's first emperor

AD

300	Yamato kingdom unifies Japan
c.600	Prince Shotoku makes Buddhism state religion and sets up constitution
710	Nara becomes Japanese capital
785	Heian (modern-day Kyoto) becomes capital (until 1868)
1192	First shogun (general) appointed
1274	Mongol invasion thwarted by typhoon (known as kamikaze, "divine wind")
1600	Tokugawa Period of national seclusion, called sakoku (until 1867)
1854	US Commander Matthew C. Perry opens two Japanese ports to US trade
1867	Shogun rule ends
1904	Russo–Japanese War (until 1905): Japan defeats Russia
1914	World War I (until 1918): Japan sides with the Allies
1937	Japan begins a war against China
1939	World War II (until 1945): Japan sides with Germany; US drops atomic bombs on Hiroshima and Nagasaki
1947	Japan adopts democratic constitution
1989	Emperor Hirohito dies; his son Akihito becomes emperor

SOUTHEAST ASIA

⟲ RETICULATED PYTHON
The reticulated python of Southeast Asia may grow to 30 feet in length.

Southeast Asia consists of a large peninsula attached to India and China, together with thousands of islands to the east and south of the peninsula. Like Eastern Asia, Southeast Asia contains several fast-developing countries, notably Singapore, Thailand, and Malaysia.

The peninsula has fertile plains, where most of the people live, and some rugged mountains. The area is drained by several major rivers. The longest is the Mekong, which rises in Tibet and flows through Laos, Thailand, and Cambodia before reaching its large delta in Vietnam. Myanmar (named Burma until 1989), has the Ayeyarwady (formerly Irrawaddy) River. Its delta is one of the world's great rice-growing areas.

Malaysia lies partly on the peninsula and partly on the island of Borneo. The small state of Singapore consists of about 50 islands; the Philippines has about 7,100 islands; and Indonesia about 13,600. The Philippines and Indonesia are largely mountainous. Both countries are liable to earthquakes, and many of the highest peaks are active volcanoes. Some of the biggest volcanic eruptions in modern times have occurred in this region. They include Tambora (1815), Krakatoa (1883), and Mount Merapi (1931), all in Indonesia, and Mount Pinatubo in the Philippines (1991).

Southeast Asia has high temperatures throughout the year and abundant rainfall. But while much of the peninsula has a wet and dry monsoon climate, the southern islands are rainy throughout the year. The wettest areas have evergreen rainforests rich in plant and animal species. Mangrove swamps thrive along many coasts.

⟲ FOREST APE
Orangutans are apes found in Borneo and Sumatra. Rainforest destruction has made them rare.

⟲ YANGON, MYANMAR
Pagodas are towers belonging to Buddhist temples. The shape is based on the Indian stupa, which covered the remains of a king or holy man.

BRUNEI
Negara Brunei Darussalam –
State of Brunei Darussalam
AREA: 2,226 sq mi.
POPULATION: 344,000
CAPITAL: Bandar Seri Begawan
OTHER CITIES: Seria, Kuala Belait
HIGHEST POINT: Bukit Betalong (2,995 ft)
OFFICIAL LANGUAGE: Malay, English
CURRENCY: Brunei dollar

CAMBODIA
Preah Reach Ana Pak Kampuchea –
Kingdom of Cambodia
AREA: 69,898 sq mi.
POPULATION: 12.7 million
CAPITAL: Phnom Penh
OTHER CITIES: Kompong Cham, Battambang
HIGHEST POINT: Phnum Aôral (5,948 ft)
OFFICIAL LANGUAGE: Khmer
CURRENCY: Riel

INDONESIA
Republik Indonesia –
Republic of Indonesia
AREA: 735,354 sq mi.
POPULATION: 212 million
CAPITAL: Jakarta
OTHER CITIES: Bandung, Surabaya, Medan
HIGHEST POINT: Puncak Jaya (16,503 ft)
OFFICIAL LANGUAGE: Bahasa Indonesian
CURRENCY: Indonesian rupiah

LAOS
Saathiaranarath Prachhathipatay Prachhachhon Lao – Lao People's Democratic Republic
AREA: 91,429 sq mi.
POPULATION: 5.6 million
CAPITAL: Vientiane
OTHER CITIES: Savannakhet, Luang Prabang
HIGHEST POINT: Mount Bia (9,242 ft)
OFFICIAL LANGUAGE: Lao
CURRENCY: Kip

↻ CRATER LAKE
The craters of some of Indonesia's many volcanoes are filled with brightly colored mineral-rich water.

↺ MOSQUE, BRUNEI
Two-thirds of the people of Brunei are Muslim. Islam is also the chief religion of Indonesia.

MYANMAR

LAOS

CAMBODIA

MALAYSIA

VIETNAM

PHILIPPINES

INDONESIA

THAILAND

↻ MOUNTAINOUS VIETNAM
Scenic mountains rise along Vietnam's borders with China, Laos, and Cambodia. But most people live on the lowlands.

SINGAPORE

BRUNEI

EAST TIMOR

↻ PENANG, MALAYSIA
Penang Island lies off the northwest coast of Malaysia. During the 1800s its chief port, George Town, was an important shipping center. Today the island is a popular tourist resort.

↻ KOMODO DRAGON
The 10-foot-long Komodo dragon is the largest living lizard.

189

A S I A

☼ RUBY PANNING
The world's finest rubies are found in river gravels in Myanmar. Thailand also produces beautiful rubies.

☼ COCONUT HARVEST
In Thailand, monkeys are trained to collect coconuts, the fruit of the coconut palm.

☼ PALACE STATUE
Many statues stand in the Royal Palace in Bangkok, Thailand. The statues reveal the natural grace of the Thai people.

☼ TOURISM
Tourism is a major industry employing many people in Thailand. Bali (in Indonesia), Malaysia, and the Philippines also attract many tourists.

There are ten countries in the Southeast Asia region. Cambodia, Malaysia, and Thailand are monarchies, with elected parliaments. Brunei is also a monarchy, ruled by a sultan. Because of the country's large oil exports, the sultan has become one of the world's richest men.

Most of the countries of Southeast Asia are republics, though not all are truly democratic. Vietnam had a Communist government after its reunification in 1975, but later moved toward a more free-market economy. The Philippines and Singapore are multi-party republics with flourishing export-based economies. Myanmar has a military government.

The largest nation in the region is Indonesia, the world's most populous Muslim country. Its ethnic and religious minorities, such as the Aceh (in Sumatra), Christians in Maluku, and the people of East Timor have faced repression and there have been outbreaks of rebellion and violence. East Timor, occupied by Indonesia after Portuguese colonial rule ended in 1975, gained independence in 2002. By then Indonesia had abandoned its authoritarian president Suharto (in power 1967–88). In such a diverse nation, with some 200 ethnic groups, achieving national unity is difficult.

About half of the people in Southeast Asia are farmers or farm workers, many of them poor. The chief crop is rice. Indonesia, Myanmar, the Philippines, Thailand, and Vietnam rank among the world's top ten rice producers.

☼ BASKETS OF FRUIT
Many tropical fruits grow on the hot island of Bali, a tourist island in Indonesia.

MALAYSIA
Persekutuan Tanah Malaysia –
Federation of Malaysia
AREA: 127,584 sq mi.
POPULATION: 22.6 million
CAPITAL: Kuala Lumpur
OTHER CITIES: Ipoh, Johor
Baharu
HIGHEST POINT: Mount
Kinabalu (13,452 ft)
OFFICIAL LANGUAGE: Malay
CURRENCY: Ringgit

**MYANMAR
(BURMA)**
Myanmar Naingngandaw –
Union of Myanmar
AREA: 261,228 sq mi.
POPULATION: 42 million
CAPITAL: Yangon (Rangoon)
OTHER CITIES: Mandalay,
Mawlamyine (Moulmein)
HIGHEST POINT: Hkakabo
Razi (19,296 ft)
OFFICIAL LANGUAGE: Burmese
CURRENCY: Kyat

PHILIPPINES
Republika ng Pilipinas –
Republic of the Philippines
AREA: 115,800 sq mi.
POPULATION: 78.6 million
CAPITAL: Manila
OTHER CITIES: Quezon City,
Cebu, Davao
HIGHEST POINT: Mount Apo
(9692 ft)
OFFICIAL LANGUAGE: Pilipino,
English
CURRENCY: Philippine peso

◯ ROYAL PALACE, BANGKOK
Thailand is an ancient monarchy. Unlike the other countries of Southeast Asia, it was never colonized by a European country.

◯ OYSTER AND PEARL
The waters off the strangely shaped island of Sulawesi, Indonesia, are the source of oysters that yield top-quality pearls.

◯ FLOATING MARKETS
Canals criss-cross Bangkok, Thailand. In places, boats loaded with produce form floating markets.

Other major products include coffee, tropical fruits such as pineapples, corn, rubber, tea, and timber. Brunei, Indonesia, Malaysia, and Vietnam produce oil and natural gas. Other resources include coal in Indonesia and Vietnam, precious stones in Myanmar, and tin in Indonesia, Malaysia, Thailand, and Vietnam.

Nearly a third of the people live in cities or towns. The largest cities are Jakarta in Indonesia, Manila in the Philippines, Bangkok in Thailand, Ho Chi Minh City and Hanoi in Vietnam, and Singapore City. Singapore is a small country, but it is the region's richest. Its highly skilled workers have made it a major center of manufacturing, producing chemicals, electronic products, scientific instruments, ships, and textiles. Indonesia, Malaysia, and Thailand have also developed industries. In contrast, neighboring Vietnam, Cambodia, and Laos are poor countries, whose economies have been badly damaged by wars.

◯ WATER BUFFALO
Farmers use water buffalo to pull plows in paddy fields. The animals like to wallow in mud and water.

◯ SINGAPORE BY NIGHT
Singapore City is a bustling center of industry, finance, and trade.

◯ TERRACED RICE FIELDS,
Terraced fields, used mainly for growing rice, have been cut like giant steps into the steep hillsides in the Philippines.

ASIA

◯ BALINESE PROCESSION
Processions are held on the mainly Hindu island of Bali.

◯ BUDDHIST MONKS, MYANMAR
About nine-out-of-ten people in Myanmar are Buddhist. Buddhism is also the chief religion in Cambodia, Laos, and Thailand.

◯ THAI CHILDREN
Primary education is free in Thailand, and 94 percent of the people over 15 years old can read and write.

Southeast Asia has about 490 million people. Most are of Chinese, Indian, or Malay descent. Many languages are spoken, especially in Indonesia, which has about 250 languages of its own.

Buddhism is the chief religion of much of the mainland peninsula of Southeast Asia. But Islam is important in Malaysia and Brunei. About 87 percent of Indonesians are Muslim, although Indonesia also has Christian and Hindu minorities. In the Philippines, about 90 percent of the people are Christian. The Philippines is the only large country in Asia with a Christian majority. The Communist governments in Laos and Vietnam have discouraged any kind of religious worship.

Ancient and modern architecture is one of the region's finest art forms. Visitors may admire the beautiful Buddhist and Hindu temples and the Muslim mosques. Music and dance are popular, especially at festivals, such as harvest celebrations and village fairs. In Indonesia, gamelan bands play drums, flutes, metal gongs, stringed, and xylophonelike instruments.

◯ TRIBAL WARRIOR
The peoples living in remote areas in the Philippines include the pygmy Negritos, descendants of people who settled there 30,000 years ago.

FACTS

SINGAPORE
Hsin-chia-p'o Kung-ho-kuo (Mandarin Chinese), Republik Singapura (Malay), Singapore Kudiyarasu (Tamil) - Republic of Singapore
AREA: 239 sq mi.
POPULATION: 3.3 million
CAPITAL: Singapore
OTHER CITIES: none
HIGHEST POINT: Timah Hill (581 ft)
OFFICIAL LANGUAGES: Chinese, Malay, Tamil, English
CURRENCY: Singapore dollar

THAILAND
Pathet Thai – Kingdom of Thailand
AREA: 299,156 sq mi.
POPULATION: 61.2 million
CAPITAL: Bangkok
OTHER CITIES: Nakhon Ratchasima, Songkhla
HIGHEST POINT: Inthanon Mountain (8,514 ft)
OFFICIAL LANGUAGE: Thai
CURRENCY: Baht

VIETNAM
Công Hòa Xã Hôi Chu Nghia Viêt Nam – Socialist Republic of Vietnam
AREA: 128,065 sq mi.
POPULATION: 80 million
CAPITAL: Hanoi
OTHER CITIES: Ho Chi Minh City, Haiphong
HIGHEST POINT: Fan Si Pan (10,311 ft)
OFFICIAL LANGUAGE: Vietnamese
CURRENCY: Dong

○ STATUE OF BUDDHA, VIETNAM

The government in Vietnam has discouraged religious worship, but many people follow Buddhist teachings.

Puppet dramas are popular in Indonesia and Malaysia. The person who operates the puppets tells the story and speaks the parts of the characters. The Philippines and Vietnam also have long literary traditions.

Leading sports include soccer, badminton, and basketball.

Traditional ox-races and bullfights are held at festivals in Indonesia. In Thailand, a version of boxing allows the boxers to use both their hands and their feet to strike their opponents.

Many people in the cities wear Western clothes. Traditional garments such as sarongs are also worn. Sarongs are long pieces of cloth that men and women wrap around their bodies. Muslim men usually wear hats, and women also cover their heads, but seldom wear veils.

Rice is the main food in Southeast Asia. It is eaten with meat, fish, and vegetables. One popular dish in Malaysia is satay. It consists of pieces of meat cooked on a skewer and dipped in a hot sauce. Adobo in the Philippines is a dish of chicken and pork cooked in soya sauce and vinegar.

○ DAYAK WOMAN

Small tribal groups live in isolated parts of Southeast Asia. They include the Dayaks of Borneo.

○ HOOKED ON PAIN

Devotees undergo pain to prove their strong religious faith at the Taipsu festival, George Town, Malaysia.

○ DANCERS IN BALI

In Bali, dance is used as a way of telling Hindu stories. The dancers use graceful movements—particularly of the hands and feet—which take years of training.

⊙ LONGHOUSE

Dayak family groups in Borneo live in longhouses. Up to a hundred people may live together in one house.

○ JAVANESE SHADOW PUPPET

Puppeteers in Java, Indonesia, enact a story by casting shadows of puppets onto a screen.

193

From about 3000 BC, people from Central Asia and southern China began to settle in Southeast Asia. The original, darker-skinned peoples were forced to live in remote areas. From about AD 100, a series of great kingdoms developed in the region, including the Funan kingdom in Cambodia. From the AD 600s, the Srivajaya kingdom arose in Sumatra and became a major sea power. But perhaps the best-known kingdom belonged to the Angkor civilization, which flourished in Cambodia between the 800s and the 1400s. It was named for its capital, the ruins of which, with its superb temples, still stand today.

◑ RAMA IV
King Mongut (Rama IV) ruled Thailand from 1851 to 1868. He allowed many Western ideas to be introduced.

◐ BRITISH BURMA
Britain gradually conquered Burma (now Myanmar) through wars in 1824–26, 1852, and 1885. Burma finally became a province of British India.

In the 19th century, Britain gradually took over Singapore, Malaysia, and Burma (now Myanmar), while France took over Indochina (now Cambodia, Laos, and Vietnam). By the early 20th century, only Thailand remained free of foreign rule. But European power in the region collapsed when Japan conquered Southeast Asia during World War II (1939–45). Following the defeat of Japan in 1945, the countries of Southeast Asia gradually won their independence from the European colonizers.

Communism attracted many people in the region and Communist guerrillas fought for independence in Indochina and elsewhere.

European influence in Southeast Asia increased after a Spanish expedition reached the Philippines in 1521. Spain gradually took control of the islands. About 100 years later, the Dutch began to take control of Indonesia, where Islam was becoming the main religion.

◑ RELIC FROM ANGKOR
Angkor was the ancient capital of a civilization that flourished in Cambodia between the 9th and 15th centuries. This guardian figure was found there.

◐ KHMER WARRIORS
In the 12th century, the Khmer rulers of Angkor conquered areas that are now in Laos, Thailand, and Vietnam.

C POL POT
*Communist leader Pol Pot
(c.1925–98) seized control
of Cambodia in the 1970s.
His forces killed thousands
of Cambodians.*

In 1954, France withdrew from Indochina, which was
divided into Cambodia, Laos, North Vietnam, and
South Vietnam. Communist North Vietnam aided
Communists in other parts of Indochina and, in the
early 1960s, the United States sent troops to stop
South Vietnam falling to the Communists. The war
ended in 1975, when Vietnam became one nation.

Although disturbed by civil war in Cambodia and
military rule in Myanmar, several countries by 2000
had made great strides in developing their
economies. The Association of Southeast Asian
Nations (ASEAN) was set up in 1967 to help its
members trade together. By 2003, all the countries of
Southeast Asia were members of ASEAN.

O RAFFLES HOTEL
*Sir Stamford Raffles
(1781–1826), the founder of
Singapore City, played an
important part in establishing
British footholds in Southeast
Asia. His name is remembered
in the Raffles Hotel.*

C ANGKOR WAT
*The temple of Angkor Wat
was the finest building in the
ancient capital of Angkor.
The city ruins were
rediscovered in 1860.*

TIMELINE

AD

800s	Powerful Hindu-Buddhist kingdom rules Cambodia with Angkor as its capital (until 1400s)
1431	Forces from the Thai Ayutthaya kingdom conquer Angkor
1525	Spain claims the Philippines (until 1898)
1898	Spain gives the Philippines to the United States
1620s	Dutch begin to control Indonesia
1800s	Britain and France take over most of the Southeast Asian peninsula
1941	Japan conquers Southeast Asia (until 1945)
1946	Laos independent from France; Philippines declared a republic
1953	Cambodia independent from France
1957	The Vietnam War (until 1975)
1963	Malaysia is formed
1965	Singapore breaks away from Malaysia
1984	Sultanate of Brunei fully independent
1986	Revolution in the Philippines
1998	Fall of Suharto regime in Indonesia
2002	East Timor, former province of Indonesia, becomes an independent nation

C IMELDA'S SHOES
*President Marcos (1917–89) fell
from power in the Philippines in
1986. He was accused of corruption.
His wife, Imelda, was criticized for
her extravagance, after the people
discovered her vast collection of
clothes and shoes.*

C HO CHI MINH
*Communist leader
Ho Chi Minh
(1890–1969) led
North Vietnam
during the
Vietnamese War
(1957–75).*

195

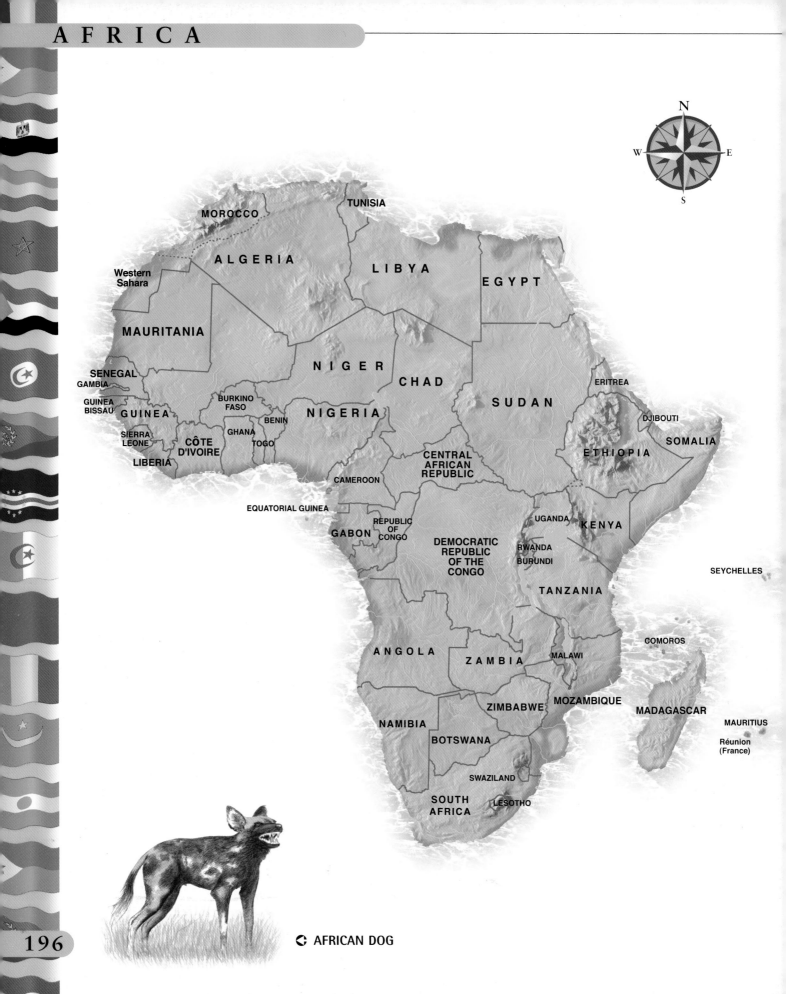

MOROCCO

TUNISIA

ALGERIA

LIBYA

EGYPT

Western
Sahara

MAURITANIA

N I G E R

CHAD

SUDAN

ERITREA

SENEGAL

GAMBIA

BURKINO
FASO

NIGERIA

DJIBOUTI

GUINEA
BISSAU

GUINEA

BENIN

SOMALIA

SIERRA
LEONE

GHANA

CÔTE
D'IVOIRE

TOGO

ETHIOPIA

LIBERIA

CENTRAL
AFRICAN
REPUBLIC

CAMEROON

EQUATORIAL GUINEA

UGANDA

KENYA

GABON

REPUBLIC
OF
CONGO

DEMOCRATIC
REPUBLIC
OF THE
CONGO

RWANDA

BURUNDI

SEYCHELLES

TANZANIA

ANGOLA

ZAMBIA

MALAWI

COMOROS

ZIMBABWE

MOZAMBIQUE

MADAGASCAR

NAMIBIA

MAURITIUS

BOTSWANA

Réunion
(France)

SWAZILAND

SOUTH
AFRICA

LESOTHO

N

W   E

S

○ AFRICAN DOG

AFRICA

⬥ Sand dune,
NAMIBIA

⬥ Niger valley,
MALI

⬥ Painted house,
GHANA

⬥ Elephant,
TANZANIA

A frica is the world's second-largest continent after Asia, covering about 20 percent of the world's land area. Most of Africa is a plateau, surrounded by narrow coastal plains. The highest peak is Kilimanjaro, a dormant (sleeping) volcano in northern Tanzania. Africa is drained by some major rivers, including the Nile, Congo, and Niger.

Northwest and southwest Africa have mild Mediterranean-type climates. Between these regions lie vast, hot deserts, tropical grassland called savanna, and dense rainforests around the Equator. The savanna is home to antelopes, elephants, lions, and zebras. Many other animals, such as gorillas and chimpanzees, are found in the rainforests. The number of animals in Africa has steadily decreased because of over-hunting and because their habitats have been cleared to create farms. Many governments have created national parks to protect their wildlife.

The continent has two main groups of people. North of the Sahara Desert, the Arab and Berber people speak Arabic and follow Islam. The black Africans to the south of the Sahara are divided into more than 1,000 ethnic groups. Some are Muslim and others are Christian, but many still follow ancient, local religions, in which spirit worship is important.

Africa contains many of the world's poorest countries. Many people are farmers, using simple farm tools. They produce little more than they need to feed their families and, when droughts occur, many starve. Agriculture employs nearly 60 percent of the people. Africa has valuable resources, such as oil and many metals, which are exported. But, apart from South Africa and Egypt, few countries have many manufacturing industries.

About 50 years ago, European countries ruled most of the continent. Today, most Africans run their own countries. But in some regions progress has been hampered by economic problems and instability.

NORTH AFRICA

⟡ FENNEC FOX

⟡ **OLD VOLCANOES**

The Ahaggar Mountains in southern Algeria contain jagged peaks formed from the necks of ancient, extinct (dead) volcanoes. These rock formations are called plugs.

North Africa, as shown on the map, makes up nearly half of Africa. It consists largely of a low plateau, between 500 and 1,970 feet above sea level. The highest peaks are in the Ethiopian Highlands in the southeast and the Atlas Mountains in the northwest. Smaller highlands made of jagged volcanic rocks rise above the plateau.

Northwestern Morocco, together with the plains along the Mediterranean Sea coast, have dry, hot summers and mild, rainy winters. The Sahara, the world's largest desert, covers more than three-fifths of North Africa. With an area of about 5.8 million square miles, it is nearly as big as the United States.

The world's highest air temperature in the shade, 136°F, was recorded in the Sahara. However, nights can be cold, and people wear thick cloaks to keep themselves warm. Several years may pass in the Sahara with hardly any rain. Then a sudden, freak storm may cause floods. But the desert contains green oases, where water from beneath the ground reaches the surface. The region with the most water is the Nile valley. South of the Sahara, the desert merges into a dry grassland region called the Sahel. South of the Sahel lie areas of savanna, with scattered trees. Some rainforests grow in the far southwest.

In the Mediterranean region, trees such as oaks and olives grow. Elsewhere, the the palm tree is common. The most important desert animal for humans is the camel, which can travel long distances without water. Other notable animals include the Barbary ape in the northeast and the gelada baboon in Ethiopia.

⟢ **DESERT, MOROCCO**

The Sahara in North Africa stretches from the Atlantic Ocean to the Red Sea.

ALGERIA
Jamhuriya al Jazairiya ad-Dimuqratiya ash-Shabiya – People's Democratic Republic of Algeria
AREA: 919,591 sq mi.
POPULATION: 30.8 million
CAPITAL: Algiers
OTHER CITIES: Oran, Constantine, Annaba
HIGHEST POINT: Mount Tahat (9,574 ft)
OFFICIAL LANGUAGE: Arabic
CURRENCY: Algerian dinar

CAPE VERDE
República de Cabo Verde – Republic of Cape Verde
AREA: 1,557 sq mi.
POPULATION: 446,000
CAPITAL: Praia
OTHER CITIES: Mindelo, São Filipe
HIGHEST POINT: Pico (9,281 ft)
OFFICIAL LANGUAGE: Portuguese
CURRENCY: Cape Verde escudo

CHAD
République du Tchad – Republic of Chad
AREA: 495,753 sq mi.
POPULATION: 8.7 million
CAPITAL: N'Djamena
OTHER CITIES: Moundou, Bongor
HIGHEST POINT: Emi Koussi (11,204 ft)
OFFICIAL LANGUAGES: Arabic, French
CURRENCY: CFA franc

DJIBOUTI
Jumhouriyya Djibouti – Republic of Djibouti
AREA: 8,957 sq mi.
POPULATION: 619,000
CAPITAL: Djibouti
OTHER CITIES: none
HIGHEST POINT: Mousaalli (6,768 ft)
OFFICIAL LANGUAGE: Arabic, French
CURRENCY: Djibouti franc

✪ LIVING BY THE NILE
The River Nile provides essential water for crop irrigation. Egypt's Nile valley is North Africa's most populated region.

EGYPT

ALGERIA

TUNISIA

LIBYA

ERITREA

✪ NIGER VALLEY, MALI
The Niger is the third-longest river in Africa. It brings water to dry areas south of the Sahara.

MOROCCO

DJIBOUTI

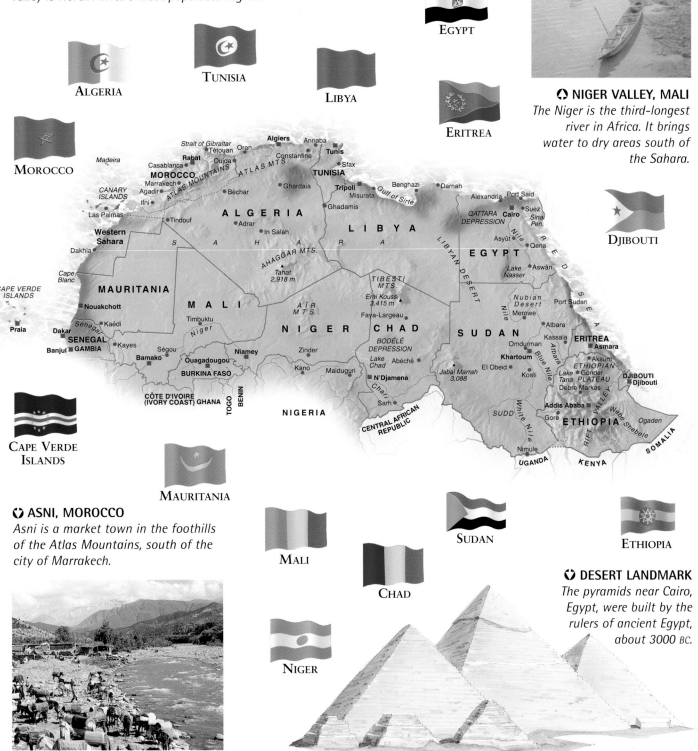

Map labels:

Strait of Gibraltar, Algiers, Annaba, Tétouan, Oran, Tunis, Constantine, Madeira, Rabat, Oujda, Sfax, Casablanca, MOROCCO, TUNISIA, Marrakech, Ghardaia, Benghazi, Darnah, Tripoli, Agadir, Béchar, Gulf of Sirte, Ifni, CANARY ISLANDS, ATLAS MOUNTAINS, ATLAS MTS., Misurata, Alexandria, Port Said, Ghadames, Suez, Las Palmas, Adrar, In Salah, QATTARA DEPRESSION, Cairo, Sinai Pen., Tindouf, ALGERIA, LIBYA, Asyût, Qena, Western Sahara, LIBYAN DESERT, EGYPT, Dakhla, S A H A R A, AHAGGAR MTS., Lake Nasser, Aswân, Cape Blanc, Tahat 2,918 m, TIBESTI MTS., Nubian Desert, Port Sudan, CAPE VERDE ISLANDS, MAURITANIA, MALI, AÏR MTS., Emi Koussi 3,415 m, Merowe, Nouakchott, Timbuktu, Faya-Largeau, SUDAN, Atbara, Kassala, ERITREA, Praia, Dakar, Sénégal, Kaédi, NIGER, CHAD, BODÉLÉ DEPRESSION, Omdurman, Asmara, SENEGAL, Kayes, Ségou, Niamey, Zinder, Lake Chad, Abéché, Khartoum, Aksum, Banjul, GAMBIA, Bamako, Kano, Maiduguri, N'Djamena, Jabal Marrah 3,088, El Obeid, Kosti, Lake Tana, Gonder, ETHIOPIAN PLATEAU, DJIBOUTI, Djibouti, Ouagadougou, BURKINA FASO, Char, Debre Markos, CÔTE D'IVOIRE (IVORY COAST), GHANA, TOGO, BENIN, NIGERIA, Sarh, CENTRAL AFRICAN REPUBLIC, White Nile, Blue Nile, Addis Ababa, Gore, SUDD, ETHIOPIA, Webe Shebele, Ogaden, SOMALIA, RIFT VALLEY, Nimule, UGANDA, KENYA, Niger, RED SEA

CAPE VERDE ISLANDS

MAURITANIA

✪ ASNI, MOROCCO
Asni is a market town in the foothills of the Atlas Mountains, south of the city of Marrakech.

MALI

CHAD

NIGER

SUDAN

ETHIOPIA

✪ DESERT LANDMARK
The pyramids near Cairo, Egypt, were built by the rulers of ancient Egypt, about 3000 BC.

○ PEANUTS

Peanuts are also called groundnuts. Sudan is a leading producer.

There are 14 independent countries in North Africa. Twelve are republics, while Morocco is ruled by a king. The government of Eritrea, which was part of Ethiopia from 1952 to 1993, is transitional—that is, its constitution has not been finalized.

The region also includes the disputed territory of Western Sahara, which was ruled by Spain until 1976. When Spain withdrew, Morocco occupied the northern two-thirds, while Mauritania took the rest. The local Saharan people demanded independence and attacked the Moroccans and Mauritanians. Mauritania withdrew from Western Sahara in 1979, leaving Morocco in charge. Fighting continued, with the rebels claiming that their territory was an independent republic. The United Nations is trying to keep the peace and solve the dispute.

Ethnic and religious differences have caused problems in North Africa, too. In Sudan, for example, Muslim government forces have fought civil wars with the people in the south, many of whom either practice traditional religions or are Christian.

○ TANNERIES, FEZ

Fez is an ancient royal capital city in Morocco. Its tanneries prepare leather, which is made into a wide range of products.

○ EMPERORS' CROWNS

Axum, a historic city in northern Ethiopia, was a royal capital from 500 BC. It has many ancient treasures.

○ MOROCCAN CARPETS

Highly decorated carpets are among the products made by skilled Arab and Berber craftspeople in North Africa.

○ DECORATED CAMEL

Tourists enjoy camel rides in North Africa. The camels here have one hump. They kneel to let riders climb on and off them.

FACTS

EGYPT
Jamhuriyat Misr al-Arabiya –
Arab Republic of Egypt
AREA: 386,660 sq mi.
POPULATION: 65.2 million
CAPITAL: Cairo
OTHER CITIES: Alexandria,
El Giza
HIGHEST POINT: Jabal
Katrinah (8,652 ft)
OFFICIAL LANGUAGE: Arabic
CURRENCY: Egyptian pound

ERITREA
State of Eritrea
AREA: 45,405 sq mi.
POPULATION: 4.3 million
Capital: Asmara
Other cities: Asseb, Keren
HIGHEST POINT: Mount Soira
(10,180 ft)
OFFICIAL LANGUAGE: None
CURRENCY: Nakfa

ETHIOPIA
Federal Democratic Republic of
Ethiopia
AREA: 426,370 sq mi.
POPULATION: 66 million
CAPITAL: Addis Ababa
OTHER CITIES: Dire Dawa,
Harar
HIGHEST POINT: Ras Dashen
(13,976 ft)
OFFICIAL LANGUAGE: None
CURRENCY: Birr

LIBYA
Jamahiriya Al-Arabiya Al-Libiya
Al Shabiya Al-Ishtirakiya Al-
Uzma – Great Socialist People's
Libyan Arab Republic
AREA: 679,370 sq mi.
POPULATION: 5.2 million
CAPITAL: Tripoli
OTHER CITIES: Benghazi,
Misurata
HIGHEST POINT: Bette Peak
(7,500 ft)
OFFICIAL LANGUAGE: Arabic
CURRENCY: Libyan dinar

◯ SUEZ CANAL
The Suez Canal, which opened in 1869, provides a valuable and significant short cut for shipping passing between the Indian Ocean and the Mediterranean Sea.

◯ ORANGES, TUNISIA
Oranges and other citrus fruits grow well in the sunny climate of North Africa.

Poverty is widespread in North Africa; the United Nations classifies most countries as poor, developing areas. The wealthier countries include Algeria and Libya, which both have reserves of oil and natural gas, and Morocco, where phosphate rock is mined and made into fertilizer. Niger, one of the poorest countries, is a major producer of uranium.

Overall, agriculture employs more than 50 percent of North Africans. Important crops include barley, citrus fruits, and olives in the Mediterranean countries; cotton and sugar cane in the Nile valley; and dates at desert oases. South of the Sahara, millet and sorghum are leading food crops, while coffee is Ethiopia's main export.

Manufacturing is unimportant in most North African countries. The chief industrial region is the Nile delta north of Cairo, the capital of Egypt. With more than ten million people, Cairo is the largest city in North Africa. About 37 percent of North Africans live in cities and towns. Other cities with populations of more than two million are Alexandria and El Giza, Egypt; Casablanca, Morocco; and Addis Ababa, Ethiopia.

◯ MARKET, ALGERIA
On market days, people buy and sell produce, meet friends, and catch up on local news.

◯ ASWAN HIGH DAM
The Aswan High Dam on the River Nile in Egypt produces hydroelectricity. The dam began operating in 1968. It holds back Lake Nasser.

◯ SNAKE CHARMER
Snake charmers and other entertainers perform at the Djemaa El Fna, a market in central Marrakech, Morocco.

FACTS

MALI
République du Mali – Republic of Mali
AREA: 478,839 sq mi.
POPULATION: 11 million
CAPITAL: Bamako
OTHER CITIES: Ségou, Mopti
HIGHEST POINT: Homboro Tondo (3,789 ft)
OFFICIAL LANGUAGE: French
CURRENCY: CFA franc

MAURITANIA
République Islamique Arabe et Africaine de Mauritanie – Islamic Republic of Mauritania
AREA: 395,954 sq mi.
POPULATION: 2.6 million
CAPITAL: Nouakchott
OTHER CITIES: Nouadhibou, Kaédi
HIGHEST POINT: Kediet Ijill (3,002 ft)
OFFICIAL LANGUAGE: Arabic
CURRENCY: Ouguiya

MOROCCO
Mamlaka al Maghrebia – Kingdom of Morocco
AREA: 172,394 sq mi.
POPULATION: 29 million
CAPITAL: Rabat
OTHER CITIES: Casablanca, Marrakech
HIGHEST POINT: Jebel Toubkal (13,665 ft)
OFFICIAL LANGUAGE: Arabic
CURRENCY: Moroccan dirham

NIGER
République du Niger – Republic of Niger
AREA: 489,189 sq mi.
POPULATION: 10.3 million
CAPITAL: Niamey
OTHER CITIES: Zinder, Maradi
HIGHEST POINT: Mount Gréboun (6,378 ft)
OFFICIAL LANGUAGE: French
CURRENCY: CFA franc

◐ MARKET DAY

A woman carries her baby through the market in Bamako, capital of Mali. Bamako is a major economic center on the Niger River.

◐ OBELISK, AXUM

Obelisks up to 100-feet tall still stand in Axum, Ethiopia. The kingdom of Axum lasted from the 2nd century AD to about 1000 AD.

Most people in Africa north of the Sahara speak Arabic and are Muslim. The countries share a common culture, with similar kinds of buildings, literature, and other art forms. Some Muslims dislike Western ideas and support groups who call for the return of fundamentalist Islamic laws and practices. In Algeria, the conflict between the government and Muslim fundamentalists led to fighting in the 1990s.

◐ SULTAN'S MOSQUE, CAIRO

Rising above the huge city of Cairo— the largest city in Africa—are the tall minarets (prayer towers) of the Sultan's mosque.

Many languages are spoken in the countries south of the Sahara, and the customs of the people vary from group to group. For example, more than 70 languages and 200 dialects are spoken in Ethiopia, which has no single official language. Several other countries use a European language for official purposes. Soccer is the leading sport throughout the region.

A food dish called ful, or fool, which consists of broad beans cooked in oil, is a favorite in Egypt and Sudan.

◐ MUAMMAR GADDAFI

Colonel Gaddafi (b.1942) became Libya's leader in 1969. He encouraged a return to the fundamental principles of Islam.

SUDAN
Jamhuryat es-Sudan – Republic of Sudan
AREA: 967,495 sq mi.
POPULATION: 36 million
CAPITAL: Khartoum
OTHER CITIES: Omdurman, Khartoum North, Port Sudan
HIGHEST POINT: Mount Kinyeti (10,456 ft)
OFFICIAL LANGUAGE: Arabic
CURRENCY: Sudanese dinar

TUNISIA
Jumhuriya at Tunisiya – Republic of Tunisia
AREA: 63,169 sq mi.
POPULATION: 9.8 million
CAPITAL: Tunis
OTHER CITIES: Sfax, Aryanah
HIGHEST POINT: Mount Chambi (5,066 ft)
OFFICIAL LANGUAGE: Arabic
CURRENCY: Tunisian dinar

WESTERN SAHARA
Western Sahara (disputed territory largely occupied by Morocco) – local nationalists have named it the Saharan Arab Democratic Republic
AREA: 102,702 sq mi.
POPULATION: 228,000
CAPITAL: El-Aaiún
OTHER CITIES: Dakhla
HIGHEST POINT: 2,700 ft
OFFICIAL LANGUAGE: Arabic
CURRENCY: Moroccan dirham

◐ HANNIBAL

In 218 BC, the great general, Hannibal—born in Carthage, Tunisia—led a surprise attack on the Romans using war elephants.

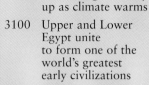

BEDOUIN CAMP
Arab herders called Bedouin roam North Africa's deserts in search of pasture for their flocks.

SAND OVEN, TIMBUKTU
Timbuktu, Mali, was once a great trading city. Many ancient traditions still survive there.

SPHINX, LUXOR
Statues of imaginary creatures called sphinxes lined avenues to temples in ancient Egyptian cities, including Karnak at Luxor.

Couscous (steamed wheat) served with fish, meat, and vegetables is popular in northwest Africa. Ethiopians enjoy wat, a spicy stew eaten with injera, a flat bread.

About 5000 BC, North Africa was wetter than it is today and the Sahara was a grassland. By 4000 BC the climate had become drier and people moved into areas with water, notably the fertile Nile valley. Here, from about 3100 BC, ancient Egypt developed into a major civilization. Other early cultures developed to the south in Sudan and Ethiopia, which became a Christian empire in the 4th century AD.

In the Middle Ages, Arab and Berber traders regularly crossed the desert in camel caravans. These traders recorded several major medieval empires ruled by Africans. They included ancient Ghana and Mali, which were based in the upper Niger River region, in what is now just Mali.

By the early 20th century, most of the North African countries, apart from Ethiopia, were under European rule. They won independence in the 1950s and 1960s. Political and economic problems have slowed development.

TUAREG
The Tuareg are a nomadic people. The men wear clothes of a distinctive blue color.

WASHING DAY, EGYPT
Egyptians in the Nile valley still use the river as they did in ancient times.

TIMELINE

BC

5000	Sahara is a grassland
4000	Sahara begins to dry up as climate warms
3100	Upper and Lower Egypt unite to form one of the world's greatest early civilizations
1400	Ancient Egypt reaches its peak
264–146	The Punic Wars between Rome and Carthage
30	Egypt and the Mediterranean coasts of North Africa come under Roman rule

AD

639	Arabs from Arabia introduce Arabic and Islam into North Africa (by 710)
1000	Large kingdoms arise in southwestern North Africa
1800s	Europeans begin to claim parts of North Africa
1882	British troops occupy Egypt
1922	Egypt becomes a partly independent monarchy
1950s	Independence won by Libya (1951), Sudan (1952), Morocco and Tunisia (1956)
1960	Chad, Mali, Mauritania, and Niger become independent from France
1962	Algeria becomes independent
1978	Egypt reaches a peace agreement with Israel, after 30 years of hostility
1991	Algeria cancels elections won by a Muslim party; civil war until 2000
1993	Eritrea breaks away from Ethiopia after a long war

203

WEST AFRICA

○ PARROT
Parrots live in West African forests.

W est Africa covers about 12 percent of Africa. It extends from Senegal and Gambia in the west to Cameroon in the east. The largest country, Nigeria, covers about a fourth of West Africa and is home to more than half of the people of West Africa. With a population of more than 126 million, Nigeria has more people than any other African country.

The landscape consists of coastal plains and a large inland plateau. The highest peak is Mount Cameroon, an active volcano. Moist winds blow from the sea up the slopes of Mount Cameroon, bringing heavy rain. With an average of 395 inches a year, the slopes of this mountain are one of the wettest places in the world.

West Africa has high temperatures throughout the year, and the southern coasts have rain all year round. Dense rainforests once covered the region, but much of the original forest has been cut down to make way for farmland. The northern part of West Africa has heavy summer rains, but winters are dry. Here, the forest merges into savanna with scattered trees, although leafy forests line the rivers.

The chief river is the Niger, which rises not far from the Atlantic Ocean, follows a huge arc through Mali and Niger, and then finally empties into the Gulf of Guinea in Nigeria. Part of Lake Chad lies in northeastern Nigeria, but the largest inland body of water entirely in West Africa is Lake Volta in Ghana. It is a reservoir, formed behind a huge dam.

BENIN
République du Bénin
AREA: 5,632,000 sq mi.
POPULATION: 6.6 million
CAPITAL: Porto-Novo
OTHER CITIES: Cotonou, Djougou, Abomey-Calavi
HIGHEST POINT: Atacora Mountains (about 2,000 ft)
OFFICIAL LANGUAGE: French
CURRENCY: CFA franc

BURKINA FASO
République Démocratique du Burkina Faso – Democratic Republic of Burkina Faso
AREA: 105,795 sq mi.
POPULATION: 12.3 million
CAPITAL: Ouagadougou
OTHER CITIES: Bobo-Dioulasso, Koudougou
HIGHEST POINT: Aiguille de Sindou (2,352 ft)
OFFICIAL LANGUAGE: French
CURRENCY: CFA franc

CAMEROON
République du Cameroun – Republic of Cameroon
AREA: 295,434 sq mi.
POPULATION: 15.8 million
CAPITAL: Yaoundé
OTHER CITIES: Douala, Bafoussam, Garoua
HIGHEST POINT: Mount Cameroon (13,353 ft)
OFFICIAL LANGUAGES: French, English
CURRENCY: CFA franc

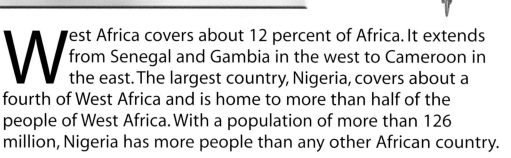

✪ STILT HOUSES
Heavy rains in West Africa often cause rivers to overflow, so many houses are built on stilts to keep them above the flood water.

◑ MERCHANT, BURKINA FASO

Farming employs 90 percent of the people of Burkina Faso. About 70 percent of the people cannot read or write.

◑ BEAUTIFUL BEACHES

West Africa has fine beaches and beautiful scenery. The Gambia has the most developed tourist industry in West Africa.

GUINEA

◑ WIDE-EYED

Bushbabies are active at night. They dart through the forest trees.

SENEGAL

GAMBIA

CÔTE D'IVOIRE

BURKINA FASO

◑ WATERFALL, NIGERIA

Waterfalls and rapids are common features on the Niger River in Nigeria—long stretches of the river are unnavigable.

NIGERIA

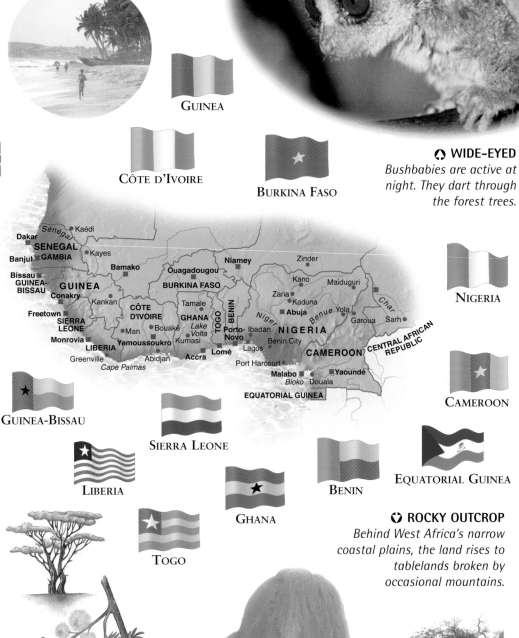

Sénégal · Kaédi
Dakar ■
■ SENEGAL · Kayes
Banjul ■ GAMBIA
Bissau ■
GUINEA-
BISSAU Bamako · · Ouagadougou Niamey · Zinder
Conakry GUINEA BURKINA FASO · Kano · Maiduguri
· Kankan · Zaria · Kaduna
Freetown CÔTE Tamale · Abuja Benue · Yola · Char
SIERRA D'IVOIRE GHANA Niger Garoua · Sarh
LEONE · Man · Bouaké Lake Porto- · Ibadan NIGERIA
Monrovia Volta Novo · Benin City
LIBERIA Yamoussoukro Kumasi Lagos CAMEROON CENTRAL AFRICAN
Greenville Abidjan Accra Lomé Port Harcourt REPUBLIC
Cape Palmas Malabo · Yaoundé
Bioko Douala
EQUATORIAL GUINEA

GUINEA-BISSAU

CAMEROON

SIERRA LEONE

LIBERIA

GHANA

BENIN

EQUATORIAL GUINEA

TOGO

◑ ROCKY OUTCROP

Behind West Africa's narrow coastal plains, the land rises to tablelands broken by occasional mountains.

◑ ACACIA TREE

Acacias are typical of tropical Africa. Many grow on the drier savanna grasslands of West Africa.

◊ LAGOS, NIGERIA

Lagos, formerly Nigeria's capital, is the largest city in West Africa. When it became too gridlocked, a new capital was built at Abuja.

There are 14 countries in West Africa. Most of them are republics, although military groups have ruled several countries for long periods. The military leaders claimed that civilian governments were inefficient or corrupt, but they, too, were often accused of the same things.

Nigeria became independent from Britain in 1960. In 1966 a military group overthrew the civilian government. Since then there has been much conflict. In 1967, the Ibo people in the southeast tried to break away from Nigeria and establish a separate country named Biafra, causing a civil war that ended in 1970. Military leaders again took over in 1983. Elections held in 1993 were cancelled by the military leaders, and Nigeria was ruled by the army until elections in 1999 brought a return to democratic government.

◊ BANANA SELLER, GHANA

Bananas are grown throughout West Africa. But Ghana's most valuable crop and export is cocoa.

Military take-overs have occurred in most West African countries, and two—Equatorial Guinea and Central African Republic—suffered periods of brutal military dictatorship. Even countries that have enjoyed relatively stable government, like Cameroon and Senegal, have had spells of violence.

The World Bank classifies the 14 countries of West Africa as "low-income economies." Agriculture employs about 55 percent of the people, but many farmers are poor, producing little more than they need to provide for their families.

EQUATORIAL GUINEA
República de Guinea Ecuatorial – Republic of Equatorial Guinea
AREA: 10,830 sq mi.
POPULATION: 486,000
CAPITAL: Malabo
OTHER CITIES: Bata, Ela-Nguema
HIGHEST POINT: Pico de Basilé (9,869 ft)
OFFICIAL LANGUAGES: Spanish, French
CURRENCY: CFA franc

THE GAMBIA
Republic of The Gambia
AREA: 4,361 sq mi.
POPULATION: 1.4 million
CAPITAL: Banjul
OTHER CITIES: Serekunda, Brikama
HIGHEST POINT: about 240 ft
OFFICIAL LANGUAGE: English
CURRENCY: Dalasi

GHANA
Republic of Ghana
AREA: 92,098 sq mi.
POPULATION: 19.9 million
CAPITAL: Accra
OTHER CITIES: Kumasi, Tamale, Tema, Sekondi-Takoradi
HIGHEST POINT: Afadjato (2,904 ft)
OFFICIAL LANGUAGE: English
CURRENCY: Cedi

GUINEA
République de Guinée – Republic of Guinea
AREA: 94,925 sq mi.
POPULATION: 7.6 million
CAPITAL: Conakry
OTHER CITIES: Kankan, Nzérékoré
HIGHEST POINT: Mount Nimba (5,748 ft)
OFFICIAL LANGUAGE: French
CURRENCY: Guinean franc

◊ CHILLIES, NIGERIA

Chilli peppers are used to make food spicy hot.

◊ RUBBER, LIBERIA

Rubber trees are grown on plantations in Côte d'Ivoire, Liberia, and Nigeria. Workers tap the trees to collect a fluid called latex, which is made into rubber.

FACTS

GUINEA-BISSAU
República da Guiné-Bissau –
Republic of Guinea-Bissau
AREA: 13,948 sq mi.
POPULATION: 1.3 million
CAPITAL: Bissau
OTHER CITIES: Bafatá, Gabú
HIGHEST POINT: Pico de
Basilé (9,869 ft)
OFFICIAL LANGUAGE:
Portuguese
CURRENCY: CFA franc

CÔTE D'IVOIRE (IVORY COAST)
République de la Côte d'Ivoire –
Republic of the Ivory Coast
AREA: 124,503 sq mi.
POPULATION: 16.4 million
CAPITAL: Yamoussoukro
OTHER CITIES: Abidjan,
Bouaké, Daloa
HIGHEST POINT: Mount
Nimba (5,748 ft)
OFFICIAL LANGUAGE: French
CURRENCY: CFA franc

LIBERIA
Republic of Liberia
AREA: 43,000 sq mi.
POPULATION: 3.2 million
CAPITAL: Monrovia
OTHER CITIES: Harbel,
Gbarnga, Buchanan
HIGHEST POINT: Nimba
Mountains (4,527 ft)
OFFICIAL LANGUAGE: English
CURRENCY: Liberian dollar

NIGERIA
Federal Republic of Nigeria
AREA: 356,667 sq mi.
POPULATION: 126.6 million
CAPITAL: Abuja
OTHER CITIES: Lagos, Ibadan,
Kano, Ogbomosho
HIGHEST POINT: Dimlang
Peak (6,700 ft)
OFFICIAL LANGUAGE: English
CURRENCY: Naira

↻ TIMBER RAFTS
In West Africa, rainforest trees are cut down so that valuable tropical hardwoods such as ebony and teak can be exported.

In the hot, wet south, important crops include bananas, cassava, cocoa, coffee, palm oil and other palm products, rubber, and yams. To the north, crops such as groundnuts, corn, millet, and sorghum are important. Livestock is raised on the savanna.

Mineral resources in West Africa include oil in Nigeria and Cameroon, bauxite (aluminium ore) in Guinea and Ghana, gold in Ghana, and iron ore in Liberia. Manufacturing has grown, especially around Abidjan in Côte d'Ivoire, Dakar in Senegal, and in Nigeria, but elsewhere it is generally on a small scale.

◑ DIAMOND MINE, GHANA
Ghana produces diamonds, bauxite (used to make aluminium), gold, and manganese. But most Ghanaians are farmers.

◑ TOURISM, THE GAMBIA
Tourists in The Gambia are able to go on organized trips, called safaris, to see wildlife in the forests.

About 38 percent of the people live in cities and towns. The largest city is Lagos, former capital of Nigeria, with a population of about 13 million. Other cities include Abidjan, Côte d'Ivoire (2.5 million); Accra, Ghana (1.8 million); Dakar, Senegal (1.7 million); and Conakry, Guinea (1.5 million).

◑ SALT SACKS, THE GAMBIA
Salt is obtained from seawater that is trapped in ponds and left to evaporate in the open air.

◐ FISHING, NIGERIA
Fish is an important food. Fishermen operate in inland waters, coastal lagoons, and on the open sea.

NIGERIAN FAMILY
Nigerians wear traditional clothes made of brightly colored fabrics, or Western clothes more usually in towns.

YORUBA SCULPTURE FROM NIGERIA
Yoruba sculpture is among Africa's finest. Some sculpture was made to decorate courts. Other pieces were made for religious purposes.

With some 210 million people, West Africa is the most densely populated part of the continent. Many different ethnic groups make up the population—there are about 250 in Nigeria alone—each with its own language. Islam is the chief religion in Gambia, Guinea, Nigeria, Senegal, and Sierra Leone, and also in the northern parts of the other countries. Around a third of the people are Christian and nearly a fifth practice traditional religions.

Music and dance are popular pastimes in West Africa, and soccer is the leading sport. Storytelling is another important part of the culture, with folk tales being passed from one generation to the next.

LION COFFIN, GHANA
To honor the dead, some Ghanaians buy impressive carved and elaborately painted coffins, resembling lions, other animals, or even Cadillac cars.

Important foods are cassava, corn, millet, plantains (a kind of banana), and yams, often eaten with spicy sauces.

One of the best known early African cultures flourished in central Nigeria between 2,200 and 1,800 years ago. There, the Nok people made beautiful, large terracotta sculptures of heads. These sculptures are the oldest known in Africa south of the Sahara.

NOK POTTERY, NIGERIA
Pottery is still made at Nok, where magnificent clay sculptures were made about 2,000 years ago. The pottery was fired in clay ovens.

SENEGAL
République du Sénégal – Republic of Senegal
AREA: 75,950 sq mi.
POPULATION: 10.3 million
CAPITAL: Dakar
OTHER CITIES: Thiès, Kaolack, Zinguinchor
HIGHEST POINT: 1,634 ft
OFFICIAL LANGUAGE: French
CURRENCY: CFA franc

SIERRA LEONE
Republic of Sierra Leone
AREA: 27,700 sq mi.
POPULATION: 5.4 million
CAPITAL: Freetown
OTHER CITIES: Koidu-New Sembehun, Bo
HIGHEST POINT: Loma Mansa (6,381 ft)
OFFICIAL LANGUAGE: English
CURRENCY: Leone

TOGO
République Togolaise – Republic of Togo
AREA: 21,925 sq mi.
POPULATION: 5.1 million
CAPITAL: Lomé
OTHER CITIES: Sokodé, Kpalimé
HIGHEST POINT: Agou (3,235 ft)
OFFICIAL LANGUAGE: French
CURRENCY: CFA franc

◑ PAINTED HOMES, GHANA
Most village homes have thick mud walls and small windows, or none at all. This keeps the insides cool by day. Many are highly decorated.

◑ AFRICAN DRUMS
Drumming plays a major part in West African music. Competing rhythms are played by several drummers.

In about AD 1000, another Nigerian culture, the Ife, produced superb bronze sculptures. But the best-known bronzes were made in the kingdom of Benin, between 1450 and 1750. Today sculpture remains important in the region—wooden masks and carvings are made for use in traditional religious ceremonies.

During the Middle Ages, northern West Africa was in contact with North Africa through Muslim traders who crossed the Sahara on camel caravans to exchange goods. Europeans explored the West African coast in the mid-15th century, and by about 1530 the trans-Atlantic slave trade from Africa to the Americas had begun. The Portuguese and later the Dutch, British, French, Swedish, Danes, and others all traded in slaves. The British abolished the slave trade in 1807, although it continued until the mid 19th century. In the late 19th century, most of West Africa came under European rule. The colonized countries gained independence in the 1950s and 1960s.

◐ MUSICAL INSTRUMENT
The kora is a kind of harp-lute often used to accompany storytellers.

◑ CHIEFS GO DEMOCRATIC
In 1957, Ghana became the first black African country to win independence. Power passed from Britain to an elected parliament. But democracy proved fragile. Ghana, like many other African countries, suffered periods of dictatorship.

TIMELINE

BC

500   Nok civilization flourishes in central Nigeria (until AD 200)

AD

1100s   Kano, in northern Nigeria, is the chief trading city for Saharan camel caravans; Islam spreads through West Africa

1440s   Portuguese reach West Africa; the slave trade begins soon afterward

1600s   Ashanti unite into a nation, which, at its peak, includes western Togo, much of Ghana, and eastern Côte d'Ivoire

1822   The American Colonization buys land in Liberia for freed slaves

1847   Liberia becomes independent

1880s   European colonization of Africa

1957   Ghana becomes independent

1958   Guinea becomes independent

1960   Benin, Burkina Faso, French Cameroon, Central African Republic, Côte d'Ivoire, Nigeria, Senegal, and Togo become independent

1961   British Cameroon becomes independent, with part joining Nigeria and part Cameroon

1965   The Gambia gains independence

1968   Equatorial Guinea and Sierra Leone become independent

1999   Civilian rule is restored in Nigeria; civil war in Sierra Leone

CENTRAL, EASTERN, AND SOUTHERN AFRICA

Central Africa forms the basin of Africa's second-longest river, the Congo. East Africa, by contrast, is a high plateau. Above this rise Africa's two highest peaks: Kilimanjaro in Tanzania and Mount Kenya in Kenya. Southern Africa also consists of a plateau, marked with some saucerlike depressions, such as the Okavango Delta in northern Botswana. Here, the Okavango River flows into an inland depression. The coastal plains are narrow, except in Mozambique and Somalia.

The region also includes Madagascar, the world's fourth-largest island, and the small island nations of the Comoros, Mauritius, and the Seychelles.

Central Africa has a hot and mostly rainy climate. Rainforests cover much of the northern part of the Congo basin, with savanna in the south. Savanna covers most of East Africa, where temperatures are lower. Much of Southern Africa is also covered by savanna, but some areas are dry. The Namib Desert in the southwest is one of the world's driest places, while the Kalahari in Namibia, Botswana, and South Africa is semi-desert. The southern parts of South Africa have a temperate climate. The area around Cape Town in the southwest has hot, dry summers and mild, rainy winters.

The Congo basin contains many rainforest animals. Some, such as the mountain gorilla of eastern Congo and Rwanda, are rare because of hunting. Other endangered animals include monkeys and the okapi, a relative of the giraffe.

⊙ ON THE LOOKOUT
Meerkats post sentries to watch out for any predators that may attack the group.

FACTS

ANGOLA
República de Angola – Republic of Angola
AREA: 481,351 sq mi.
POPULATION: 11 million
CAPITAL: Luanda
OTHER CITIES: Huambo, Benguela, Lobito
HIGHEST POINT: Môco (8,952 ft)
OFFICIAL LANGUAGE: Portuguese
CURRENCY: Kwanza

BOTSWANA
Republic of Botswana
AREA: 224,606 sq mi.
POPULATION: 1.6 million
CAPITAL: Gaborone
OTHER CITIES: Francistown, Selebi-Pikwe
HIGHEST POINT: Otsa Mountain (4,885 ft)
OFFICIAL LANGUAGE: English
CURRENCY: Pula

BURUNDI
Republika y'Uburundi, République du Burundi – Republic of Burundi
AREA: 10,747 sq mi.
POPULATION: 6.2 million
CAPITAL: Bujumbura
OTHER CITIES: Gitega, Bururi
HIGHEST POINT: Mount Teza (8,747 ft)
OFFICIAL LANGUAGES: Rundi, French
CURRENCY: Burundi franc

CENTRAL AFRICAN REPUBLIC
République Centrafricaine – Central African Republic
AREA: 240,534 sq mi.
POPULATION: 3.6 million
CAPITAL: Bangui
OTHER CITIES: Berbérati, Bouar
HIGHEST POINT: Mount Toussoro (4,363 ft)
OFFICIAL LANGUAGE: French
CURRENCY: CFA franc

⊙ ISALO MASSIF, MADAGASCAR
Madagascar is home to many unique plants and animals that are found nowhere else.

⊙ MOUNT KILIMANJARO, TANZANIA

NAMIB DESERT
Huge sand dunes build up and shift across the Namib Desert on Namibia's coast. Few living things can survive there.

THE VICTORIA FALLS
These falls thunder down the Zambezi River between Zambia and Zimbabwe.

CENTRAL AFRICAN REPUBLIC

KENYA

BURUNDI

CHIMPANZEE
Chimpanzees live in Central Africa's forests.

UGANDA

RWANDA

SOMALIA

GABON

CONGO, REP. OF

SOMALIA

CONGO, DEM. REP. OF

TANZANIA

ZAMBIA

SEYCHELLES

ANGOLA

MALAWI

NAMIBIA

MAURITIUS

GIRAFFE
Giraffes stride across the African savanna—a rich habitat for wildlife, including lions, elephants, zebras, and warthogs.

BOTSWANA

MOZAMBIQUE

SOUTH AFRICA

LESOTHO

ZIMBABWE

SWAZILAND

MADAGASCAR

RURAL ZIMBABWE
Rolling tablelands broken by rocky mountains like these in Zimbabwe are typical of the southern African landscape.

THE BAOBAB
Africa's baobab trees—recognizable by their swollen trunks, which store water—can live more than 1,000 years.

Map labels

CHAD · CENTRAL AFRICAN REPUBLIC · Bozoum · Bangassou · Bomu · SUDAN · Bangui · Uele · Congo · CAMEROON · REP. OF CONGO · UGANDA · Margherita Peak 5,709m · Kampala · KENYA · Lake Turkana · Cape Caseyr · Berbera · ETHIOPIA · Juba · Mogadishu · SÃO TOMÉ & PRÍNCIPE · Libreville · Mbandaka · Kisangani · RWANDA · Kigali · Kisumu · Mt. Kenya 5,199m · Tana · Cape Lopez · GABON · DEMOCRATIC REP. OF CONGO · Lake Victoria · Nairobi · Kismayu · INDIAN OCEAN · Brazzaville · Kinshasa · Bujumbura · BURUNDI · Bukavu · Mwanza · Kilimanjaro 5,895m · Mombasa · Cabinda (ANGOLA) · Matadi · Kananga · Kasai · Sankuru · Lake Tanganyika · Dodoma · Zanzibar · Dar-es-Salaam · SEYCHELLES · Luanda · ANGOLA PLATEAU · Likasi · Lake Mweru · Rufiji · TANZANIA · Aldabra Is. · Lubumbashi · Lake Nyasa · C. Delgado · COMOROS · C. d'Ambre · ANGOLA · Ndola · ZAMBIA · MALAWI · Antsiranana · Lobito · Huambo · Lilongwe · Moçambique · Cunene · Cubango · Cuito · Lusaka · Blantyre · Mahajanga · Namibe · Zambezi · MOZAMBIQUE · Mozambique Channel · Toamasina · Etosha Pan · Harare · Livingstone · Beira · MADAGASCAR · MAURITIUS · NAMIBIA · Windhoek · Okavango Delta · ZIMBABWE · Bulawayo · Limpopo · Antananarivo · Fianarantsoa · Réunion (France) · BOTSWANA · KALAHARI DESERT · Gaborone · NAMIB DESERT · Pretoria · Maputo · C. Ste. Marie · Johannesburg · Mbabane · High Veld · SWAZILAND · Orange · Kimberley · Maseru · Durban · LESOTHO · DRAKENSBERG · SOUTH AFRICA · Great Karoo · Cape Town · East London · Cape of Good Hope · Cape Agulhas · Port Elizabeth

FACTS

COMOROS
République Féderale Islamique des Comores – Federal Islamic Republic of the Comoros
AREA: 836 sq mi.
POPULATION: 560,000
CAPITAL: Moroni
OTHER CITIES: Mutsamudu
HIGHEST POINT: Mount Kartala (7,746 ft)
OFFICIAL LANGUAGES: Comorian, Arabic, French
CURRENCY: Comorian franc

CONGO, DEMOCRATIC REPUBLIC OF THE
République Démocratique du Congo – Democratic Republic of the Congo
AREA: 905,350 sq mi.
POPULATION: 53 million
CAPITAL: Kinshasa
OTHER CITIES: Lubumbashi, Mbuji-Mayi, Kisangani
HIGHEST POINT: Mount Ruwenzori (16,762 ft)
OFFICIAL LANGUAGE: French
CURRENCY: Congolese franc

CONGO, REPUBLIC OF
République du Congo – Republic of Congo
AREA: 132,046 sq mi.
POPULATION: 2.9 million
CAPITAL: Brazzaville
OTHER CITIES: Pointe-Noire, Loubomo
HIGHEST POINT: Létéki (16,762 ft)
OFFICIAL LANGUAGE: French
CURRENCY: CFA franc

GABON
République Gabonaise – Gabonese Republic
AREA: 103,346 sq mi.
POPULATION: 1.2 million
CAPITAL: Libreville
OTHER CITIES: Port-Gentil, Franceville
HIGHEST POINT: Mount Iboundji (3,904 ft)
OFFICIAL LANGUAGE: French
CURRENCY: CFA franc

KENYA
Jamhuri ya Kenya – Republic of Kenya
AREA: 220,625 sq mi.
POPULATION: 30.7 million
CAPITAL: Nairobi
OTHER CITIES: Mombasa, Kisumu, Nakuru
HIGHEST POINT: Mount Kenya (17,060 ft)
OFFICIAL LANGUAGES: Swahili, English
CURRENCY: Kenya shilling

◊ FISHING, LUANDA
Fishing is important along Angola's coast.

◊ SOUTH AFRICAN APPLES

◊ CAPE TOWN, SOUTH AFRICA
Flat-topped Table Mountain overlooks Cape Town, South Africa's legislative capital. Cape Town is also a major port and industrial city.

◊ MOMBASA, KENYA
Sunshine and beaches attract tourists to tropical Africa. Camel rides and boat trips are added attractions.

In Central, Eastern, and Southern Africa there are 24 independent countries and one French island territory named Réunion. The countries are all republics, except for Lesotho and Swaziland in the south, which have kings as their heads of state.

The boundaries between the countries were drawn in colonial times, when the region was ruled by European powers. Some boundaries divide people belonging to the same ethnic group. Somali people, for example, live not only in Somalia, but also in Djibouti, Ethiopia, and northern Kenya. This has created problems along Somalia's borders.

Many countries have a large number of ethnic groups, and this has led to violent clashes. In Burundi and Rwanda, for example, fighting broke out between the two main groups, the Tutsi and the Hutu, resulting in thousands of deaths. Other countries to have suffered from ethnic civil wars in recent years include Angola, the Democratic Republic of the Congo (formerly Zaire), and Uganda.

In South Africa, European colonizers introduced a policy called apartheid, under which white people ruled, while non-whites had little or no power.

◐ GOLD MINE
Gauteng province in South Africa is famous for its gold mines.

This led to a civil war. But, in 1994, a government with a black majority took power. Nelson Mandela, the leading black opponent of apartheid, was president from 1994 until 1999.

◐ CIVIL UNREST
Conflict between Hutus and Tutsis in Rwanda and Burundi has shattered the countries' economies.

Agriculture employs about two-thirds of the people in this part of Africa. However, many farmers produce barely enough to support their families. Different crops are grown depending on the climate. Corn is a major food crop, while coffee, tobacco, tea, and various fruits are important exports.

Natural resources include oil in Gabon and Congo; copper in Zambia; diamonds in Botswana, the Democratic Republic of the Congo, South Africa, and Namibia; gold in South Africa; and uranium in Namibia and South Africa. However, apart from South Africa, the region lacks large-scale manufacturing centers. South Africa is the most developed country in this part of Africa, but many of its black Africans are poor.

In 2001, the Organization of African Unity met for the last time in Zambia. After 38 years, this organization of African states was transforming itself into the African Union, with its own parliament, court, currency, and laws.

◐ HYDROELECTRIC DAM, ZIMBABWE
Hydroelectric plants at dams on Africa's great rivers produce large amounts of cheap electricity.

◑ OSTRICH CHICKS, SOUTH AFRICA
Ostriches were once prized for their feathers, but today farmers rear them mainly for their hides.

FACTS

LESOTHO
Kingdom of Lesotho
AREA: 11,720 sq mi.
POPULATION: 2.2 million
CAPITAL: Maseru
OTHER CITIES: Maputsoe, Teyateyaneng
HIGHEST POINT: Thabana Ntlenyana (11,425 ft)
OFFICIAL LANGUAGES: Sotho, English
CURRENCY: Loti

MADAGASCAR
Repobikan'i Madagasikara, République de Madagascar – Republic of Madagascar
AREA: 226,658 sq mi.
POPULATION: 16 million
CAPITAL: Antananarivo
OTHER CITIES: Toamasina, Antsirabe, Mahajanga
HIGHEST POINT: Maromotro (9,436 ft)
OFFICIAL LANGUAGES: Malagasy, French, English
CURRENCY: Malagasy franc

MALAWI
Dkiko la Malawi – Republic of Malawi
AREA: 45,747 sq mi.
POPULATION: 10.5 million
CAPITAL: Lilongwe
OTHER CITIES: Blantyre, Mzuzu
HIGHEST POINT: Sapitwe (9,843 ft)
OFFICIAL LANGUAGE: English
CURRENCY: Malawi kwacha

MAURITIUS
Republic of Mauritius
AREA: 788 sq mi.
POPULATION: 1.2 million
CAPITAL: Port Louis
OTHER CITIES: Beau Bassin-Rose Hill, Vacoas-Phoenix
HIGHEST POINT: Piton de la Rivière Noire (2,711 ft)
OFFICIAL LANGUAGE: English
CURRENCY: Mauritian rupee

MOZAMBIQUE
República de Moçambique – Republic of Mozambique
AREA: 309,496 sq mi.
POPULATION: 19.4 million
CAPITAL: Maputo
OTHER CITIES: Beira, Nampula
HIGHEST POINT: Mount Binga (7,992 ft)
OFFICIAL LANGUAGE: Portuguese
CURRENCY: Metical

MBUTI DANCER
The Mbuti are a pygmy people who live in the northeastern part of the Democratic Republic of the Congo.

FACTS

NAMIBIA
Republic of Namibia
AREA: 318,259 sq mi.
POPULATION: 1.8 million
CAPITAL: Windhoek
OTHER CITIES: Swakopmund, Rundu
HIGHEST POINT: Brandberg (8,465 ft)
OFFICIAL LANGUAGE: English
CURRENCY: Namibian dollar

RWANDA
Republika y'u Rwanda, République Rwandaise – Republic of Rwanda
AREA: 10,169 sq mi.
POPULATION: 7.3 million
CAPITAL: Kigali
OTHER CITIES: Ruhengeri, Butare
HIGHEST POINT: Mount Karisimbi (14,786 ft)
OFFICIAL LANGUAGES: Kinyarwanda, French
CURRENCY: Rwanda franc

SAO TOME & PRINCIPE
República Democrática de São Tomé e Príncipe – Republic of São Tomé and Príncipe
AREA: 372 sq mi.
POPULATION: 147,000
CAPITAL: São Tomé
OTHER CITIES: Trinidade, Santana
HIGHEST POINT: Pico de São Tomé (6,640 ft)
OFFICIAL LANGUAGE: Portuguese
CURRENCY: Dobra

SEYCHELLES
Repiblik Sesel, République des Seychelles – Republic of the Seychelles
AREA: 176 sq mi.
POPULATION: 80,000
CAPITAL: Victoria
OTHER CITIES: none
HIGHEST POINT: Morne Seychellois (2,969 ft)
OFFICIAL LANGUAGES: Creole, French, English
CURRENCY: Seychelles rupee

Most people in Central, Eastern, and Southern Africa speak a Bantu-related language—Kongo in Central Africa; Swahili in East Africa; and Xhosa and Zulu in South Africa, for example.

The ancestors of the Bantu-speaking people originated in an area around the Cameroon–Nigeria border. They were farmers, who used iron tools. More than 2,000 years ago they began to spread east and south, taking over the land from earlier peoples, including pygmies, who were forest hunters, and the Khoikhoi and San (also called Hottentots and Bushmen) in the southwest. A few of these people survive, mainly in remote areas. But the main minority groups today are people of European and Asian origin.

Christianity was introduced to the region by European missionaries, and today more than three-fifths of the people are Christian. About 22 percent follow ancient religions, most of which include the worship of ancestors and spirits. Muslims, who make up 12 percent of the population, are found mostly in Eastern Africa.

Music, especially drumming, is a major traditional art form.

HUTU WOMAN
Rwanda and Burundi have three ethnic groups: the majority Hutu, the Tutsis, and a few pygmies.

ZULU WOMAN
Many Zulu men work in mines and industries. Their wives stay at home and bring up the children.

A SAMBURU MAN FROM KENYA
Kenya has about 40 ethnic groups. The Samburu are related to the Masai.

⟲ CONGO MASK
Masks are used in ceremonies by people who follow traditional religions.

⟲ TOWNSHIP
Huge "townships," where shelters are made from whatever people can find, have grown up near South African towns. Poverty and crime are major problems.

In recent years, several kinds of African jazz have developed. Dance is another popular pastime. Soccer is the leading sport, but cricket and rugby football are also widely played in South Africa, Zimbabwe, and other countries.

The carving of wooden statues and masks is an art form in the region, especially in Central Africa. Many beautiful carvings are made for use in traditional religious ceremonies, and are then thrown away. Pottery, baskets decorated with beads and shells, and shields used in ritual dances are other items of great beauty made throughout the region.

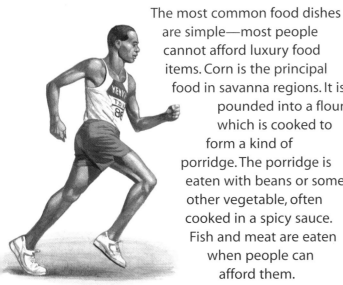

The most common food dishes are simple—most people cannot afford luxury food items. Corn is the principal food in savanna regions. It is pounded into a flour, which is cooked to form a kind of porridge. The porridge is eaten with beans or some other vegetable, often cooked in a spicy sauce. Fish and meat are eaten when people can afford them.

◐ CATHEDRAL, GABON
Christianity is the leading religion in Central, Eastern, and Southern Africa. It was introduced by European missionaries, including the explorer David Livingstone.

◐ KENYAN ATHLETE
East Africa has produced many fine athletes. They excel at long-distance running, especially at high altitudes.

⟲ XHOSA VILLAGE
Most Xhosa live in villages in southeastern South Africa. Many depend on money sent from relatives working in the cities.

FACTS

SOMALIA
Jamhuriyadda Dimugradiga ee Soomaaliya –
Somali Democratic Republic
AREA: 246,200 sq mi.
POPULATION: 7.5 million
CAPITAL: Mogadishu
OTHER CITIES: Hargeisa, Kismayu, Berbera
HIGHEST POINT: Surud Ad (2,969 ft)
OFFICIAL LANGUAGES: Somali, Arabic
CURRENCY: Somali shilling

SOUTH AFRICA
Republic of South Africa
AREA: 471,443 sq mi.
POPULATION: 43.5 million
CAPITAL: Pretoria (executive), Cape Town (legislative), Bloemfontein (judicial)
OTHER CITIES: Johannesburg, Durban, Port Elizabeth
HIGHEST POINT: Mount aux Sources (10,768 ft)
OFFICIAL LANGUAGES: Afrikaans, English, Ndebele, North Sotho, South Sotho, Swazi, Tsonga, Tswana, Venda, Xhosa, Zulu
CURRENCY: Rand

SWAZILAND
Umboso weSwatini –
Kingdom of Swaziland
AREA: 6,704 sq mi.
POPULATION: 1.1 million
CAPITAL: Mbabane
OTHER CITIES: Manzini, Nhlangano
HIGHEST POINT: Mount Emlembe (6,109 ft)
OFFICIAL LANGUAGES: Swazi, English
CURRENCY: Lilangeni

TANZANIA
Jamhuri ya Muungano wa Tanzania – United Republic of Tanzania
AREA: 341,216 sq mi.
POPULATION: 36.2 million
CAPITAL: Dodoma
OTHER CITIES: Dar es Salaam, Mwanza, Tanga
HIGHEST POINT: Kilimanjaro (19,340 ft)
OFFICIAL LANGUAGES: Swahili, English
CURRENCY: Tanzania shilling

THE GREAT TREK
In 1836, Boer (Afrikaner) settlers moved inland from the Cape to escape British rule.

Scientists have found fossils of humanlike creatures that lived in East Africa over two million years ago. Some experts think that this was the place where the first modern human beings appeared.

In prehistoric times, people in Central, Eastern, and Southern Africa lived by hunting animals and gathering nuts and berries. From about 2,000 years ago, Bantu-speaking farmers entered the region from the northwest. They intermarried with the original people, although some small groups of hunter-gatherers survived in remote areas.

The Bantu-speaking people developed large and powerful kingdoms. From the 15th century, however, most of these kingdoms were weakened by the demand for slaves made by Europeans. The Europeans themselves rarely ventured inland, but Africans from the coast attacked the inland kingdoms and took captives, who they sold as slaves to the European traders on the coasts. Large areas were devastated by these slave wars.

FORT JESUS, KENYA
Fort Jesus, built by the Portuguese in the 1590s, helped them win control over the East African coast.

GREAT ZIMBABWE
This great walled citadel, now in ruins, was built by the Shona in Zimbabwe in the 1300s.

AUSTRALOPITHECUS
Remains of early humans have been found in Eastern and Southern Africa.

ZULU WARS
The Zulus of South Africa clashed with white settlers, called Boers, in 1836. Zulu resistance to European rule continued until 1879, when British troops finally defeated the Zulu army.

FACTS

UGANDA
Republic of Uganda
AREA: 93,065 sq mi.
POPULATION: 24 million
CAPITAL: Kampala
OTHER CITIES: Jinja, Mbale, Masaka
HIGHEST POINT: Mount Ruwenzori (16,762 ft)
OFFICIAL LANGUAGE: English
CURRENCY: Uganda shilling

ZAMBIA
Republic of Zambia
AREA: 290,586 sq mi.
POPULATION: 9.7 million
CAPITAL: Lusaka
OTHER CITIES: Ndola, Kitwe, Mufulira
HIGHEST POINT: 6,781 ft
OFFICIAL LANGUAGE: English
CURRENCY: Zambian kwacha

ZIMBABWE
Republic of Zimbabwe
AREA: 150,871 sq mi.
POPULATION: 11.3 million
CAPITAL: Harare
OTHER CITIES: Bulawayo, Chitungwiza, Mutare
HIGHEST POINT: Mount Inyangani (8,507 ft)
OFFICIAL LANGUAGE: English
CURRENCY: Zimbabwe dollar

REUNION (FRANCE)
Département de la Réunion –
Department of Réunion
AREA: 969 sq mi.
POPULATION: 664,000
CAPITAL: Saint-Denis
OTHER CITIES: Le Port, Le Tampon
HIGHEST POINT: Piton des Neiges (10,070 ft)
OFFICIAL LANGUAGE: French
CURRENCY: Euro

One important European settlement was made by the Dutch in 1652—Cape Town. It served as a supply station for Dutch ships sailing between Europe and Southeast Asia, and became the nucleus of what is now South Africa.

During the 19th century, explorers mapped the African interior. In the late 1800s, European countries divided the region among themselves, in what became known as the "Scramble for Africa." Most of these colonies won their independence in the 1960s and 1970s. Zimbabwe (formerly Rhodesia) did not get majority rule until 1980, and Namibia, formerly ruled by South Africa, became independent in 1990.

In 1948, South Africa's white's-only government began a policy known as apartheid. Whites controlled the government and the economy. Blacks had no right to vote and their lives were strictly controlled. From the 1960s, most other countries condemned South Africa's policies, while opposition from black groups in South Africa gradually increased.

Apartheid was ended in the early 1990s and, in 1994, all the people of South Africa voted in elections that resulted in a black majority government. However, the new South Africa faces huge problems, including poverty and the threat of HIV/AIDS infection

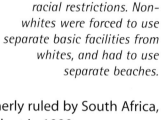

◐ RACIAL DISCRIMINATION
From 1948, life in South Africa was dominated by racial restrictions. Non-whites were forced to use separate basic facilities from whites, and had to use separate beaches.

◑ BARTOLOMEU DIAS MEMORIAL
Dias (1450–1500) was the first European to reach the southern tip of Africa.

◑ NELSON MANDELA
Nelson Mandela led the African National Congress to victory in South Africa's first non-racial elections in 1994. Mandela had been imprisoned from 1962 to 1990 for his opposition to apartheid.

TIMELINE

AD

1100	Arab traders settle East Africa
1250	Great Zimbabwe develops
1487	Bartolomeu Dias rounds the southern tip of Africa
1652	Dutch find Cape Town
1800s	European colonization
1958	Central African Republic becomes independent
1960	Democratic Republic of the Congo, Republic of the Congo, Gabon, and Somalia gain independence
1962	Burundi, Rwanda, and Uganda become independent
1963	Kenya becomes independent
1964	Lesotho, Malawi, Tanzania, and Zambia become independent
1966	Botswana becomes independent
1968	Swaziland becomes independent
1975	Angola and Mozambique become independent
1990	South Africa grants independence to Namibia
1994	South Africa's first fully democratic elections
2002	The Organization of African Unity renamed itself the African Union

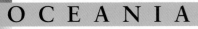

Northern
Mariana
Islands
(U.S.A.)

Wake Ieland
(U.S.A.)

Guam (U.S.A)

MARSHALL
ISLANDS

M I C R O N E S I A

PALAU

Caroline Islands

Line
Islands

M E L A N E S I A

NAURU

KIRIBATI

INDONESIA

West
Papua

PAPUA
NEW
GUINEA

SOLOMON
ISLANDS

TUVALU

French
Polynasia
(Franca)

VANUATU

SAMOA

American
Samoa
(U.S.A.)

Cook Islands
(N.Z.)

FIJI

M
E
L
A
N
E
S
I
A

TONGA

Pitcairn
(U.K.)

NEW
CALEDONIA
(France)

AUSTRALIA

Kermadec Is.
(N.Z.)

Norfolk Is.
(Australia)

NEW
ZEALAND

Chatham
Islands
(N.Z.)

218

↻ KANGAROO

OCEANIA

◊ Great Barrier Reef,
AUSTRALIA

◊ Sydney Opera House,
AUSTRALIA

◊ Uluru (Ayers Rock),
AUSTRALIA

◊ Beach houses,
FIJI

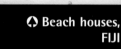

The continent of Oceania is also known as Australasia. It takes in a vast swathe of the Pacific Ocean, stretching from the Tropic of Cancer in the north to Stewart Island (New Zealand) in the south.

Australia takes up 90 percent of the land area. Too large to be called an island, it is normally rated as the smallest of the world's major landmasses. Australia is a land of empty deserts, ringed by temperate grassland and rainforest, scrub, and tropical rainforest.

To its north lies the island of New Guinea. The western part of the island (West Papua) is ruled by the Asian nation of Indonesia, while the eastern part forms the independent state of Papua New Guinea. To the southeast lies the island chain of New Zealand, dominated by North and South Island. These are beautiful, cooler lands with volcanic mountains, deep sea inlets, forests, and grassy plains.

Strung out across the open Pacific Ocean are thousands of tiny coral and volcanic islands, grouped into nations and dependent territories. They are sometimes divided into ethnic regions. Micronesia includes Guam, Kiribati (pronounced Kiribass), and the Mariana, Marshall, and Caroline islands. Melanesia includes Papua New Guinea, Vanuatu, New Caledonia, Fiji, and the Solomon Islands. Polynesia includes Tonga, Samoa, the Line Islands, Tuvalu, French Polynesia, and Pitcairn Island.

AUSTRALIA

☢ THORNY DEVIL

FACTS

AUSTRALIA
Commonwealth of Australia
AREA: 2,966,139 sq mi.
POPULATION: 19.3 million
CAPITAL: Canberra
OTHER CITIES: Sydney,
Melbourne, Brisbane,
Adelaide, Perth
HIGHEST POINT: Mt
Kosciusko (7,313 ft)
OFFICIAL LANGUAGE: English
CURRENCY: Australian dollar

☢ PHILLIP ISLAND
Collapsing rock has formed stacks and pinnacles off Phillip Island, near Melbourne. Bordered by Western Port and the Bass Strait, the island is famous for its fairy penguins.

☢ GREAT BARRIER REEF
Divers explore this magical world of corals, brilliantly colored fish, giant clams, and starfish.

Australia lies between the Indian and Pacific Oceans. Its northern shores are washed by warm, tropical seas, while the island of Tasmania to the south lies in cooler, stormier waters. Its northeastern coast is protected by the world's longest coral reef, the Great Barrier Reef, which extends for 1,260 miles from north to south.

Running parallel to the east coast are the mountains of the Great Dividing Range. At the southern end of this range are the Australian Alps. Australia's longest river, the Murray, whose chief tributary is the Darling, rises near Mount Kosciusko.

The interior of Australia is mostly wilderness, made up of the Great Victoria Desert, the Gibson, and the Great Sandy Desert. There are rocky outcrops, salt pans, dried-out lakes, and, along the Great Australian Bight, the flatlands of the Nullarbor Plain. Surrounding the deserts are regions of dry scrub, savanna grassland, tropical rainforest, temperate grassland, and eucalyptus forest. Australia's habitats are home to many species of animal and bird found nowhere else on Earth, such as koalas, kangaroos, Tasmanian devils, and duck-billed platypuses.

The great majority of Australians live in the big cities along the east, south, and southwest coasts, where the temperature is pleasant and the ground fertile. Where conditions permit in the interior, or "outback," there are huge cattle and sheep stations, and also mines.

☢ BYRON BAY
Unspoilt sands and rolling breakers extend for huge distances along the northern coast of New South Wales.

↻ THE OLGAS
Known to the Aborigines as Kata Tjuta (meaning "many heads"), these strange, rounded domes of rock rise 30 miles to the west of Uluru (Ayers Rock) in central Australia.

↻ UP A GUM TREE
The furry, gray koala spends most of its time in eucalyptus trees. Babies remain in a pouch on their mother's body for six months after birth.

Map labels

Torres Strait
C. York
Melville I.
Bathurst I.
Darwin
C. Arnhem
Gulf of Carpentaria
CAPE YORK PENINSULA
Arnhem Land
Groote Eylandt
Roper
Wellesley Is.
Mitchell
Gilbert
Norman
Cairns
Townsville
Great Barrier Reef
Bonaparte Archipelago
Joseph Bonaparte Gulf
Daly
Victoria
KIMBERLEY PLATEAU
BARKLY TABLELAND
Broome
Fitzroy
NORTHERN TERRITORY
Mount Isa
Flinders
G R E A T   D I V I D I N G   R A N G E
Proserpine
Mackay
C.Townsend
Eighty Mile Beach
Port Hedland
De Grey
Barrow I.
Fortescue
Ashburton
Mt. Bruce
GREAT SANDY DESERT
MACDONNELL RANGES
Alice Springs
QUEENSLAND
Georgina
Rockhampton
Bundaberg
GIBSON DESERT
Uluru (Ayers Rock) 867m
Diamantina
Thomson
Barcoo
Belyando
Lake Macleod
Carnarvon
Murchison
SIMPSON DESERT
Finke
MUSGRAVE RANGES
Alberga
L.Eyre
Cooper Creek
Warrego
Brisbane
Toowoomba
Gold Coast
Dirk Hartog I.
WESTERN AUSTRALIA
GREAT VICTORIA DESERT
SOUTH AUSTRALIA
Culgoa
Barwon
Grafton
Geraldton
Laverton
L.Everard
L. Torrens
Broken Hill
Darling
NEW SOUTH WALES
Coffs Harbour
NULLARBOR PLAIN
L.Gairdner
FLINDERS RANGE
Lachlan
Maitland
Kalgoorlie-Boulder
Great Australian Bight
Perth
Fremantle
C. Naturaliste
Bunbury
Archipelago of the Recherche
Port Lincoln
Spencer Gulf
Adelaide
Milgura
Wagga Wagga
Murray
Newcastle
Sydney
Wollongong
C. Leeuwin
Albany
Kangaroo I.
VICTORIA
Canberra
AUSTRALIAN CAPITAL TERRITORY
Bendigo
Mt. Kosciusko 2,228m
Ballarat
Melbourne
C. Howe
Mount Gambier
Geelong
C. Otway
Wilson's Promontory
TASMAN SEA
King I.
Bass Strait
Flinders I.
Davenport
Cape Barren I.
Burnie
Launceston
TASMANIA
Queenstown
Hobart
South East C.

AUSTRALIA (flag)

↻ WAVE ROCK
Like a wave frozen in stone, this rock in Western Australia has been shaped by wind and rain.

↻ MURRAY RIVER TURTLE

↻ LAKE EYRE
This vast salt lake lies below sea level in South Australia. It is normally dry, as the river waters that feed it soon evaporate, leaving the ground encrusted with mineral salts.

OCEANIA

◑ PINEAPPLE PLANTATION
Queensland's hot, moist climate produces tropical crops such as pineapples, bananas, and sugarcane.

Australia is an independent nation organized on federal lines. Canberra is its purpose-built center of government, located in Australian Capital Territory (ACT) in the southeast of the country. The most populous states are New South Wales and Victoria in the southeast, followed by Queensland in the northwest, Western Australia, South Australia, and the island of Tasmania. The wilderness of Northern Territory is very sparsely populated.

Australia also governs some outlying ocean territories, including Norfolk Island, Christmas Island, Cocos (Keeling) Islands, the Ashmore and Cartier Islands, the Coral Sea Islands, Heard Island, and Macdonald Island.

◔ CAMELS IN THE DESERT
Dromedaries (single-humped camels) were first brought to Australia in the 1860s. They were used by the explorer Robert O'Hara Burke (1820–61) and may still be seen in the deserts today.

Originally a group of British colonies, the Commonwealth of Australia still has the British monarch as its head of state. However, republicanism has widespread political support. Although cultural links with the British Isles are still strong, Australia now sees itself as a Pacific nation and part of the Pacific regional economy.

◔ CHRISTMAS ISLAND
A territory of Australia, tiny Christmas Island lies in the Indian Ocean about 185 miles south of Java. Its population is mostly made up of Malays and Chinese, who mine phosphates or work in tourism.

◔ WIND POWER
A windmill stands as a landmark in the empty outback. In these dry and dusty lands, wind may be used to raise precious underground reserves of water, for storage in tanks.

◑ WILDFIRE!
When the bush is as dry as tinder, one stray spark can set off a blaze. Vast bushfires are all too common, threatening property and life.

○ ROAD TRAIN

With no other vehicles in sight, thundering long-distance truck-trains kick up clouds of dust as they haul multiple trailers across the wilderness.

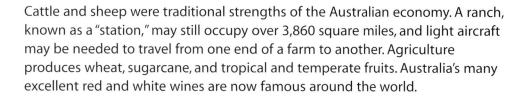

○ SHEEP SHEARING

Part of Australian folklore, the sheep shearer was once the mainstay of the Australian economy. He is still kept busy today.

○ A BIRDS-EYE VIEW

A helicopter carries tourists over blue seas and reefs off Cairns, in northern Queensland. Australia is becoming a major world tourist destination.

Cattle and sheep were traditional strengths of the Australian economy. A ranch, known as a "station," may still occupy over 3,860 square miles, and light aircraft may be needed to travel from one end of a farm to another. Agriculture produces wheat, sugarcane, and tropical and temperate fruits. Australia's many excellent red and white wines are now famous around the world.

○ AUSTRALIAN WINES

Vineyards were planted in South Australia's Barossa Valley in the 1840s. Quality has steadily improved and today Australia produces a wide variety of excellent wines, which are exported around the world.

The gold rush of the 1850s opened up Australia to mining, and today the country is a major exporter of iron ore, nickel, bauxite, gold, tin, uranium, zinc, and tungsten. There are reserves of coal, oil, and timber, and the rivers of the Snowy Mountains—part of the Great Dividing Range—provide hydroelectric power.

Manufactured goods include textiles, chemicals, and vehicles. Australia has become a major center of television and movie making, and newspaper publishing. It has also become a popular tourist destination, with people flying in to enjoy sun and surf, watersports, wilderness trekking, and lively city entertainments.

○ KANGAROOS

There are over 50 species of Australian kangaroo, large and small, gray and reddish-brown, living in forests, grasslands, and coastal regions. All leap on immensely powerful back legs.

○ HARBOR BRIDGE

This Sydney landmark, built in 1932, links the north and south of the city.

223

◑ AUSSIE FOOTBALL
Australian Rules football is a tough, fast game with 18 players per side.

◑ NEW AUSTRALIANS
Since 1974, many immigrants have arrived in Australia from Southeast Asia. This Vietnamese mother and child live in the west Melbourne suburb of Footscray.

◑ IN REMEMBRANCE...
The National War Memorial is linked by Anzac Parade to the new parliament building in Canberra. Anzac Day (April 25th) commemorates members of the Australia and New Zealand Army Corps killed in World War I (1914–18).

People descended from the first Australians are known as Aborigines. Various Aboriginal cultures and languages exist in different parts of Australia. Traditionally the Aborigines are experts at desert survival. The Torres Strait islanders of the far north form another ancient, related ethnic group.

The Aboriginal peoples experienced persecution and violence in the years following the arrival of the British in the 1770s. They were excluded from citizenship until 1967. Today Aborigines number only about one percent of the population. They face many economic and political problems, and are lodging claims to possession of their ancient lands. There has been a great revival of Australian and international interest in their culture and traditions in recent years.

The great majority of Australians are of English, Scottish, Irish, or Welsh descent. The English language is spoken throughout the country, but with its own accent and many local phrases and expressions. In the last 20 years, Australia has become much more of a multi-ethnic society. It has also been settled by Scandinavians, Poles, Dutch, Germans, Italians, Greeks, Lebanese, Indians, Chinese, Thais, and Vietnamese.

◑ EXPLORING AUSTRALIA
More and more city-based Australians are beginning to explore their own vast back country, with its extraordinary landscapes.

◐ BARBIE TIME
The barbecue has become a famous Australian tradition—nothing can beat freshly caught seafood or meat grilled in the open air.

◑ THE FLYING DOCTOR
Australia pioneered airborne medical services. The Flying Doctor Service provides medical advice by radio and aircraft for emergencies on remote farms.

○ CITIZENS

Aborigines may be greatly outnumbered in their own land, but at least they now face the future as full citizens.

○ IN THE SURF

These days, Australian life centers on the beach as much as the outback. Swimmers, lifeguards, rowers, and surfers like to show off their muscles to the crowds.

Many Australians enjoy outdoor activities and sports, such as tennis, sailing, swimming, surfing, cricket, rugby, and Australian rules football. Cities such as Sydney and Melbourne have become centers for the arts in recent years. While 85 percent of Australians live in the modern coastal cities or in other towns, there is still a widespread fascination with the folklore and traditions of the outback. Life in the more remote areas can be tough. If there is an accident at a remote sheep station, doctors may have to fly in by plane. A teacher may have to give lessons to his or her pupils from hundreds of miles away, over a two-way radio link.

○ ABORIGINAL ART

Traditionally, the Aborigines used natural pigments for their paintings on rock faces and on panels of bark. Many paintings featured the animals that the people hunted for food.

○ ARTIST AT WORK

Recent years have seen great international interest in contemporary Aboriginal art. Today, painters use modern paints and materials, but the abstract patterns they produce often refer back to ancient spiritual beliefs.

○ SYDNEY OPERA HOUSE

Completed in 1973, this inspiring building rises from Sydney harbor like a series of billowing white sails.

225

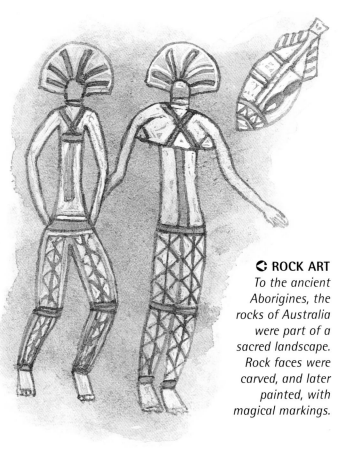

○ VICTORIAN AGE
As part of the British Empire, Australia developed rapidly during the reign of Queen Victoria (1837–1901).

○ ROCK ART
To the ancient Aborigines, the rocks of Australia were part of a sacred landscape. Rock faces were carved, and later painted, with magical markings.

Explorers began to set out into the harsh lands of the interior. During the 1850s, the transportation of prisoners ended and free settlers from the British Isles arrived in their thousands, lured by the discovery of gold. New colonies were founded in Western and South Australia, and Victoria and Tasmania broke away from New South Wales. Many Aborigine populations were killed or treated with violence. In Tasmania, all the original inhabitants were slaughtered by British settlers.

Humans may have first entered Australia over 50,000 years ago, when low ocean levels made it easier to cross from Southeast Asia. Over the ages, waves of Aboriginal peoples moved across the land, following river valleys as they hunted, fished, and traded.

Portuguese, Spanish, and Dutch explorers sailed into Australian waters, but it was the British who settled there. In 1770 Captain James Cook (1728–79) landed at Botany Bay, and explored the east coast, which he named New South Wales.

In 1787 the British founded a prison colony at Sydney Cove. By 1823 New South Wales had become a full colony.

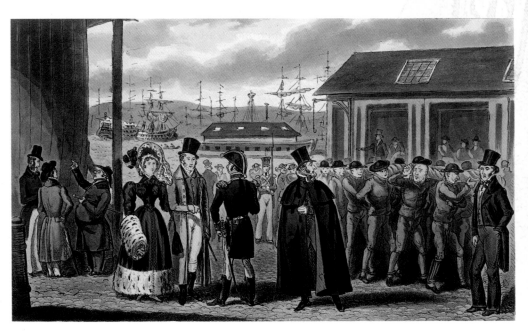

○ THE CONVICTS
Transported across the world, often for petty crimes, British prisoners arrived to a regime of brutal punishment.

THE RUSH FOR GOLD
In the 1850s, gold was discovered in New South Wales and Victoria. Prospectors arrived from around the world, hoping to make their fortunes.

NED KELLY (1855–80)
Outlaw, bushranger, and bank robber, the notorious Ned Kelly was hunted by police before a final shoot-out in which he wore home-made iron armor. Kelly was hanged in Melbourne jail.

The separate colonies federated as the Commonwealth of Australia in 1901. During the century that followed, Australia fought as part of the British Empire in World Wars I and II (1914–18 and 1939–45). During World War II, Australia was threatened by the Japanese invasion of Southeast Asia. In the 1950s, there was a new wave of settlement from Britain.

After the 1960s, Australia gradually moved away from its close political and commercial links with Britain. Japan and the United States became its major trading partners. New immigrants from Asia and the Pacific came to Australia, and Aborigines' rights were more fully recognized.

VOICES TO BE HEARD
In the last 20 years Australia's Aborigines, with their flag of black, yellow, and red, have been vocal in their demand for social justice and land rights. Many white Australians are looking again at their country's history.

TIMELINE

BC

50,000 Possible first Aboriginal settlement

12,000 Waves of settlers

AD

1606 Dutch discover Australia

1644 Abel Tasman maps Australian coast

1770 James Cook claims New South Wales for Britain

1788 Prison colony founded at Sydney

1825 Tasmania becomes separate colony

1829 Western Australia colonized

1836 South Australia colonized

1840 Transportation of convicts draws to an end (by 1868)

1851 Australian Gold Rush (until 1861)

1851 Victoria becomes separate colony

1855 Self-government (by 1856)

1859 Queensland becomes new colony

1901 Commonwealth of Australia founded

1914 World War I (until 1918): many Australian troops die at Gallipoli

1927 Federal government moves to Canberra

1931 Statute of Westminster: Australia confirmed as independent

1939 World War II (until 1945)

1950s Large-scale immigration from Europe

1967 Aborigines recognized as citizens

1970s New immigrants from Asia and the Pacific

1992 Court confirms Aboriginal right to ancestral lands

227

NEW ZEALAND
AND THE PACIFIC ISLANDS

◯ KIWI

The Pacific Ocean is surrounded by a "ring of fire," a region of intense volcanic activity. Erupting volcanoes under the ocean have thrown up chains of small islands. In the warm waters of the South Pacific, many of these have become rimmed with growths of coral. Sometimes the volcanic rock has then collapsed, leaving a coral ring called an atoll.

◯ CLOUDS OF STEAM

There are seven spectacular geysers at Whakarewarewa, near Rotorua, on North Island, New Zealand.

New Zealand lies about 1,200 miles to the southeast of Australia. It is home to many unusual animals, including the kiwi, a flightless bird. Its two main parts, North Island and South Island, are separated by Cook Strait. North Island has rich farmland, active volcanoes, geysers, and hot springs. Its major cities are Wellington, the capital, and Auckland. South Island has the snowy peaks of the Southern Alps, the fertile Canterbury Plains, and the cities of Christchurch and Dunedin.

Papua New Guinea is another volcanic country, with remote, forested mountains and lush, tropical valleys—a habitat for the world's biggest butterflies. Mount Wilhelm is the highest point in Oceania. National territory also includes many smaller islands, including the Bismarck archipelago and the northern Solomon Islands.

The nations and territories of the open Pacific are made up of thousands of tiny, scattered islands. Some are low-lying coral reefs and atolls, while others are mountainous, with tropical forest.

◯ NAVILU ISLAND, FIJI
Fiji is made up of 800 or so small tropical islands, many of them uninhabited.

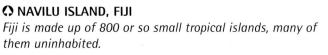

◯ FRILLED LIZARD

AMERICAN SAMOA
Territory of American Samoa
UNINCORPORATED US TERRITORY
LAND AREA: 77 sq mi.
POPULATION: 0.06 million
CAPITAL: Pago Pago
OFFICIAL LANGUAGES: Samoan, English
CURRENCY: US dollar

FIJI
Republic of Fiji
LAND AREA: 7,055 sq mi.
POPULATION: 0.8 million
CAPITAL: Suva
OTHER TOWNS: Lautoka, Nadi, Ba, Labasa
HIGHEST POINT: Mt Tomanivi (4,340 ft)
OFFICIAL LANGUAGE: English
CURRENCY: Fiji dollar

FRENCH POLYNESIA
Térritoire de la Polynésie Française
OVERSEAS TERRITORY OF FRANCE
LAND AREA: 1,263 sq mi.
POPULATION: 0.2 million
CAPITAL: Papeete
OFFICIAL LANGUAGES: French, Tahitian
CURRENCY: CFP franc

KIRIBATI
Republic of Kiribati
LAND AREA: 277 sq mi.
POPULATION: 0.08 million
CAPITAL: Bairiki
HIGHEST POINT: Banaba summit (266 ft)
OFFICIAL LANGUAGE: English
CURRENCY: Australian dollar

MARSHALL ISLANDS
Republic of the Marshall Islands
LAND AREA: 70 sq mi.
POPULATION: 0.1 million
CAPITAL: Majuro
OTHER TOWN: Ebeye
HIGHEST POINT: Nowhere more than 20 ft
OFFICIAL LANGUAGES: English, Marshallese
CURRENCY: US dollar

KIRIBATI

PAPUA NEW GUINEA

MARSHALL ISLANDS

NAURU

MICRONESIA

PALAU

SOLOMON ISLANDS

VANUATU

SAMOA

TUVALU

FIJI

TONGA

BERING SEA

Gulf of Alaska

SEA OF JAPAN

Yellow Sea

East China Sea

NORTH PACIFIC OCEAN

Midway Island (USA)

Northern Mariana Islands (USA)

Wake Island (USA)

Hawaii (USA)

SOUTH CHINA SEA

Guam (USA)

Federated States of Micronesia

Palau

Philippine Sea

Celebes Sea

West Papua (Indonesia)

Papua New Guinea

Marshall Islands

Nauru

Kiribati

Galapagos (Ecuador)

Solomon Islands

Tuvalu

SOUTH PACIFIC OCEAN

Arafura Sea

Port Moresby

Coral Sea

Samoa

American Samoa

French Polynesia

AUSTRALIA

Vanuatu

Fiji

New Caledonia (France)

Tonga

Cook Islands (New Zealand)

Pitcairn Island (UK)

Easter Island (Chile)

TASMAN SEA

NEW ZEALAND

SOUTHERN ALPS

This range forms a backbone to New Zealand's South Island, extending over 186 miles. Many of its snowy peaks top 9,800 feet.

STILL WATERS

New Zealand's South Island borders Cook Strait, with its deeply indented coastline. This is Queen Charlotte Sound.

ROTORUA

Health-giving warm springs and bubbling mud pools may be visited at Rotorua, on New Zealand's North Island.

North Cape

Whangerai

Gt. Barrier Island

Auckland

Manukau

Bay of Plenty

Hamilton

Waikato

East Cape

NORTH ISLAND

Rotorua

New Plymouth

L. Taupo

Gisborne

Ruapehu 2,797m

Napier

Wanganui

Hastings

Cape Farewell

Palmerston North

Nelson

Cook Strait

Wellington

Westport

Blenheim

Greymouth

SOUTHERN ALPS

SOUTH ISLAND

Mt.Cook 3,764m

Canterbury Plains

Christchurch

Timaru

NEW ZEALAND

N
W   E
S

Clutha

Dunedin

Invercargill

Foveaux Strait

Stewart Island

TUATARA

229

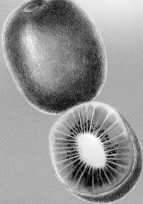

◊ KIWI FRUIT
The juicy green Chinese gooseberry, marketed under a name more associated with New Zealand, has become a major export.

◊ SAND AND SUN
Vanua Levu and its surrounding islands, in northern Fiji, attract tourists to their palm-fringed, tropical beaches.

FACTS

MICRONESIA
Federated States of Micronesia
LAND AREA: 271 sq mi.
POPULATION: 0.1 million
CAPITAL: Palikir
OTHER TOWNS: Weno, Kolonia
HIGHEST POINT: Totolom (2,359 ft)
OFFICIAL LANGUAGE: English
CURRENCY: US dollar

NAURU
Republic of Nauru, Naoero
LAND AREA: 8 sq mi.
POPULATION: 0.01 million
SEAT OF GOVERNMENT: Yaren
HIGHEST POINT: Western Nauru (225 ft)
OFFICIAL LANGUAGES: Nauruan
CURRENCY: Australian dollar

NEW CALEDONIA
Nouvelle Calédonie et Dépendances
OVERSEAS TERRITORY OF FRANCE
LAND AREA: 1,173 sq mi.
POPULATION: 0.2 million
CAPITAL: Nouméa
OFFICIAL LANGUAGE: French
CURRENCY: CFP franc

New Zealand is an independent nation, and has the British monarch as its head of state, reflecting its historical links with the British empire. It rules over two self-governing Pacific territories, Niue and the Cook Islands.

New Zealand has become one of the most important economies on the Pacific "rim." It raises large numbers of sheep and cattle and exports wool, meat (especially lamb), and dairy products. It also produces grain, vegetables, and fruit, including apples and kiwi fruit. Power is generated from hydroelectric schemes and from geothermal plants, which convert the heat from underground volcanic activity into electricity. Tourism is a fast-growing industry.

Papua New Guinea is another independent democracy, formally headed by the British monarch. The plantations of Papua New Guinea produce coffee, tea, rubber, palm-oil, and copra (dried coconut). Villagers clear forest to grow crops such as sweet potato, corn, and bananas for their own needs. The country has rich mineral reserves, including gold, silver, and copper.

◊ PEARL FISHERS
The warm waters of the South Pacific are ideal for oysters—and pearls. Pearls develop around small grains of sand inside oyster shells.

◷ HARVESTING COCONUTS
Dried coconut flesh, or copra, is produced on many Pacific islands. The hairy brown coconuts are the seeds of large green fruits, which grow at the tops of the palm trees.

⟳ NORTHERN SKYLINE
Auckland is New Zealand's largest city. Founded in 1840, it is an important seaport and industrial center.

⟲ SHEARING TIME
The New Zealand climate and terrain is ideal for raising sheep. Meat and wool are exported all over the world.

FACTS

NEW ZEALAND
Dominion of New Zealand
AREA: 103,288 sq mi.
POPULATION: 3.8 million
CAPITAL: Wellington
OTHER CITIES: Auckland,
Christchurch, Dunedin
HIGHEST POINT: Mt Cook
(12,394 ft)
OFFICIAL LANGUAGE: English
CURRENCY: NZ dollar

PALAU
Belu'u Era Balau
LAND AREA: 196 sq mi.
POPULATION: 0.02 million
CAPITAL: Koror
OTHER TOWNS: Melekeiok,
Garusuun, Malakal
HIGHEST POINT: (712 ft)
OFFICIAL LANGUAGES: English,
Palauan
CURRENCY: US dollar

The smaller islands of the Pacific include independent monarchies and republics as well as overseas territories such as New Caledonia and French Polynesia. Scattered locations, small populations, and lack of fertile land offer limited economic opportunities for the islanders. Many grow coconuts and tropical fruits, raise pigs and chickens, and catch fish. Local dishes are often made with breadfruit, cassava, or sweet potatoes. Sugarcane is grown as a cash crop in Fiji, and cocoa in the Solomon Islands. Islands such as Tahiti in French Polynesia have developed a tourist industry. Nickel is mined in New Caledonia. Tiny Nauru has been mined into a desert for its phosphates, which are used in the manufacture of fertilizers. Phosphate supplies in Kiribati have already been exhausted.

◐ IN PAPUA NEW GUINEA
Local markets may sell pigs, poultry, yams, taro (a root vegetable), sago (cereal from the sago palm), bananas, and sweet potatoes.

◑ WEDDING PARTY, TONGA
Guests gather for a royal wedding in Tonga. The chiefdoms of this Polynesian island group were united as a single kingdom in 1845.

231

⟳ MAORIS

The first inhabitants of the south Pacific were the ancestors of today's Melanesian, Micronesian, and Polynesian peoples. Over several thousand years, they explored the world's largest ocean in their canoes, settling land from the Hawaiian islands in the north to Easter Island in the east, where they carved large, mysterious stone statues. Their last great expansion took place over a thousand years ago, when a Polynesian people called the Maoris settled New Zealand.

The tattooed Maoris were fierce warriors. They hunted the islands' gigantic flightless birds, called moas (now extinct). Today Maoris make up about nine percent of New Zealand's population. They have preserved a keen sense of their history and culture.

The Dutch explored New Zealand's coasts in 1642. The next European visitor was the English navigator Captain James Cook (1728–79), in 1769.

⟳ TREE CARVING
Carvings, customs, and spiritual beliefs link many widely scattered Pacific islands, revealing a common ancestry.

⟳ FIJI TRADITIONS
Fiji was settled by both Melanesians and Polynesians, and later by Indians.

⟳ MEETING-HOUSE
The wharerunanga, with its elaborately carved roof and doorposts, is a Maori meeting-house built in the traditional style.

FACTS

SOLOMON ISLANDS
LAND AREA: 10,656 sq mi.
POPULATION: 0.4 million
CAPITAL: Honiara
OTHER TOWNS: Gizo, Kieta, Auki
HIGHEST POINT: Mt Popomanaseu (7,648 ft)
OFFICIAL LANGUAGE: English
CURRENCY: Solomon Islands dollar

TONGA
Kingdom of Tonga;
Pule'anga Fakatu'i'o Tonga
LAND AREA: 290 sq mi.
POPULATION: 0.1 million
CAPITAL: Nukualofa
OTHER TOWNS: Neiafu, Pangai
HIGHEST POINT: 3,432 ft
OFFICIAL LANGUAGES: Tongan, English
CURRENCY: Pa'anga

TUVALU
Southwest Pacific State of Tuvalu
LAND AREA: 9 sq mi.
POPULATION: 0.01 million
CAPITAL: Fongafale
OTHER TOWNS: Vaitupu, Niutao
HIGHEST POINT: Nowhere more than 20 ft
OFFICIAL LANGUAGES: English, Tuvaluan
CURRENCY: Australian dollar

VANUATU
Ripablik blong Vanuatu
LAND AREA: 5,714 sq mi.
POPULATION: 0.2 million
CAPITAL: Port-Vila
OTHER TOWN: Luganville
HIGHEST POINT: Tabwémasana (6,165 ft)
OFFICIAL LANGUAGES: Bislama, English, French
CURRENCY: Vatu

SAMOA
Independent State of Samoa
LAND AREA: 1092 sq mi.
POPULATION: 0.02 million
CAPITAL: Apia
OTHER TOWNS: Lalomanu, Falevai, Tuasivi, Falealupo
HIGHEST POINT: Mt Sisili (6,100 ft)
OFFICIAL LANGUAGES: Samoan, English
CURRENCY: Tala

◎ MAORI CRAFTS
Intricate, swirling designs are a part of the Maori tradition, carved in wood, whale ivory, or stone.

◎ EUROPEAN ENCOUNTER
In 1769 the English explorer Captain James Cook sailed around New Zealand, charting the waters and meeting tattooed Maori warriors.

In the following century, many British settlers came to New Zealand, attracted by the moderate climate, green pastures, and gold. They met with warlike resistance from the Maoris. By 1852 New Zealand was a self-governing British colony, and in 1907 it became a Dominion within the British Empire (having a similar status to Canada).

New Zealand fought in the two World Wars (1914–18 and 1939–45), and maintained close ties with Britain. By the 1970s, however, New Zealand saw itself more as a Pacific nation, expanding its trade with Japan, the USA, and Australia. Today's New Zealanders enjoy a good standard of living and an outdoor life, sailing, skiing, and playing team sports such as rugby and cricket.

◎ THE ALL BLACKS
In rugby football, New Zealand's national team has regularly been a world beater. Games start with a Maori chant and dance, the haka.

◎ GOING TO CHURCH
The Tongans had converted to the Christian faith by 1860. Today, Protestant churches are well attended.

◯ THE WARRIOR AGE
The Maoris defended their lands with war canoes. Fortifications called pa were surrounded by ditches and fences of stakes, or palisades.

233

The smaller Pacific islands were colonized in the 1800s, mostly by Germans, French, British, and Americans. Some of the Europeans came to live on the islands, but most merely acted as colonial governors. Workers were brought to Fiji from India, and their descendants became a large part of that island's population. Some colonies passed from British to Australian or New Zealand rule, but by the 1980s large areas of the Pacific were ruled as small, independent states.

⊙ HOUSE OF SPIRITS
Most people in Papua New Guinea are Christian, but traditional beliefs in spirits and magic are still widespread.

Ancient customs on the Pacific islands changed greatly during the colonial period. Christian missionaries banned traditional forms of worship, and people found work on plantations or in mines.

⊙ FACES OF PAPUA
Papua New Guinea is home to hundreds of different ethnic groups. Many of them wear elaborate face and body decorations.

The last land in the region to be opened up to the outside world was Papua New Guinea. Its forest and mountain communities were so isolated from each other that as many as 800 different languages had grown up there. The tribal costumes worn by many of the communities may still be seen at festivals today. They include spectacular feathers, bone ornaments, and body paint.

The way of life in the Pacific today is a mixture of the traditional and the modern. Social life is still marked by feasting, dancing, and singing. However modern communications have shrunk the great distances between one group of islands and another, and transportation is by aircraft and motor-boat as well as by canoe.

⊙ OCEAN RIDER
This canoe is of Samoan design. The Samoan Islands were colonized by Lapita seafarers, ancestors of today's Polynesians, as early as 1000 BC.

⊙ TROBRIAND ISLANDER
The people of the Trobriand or Kiriwina Islands are taller and lighter-skinned than most other Melanesians.

234

TIMELINE

AD
c.900	Polynesians (Maoris) settle New Zealand
c.1200	Rise of Polynesian chiefdoms
1526	Portuguese discover Papua New Guinea
1642	Tasman discovers New Zealand
1769	James Cook explores New Zealand coast (until 1777)
1815	First British settlers in New Zealand
1840	Treaty of Waitangi: New Zealand linked to Australia
1842	Formation of French Polynesia
1845	Maori uprising (until 1847)
1851	New Zealand becomes a separate British colony
1860	Maori uprisings (until 1872)
1884	British and Germans claim New Guinea
1907	New Zealand self-governing
1914	World War I (until 1918): Australia occupies German New Guinea
1939	World War II (until 1945)
1970	Tonga becomes independent
1975	Papua New Guinea and Tuvalu become independent
1978	Solomon Islands become independent
1980	Vanuatu becomes independent
1983	Kiribati becomes independent
1990	Federated States of Micronesia become independent
1991	Marshall Islands become independent
1994	Palau becomes independent

PACIFIC OCEAN

The Pacific Ocean is the largest body of water in the world, with an area of approximately 11.1 million square miles. It is bordered by Asia to the west and the Americas to the east, and is artificially linked to the Atlantic Ocean by the narrow Panama Canal.

The ocean floor is marked by extreme differences in relief. The Marianas Trench plunges to 36,200 feet, the deepest place on the planet, while massive volcanic mountains rise from the ocean floor to form the Hawaiian island chain.

Beneath the Pacific, the cracked crust of the Earth is moving apart at the rate of 8 inches a year. Intense activity surrounds the plates, or sections of crust, around the Pacific. This is an area of volcanoes and earthquakes, which in turn may create massive waves called tsunamis. Underwater lava creates chains of volcanic islands, often surrounded by coral reefs.

Ocean currents, including the Californian and Kuroshio, circulate clockwise around the North Pacific, while the Humboldt and East Australian currents move anti-clockwise around the South Pacific. Cycles of warming (an effect known as El Niño) and cooling (La Niña) of waters in the Pacific Ocean have a major effect on global climate, creating severe storms.

SEPIK TURTLE
This reptile takes its name from the Sepik River in northern Papua New Guinea.

SCORPION FISH, FIJI
Camouflage often conceals venomous spines on these tropical fish.

STONE MYSTERIES
Giant figures were carved on Easter Island, the most easterly of the Polynesian settlements, between AD 1000 and 1600.

BIKINI ATOLL
From the 1950s until the 1980s, places in the South Pacific like this atoll were used as testing grounds for nuclear weapons, amid protests worldwide.

ATLANTIC
OCEAN

◐ MANTA RAY
Manta rays live near the surface in the open sea. They feed on plankton.

The Atlantic is the world's second-largest ocean. It covers a total area of more than 41 million square miles. Its average depth is 11,745 feet, but depths of more than 29,500 feet occur in some trenches. The many islands in the Atlantic include Greenland, Iceland, and the British Isles.

The ocean's main feature is the Mid-Atlantic Ridge, an underwater mountain range that stretches from north to south. Running through the ridge is a rift valley, where earthquakes are common.

◑ OIL RIGS
The Atlantic has vast reserves of oil and natural gas, mined by offshore drilling platforms.

◑ VIKING SETTLERS
After sailing across the North Atlantic from Norway to Iceland, and then Greenland, Viking explorers built settlements.

◑ TRAWLER
From Atlantic waters come about a third of the world's annual catch of fish and shellfish.

This rift valley is the border between huge plates that are widening the Atlantic by about 1 inch a year. Lava from beneath the Earth's crust flows to the surface in places along the rift valley, creating new crustal rock.

Strong currents flow around the Atlantic Ocean. One famous current, the Gulf Stream, flows from the Gulf of Mexico to northwestern Europe. Its waters bring mild weather to places such as the Norwegian coast. The Atlantic contains important fishing grounds, though some places have been overfished. The Atlantic is also the busiest ocean for shipping.

◑ SQUID
Atlantic fishermen regard the many species of squid as pests, because they eat herring and mackerel.

◑ HUMPBACK WHALE
Humpback whales live in coastal waters in all the oceans.

INDIAN
OCEAN

◐ GREEN TURTLE
Hunting has greatly reduced the number of green turtles in the Indian Ocean.

The Indian Ocean, the world's third-largest ocean, lies between Africa to the west, Indonesia and Australia to the east, and Antarctica to the south. It covers an area of about 28.5 million square miles. Major islands include Madagascar and Sri Lanka. India and Sri Lanka divide the ocean's northern part into the Bay of Bengal and the Arabian Sea.

The average depth is 12,500 feet, but the deepest point is in the Java Trench, where depths of more than 24,300 feet have been recorded. Like the Atlantic, the Indian Ocean contains ocean ridges.

New crustal rock is being formed along the central rift valleys of the ridges—and earthquakes are common.

The northern part of the Indian Ocean lies in the tropics. Water temperatures are high in some areas, especially in the Red Sea and the Persian Gulf. The ocean currents are determined by the winds. North of the equator, the direction of the currents varies every year when wind directions change because of the monsoon.

◐ MORAY EEL
Moray eels live in tropical waters, lurking in the crevices of coral reefs.

◑ SEA CUCUMBER
Despite their name, sea cucumbers are animals! In the warm waters of the Indian Ocean, they reach lengths of up to 35 inches.

◐ GREAT WHITE SHARK
Great white sharks are among the most dangerous sharks, and have attacked people and small boats.

◑ TRADITIONAL FISHING
In the rich coastal waters of the Indian Ocean, fishermen catch sardines, anchovies, and bummalo, or Bombay duck, among other fish.

237

ARCTIC
OCEAN

ARCTIC
AREA: 4,633,236 sq mi.
AVERAGE DEPTH: 3,675 ft
GREATEST KNOWN DEPTH:
17,880 ft

◊ **INUIT**
The Inuit live in the Arctic region of North America. In 1999, they took control of a new Canadian territory named Nunavut.

The Arctic is a bitterly cold region and the Arctic Ocean is largely covered with thick ice throughout the year. This ice blocked early explorers trying to find sea routes around North America and northern Asia. Today, ice-breakers can force a passage through the ice. The first expedition to reach the North Pole was led by Commander Robert Edwin Peary (1856–1920) of the US Navy in 1909.

The average depth of the Arctic Ocean is about 3,675 feet and the greatest depth is 17,880 feet. Whales and many fishes, including cod and halibut, live in the Arctic Ocean. Polar bears live on the polar ice, where they hunt seals and fish in the freezing waters.

The Arctic is the region that lies north of the Arctic Circle. It includes the northern parts of Asia, North America, and Europe, together with most of the world's largest island, Greenland. These land areas enclose the world's smallest ocean, the Arctic Ocean. Near its ice-covered center is the North Pole.

◊ **ICEBERGS**
Icebergs break away from valley glaciers and from Greenland's huge ice sheet. Some drift south into the Atlantic Ocean.

Mainland areas within the Arctic Circle are covered in a treeless wilderness called tundra. The most common animals are caribou and reindeer, which graze there during the short summers. Other animals include bears, foxes, hares, lemmings, and voles. Many birds migrate to the Arctic in summer to breed, feeding on small animals or the swarms of insects that thrive in the marshy summer environment.

Greenland is a dependency of Denmark, but has been self-governing since 1981. With the exception of Antarctica, it is the world's least-populated land. Temperatures on the central ice cap can drop below -85°F, but ocean currents keep the southwest coast relatively mild. The fishing industry is a major employer. As well as the Inuit of Greenland and northern Canada, other Arctic peoples are the Saami (or Lapps) in northern Scandinavia, and the Samoyeds, Tungus, and Yakuts of northern Asia. In the past, most lived by fishing and hunting. But many now live in permanent settlements.

◊ **INUITS AND THEIR DOGS**
Traditionally, the Inuits used teams of dogs to pull their sleds across the snow. Today, motorized snowmobiles are more commonly used to travel over the ice.

◐ DRYING WHITE FISH
Fishing and hunting seals and whales are traditional activities of Arctic peoples. But today, many people live more comfortable lives in permanent settlements.

◐ ICEBOUND SHIPS
Ships can become locked in the frozen waters of the Arctic Ocean.

◐ HARP SEALS
Newly born harp seals were hunted for their valuable soft, white pelts.

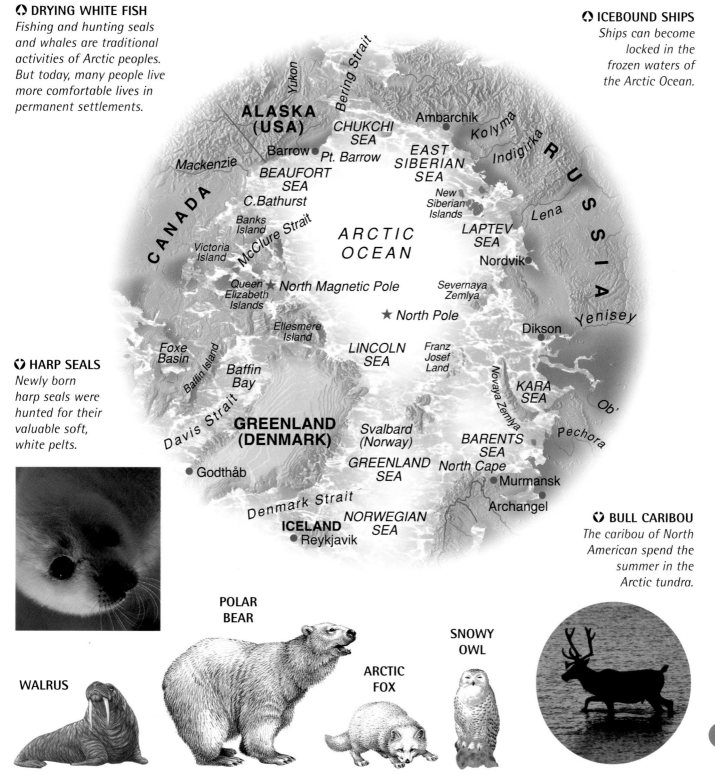

Yukon
Bering Strait
ALASKA (USA)
CHUKCHI SEA
Ambarchik
Kolyma
Barrow • Pt. Barrow
EAST SIBERIAN SEA
Indigirka
RUSSIA
Mackenzie
BEAUFORT SEA
CANADA
C.Bathurst
New Siberian Islands
Lena
Banks Island
McClure Strait
LAPTEV SEA
Victoria Island
ARCTIC OCEAN
Nordvik
Queen Elizabeth Islands
★ North Magnetic Pole
Severnaya Zemlya
★ North Pole
Yenisey
Ellesmere Island
Dikson
Foxe Basin
LINCOLN SEA
Franz Josef Land
Baffin Island
Baffin Bay
Novaya Zemlya
KARA SEA
Davis Strait
Ob'
GREENLAND (DENMARK)
Svalbard (Norway)
BARENTS SEA
Pechora
GREENLAND SEA
North Cape
• Godthåb
Murmansk
Denmark Strait
NORWEGIAN SEA
Archangel
ICELAND
• Reykjavik

◐ BULL CARIBOU
The caribou of North American spend the summer in the Arctic tundra.

WALRUS

POLAR BEAR

ARCTIC FOX

SNOWY OWL

239

ANTARCTICA

FACTS

ANTARCTICA
AREA: about
5,405,405 sq mi.
POPULATION: none permanent
HIGHEST POINT: Vinson
Massif (16,864 ft)

✪ WEATHER BALLOONS
Weather studies are important, because conditions in Antarctica affect the world's weather.

↻ ROALD AMUNDSEN
Amundsen, a Norwegian explorer, led the first expedition to reach the South Pole on December 14, 1911.

The Antarctic is the region lying south of the Antarctic Circle. It includes most of the world's fifth-largest continent, Antarctica, in the middle of which is the South Pole. Only the tip of the Antarctic Peninsula, jutting out toward South America, lies outside the Antarctic Circle. The waters around Antarctica are sometimes called the Antarctic or Southern Ocean. But most geographers regard these waters as parts of the Pacific, Atlantic, and Indian oceans.

Ice covers about 98 percent of Antarctica, although mountain peaks jut through the ice in places. The average thickness of the ice is 7,200 feet, but in places it is 15,750 feet thick. Antarctica is bitterly cold—the world's lowest air temperature, -128°F, was recorded at the Russian Vostok Station in 1983. Few plants and animals are found on Antarctica. The best-known creatures are penguins—flightless birds that feed mainly on fish in the waters around the continent.

Early explorers in Antarctica faced great hardship. An expedition first reached the South Pole in 1911.

It was led by the Norwegian Roald Amundsen (1872–1928). A British expedition led by Robert Falcon Scott (1868–1912) reached the pole five weeks later, but Scott and all his team perished on the way back. Later explorers used aircraft. The first flight over the South Pole was made in 1929 by Richard E. Byrd (1888–1957), a US naval officer.

Several countries have claimed parts of Antarctica, but none of the claims is recognized under international law. Many people would like to make the continent a huge international park, a protected wilderness safe from development and pollution.

Today, scientists from several countries work in Antarctica. In the 1980s, scientists discovered that the ozone layer above Antarctica was being thinned by chemicals called fluorocarbons. The ozone layer is important because it protects our planet from harmful ultraviolet rays. International action has been taken to reduce the release of fluorocarbons into the atmosphere.

↻ TRAWLING NEAR ANTARCTICA
The waters around Antarctica are rich in marine life, including krill (tiny, shrimplike creatures), squid, seals, fish, and whales.

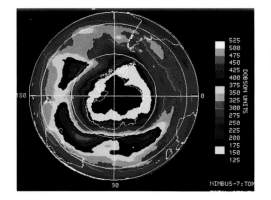

⟳ OZONE LAYER

The ozone layer in the upper atmosphere of the Earth blocks most of the Sun's harmful ultraviolet rays. Since the 1980s, pollution has created "holes" in the ozone layer over Antarctica.

⟳ VITAL SUPPLIES

Supplies for scientists are flown or shipped in to Antarctica.

⟳ WANDERING ALBATROSS

⟳ ICE CAVE

Around the coast of Antarctica, the sea hollows out spectacular caves in the ice.

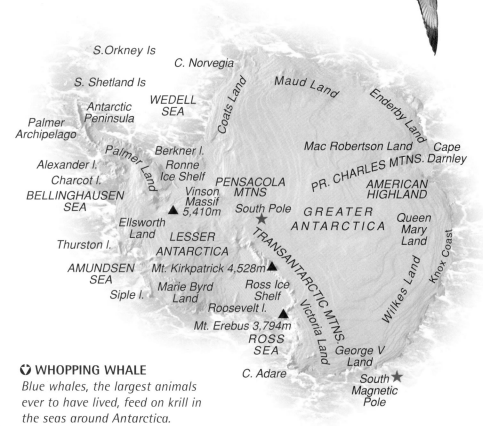

S.Orkney Is
C. Norvegia
Maud Land
Enderby Land
S. Shetland Is
WEDELL SEA
Coats Land
Antarctic Peninsula
Palmer Archipelago
Mac Robertson Land
Cape Darnley
Palmer Land
Berkner I.
PR. CHARLES MTNS.
Alexander I.
Ronne Ice Shelf
PENSACOLA MTNS
AMERICAN HIGHLAND
Charcot I.
BELLINGHAUSEN SEA
Vinson Massif ▲ 5,410m
South Pole ★
GREATER ANTARCTICA
Queen Mary Land
Ellsworth Land
LESSER ANTARCTICA
TRANSANTARCTIC MTNS.
Thurston I.
Knox Coast
AMUNDSEN SEA
Mt. Kirkpatrick 4,528m ▲
Wilkes Land
Siple I.
Marie Byrd Land
Ross Ice Shelf
Roosevelt I. ▲
Victoria Land
Mt. Erebus 3,794m
ROSS SEA
George V Land
C. Adare
South Magnetic Pole ★

⟳ WHOPPING WHALE

Blue whales, the largest animals ever to have lived, feed on krill in the seas around Antarctica.

⟳ PENGUIN PARADE

Adélie penguins, the most common penguins in Antarctica, build nests of pebbles on the coast.

⟲ TENTS IN THE SNOW

Scientists use special tents when they are making research journeys across Antarctica.

GLOSSARY

ABYSSAL PLAIN The deepest part of the ocean, below the continental slope.

AMMONITES Extinct mollusks whose fossils are common in rocks formed during the Mesozoic era. Like the dinosaurs, they became extinct about 65 million years ago.

ASTEROID A very small planet in orbit around the Sun. Most are found between the orbits of Mars and Jupiter.

ATMOSPHERE The layer of air that surrounds the Earth.

AUTOMATION The use of machines—or robots—to perform tasks that are too repetitive, complex, dangerous, or costly for people to undertake.

BIOME A plant and animal community that covers a large area. Biomes include the tundra, coniferous forests, temperate forests, temperate grasslands, deserts, savanna, and tropical rainforests.

BIRTH AND DEATH RATES The number of births and deaths in a year for every 1,000 people.

BLOCK MOUNTAIN A mountain system formed when a block of land is pushed upward between sets of roughly parallel faults.

CIRCUMFERENCE The distance around a circle.

COLONY A territory ruled by a foreign power.

COMET A heavenly body usually consisting of a nucleus and tail. It is composed of frozen gases of ice and dust, and follows a definite path through space.

COMMUNISM A political system where land, industry, and all property and goods are controlled by the government.

COMPASS Instrument used to measure direction. Magnetic compasses have needles that point to the magnetic North Pole.

CONDENSATION A change of state that occurs when a gas or vapor is turned into a liquid. Invisible water vapor in the air condenses into water droplets when the air is chilled.

CONIFEROUS FOREST Forests of mostly evergreen, cone-bearing trees. Common coniferous trees include fir, larch, pine, and spruce.

CONTINENT A very large land mass. The world has seven continents in all. In order of size they are Asia, Africa, North America, South America, Antarctica, Europe, and Australia.

CORAL A rock formed from the external skeletons of tiny sea creatures called coral polyps.

CUMULONIMBUS CLOUD A high, often anvil-shaped thundercloud formed when warm, moist air rises quickly.

DELTA A flat area at the mouth of a river, formed from muddy sediments deposited by the river.

DEPRESSION A region of low air pressure associated with changeable, and often stormy, weather.

DIALECT A variation of a language used by a group of people in a particular area.

DIAMETER A line which dissects a circle, passing through its center.

DECIDUOUS TREES Trees that shed their leaves during a certain season. Deciduous trees such as elms and oaks in the mid-latitudes shed their leaves in the fall. In monsoon regions, deciduous trees shed their leaves in the dry season.

EARTHQUAKE Sudden movements or tremors in the Earth's crust that make the ground shake.

ENVIRONMENT The external conditions that influence the growth and development of plants, animals, and people.

EROSION The process by which natural forces, including weathering, running water, ice, winds, and the sea, constantly wear down the land and carry the worn material, only to deposit it elsewhere.

ETHNIC GROUP A group of people with common characteristics, such as ties of ancestry, culture, language, nationality, or religion. These characteristics distinguish them from other people in the same country or society.

EVAPORATION A change of state that occurs when a liquid turns into a gas or vapor. For example, heat evaporates water to create invisible water vapor.

FAULT A fracture or break in rocks that make up the Earth's crust, along which the rocks have moved. Sudden movements along faults cause earthquakes.

FOSSIL Evidence of ancient life found in rocks. They include traces of leaves, shells, or bones, together with footprints made by animals. Sometimes, whole animals or plants are preserved.

FOSSIL FUELS Fuels such as coal, oil, and natural gas that are formed from the remains of once-living organisms.

GLOBE A spherical model of the Earth showing the land and seas. Some mounted globes can be rotated around a central axis.

HABITAT The type of place or environment to which a plant or animal is adapted. Habitats are usually defined in terms of their vegetation, altitude, or climate.

HOMO SAPIENS The scientific name for human beings, distinguishing them from early humanlike creatures such as *Homo erectus* and *Homo habilis*.

HURRICANE A severe tropical storm that forms over the oceans north and south of the Equator. When it reaches land, the hurricane often does much damage.

HYDROELECTRICITY Electricity that is generated at power plants by the force of water flowing through turbines at dams.

INDUSTRIAL REVOLUTION An important event in history involving the use of power-driven machines and the growth of factories. It began in the late 18th century in Britain and, by the mid-19th century, had spread through much of western Europe and North America. Progress in industrial development is still continuing in some developing countries.

INTERNATIONAL DATE LINE An imaginary line around 180 degrees east and west longitude. To the east of the line, the day is one day ahead of places to the west of the imaginary line.

MAGMA Molten rock inside the Earth's crust. When magma rises to the Earth's surface and spills out through volcanoes, it is called lava.

MAGNETIC POLE The Earth is like a giant magnet. It has two magnetic poles, north and south, just like the ends of a magnet.

MANGROVE SWAMP Coastal swamp in tropical regions, in which mangrove trees grow in the salty water along the coasts. The stiltlike roots sent down from their branches trap silt, which may build up to form new land.

MAP A representation of the Earth—or a large or small part of it—on a flat surface such as a sheet of paper. Navigators use maps.

METEOR A streak across the sky, also known as a shooting star, caused by a lump of rock burning up as it enters the Earth's atmosphere. Meteoroids that reach the surface are called meteorites.

MID-LATITUDES The mostly temperate climatic zones between the hot tropics and the cold polar regions.

243

MIGRATION The movement of animals and people from one location to another. People usually migrate to escape from something they do not like, or to go somewhere that seems to be more attractive.

MINORITIES Groups of people who differ in some ways, for example in culture or language, from the main group in a society.

NATURAL RESOURCES Materials that occur naturally and can be used by people, such as energy sources, forests, minerals, and fertile soils.

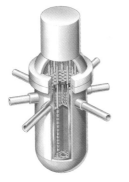

⚛ NUCLEAR POWER Energy that is released from a controlled nuclear reaction in a nuclear power plant.

OZONE An unstable form of the gas oxygen. It is produced when electricity is discharged through air.

PENINSULA Part of the land that juts out into the sea.

PINGO A mound that occurs in polar regions when freezing water beneath the surface pushes up the overlying soil.

PLANET In our Solar System, a heavenly body that orbits the Sun. Astronomers have identified other distant stars that have planets orbiting them.

PLANKTON Microscopic plants and animals that float near the surface of oceans. They are the food for many marine creatures.

PLATEAU An large upland region with a generally level surface.

⚛ PRAIRIE A mid-latitude grassland region in North America. It is the equivalent of the pampas in South America and the veld in South Africa.

RIFT VALLEY A valley formed when a block of land sinks between sets of roughly parallel faults.

SATELLITE In astronomy, a body that orbits a planet. Artificial satellites are manufactured objects that orbit the Earth or some other heavenly body. They may be used to send and receive radio signals.

SMOG A fog that is mixed with smoke. Photochemical smog is caused by the action of sunlight on exhaust gases from cars and factories.

SOIL EROSION The removal of the topsoil as the result of human interference with the land, such as deforestation. Soil erosion occurs quickly on exposed areas, especially on sloping land. By contrast, natural erosion is a much slower process.

STEPPE A mid-latitude grassland extending from the Ukraine into Central Asia. The term is often used for grasslands that are drier than prairies, with shorter and coarser grasses.

STRATOSPHERE The part of the atmosphere above the troposphere, extending to about 427 ft above ground level. It contains the ozone layer, which blocks most of the Sun's harmful ultraviolet rays.

SUBSISTENCE FARMING The farming of crops in order to support a farmer and his/her family. Often there is little surplus left to trade. It is the chief activity in many developing countries.

TELECOMMUNICATIONS The communication of information over long distances, by a wide variety of electrical and electronic systems, including telephone, telegraph, radio, television, and satellite.

VOLCANO A hole (or vent) in the ground through which lava, steam, and gases are ejected. The term volcano is also used for the mountains of ash and lava that form around the vent.

WATER VAPOR Invisible moisture in the air. It has the properties of a gas, until it condenses into droplets of water.

WIND The movement of air either across the Earth's surface or within the atmosphere. For example, the jet stream is a powerful wind that blows in the upper atmosphere.

TEMPERATURE The measurement of the hotness or coldness of a gas, liquid, or solid. It is normally measured on the Celsius or Fahrenheit scales.

TORNADO A small, intense storm, or whirlwind, with wind speeds of up to 404 mph.

TRADE The buying and selling of both goods and services.

URBAN AREA A built-up area such as a town or city and the suburbs around it.

INDEX
OF PLACE NAMES

(Page numbers in **Bold** refer to the maps)

A

Aberdeen **45**, 46, 47
Abu Dhabi **159**, 164
Abuja **205**, 206, 207
Acapulco **117**, 118
Accra **205**, 206, 207
Aconcagua 11, 142, **143**
Addis Ababa **199**, 200, 201
Adelaide 220, **221**
Aden **159**, 164
Adriatic Sea 92
Aegean Sea 92, **93**
Afghanistan **28-29**, **148**, 157, 159, 166-173
Africa 11, 42, 126, 127, **196**-217, 237
  British Empire 51
  Canary Islands 68
  Central 210-217
  Eastern 210-217
  economy 22, 23
  North 198-203
  rainforests 24
  religion 21
  savanna 18, 19
  Southern 210-217
  West 204-209
Agra **167**, 172
Ahaggar Mountains 198, **199**
Aksum 199, **200**, **202**
Alabama **107**
Alaska 27, 98, 99, 101, 106-115, 239
Albania 28-29, 31, 92, 93, 94, 97
Alberta 101, 103, 105,
Albuquerque 107
Aleutian Islands 28-29, 107
Alexandria 97, 199, 200, 201
Algarve 69, 71
Algeria **28-29**, **196**, 198-203, **199**
Algiers 198, **199**
Alicante **69**
Alice Springs **221**
Alps 60,
  formation 14
  France 52, 53
  Italy 76, **77**, 78

Altai Mountains 28-29, 151, 174, 175
Amarillo 107
Amazon River 27, 28-29, 98, 128, **129**, 134, **135**, 137
Americas 21, **98,** 99-147
Amman **159**, 160
Amritsar 167, 172
Amsterdam 38, 39, 40, 43
Amur River **151**, **175**
Anchorage **107**
Andalucia 69, 72, 73
Andes 98
  Brazil 134
  Northern 128, **129**, 129, 130
  Southern 142, 143, 145, 146, 147
Andorra **28-29**, 31, 53, 68, 69, 70, 72, 75
Angara River 27, **151**
Angel Falls 27, 134, 135
Angkor 194, 195
Angola **28-29**, 197, 210-217
Ankara **159**, 161, 164
Antarctica 10, 11, 28-29, 13, 26, 27, 98, 240, **241**
Antigua 123
Antwerp **39**
Apennines 76, 77, 79
Appalachian Mountains 107, 108
Arabian Peninsula 158, 164
Arabian Sea 237
Araguaia River **135**, 139
Aral Sea 150, 151, 153, 156
Archangel **239**
Arctic
  Alaska 106
  Europe 30
  Iceland 32
  Ocean 27, 100, 100, 101, 105, 107, 238, **239**
  Russia 150
  Scandinavia 32
  USA 109
Ardennes Mountains 38, **39**, 41, 52, 53

Argentina 23, 26, 28-29, 98, **99**, 135, 138, 142-147,
Arizona 22, 27, 107, 107, 109, 110
Arkansas 28-29, 107
Armagh 45, 47
Armenia 28-29, 148, 150, 151, 157, 165
Aruba 122, 123, 124, 125
Ashgabat 151, 155
Ashmore Islands 222
Asia 11, **148**, 148-195, 159
  Arctic 238
  China 174-181, **175**
  continental drift 13
  economy **22**, 23
  Japan 182-187, **183**
  rainforests **24**
  religion 21
  Russia 150
  Southeast 188-195
  Southwest 158-165
  steppes 19
Asunción 142, 143, 147
Aswân 159, 199, 200
Atacama Desert 26, 142, **143**, 144, 146
Athens 92, **93**, 96
Atlantic Ocean 10, 27, 28-29, 236
Africa 198, 204
Americas 99
Antarctica 240
British Isles 44, **45**
  Caribbean 122
  Central America 117
  continental drift 13
  Europe 30
  France 52, 53
  Iberian Peninsula 68, 69
  Iceland 32
  North America 100, 101, 106
  South America 129, 134, 135, **141**, 142
Atlas Mountains 28-29, 198, 199
Auckland 28-29, 228, 229, 230, 231
Australasia, 218
Australia 11, 21, 28-29, 218, 220-227, 228, 234, 237
  British Empire 51
  continental drift 12
Australian Capital Territory 221, 222
Austria 28-29, 31, 39, 43, 60-67, 76-83, **77**, **93**, **97**
  World War I 51
Axum 199, 200, 203
Ayers Rock 221

Ayeyarwady River 188, 189
Azerbaijan 28-29, 148, 150, 151, 157

B

Baden-Baden **61**
Baffin Bay 28-29, 101, 239
Baghdad 158, **159**, 161
Bahamas 28-29, 99, 122, 123, 126, 127
Bahrain 158, **159**, 160
Baja California 116, 117
Balearic Islands 68, 69, 71
Bali **189**, 190-191, **193**
Balkans 92-97
Baltic Sea 28-29
  Central Europe 84, 88, 90
  Germany 60, **61**
  Scandinavia 32, **33**,
Baltic States 84-91, 157
Bamako 199, 201, 202, 205
Bamberg **167**, 169
Bangassou 211
Bangkok 189, 190-195
Bangladesh **28-29**, **148**, 166-173, **167**
Bangui 210, **211**
Banja Luka 92, 93
Banjul 199, 206
Banks Island 101, 239
Barbados 122, 123, 124
Barcelona 28-29, 69, 71, 72, 73, 75
Barents Sea 28-29, 239
Barranquilla 128, 129
Bass Strait 221
Bavaria 60, 61, 64, 65
Bay of Bengal **28-29**, 169, 237
Bay of Biscay 53, 68, 69
Bay of Campeche 116, 117
Bay of Naples 77
Beaufort Sea 28-29, 100, 101, 239
Beijing 28-29, 174, 175, 176, 178, 179, 180, 181
Beira 211, 213
Beirut 159, 160
Belarus 28-29, **30**, 84, 85, 150, 151
Belfast 45, 47
Belgium 28-29, 30, 31, 38-43, 53, 61
Belgrade 93, 94, 95
Belize 28-29, **98**, 99, 116, 117, 119,
Belmopan 116, 117

Belo Horizonte 28-29, 134, 135
Ben Nevis Mountain 44, 45
Benghazi 199, 200
Benin 28-29, **196**, **205**, 208, 209
Berbera **211**, 215
Bergen 33, 35
Bering Sea 27, 28-29, 151
Bering Strait 28-29, 239
Berlin 28-29, **61**, 63, 67
Bermuda 106
Bern 61, 62
Bhopal 167
Bhutan **28-29**, **148**, 166, **167**, 168, 170, 171, **175**
Biarritz 53
Bilbao 69, 73
Birmingham, UK 45, 47
Birmingham, USA 107
Bissau 205, 207
Black Forest 60, 61, 92, 93
Black Hills 107
Black Sea 28-29, 30, 150-151, 158-159
Blackpool 45, 46
Blantyre 211, 213
Blue Nile River 199
Bogotá 28-29, 128,129, 131
Bohemia **85**, 87, 90
Bohemian Forest 60, 61, 84
Bolivia 28-29, 98, 124, 128-133, 138, 147
Bologna 77, 81
Bombay 28-29, **167**, 169
Bonn 61
Bordeaux 53, 55
Borgarnes 33
Borneo 188, 189, 193
Bornholm 33
Bosnia-Herzegovina 28-29, 31, 92, 93, 94, 97
Boston 28-29, 107, 115
Botany Bay 226
Botswana 28-29, 197, 210, 211, 213, 217
Boulogne 53
Brahmaputra River 148, 166, 167
Brasília 28-29, 134, 135, 141
Brasov 93, 94
Bratislava 85, 86
Brazil 28-29, 99, 129, 134-141, 143
Brazzaville **211**, 212
Bremen **61**

Brest **53**
Brighton **45**
Brisbane 220, **221**
Bristol **45**
British Columbia 100, **101**, 102, 105
British Isles 31, 37, 44-51, 236
Brittany 50, 52, **53**, 58
Brno 84, **85**
Brooks Range 28-29, 107
Bruges 39, 40
Brunei **28-29**, **148**, 188-195
Brussels 38, **39**, 40
Bucharest 93, **93**, 94
Budapest 84, 85, 87, 88
Buenos Aires 28-29, 142, **143**, 144, 145, 146, 147
Bujumbura 210, **211**
Bukhara **151**, 155
Bulawayo **211**, 216
Bulgaria **28-29**, 31, 92-97, **93**
Burkina Faso **28-29**, 196, 199, 204, 205, 209
Burma see Myanmar
Burundi 28-29, 196, 210-217

C

Cádiz **69**, 72
Cairo 28-29, **199**, 200, 201, 202
Calais **53**
Calama **143**
Calcutta (see Kolkata)
Calgary 28-29, 101,104, 105
Cali 128, 129
California 13, 106-115, **107**
  Callao 128, **129**
Camagüey 123
Cambodia 28-29, 149, 188-195
Cambrian Mountains 45
Cambridge 45
Cameroon 28-29, 197, 204-209, 211, 214
Canada 28-29, 98, 99, 100-105, **101**, 106, 107
  Arctic 238, **239**
  USA 111
Canary Islands **28-29**, 68, 71, 72, 199
Canberra 220, **221**, 222, 224, 227
Cancún **117**
Cannes **53**
Cantabrian Mountains 68, **69**
Canterbury **45**
Canterbury Plains 228, 229

Cape Blanc **199**
Cape Canaveral 107, 111
Cape Darnley **241**
Cape Finisterre **69**
Cape Horn **143**
Cape of Good Hope 42, **211**
Cape Town 210, **211**, 212, 213, 215, 216, 217
Cape Verde Islands 198, **199**
Cape York **221**
Capri 76, **77**
Caracas **135**, 136, 137, 139
Cardiff **45**, 46, 47
Caribbean Sea 27, 122-127, Americas 98 Brazil 134 Central America 116, 119 South America 128, 136, 138, 140 USA 110, 113
Carlisle **45**
Carpathian Mts. **85**, 92, **93**, 150
Carrauntoohil 44, **45**
Casablanca **199**, 201
Cascade Mountains **107**, 109
Caspian Sea **28-29**, 30, 150, 151, 153, 159
Caucasus Mountains 31, 150, **151**
Cayenne **135**, 136, 137, 141
Cayman Islands 122, **123**, 125
Cebu **189**, 190
Celebes Sea **28-29**, 189
Central Africa 27, 210-217, **211**
Central African Republic **28-29**, 197, 199, 204, 205, 206, 209, 210, **211**, 217
Central America 113, 116-121
Central Asia 27, 148
Central Europe 84-91, **85**
Cévennes Mountains 53, 53
Chad **28-29**, **196**, 198, **199**, 203
Chang Jiang River 27, 28-29, 174, 175
Channel, English **45**, 47, 50, 52
Channel Islands **45**,
Chartres 53
Chatham Islands **218**
Chattanooga **107**
Chelmsford **45**
Chengdu **175**

Chennai (Madras) 166, **167**, 169
Cherbourg **53**
Chernobyl **151**, 152
Chicago 28-29, 106, 107, 110, 115
Chiclayo 128, 129, 131
Chile 26, **28-29**, 99, **129**, 142-147
Chimborazo 128, **129**, 130
China 27, **28-29**, 149, 174-181, 177 economy 23 population 21 Russia 151, 152, Southeast Asia 188, 194 Southern Asia 166, 167, 168
Christchurch 28-29, 228, **229**, 231
Chukchi Sea 28-29, **239**
Cidad del Este 143
Cittagong 166, **167**
Clermont-Ferrand **53**
Clyde River **45**, 47
Coast Mountains 100, **101**, 109
Coats Land **241**
Coatzalcoalcos **117**
Cochabamba 128, **129**
Cocos Islands 222
Cognac **53**
Coimbra **69**
Cold Lake 103
Cologne 61, **61**, 63, 65, 66
Colombia 28-29, 99, 128-133
Colombo **167**, 169
Colorado 28-29, 107, 108
Colorado River, Argentina **143**
Colorado River, USA 107, 109, 109
Columbia 28-29
Columbus **107**
Comoros 197, 210, 211, 212
Conakry **205**, 206
Concepción 142, **143**
Congo, Democratic Republic of the (Zaire) 28-29, 197, 211-217
Congo, Republic of the 28-29, 197, 211, 212, 213, 217
Congo River 27, 28-29, 196, 210, **211**
Connecticut **107**
Constanta **93**
Constantine 198, **199**
Cook Islands 219, 229, 230
Cook Strait 228, 229
Copenhagen 32-37

Coral Sea **28-29**, 222
Córdoba 28-29, **69**, 142, **143**
Corfu **93**
Cork 44, **45**
Corrientes **143**
Corsica 52, **77**
Cos **93**
Costa Brava 69
Costa del Sol **69**, 71
Costa Rica 28-29, 99, 116-120
Coventry **45**
Crete 92, **93**, 95, 96
Cristobal Colón Mountain 128, **129**
Croatia **28-29**, 31, 85, 92-97
Cuba **28-29**, 99, 122, 123, 124, 125, 127
Cuenca 128, 129
Cuzco **129**, 132
Cyprus 28-29, 158, 159, 160, 162
Cythera **93**
Czech Republic **28-29**, 61, 84-87, 90, 91
Czestochowa 85, 89

D
Dakar **199**, 205, 207, 208
Dakhla **199**, 202
Dallas **107**
Damascus **159**, 160, 161
Danube River 60, 61, 84, **85**, 90, 92, **93**
Dar es Salaam 28-29, **211**, 215
Darhan 174, 175
Darling River 220, 221
Darwin **221**
Daugavpils 84, 85
Davao **189**, 190
Davis Strait 28-29, 100, **101**
Death Valley **107**
Debrecen 84, **85**
Deccan 166, 167
Delaware **107**
Delft **39**
Delhi 28-29, 167, 169
Denmark 28-29, 31-37, 100, 102
Denmark Strait 28-29, 239
Denver **107**
Detroit 28-29, **107**, 111
Dhaka 166, **167**
Dieppe **53**
Dinaric Alps 92, **93**
Diyarbakir **159**
Djibouti 197, 198, 212
Dnepr River **151**, 156
Dobruja 93
Dodoma **211**, 215
Doha **159**, 161
Dominican Republic **28-29**, 99, 122-123

Don River 28-29, 150, **151**
Donegal 45
Dordogne River **53**
Douglas **107**
Douro River **69**
Dover **45**
Drakensberg Mountains **211**
Drava River **93**
Dresden **61**, 67
Dubai **159**, 164
Dublin 28-29, 44, **45**, 47, 51
Dubrovnik **93**
Duero River 68, **69**
Duisburg **61**
Dundee **45**
Dunedin 228, **229**, 231
Durban 28-29, 211, 215
Durham **45**
Durrës 92, **93**
Dushanbe **151**, 153
Düsseldorf **61**
Dvina River **151**

E
East Anglia 44, **45**
East China Sea **28-29**, 175
East Indies **28-29**
East Siberian Sea 28-29, **239**
Easter Island 232, 235
Eastern Africa 210-217, **211**
Eastern Asia 148, 174-181
Ebro River 68, **69**
Ecuador 26, 28-29, 99, 128-133
Edinburgh **45**, 47, 51
Egypt **28-29**, **196**, 197, 199, **199**, 200-203, Alexander 96 Asia **159**, 165 France 59
Eindhoven **39**, 40
El Salvador **28-29**, 99, 116, 117, 119, 120
Elba Island 76, **77**
Elbasan 92, **93**
Elbe River 60, 61, 84, 85
Elburz Mountains 158, **159**
Ellesmere Island 101, 239
Emi Koussi Mountain 198, 199
Enderby Land **241**
England **30**, 44-51, 59
English Channel see Channel
Equitorial Guinea 28-9, 196-197, 204, 205, 206, 209
Erdenet 174, **175**
Erebus, Mount **241**

Eritrea **28-29**, **196**, 200, 203
Esfahan 158, 159
Essen **61**
Estonia 28-29, 31, 84, 85, 86, 91
Ethiopia **28-29**, **196**, 198, **199**, 200, 201 202, 203, **211**, 212
Etna volcano **77**
Euphrates River 158, **159**, 163, 164, 165
Europe 11, 30-31, 53, 61, 69 Arctic 238 Asia 148 Central 84-91 France 52-59 Iberian Peninsula 68-70 Low Countries 38-43 religion 21 Russia 150 Scandinavia 32-37 steppes 19
Everglades 108
Exeter **45**

F
Faeroe Islands 34
Faisalabad 167, 169
Falkland Islands **28-29**, 142, 143, 144, 147
Falster 32
Fiji **28-29**, 218, 219, 228-234, 235
Finland 28-29, 31, 32-37, 151
Florence **77**, 83
Flores Sea **189**
Florida 106-115, **107**
Formosa **143**
Forth River **45**
France **28-29**, 52-60, Canada 100 Low countries **39**, 38, 43 Germany 61 Iberian Peninsula 69, 72 Italy 77 trade 22 UK 46, 50
Frankfurt am Main **61**, 63
Franz Josef Land **239**
Freetown **205**, 208
French Guiana 98, 134-141
French Polynesia 218, 219, 228-234

G
Gabon **28-29**, 197, **211**, 212, 213, 214, 217
Gaborone 210, **211**
Galápagos **28-29**, 128
Galati **93**

Galdhøpiggen **33**, 35
Gambia **28-29**, 196, 199, 204-209, **205**
Ganges River 28-29, 148, 166
Gdansk 85, 86, 91
Geneva **77**
George Town 125, **189**, 189, 193
Georgetown **135**, 140
Georgia, Asia 28-29, 148, 150, 151, **151**, 153
Georgia, USA 107, 108
Germany 22, **28-29**, 60-67, **61** Baltic 84, **85** France 52, 53, 59 Italy 83 Low countries 38, **39** Russia 150 Scandinavia 33 World Wars 51
Ghana 28-29, 196, 203, 204-209, **205**
Ghats Mountains 166, 167
Ghent **39**
Gibraltar 68, **69**, 75
Gibson Desert 220, **221**
Glasgow **45**, 47
Gobi Desert 28-29, 174, 175
Gomel **151**
Göteborg **33**, 35
Gotland 33
Grampian Mountains 45, **45**
Gran Chaco 142, **143**
Granada 69, 72, 75, 118
Grand Canyon 27, **107**, 109
Graz 61
Great Australian Bight 220, 221
Great Barrier Reef 220, 221
Great Basin 107
Great Bear Lake 28-29, **101**
Great Britain 44, 45
Great Dividing Range 28-29, 220, 221, 223
Great Lakes 28-29, 100, 108
Great Plains 28-29
Great Salt Lake 107
Great Sandy Desert 28-29, 220, **221**
Great Slave Lake 28-29, 101
Great Victoria Desert 220, **221**
Great Zimbabwe 216
Greater Antilles Islands 98, 122, **123**

247

Greece 26, 28-29, 31, 92-97, **93**
Greenland **28-29**, 34, 37, 100-105, 236, 238, 239
Grenada **123**, 127
Grenoble **53**
Groningen **39**
Groznyy **151**
Guadalajara **117**, 118
Guadaloupe **123**, 125
Guadalquivir River 68, **69**
Guadiana River 68, **69**
Guangzhou 175, 181
Guatemala 28-29, 99, 116-121
Guayaquil 128, **129**
Guinea **28-29**, 196, 204, **205**, 206, 207, 208, 209
Guinea-Bissau **28-29**, **196**, **205**, 207
Gulf of Mexico 10, 27, **28-29**, 108, 107, 110, 118, 122
Guyana **28-29**, 98, 134-141,

H
Haiti **28-29**, 98, 122-127
Hamburg 61, 63
Hanoi 28-29, **189**, 190-192
Harare **211**, 216
Havana 28-29, 122, 123
Hawaii 26, **107**, 109, 113
Hawaiian Islands 28-29, 107, 109, 113, 115, 232, 235
Hebrides 44, **45**
Helsinki 28-29, 33, **33**
Himalayas 14, 27, 28-29, 148, 166, **167**, 167, 175
Hindu Kush 28-29, 151, 166
Hiroshima **183**, 187
Ho Chi Minh City 28-29, **189**, 191, 192
Hobart 28-29, **221**
Hokkaido 182 **183**, 186
Holland 40, 41
Honduras **28-29**, 99, 117, 118, 119, 120
Hong Kong 28-29, 149, **175**, 176, 177, 178, 181
Honolulu **107**
Houston 28-29, **107**
Huang He River 27, 28-29, 174, **175**, 181
Hudson Bay 28-29, 100, **101**, 105

Hungary 28-29, 31, 84-91
Balkans 93
Germany 61
Hyderabad **167**

I
Iberian Peninsula 68-70, **69**
Ibiza **69**
Iceland **28-29**, 30, 32-37, 236, 239
Illinois **107**
India 26, 27, **28-29**, 51, 96, 127, 166-173, **167**, 237
Antarctic 240
Asia 148, 149, 175, 188
British Empire 51
continental drift 12
economy 23
religion 21
Indian Ocean 10, 27, 28-29, 237
Africa 211
Asia 148, 167
Australia 220
Indonesia 26, 28-29, 188-195
Asia 149,
Europe 42
Indian Ocean 27, 237
Oceania 218
Indus River 28-29, 166, 167, 172
Ionian Sea 92, 93
Iran 28-29, 148, 151, 158-165, **159**
Iraq **28-29**, 148, 158, 159, 161, 163-165
Ireland **28-29**, 30, 44-51
Irrawaddy River 28-29, 188, 189
Irtysh River 27, 28-29, 150, **151**
Islamabad 167, 169
Isle of Man 44-51, **45**,
Israel **28-29**, 159, 160, 161, 162, 165
Asia 148
religion 21
Istanbul 96, **159**, 161, 164
Italy **28-29**, 30, 53, 60, 61, 76-83
Ivory Coast **28-29**, 196, 199, 205, 206, 207, 209

J
Jaipur **167**, 168,
Jakarta 188, **189**, 191
Jamaica **28-29**, 99, 122, 123, 124, 126, 127
Japan **28-29**, 182-187, 183
Asia 148, 149, 174, 177, 180, 181, 194

Industrial Revolution 22
manufacturing 23
religion 21
trade 22
World War I 51
Java **189**
Jerusalem 159, 160, 162, 164, 165
Johannesburg **211**, 215
Jordan 28-29, 148, 159, 160, 165
Jura Mountains 52, 53, 61

K
K2 Mountain 27, **167**, 168, **175**
Kalahari Desert 28-29, 210, **211**
Kaliningrad 84, **85**
Kamchatka 26, 151
Kamchiya River 93
Kampala 211, 216
Kanpur **167**, 171
Kansas **107**
Karachi 28-29, 167, 168, 169
Karakoram Mountains 148, 166, 167, 175
Kashmir **167**, 168,
Katmandu **167**, 169
Kaunas **85**, 86, 90
Kazakhstan **28-29**, 148-149, 150-151, 175
Kentucky 27, 110, **107**
Kenya **28-29**, 197, 210-217
Khartoum 28-29, **199**, 202
Kiev **151**, 155, 156
Kigali **211**, 214
Kilimanjaro Mountain 11, 28-29, 196, 197, 210, 211, 215
Kinshasa 28-29, 211
Kiribati 218, 219, 228, 231, 234
Kisangani **211**, 212
Klaipeda **85**, 87
Kobe 182, **183**
Kolkata (Calcutta) 166, **167**, 169
Kosovo **93**, 97
Krakatoa Mountain 26, 188
Krakow 85, 87
Krygyzstan 28-29
Kuala Lumpur 28-29, **189**, 190
Kuwait **159**, 160, 165
Kyoto 183, 186, 187
Kyrgyzstan 149, 150, **151**, **175**
Kyushu 182, **183**, 183

L
La Paz 28-29, 128, 129, **129**, 132

Labrador 100, **101**, 105
Lagos **205**, 207
Lahore 28-29, **167**, 168, 169
Lake Baykal 28-29, **151**
Lake Chad 28-29, **199**, 204, 205
Lake Constance **61**
Lake District 44, **45**
Lake Erie 101, 107
Lake Eyre 28-29, **221**, 221
Lake Geneva
Lake Huron **101**, 107
Lake Maracaibo 134, **135**, 136
Lake Michigan **107**
Lake Nasser **199**
Lake Nyasa **211**
Lake Ontario 100, **101**
Lake Superior 28-29, 101, **101**, **107**
Lake Tanganyika 28-29, **211**
Lake Titicaca 128, 129, 131
Lake Victoria **211**
Lake Volta **205**
Laos 28-29, 149, 175, 188-194,
Las Vegas **107**
Latvia **28-29**, 30, 84, 85, 91
Le Havre **53**
Le Mans **53**
Lebanon 28-29, 148, **158**, 159, 160, 162, 165
Lena River 28-29, **151**, **239**
Lesotho 28-29, 197, 210-217
Lesser Antilles Islands 98, 122, **123**
Lhasa 174, **175**
Liberia 28-29, 196, 204, 205, 206, 207, 209
Libreville **211**, 212
Libya 26, **28-29**, 197, 199-203
Liechtenstein 76, **77**
Lima 28-29, 128, **129**, 131
Limerick 44, **45**
Lipari Islands 76, **77**
Lisbon 28-29, 31, 68
Lithuania 28-29, 31, 84-91
Liverpool **45**, 46, 47, 49
Ljubl Jana 92, **93**, 94
Llanos 98, **135**, 136
Loire River 53, **53**, 55
London 28-29, 44, **45**, 46-50
Los Angeles 28-29, 106, **107**
Louisiana **107**, 115

Low Countries 38-43
Luanda 28-29, 210, **211**, 213
Luxembourg 28-29, **30**, 38-43, 53, 61
Lyon 52, **53**

M
Maastricht **39**
Macao 174, **175**, 176, 181
Macedonia 28-29, 30, 92-97
Mackenzie River 28-29, **101**, **239**
Madagascar **28-29**, 197, 210, 211, 213, 237
Madeira 68, 199
Madras 28-29, 167, 169
Madrid 28-29, 68, **69**, 71
Maine **107**, 113
Mainz 60, **61**
Majorca 69, 71
Malawi 28-29, 197, 211, 213, 217
Malaysia 28-29, 149, 188-195, 189, 193
Maldives 166, **167**, 168, 169, 170, 171
Mali **28-29**, **196**, **199**, 199, 201, 202, 203, 204
Malta 31, 76, 77, 79, 81, 82, 83
Malvinas Islands 28-29, **143**, 144
Managua 28-29, **117**, 118
Manchester **45**, 47, 49
Mandalay **189**, 190
Manila 28-29, 189, 190, 191
Manitoba **101**, 105
Marrakech **199**, 199, 201
Marseille 52, **53**, 54
Marshall Islands 218, 219, 228, 234
Martinique **123**, 125
Massachusetts **107**, 114
Massif Central 52, 53
Mato Grosso 134, 135
Matterhorn 60, 61, **77**
Mauna Loa Mountain 26, 107
Mauritania **28-29**, **196**, **199**, 198-203
Mauritius **28-29**, 197, 210, 211, 213
Mecca **159**, 161, 164, 203
Medellin 28-29, 128, 129
Mediterranean Sea 27, 28-29
Africa 198
Asia 148

Balkans 92, 93
Europe 30
France 52, 53, 54
Iberia 68, 69
Italy 76, 77, 79
Middle East 158, 165
Suez 200
Mekong River 27, 188, 189
Melbourne 220, **221**, 224, 225
Melanesia 218-219
Mendoza **143**, 144, 145
Mexico 28-29, 98-99, 116-121
Mexico City 28-29, **117**, 118, 119, 120
Miami 28-29, **107**
Micronesia 218, 219, 230, 234
Middle East 37, 158-165
Milan 76, 77, 79
Minneapolis 28-29, **107**
Minsk 150, **151**
Mississippi 27, 28-29, 98, 107, 108
Missouri 27, 28-29, 98, **107**, 108
Mogadishu **211**, 215
Moldova 28-29, 31, 93, 150-167
Mombasa 211, 212
Monaco 31, 52, 53, 55, 77
Mongolia 28-29, 149, 151, 152, 174-181
Mont Blanc 52, 53, 76, 77
Monte Carlo 52, 55
Monte Rosa 61, 62, 77
Montenegro 93, 94
Monterrey 28-29, 117, 118
Montevideo 28-29, 142, 143, 147
Montréal 28-29, 100, **101**, 102, 103, 104, 105
Montserrat **123**, 126, 127
Morocco **28-29**, 68, 196, 198-203
Moscow 28-29, **151**, 152-157
Moselle River **39**, 53, 60, 61, 63
Mt. Cook 28-29, **229**, 231
Mt. Everest 11, 26, 28-29, 148, 166, 167, 168, 174, 175, 178
Mt. Fuji 182, **183**
Mt. Kenya 210, 211, 213
Mt. McKinley 28-29, 106, 107
Mt. Olympus 92, **93**
Mt. Pinatubo 188, **189**

Mt. Vesuvius **77**
Mozambique 14, 28-29, 197, 210, 211, 213, 217
Munich **61**, 63
Murmansk 151, **239**
Murray River 220, **221**
Myanmar (Burma) **28-29**, 149, 166, 167, 175, 188-195,

N
Nagasaki **183**, 187
Nairobi 28-29, **211**, 213
Namib Desert 210, **211**, 211
Namibia **28-29**, 196, 210, 211, 213, 214, 217
Nancy **53**
Nanjing **175**
Nantes **53**
Naples 76, **77**
Near East 158-165
Nebraska **107**
Negro River **28-29**, 135, 141
Nepal **28-29**, **148**, 167, 168, 169, 170, 171, 174
Netherlands **28-29**, 31, 38, 39, 40, 42, 43, 61
Netherlands Antilles 123, 124, 126
New Brunswick **101**, 105
New Caledonia 28-29, 218, 219, 230, 231
New Delhi 166, **167**
New Guinea **189**, 218
New Mexico 107, 115, 120
New South Wales 220, **221**, 222, 226, 227,
New York 28-29, 106, 107
New York City 106, 107, 110, 111, 112, 113
New Zealand 26, 28-29, 218, 219, 228-234, 229, 230
Newfoundland **28-29**, 100, 101, 102, 103, 105
Niagara Falls **101**, 107
Niamey **199**, 201, **205**
Nicaragua 28-29, 99, 117-121
Nice 53
Nicosia 158, **159**
Niger **28-29**, **199**, 201, 203, 204
Niger River 197, **199**, 202, 204, 205
Nigeria **28-29**, **196**, 197, 204-209, 214

Nile River 27, 28-29, 196, 198, **199**, 199, 201, 203
Normandy 52, **53**, 54, 57
North Africa 27, 68, 72, 198-203
North America 98, 101, 106, 118
Arctic 238
prairies 19
Vikings 37
North Andes 128-133
North Atlantic Ocean 28-29, 30, 35
North Carolina 107
North Dakota 107
North Island 28-29, 218, 228, 229
North Korea 28-29, 149, 174, 175, 177, 181
North Pole 6, 7, 238, 239
North Sea 28-29, 31, 32, 61
Germany 60
Iceland 32
Low Countries 38
Scotland 47
trade 34
Northern Ireland 45, 46, 47, 51
Northern Territory 221, 222
Northwest Territories **101**
Norway 28-29, 30, 32-37, 239
Norwegian Sea **28-29**, **33**
Norwich **45**
Nouakchott **199**, 201
Nova Scotia **101**, 105
Novaya Zemlya 28-29, 151, 239
Novi Sad **93**, 94
Novosibirsk 28-29, **151**, 153
Nubian Desert **199**
Nullarbor Plain 220, **221**
Nuremberg **61**

O
Ob' River 27, 28-29, **150**, 151, **239**
Oceania 218-219
Oder River 60, **61**
Odessa, Russia **151**, 155
Odessa, USA **107**
Ohio **107**
Okavango 210, **211**
Oklahoma **107**
Oman 28-29, **159**, 158-165,
Omdurman **199**, 202
Omsk **151**
Ontario **101**
Oregon **107**

Orinoco River 28-29, 128, 134, 135
Orkneys 44, **45**
Orlando **107**
Orléans **53**
Osaka 182, **183**
Oslo **33**, 35
Ostend **39**
Ottawa 28-29, 100, **101**, 105
Ouagadougou 199, 205
Oxford **45**

P
Pacific Ocean 10, 27, **28-29**, 106, 235
Americas 98
Andean countries 128, 129
Antarctic 240
Asia 148
Australia 220
Central America 116
Oceania 218, 228-235
Russia 150
South America 142, 143
USA 106, 109, 110
Pakistan **28-29**, **148**, 166, **167**, 167, 170, 171, 172, 173
Palestine 164, 165
Pampas 28-29, 98, 143
Panama 28-29, 99, 116-121, **117**, **129**
Panama Canal 98, 235
Papua New Guinea **28-29**, **219**, 228-234, 235
Paraguay **28-29**, 99, 129, 138, 142-147
Paraguay River 138, 142, 143
Paramaribo 134, **135**, 136
Paraná River 27, 28-29, 134, 135, 142, 143
Paris 28-29, 52, **53**, 54, 56
Patagonia 142, **143**, 143, 144, 145, 146
Pennines 44, **45**
Pennsylvania **107**
Perth, Australia 220, **221**
Peru **28-29**, 99, 128-133
Philadelphia 28-29, **107**
Philippines **28-29**, 149, 188-195
Phnom Penh 188, **189**
Phoenix **107**
Pico Bolívar Mountain **135**, 136
Pidurutalagala Mountain **167**, 169

Pindus Mountains 92, **93**
Pitcairn Island **218**, 219
Plate River 142, **143**, 147
Po River 76, **77**
Poitiers 53, 55
Poland **28-29**, 31, 60, 61, 84-91, 156
Polynesia **218**, 219
Port Elizabeth **211**, 215
Port Sudan **199**, 202
Porto 68, **69**, 70
Porto Novo 204, 205
Pôrto Alegre 28-29, 134, **135**
Portugal 28-29, 30, 31, 68-75, 174
Prague 84, **85**, 87, 90,
Pretoria **211**, 215
Prince Edward Island **101**, 105
Puerto Rico 28-29, 98, 122, **123**, 124, 126, 127
Pyrenees Mountains 52, **53**, 68, **69**

Q
Qatar **28-29**, **148**, **159**, 160, 161
Québec 28-29, 101, 103, 105
Queen Charlotte Islands **101**
Queensland 221, 222, 227

R
Rabat 28-29, **199**, 201
Rangoon **189**, 190
Red Sea **28-29**, 148, 158, 198, 199, 237
Réunion 28-29, 197, **211**, 212, 216
Reykjavik 28-29, **33**, 35, **239**
Rhine River 38, 43, 58, 60, 61, 63
Rhodes **93**
Rhodesia see Zimbabwe
Rhodope Mountains
Rhône River 52, **53**, 61
Rio de Janeiro 28-29, 134, **135**, 137, 138, 139, 141
Rio Grande 28-29, **107**, 116, 117
Rio Negro 141, 142
Riyadh **159**, 161
Rocky Mountains 14, 28-29, 98, 100, **101**, 107, 108, 109
Romania **28-29**, 31, 85, 92-97
Rome 28-29, 76, 77, 78, 82, 83

Ross Sea **241**
Rostock 28-29, 61
Rotorua 228, **229**
Rotterdam **39**, 41
Rub 'al Khali Desert 158, **159**
Russia 27, 28-29, 31, 150-157
Arctic **239**
Asia 148, 149, 175, 183
Europe 33, 59, 60, 61, 84, 85, 86
Vikings 37
Russian Federation 26, 150-152
Rwanda 28-29, 197, 210-217

S
Sahara Desert 27, 28-29, 196, 198, **199**, 200, 202, 203, 209
St. Kitts & Nevis **123**, 124
St. Lawrence River 100, **101**, **103**, 105
St. Lucia 122, **123**, 124, 125
St. Petersburg 28-29, **151**, 152-156
St. Pierre & Miquelon 100, 101
St. Vincent & The Grenadines 123, 124
Salvador 28-29, 134, **135**, 140
Salzburg 64
San Diego **107**
San Francisco 28-29, **107**, 109
San Marino 30, 76, 77, 79, 83
San Salvador 116, 117
San'a 158, **159**, 161, 164
Santa Cruz 128, **129**
Santiago 28-29, 142, **143**, 144, 145
Santo Domingo **123**, 127
São Paulo 28-29, 134, **135**, 139
São Tomé & Príncipe **211**, 214
Sarajevo 92, 93, 97
Sardinia 76, **77**, 78
Saskatchewan 101, 105
Saudi Arabia 28-29, **148**, 158-165, **159**
Scandinavia 32-37, 238
Scilly Isles **45**
Scotland 30, 44-51
Seine River 52, 53, 54
Senegal 28-29, 196, 199, 204-209, **205**
Seoul 28-29, 175, 176

Serbia 93, 94, 95, 97
Severnaya Zemlya **151**, **239**
Seville **69**, 69, 72
Seychelles **196**, 210, 211, 215
Shanghai 28-29, 174, **175**
Shenyang 28-29, 174, 175
Siberia 28-29, 151, **151**, 152, 156
Sicily 76, **77**, 78, 83
Sierra Leone **28-29**, **196**, 205, 208, 209
Sierra Madre 28-29, 116, **117**
Sierra Nevada 68, 69, 109
Singapore 28-29, **148**, 188-195, 189
Skye 45
Slovakia 28-29, 31, 84-87, 90, 91
Slovenia 31, 61, 76, 77, 92-95
Solomon Islands 28-29, 218, 219, 228, 229, 231, 233, 234
Somalia **28-29**, **196**, 210, 211, 212, 215, 217
South Africa **28-29**, **196**, 197, 210-217
South America 24, 27, 98, 122, 128-147
South Atlantic Ocean 28-29, 144
South Australia 221, 222, 226, 227
South China Sea 27, 28-29, 175
South Georgia 28-29, 143, 241
South Island 28-29, 218, 228, 229
South Korea **28-29**, 149, 174-181
South Pacific 142, 228, 231, 235
South Pole 6, 241, 240
Southeast Asia 27, 127, 148, 188-195, 226, 227
Southern Alps 219, 228, **229**, 229
Southern Ocean 10, 240
Southwest Asia 148, 158-165
Spain 28-29, **30**, 31, 52, 53, 56, 59, 68-75
Sri Lanka **28-29**, **148**, 166-173, **167**, 237
Stanley 142, 143
Stewart Island 218, **229**
Stockholm 28-29, **33**, 34, 35
Strasbourg **53**, 66
Stuttgart **61**

Sudan **28-29**, 197, 199-203, 211
Suez Canal **199**, 200
Sulawesi Island 189,190
Sumatra 188, **189**,
Surinam 42, 99, 134, 135, 136, 138, 139, 141
Surtsey **33**
Svalbard 28-29, 34, 239
Swansea **45,** 46, 47
Swaziland **28-29**, 197, 211, 212, 215, 217
Sweden **28-29**, 31, 32-37
Switzerland **28-29**, 30, 39, 52, 53, 60-67, 77, 80
Sydney 219, 220, **221**, 223, 225, 227
Syria 28-29, 148, 158, 158-165

T

Tagus River **69**, 71
Tahiti 231
T'ai-pei 28-29, 175, 176
Taiwan **28-29**, 149, 174, **175**, 176, 177
Tajikistan 28-29, 149, 151,153, 166, 167
Tanzania **28-29**, 196, 197, 210-217
Tashkent 151, 155
Tasman Sea **28-29**, 221
Tasmania 220, 221, 222, 226, 227
Tegucigalpa 117, 118
Tehran **159**, 161
Tel Aviv 159, 160
Texas 26, **107**, 110,
Thailand 28-29, 149, 188-195
Thames River 44, **45**
Thar Desert 166, **167**, 171
The Gulf **159**
The Hague 39, 40
Thessaloníki 92, **93**
Thíra 26, **93**, 95
Tibet 27, **28-29**, 167, 174, 175, 176, 188
Tierra del Fuego 98, 128, 142, **143**
Tigris River 158, 159, 163, 164, 165
Tijuana 116, 117
Timbuktu **199,** 202
Togo **28-29**, **196**, 205, 208, 209
Tokyo 28-29,182, 183, 186
Tonga 218, 219, 231, 233, 234
Toronto 28-29, 99, 100-103
Torres Strait 221, 224

Transantarctic Mountains 241
Transylvanian Alps 92, 93
Triglav Mountain 92, 93, 94
Trinidad & Tobago 28-29, 122-127
Tripoli 28-29, 159, 160, 199
Trondheim 33, 35
Tunisia 28-29, 197, 199, 199, 202, 203, 203
Turkey 14, 28-29, 94, 96, 97, 148, 158-165
Turkmenistan 28-29, 148, 150, 151, 155, 166, 167
Turks & Caicos 122, 123, 126
Tuscany 76, 77, 78, 83

U

Uganda 28-29, 197, 199, 210-217
Ukraine 28-29, 31, 85, 93, 150, 151, 151, 152, 155, 157
Ulan Bator 28-29, 174, 175
Uluru (Ayers Rock) 218, **221**, 221
United Arab Emirates **28-29**, **148**, 159, 160, 164
United Kingdom 23, **28-29**, 44, 46, 47, 48, 51
United States of America 10, 22, 26, 26, 27, **28-29**, 98, 99, 100, 106-115, **101**, 116, 117
earthquakes 13
manufacturing 23
trade 22
Yellowstone River 15
Uppsala 33
Ural Mountains 28-29, 30, 148, 150-151, 153
Ural River 28-29, 151
Uruguay **28-29**, 142-147
Uruguay River 135, 142, 143
Ushuaia 142, 143, 145
Utah 106, 107, 109
Utrecht 39
Uzbekistan 28-29, 148, 150, 151,

V

Vaduz 60, 61, 64
Valdés **143**, 144
Valencia 69, 72, 74, 71
Valletta 76, **77**, 77
Valparaiso 142, 143, 145, 147

Vancouver 28-29 100, **101**,104
Vatican City 30, 76, 77, 79
Venezuela 27, **28-29**, 98, 99, 122, **129**, 134-141
Venice 76, **77**, 78, 80, 81
Victoria, Australia **221**, 222, 226, 227
Victoria Island 101, 239
Vienna 61, 62, 65
Vientiane 188, 189
Vietnam 28-29, 149, 175, 188-195
Vilnius **85**, 86
Vinson Massif 240, 241
Virgin Islands 122, **123**, 126
Virginia 50, 107, 115
Vladivostok **151**, 152, 152
Volga River 28-29, 150, **151**, 156
Vosges Mountains 52, **53**

W

Wales **30**, 44-51
Warsaw **85**, 86
Washington 28-29, 106, 107
Wedell Sea **241**
Wellington 228, 229, 231
Weser River 60, **61**
West Africa 204-209
West Frisian Islands 38, **39**
West Indies 28-29, 127
West Virginia 107
Western Australia 221, 222, 226, 227
Western Sahara 28-29, 196, 199, 200, 202
White Nile River 28-29, 199
Wilkes Land **241**
Windhoek **211**, 214
Winnipeg 28-29, **101**
Wisconsin **107**
Wrexham **45**, 47
Wroclaw **86**
Wuhan 28-29, 174, 175
Wyoming 15, **107**

X

Xi Jiang River **175**
Xingu River 28-29, **135**, 138

Y

Yakutsk 28-29, **151**
Yamoussoukro **205**, 207

Yangon 149, 189, 190
Yemen **28-29**, **148**, 149, 158-165
Yenisey River 27, 28-29, **151**, **239**
Yokohama 182, 183
Yorkshire **45**
Yucatán 116, 117, 118, 119
Yugoslavia see Serbia and Montenegro
Yukon River **101**
Yukon Territory 28-29, 101

Z

Zagreb 92, **93**
Zagros Mountains 158, **159**
Zaire see Congo, Democratic Republic of
Zambezi River **211**,
Zambia **28-29**, 197, 211, 213, 216, 217
Zanzibar **211**
Zemlya Frantsa Iosifa 28-29, 151
Zimbabwe 28-29, 197, 210-217
Zinder **199**, 201
Zurich **77**

GENERAL INDEX

A

Aalto, Alvar 37
Aboriginal people 220 - 227
abyss 11, 242
acid rain 24
Act of Union 51
aerospace industry 103, 111
African National Congress Party 217
Afrikaners 216
Afro-Caribbeans 126, 127
British Isles 49
Canada 105
agriculture 22, 23
Africa 196, 201, 202, 207, 208, 213, 214
Australia 222, 223
Europe 35, 54, 78
South America 140, 142
Ainu people 186
air 16, 17
greenhouse effect 24, 25
pollution 24, 25
Ajax soccer team 43
Akashi Kaikyo road bridge 184
Akihito, Emperor of Japan 187
Albanians 94
Albert II of Austria 66
Aleuts 112
Alexander I of Russia 157
Alexander the Great, Balkans 96, 97
Middle East 164, 165
Russian Federation 151
Southern Asia 172, 173
Alhambra palace 72
Allah 21
Allende, Isabel 147
Allied Forces,
Canada 105
Germany 67
Italy 83
Japan 187
Russia 157
USA 115
alpenhorn 64
Altamira cave paintings 74
Althing parliament 37
altitude 19
Alvin 11
American football 113
Amish farmer 112
ammonites 14, 242
amphitheatre 82

Amundsen, Roald 240, 241
ancestor worship 193, 214
Ancient Egyptians 14,15, 199, 203
Ancient Greeks 58, 74, 80, 81, 94, 96
Angel of the North 49
Angkor civilization 194, 196
Angles 48
Anglo-Saxon language 48
animals 12, 18-19, 24
Anna Karenina 155
Antarctic Circumpolar Current 10
Anzacs 224
apartheid 213, 217
Apple computers 111
aqueduct 52
Arab people,
Africa 197, 202, 203, 217
Asia 149
France 58
Iberia 74
Italy 80, 81, 83
Middle East 160, 162
Arabic language 196, 202
Arafat, Yasir 165
Araucanians 146
Arawaks 126, 127
Arecibo radio telescope 124
Armani 78
Armenian people 154
Arpad, Magyar chief 88
arts,
Asia 170, 179,186
Australia 224
France 52
Iberia 70, 73
Italy 79, 80, 81
Low Countries 40, 42
Middle East 162
Russian Federation 154, 155
USA 113
Aryan people 172
ASEAN 195
Ashanti nation 209
Asoka, Mauryan emperor 173
Assyrians 164
asteroids 8, 242
Atahualpa, Inca emperor 132
athletes 215
atmosphere 12, 16, 242
formation 12
greenhouse effect 25

ozone layer 240, 241
pollution 25
atolls 228
atomic bombs 187
Atomium 39
aurora borealis 32
Australian Current 10
Australopithecus 216
Austrian empire 94
axis, Earth's 6, 9, 26
Axis powers 51
Ayatollah 165
Aymara people 131
Azeri people 154
Aztecs 119, 120, 121

B

Babylonians 164
backgammon 162, 163
badminton 193
bagels 163
balalika 155
ballet 154, 155
Bantu language 214, 216
baroque churches 64
basalt 15, 45
baseball 112, 113, 127, 179, 186
Bashkir people 154
basket-making 94, 168
basketball 113, 163, 179, 193
Basque people 56, 72, 73, 75, 146, 147
Batista, Fulgencio 125, 127
Bayeux tapestry 50
bazaars 161
Bedouin people 203
beer 41, 47, 63, 85, 87, 110
Beethoven 65
Benedictine abbey 52
Benelux countries 40, 43
Berber people 196, 200, 203
France 58
Iberia 72, 74
Berlin wall 67
Bernadone, Giovanni 81
Bible 66
Big Bang 8
Big Ben 46
biomes 16, 242
Biosphere 22, 111
Bismark, Otto von 67
Black Madonna 89
black smokers 11
Blackpool Tower 46
block mountains 14 242
Boers 216
Bokmål language 36

Bolívar, Simón 133, 140
Bolsheviks 156, 157
Bonaparte, Napoleon 59, 59
Bonny, Anne 127
bonsai tree 183
Borges, Jorge Luis 147
Boston Tea Party 115
Boudicca, queen of the Iceni 50
boxing 193
Brazil Current 10
Brazil nuts 136
Breton people 48, 56
Breughel, Pieter 43
brewing industry 41, 47
British East India Company 173
British Empire 51
Asia 173, 194, 195
Australia 222, 226, 227
Canada 105
Caribbean 126
India 172
New Zealand 230, 233
North Africa 203, 209
Pacific islands 234
South America 140
USA 115
Britons 50
Buddhism 21
Eastern Asia 178, 179
Japan 182, 186, 187
Russia 155
Southeast Asia 188, 192
Southern Asia 167,170,171, 172, 173
Bulgars 94
bullfighting 72, 73, 193
Burke, Robert O'Hara 222
Burns, Robert 48
Buryats 154
bushfires 222
Bushmen 214
Byrd, Richard E 240
Byzantine Empire 82, 96, 97

C

Cabot, John 105
Cabral, Pedro Alvares 140
Calgary Stampede 104
Californian current 235
calligraphy 162, 186
calypsos 127

camel caravans 203, 209
Canaries Current 10
Candomblé spirit religion 139
canoes 232, 233, 234
carbon dioxide 24
Carib people 121, 126, 127, 138
Caricom 124
carnival 81, 126,127, 139
Cartier, Jaques 105
cassava 137, 207, 208, 231
Castilan language 72
Castle of the Knights 164
castles 53, 54, 55, 59
Castro, Fidel 125, 127
Catalans 56, 72
cattle 136, 144, 220, 223, 230
Caucasoids 21
cave paintings 58, 74
Ceausescu, Nicolae 94
Celtic people,
British Isles 48, 49, 50
France 57, 58
Germany 66
Iberia 72, 74
Italy 80
Central Powers 51
ceramics 89, 162
CERN 62
Channel Tunnel 46
chaparral 16
chapati 171
Charles I, king of England 51
Charles II, king of England 51
château 53, 55
Chavín civilization 132, 133
Chechens 154
Cherkess people 154
Chiang Kai-shek 180
Chimú civilization 132, 133
Chinese language 20, 21, 178
chlorofluorocarbons 25
chocolates 40, 41
Chopin, Frédéric 89

Christian churches 48, 89, 112
Christian Crusaders 164, 165
Christianity 21
Africa 200, 203, 214
America 112, 121, 127
Asia 171, 178, 187, 192
Baltic States 89
British Isles 50, 51
Italy 82
Middle East 164, 165
Pacific islands 233, 234
Russia 155
Scandinavia 37
Church of England 50
Chuukchee people 154
cinema industry 111
civil war,
Africa 200, 202, 206, 212, 213
Australia 227
British Isles 51
Central America 120
Iberia 75
Russia 156, 157
Southeast Asia 195
Southern Asia 169, 173
USA 114, 115
climate 16-17, 18, 26
global warming 25
Clinton, Bill, President USA 115
clouds 16, 17
CN Tower 102
cola drinks 110
Cold War 115, 157
Colosseum 82
Columbus,
Christopher 126,127
comets 8, 242
Commonwealth,
British 51
Commonwealth of Australia 227
Commonwealth of Independent States 152
Communism 65, 242
Balkans 94, 97
Baltic States 86, 91
Caribbean 124

Eastern Asia 176, 177, 180, 181
Germany 67
Russian Federation 152, 153, 157
Southeast Asia 190, 192, 195
Southern Asia 173
compact discs 63
compass 6, 242
computer industry, Brazil 136
British Isles 47
Japan 185
Southern Asia 169
USA 111
concentration camp 43
condensation 242
Confederates 114
Confucianism 21, 179
coniferous forest 16, 18, 242
conquistadors 132
continental drift 12
continental shelf 10, 11, 44
Cook, Captain James 226, 227, 232, 233, 234
Copernicus, Nicolaus 88
coral 10, 242
islands 219, 228
reefs 19, 118, 122, 123, 220, 235, 237
core, Earth's 12, 13
Corneille 56
Corsican people 56
Cossaks 154
Costa, Lucio 141
couscous 202
crafts 64, 119, 160, 200
Cree people 101, 104
Creole dialect 127
cricket,
Africa 215
Australia 225
British Isles 48
Caribbean 127
New Zealand 233
crime 20, 215
Croatians 94
crown jewels 46, 200
Crusades 164, 165
crust 12, 13, 235, 236, 237
Cuban Missile Crisis 127
cumulonimbus clouds 17, 242
Cuna people 121
Curie, Marie 88
currents 10, 13, 15
Atlantic ocean 236
Indian ocean 237
Europe 30

Pacific ocean 235
cycle race 57

D

Dagestanis 154
Dalai Lama 176
dams 145, 201, 213
dance,
Africa 215
Japan 186
Southeast Asia 192
Southern Asia 170
West Africa 208
Danes 36, 48, 209
Dante, Alighieri 81
da Vinci, Leonardo 81
Dayak people 193
de Camões, Luis 73
de Cervantes, Miguel 73
de Champlain, Samuel 105
de Gama, Vasco 71
de Gaulle, Charles 59
de Goya, Francisco 73
de' Medici, Catherine 83
de San Martin, José 74
de Valera, Eamon 51
Debussy 56
deciduous trees 18, 182, 242
Dégas 56
Delta Project flood defences 43
Dene people 104
Deng Xiaoping 181
dervishes 162
dhotis 170
Dias, Bartolomeu 216, 217
Díaz, Rodrigo 74
Diderot, Denis 56
Disney, Walt 111
Disneyworld 99, 111
Diwali festival 17, 171
dogsleds 105, 155, 182, 238
Domesday Book 50
Domingo, Placido 80
Don Quixote 73
Dracula legend 97
dragon festivals 178
Dravidians 170
Dürer, Albrecht 65
Dushan, Stephen 97
Dutch East India Company 42, 43
Dutch influence,
Africa 217
Australia 225, 226, 227
Canada 105
Caribbean 126
New Zealand 233
South America 139, 140

Southeast Asia 194, 195
USA 113, 114
West Africa 209
Dutch language 42
Dvořák, Antonín 89
dykes 38
dynasties 180

E

Earth,
age 26
formation 8, 12-13
planet 6-7, 8-9
plate movements 13
structure 12-13
surface 10-11, 14-15
tides 9
water cycle 17
weather 16,17
Earth Summit 141
East Australian current 235
Easter 72, 88
Easter Rising 51
easterlies 16, 17
Eastern Orthodox Church 96, 97, 155
education 177, 179, 192
Eighty Years War 43
eisteddfodau 48
El Cid 74
El Niño 235
electronic goods 40, 185, 191
Elfstedentocht 42
Elizabeth I, Queen of England 50
emirs 160
endangered animals 210
English language 20, 30
Canada 103
Caribbean 126
South America 138
USA 112
environment 18, 24-25, 243
Biosphere 23, 111
Epona 49
Equator 6, 10, 16, 17, 26, 237
weather 16, 17
equniox 9
Erasmus 43
Estonian language 88
Etruscans 80, 82
eucalyptus trees 220, 221
euro 31
European Court of Justice 41
European Economic Community,
Balkans 97

France 54
Iberia 75
Italy 78, 83
Low Countries 40, 43
Scandinavia 37
European Parliament 41
European Space Agency 137
European Union 31
Austria 83
Balkans 95, 97
British Isles 46, 51
France 54, 59
Germany 62, 67
Iberia 70, 75
Italy 78, 83
Low Countries 40, 41, 43
Scandinavia 34, 37
Euskara language 72
Evangelical Lutheran People's Church of Denmark 34
evaporation 243
Evenk people 154
evergreen trees 18, 149, 182, 188
evolution 12
Evzone guards 95
extinction 12

F

Fabergé, Carl 153
Falklands War 144, 147
fan 184
Fangio, Juan 147
fascism 83
fashion 54, 55, 79
fast-food 110, 113
faults 13, 14, 243
Federal Republic of Germany 67
Ferdinand, Archduke Franz, of Austria 97
Ferrari, Enzo 79
film industry 111, 223
Finnish language 36, 88
Finns 36, 37
fiords 32
first peoples,
Canada 104
Australia 226
Brazil 138
flamenco dancing 72, 73
Fleming people 42
Flemish language 42
fluorocarbons 240
flying doctor 225
fold mountains 14, 152
folkdances 64, 88, 89
football 81, 138, 225

Forbidden City 176, 178
foreign debt 119
forest destruction 92
forest people 234
Forth Bridge 45
fossil fuels 24, 25, 243
fossils 12, 13, 14, 15, 242, 243
Africa 216
Franciscan monks 80
Franco, General Francisco 75
Frank, Anne 43
Frankish Empire 42, 66
Franks 43, 56, 58, 74
French colonies 105, 114
French influence,
North Africa 203
Pacific islands 234
South America 140
Southeast Asia 194, 195
USA 113
West Africa 209
French language 20, 31, 42
British Isles 48
Canada 103, 105
Caribbean 127
France 56
South America 138
French Revolution 58, 59
Freud, Sigmund 65
Frisian language 42
fruits, South America 145
fuels 22, 24, 25
Funan kingdom 194
fundamentalists 202
fur trade 130
Futuroscope 55

G

Gaddafi, Colonel 202
Gaelic people 49, 50
galaxies 8, 9
Galician people 72
gamelan bands 192
Gandhi, Mahatma 172, 173
Garibaldi, Giuseppe 83
Garifuna people 121
gauchos 146
Gaudí, Antonio 73
Gauls 56, 58
Gautama Buddha 21
geisha 186
Georgian people 154
geothermal power 230
German language 42, 65
Germanic people,

British Isles 48, 50
France 58
Germany 66
Iberia 74, 75
Italy 82
Low Countries 42
Scandinavia 37
geysers 32, 228
glaciers 15
Arctic ocean 239
Canada 100
Scandinavia 32
South America 143
USA 107
gladiators 82
glass-making 47, 78, 87, 162
global climate 25, 235
Globe Theatre 48
Goethe 65
Gold Rush
Australia 223, 227
Klondike 105
USA 115
Golden Gate Bridge 109
Golden Temple 173
Gondwanaland 12
Gorbachev, Mikhail 157
Gormley, Antony 49
gospel music 112
Goths 80
goulash 87
Grand Canyon Gorge 109
Grand Prix,
France 55
South America 147
granite 15
Great Northern War 37
Great Wall of China 175, 181
Greek Cypriots 160
greenhouse effect 25
gross national product 23
Grundtvig, Nikolai 34
guacamole 118
Guanche people 72
guano 143
Guaraní language 147
Guaymi people 121
Gucci 78
guerilla warfare 97, 130, 195
Guevara, Che 124
Gulf Stream 10, 236
Guru Nanak 21
Gustavus Adolphus, King of Sweden 36
Gutenburg, Johannes 66
Gypsies,
Balkans 94
Baltic States 88, 89
British Isles 49

France 57
Iberia 72

H
habitat 19, 220, 243
Habsburg empire 43, 66, 75
Haile Selassie, Emperor of Ethiopia 127
haka 233
hamburgers 110
Han dynasty 180, 181
Han people 178
Handy Man 20
Hannibal 203
Harley Davidson motor bike 99, 111
Harold, King of England 50
Hebrew language 162
Heguy, Eduardo 147
Henry II, King of France 83
Henry VIII, King of England 51
high-income economies 23
high-rise building 110
Hindi language 20, 21, 170
Hindu architecture 167
Hindu Tamils 173
Hindu temples 170, 192
Hinduism 21,172
   Asia 149
   Brazil 139
   British Isles 48
   Southern Asia 167, 170, 171, 173
Hirohito, Emperor of Japan 184, 187
Hiroshige 187
Hispanics 113, 127
Hitler, Adolf 67
Hittites 164
Ho Chi Minh 195
Holi festival 171
Holy Roman Empire 36, 43, 66, 82, 90
Homo erectus 20, 243
Homo habilis 20, 243
Homo sapiens 20, 243
Homo sapiens neanderthalensis 20, 243
Homo sapiens 20, 243
hot air balloons 56
hot dogs 110
Hottentots 214
Hoxha, Enver 97
Hubble telescope 8
Hudson's Bay Company 105
Hugo, Victor 56

human evolution 20, 216
human rights 190
Humbolt current 235
Hunchback of Notre-Dame, The 56
Hundred Years War 51
hunter gatherers 20, 216
Hurricane Mitch 117
hurricanes 17, 243
   Caribbean 122, 123, 124
   Central America 117
   USA 108
Hussein, Sadam 165
Hutu people 212, 214

I
Ibo people 206
Ice Age 32
ice cream 78
ice hockey 105, 154
ice skating 42, 105
ice-breakers 238
icebergs 100, 238
Iceni tribe 50
Ife culture 209
igneous rocks 15
Inca empire 132, 133
Indo-Aryan people 170
Indo-European languages 21
Industrial Revolution 21, 22, 243
Inter Milan football team 80
International Date Line 6, 243
Inuit people 104, 105, 112, 238, 239
Iran-Iraq War 165
Iranians 160
Ireland, Republic of 44, 47
Islam 21
   Africa 196
   Brazil 139
   British Isles 49
   Middle East 160, 162, 163, 164, 165
   North Africa 202
   Southeast Asia 189, 192
   Southwest Asia 162 163
   Southern Asia 173
   West Africa 208, 209
Italian influence,
   Australia 224
   British Isles 49
   Canada 105
   South America 146
   USA 113
Italian language 80
Ivan the Great of Russia 157

Ivan the Terrible of Russia 157

J
Jahan, Shah 172
Jainism 171
Japanese people 21, 113, 138
Jefferson, President 110
Jesus Christ 21, 164
Jews,
   Anne Frank 43
   Baltic States 88
   British Isles 49
   France 57
   Germany 67
   Iberia 74
   Middle East 160, 162, 163, 165
   Russia 154, 155
   South America 146, 147
   USA 112, 113
Jimmu Tenno 187
Jinnah, Mohammed Ali 173
Joan of Arc 58
John Paul II, Pope 79
Joseph II of Austria 64
Judaism 21, 112, 162
Jupiter 8

K
kabuki theatre 186
Kalmuk people 154
Kayapo people 138
Kazak people 178
Kelly, Grace 55
Kelly, Ned 227
Kennedy, J F President USA 115
Ket people 154
Khmer rulers 194
Khoikhoi people 214
Khomeini, Ruhollah 165
Kibbutz 163
Kiel Canal 60
King, Martin Luther 115
Klondike gold rush 105
Knights of St. John 81, 83
Korean people 113, 178, 186
Korean War 176, 181
Kremlin 157
Kurds 165
Kuroshio current 10, 235
Kwakiutl people 104

L
La Niña 235
Labrador Current 10

lacemaking 41
Ladin language 80
Lamaism 171
language 20, 21
   Africa 202, 214
   Americas 112, 131, 139, 147
   Asia 162, 170, 178, 186, 192
   Australia 225
   Baltic States 88
   Belgium 42
   British Isles 48, 49
   Canada 105
   Europe 30
   France 56, 57
   Germany 64, 65
   Iberia 72
   Italy 80
   Low Countries 42
   Oceania 234
   Scandinavia 36
Lao Tzu 21
Lapita seafarers 234
Lapps 238
Lascaux cave paintings 58
latex 206
Latin America 139
Latin language,
   British Isles 48
   France 56, 58
   Iberia 74
   Italy 80
latitude 6, 7, 9
Laurasia 12
lava 11, 15
   Atlantic ocean 236
   Iceland 32
   Pacific ocean 235
   USA 109
Lawrence of Arabia 165
Lebanese people 225
Lenin 156, 157
Les Misérables 56
Letzebuergesch language 42
life on Earth 12
lighthouses 45
lightning 17
limestone 15
Lincoln, Abraham, President USA 111, 114, 115
Little Big Horn, Battle of the 115
Livingstone, David 214
Lombards 80, 82, 83
Long March 181
longitude 6, 7
Louis XIV of France 56, 58, 59
Louvre museum 56
Luther, Martin 66, 67
Lützen, Battle of 36

M
MacAlpin, Kenneth 51
Mafia 83
Magellan, Ferdinand 74
maglev train 184
magma 11, 13, 15, 243
magnetic pole 243
Magyar people 88, 90, 91
mah jong 178
Mahal, Mumtaz 172
Malay people 222
Maltese cross 81
Manchus 180, 181
Mandela, Nelson 213, 217
mangrove swamp 188, 243
Mangut of Thailand 194
Mansa Musa 203
mantle 12, 13, 14
Manx people 49
Mao Zedong 180, 181
Maori people 218, 232, 233, 234
maps 7, 243
Mapuche 146
Marcos, Imelda 195
Maria Theresa of Austria 67
mariachi music 121
Mars 8
Marsh Arabs 163
martial arts 186
Marx, Karl 65
Marxism 156
Masai people 214
Maurya empire 172
Mayan civilization 117, 120, 121
Mbuti people 215
Meir, Golda 165
Melanesian people 232
Mercator's projection 7
Mercury 8
meridians 6, 7
mesas 116
mestizos 121, 132, 138
metamorphic rocks 15
meteors 8, 243
Michelangelo 81
Micmac people 104
Micronesian people 232
mid-ocean ridge 11, 236, 237
Milky Way galaxy 8, 9
Milosevic, Slobodan 97
Ming Dynasty 180, 181
Minoan Civilization 96
Miskito people 121

Mixtec people 120, 121
Moche Civilization 132, 133
Modern man 20
Mohawk people 104
Mohenjo-daro Civilization 172
Moldovan people 154
Molière 56
Mondrian, Piet 43
Monet 56
Mongoloid people 21
Mongols,
   Eastern Asia 178, 180, 181
   Japan 187
   Russian Federation 155, 156, 157
   Southern Asia 172, 173
Monsoon Drift 10
monsoons 148, 166, 188, 237
Monster Mash 105
Montenegrin people 94
Monteverdi 81
Montgolfier brothers 56
Moors,
   Alhambra palace 72
   France 58
   Iberia 74, 75
mosques,
   Asia 170, 192
   British Isles 49
   Middle East 159, 162
   North Africa 202
motor racing 55, 147
Mozart, Wolfgang Amadeus 65
Muhammed 21, 164
mummies 120, 146
music,
   Africa 208, 215
   Americas 113, 120, 127, 131
   Asia 170, 192
   Baltic States 89
   France 56
   Italy 80, 81
   Russian Federation 154, 155
Muslims 21
   Africa 196, 202, 209
   Balkans 97
   Eastern Asia 179
   France 57, 58
   Iberia 74
   Middle East 162, 163, 164, 165
   Russia 155
   Southeast Asia 189, 192, 193
   Southern Asia 170, 171, 172, 173

253

Mussolini, Benito 83

N

NAFTA,
  Canada 102, 105
  Central America 118, 121
  USA 111, 115
Nahua people 121
Native American people,
  Caribbean 127
  South America 146
  USA 112, 113, 114
native peoples,
  Brazil 137
  Canada 104
  Andes 131
  Central America 120
Nautilus 238
Nazca Civilization 133
Nazi Party 67, 75, 89, 157
Neanderthal man 20
Negrito people 193
Negroid people 21
Nehru, Jawaharlal 173
Nenet people 154
Neptune 8
Niagara falls 106
Nobel Peace Prize 165
Nok culture 209
Norman people 49
  British Isles 50, 51
  France 57
  Italy 80, 81, 82, 83
Norse invaders 49
North Atlantic Drift 10
North Equatorial Current 10
North Pacific Current 10
North Pole 6, 7, 16, 238
northern lights 32
Norwegian language 36
nuclear power 22, 244
  France 54
  Japan 185
  Russia 152
nuclear waste 63
nuclear weapons 173, 235
Nyatapola temple 167
Nynorsk language 36

O

oases 198, 201
obelisks 202
Oberammergau Passion Play 65
oceanic crust 10, 11, 12, 13
oceans 10, 11, 27
  Arctic 238
  Atlantic 236
  biomes 16

formation 13
hurricanes 17
Indian ocean 237
Pacific 235
tides 9
water cycle 17
October Revolution 156, 157
Okefenokee Swamp 109
Olmecs 120
opera 80, 81, 179
Oregon Trail 115
Orthodox Church 157
Osset people 154
Otomi people 121
Ottoman Turks 94, 164, 165
outback 220, 225
Oyashio Current 10
ozone layer 25, 240, 241, 244

P

Pajamies, Esko 37
Palace of the Winds 169
Pampas 142, 144, 146
Pan-American highway 131
Pangaea 12
panpipes 130, 131
Parthenon temple 96
pasta 78, 80
pâté 55
Pavarotti, Luciano 80
Peary, Robert Edwin 238
Perez, Carlos Andréas 141
perfumes 55, 94, 95
Perón, Juan 147
Perry, Matthew C 187
Persia 21, 96, 164, 165
Peru Current 10
pétanque 57
Peter the Great of Russian Federation 152, 156
Peter's projection 7
Philip II of Spain 74
Phoenicians 74, 81
Picasso, Pablo 73
Picts 48, 51
Pilgrim Fathers 114, 115
Pinochet, Augusto 147
pirates 121, 126, 127
pizza 78, 79
plankton 236, 244
plants 12, 16, 18, 19, 24, 150
plate movements 13, 14, 182, 235, 236
PLO 165
Pluto 8

Pol Pot 195
polar easterlies 16, 17
polders 38
police 70, 104, 112
pollution 19, 20, 24
  Antarctica 241
  Central America 118
  Russia 153
polo 146
Polynesian people 232, 234, 235
  USA 112, 113
Pompeii ruins 82
Pont du Gard 52
Poquelin, Jean Baptiste 56
Portuguese influence,
  Africa 217
  Australia 226
  Brazil 140, 141
  Japan 187
  Papua New Guinea 234
  West Africa 209
Portuguese language 72, 138
Prada 79
prairies 18, 19, 244
  Americas 98
  Canada 100, 102
  USA 108
Pravicky Cone 85
prime meridian 6, 7
printing 177
prison colonies 226, 227
Protestant Church,
  Baltic States 90
  Brazil 139
  British Isles 50, 51
  Germany 64, 66
  Low Countries 42
  Pacific islands 233
  Scandinavia 36, 37
  South America 147
  Switzerland 64
  USA 112
Pu Yi of China 181
puppet theatre 192
pygmy people 193, 214, 215
pyramids,
  Africa 197, 199
  Americas 120, 132

Q

Qin dynasty 180
Qing dynasty 179, 180
Quechua people 131
Querandí people 146

R

Rabin, Yitzhak 165
Racine 56
Raffles, Sir Stamford 195
railways 104, 130, 153, 173, 185

rainforests 16, 18, 19, 24, 27
  Africa 196, 198, 204, 210
  Andes 128
  Australasia 218
  Brazil 134, 135, 136, 137, 138, 140
  Central America 117
  people 138, 140
  Southeast Asia 188
Rainier, Prince 55
Raleigh, Sir Walter 50
Rama IV of Thailand 194
Rastafarians 127
Read, Mary 126
Red Army 156
Red Cross 62
regattas 78
reggae music 127
religious wars 42
Rembrandt van Rijn 43
Renaissance 83
revolution,
  Caribbean 124
  Central America 119, 120
  France 59
  Russian Federation 156, 157
rice farming,
  Eastern Asia 177, 179
  Japan 185
  Southeast Asia 190, 191, 193
  Southern Asia 168, 169
rickshaw 131, 169
rift valleys 11,13, 14, 244
  Atlantic ocean 236
  Indian ocean 237
Ring of Fire 148, 182, 228
road train 222
Roma people 49, 57, 72, 88, 94
Roman Catholic Church,
  Andes 131, 133
  Baltic States 89
  Brazil 139
  British Isles 51
  Central America 121
  France 57
  Germany 65, 66
  Iberia 72, 73
  Italy 79, 81, 82
  South America 147
  USA 112
Roman Empire 82
  Balkans 96, 97
  British Isles 50, 51
  France 52, 56, 58
  Iberia 74

Italy 80, 82, 83
Low Countries 43
Middle East 164, 165
North Africa 203
Romanians 94, 154
Romansch language 80
Ronaldo 80
Roosevelt, President 110
Royal Greenland Trading Company 105
rugby football 215, 225, 233
Rus people 156
Russian language 20
Russian revolution 156

S

Saami people 36, 154, 238
Sacré Coeur Church 56
safaris 207
St Basil's Cathedral 155
St Cyril 155
St Lucy 37
St Nicholas 65
Saladin 164, 165
salsa music 127
samba music 139
Samburu people 214
Samoyed people 238
samurai 186, 187
San Andreas Fault 13
San people 214
Sards 80
saris 170
sarongs 193
satay 193
satellites 157, 244
  communications 23
  weather 16, 123
Saturn 8
sausages 63, 70
savanna 16, 18, 19
  Africa 197, 210, 211, 215
  Australia 220
  North Africa 198
  West Africa 204, 207
Saxons 22, 48, 50
Schiller 65
Scotch whisky 47
Scott, Robert Falcon 240
Scottish people 50, 51, 113, 225
Scythians 156
sedimentary rocks 15
Serbs 94
service industries 22, 23, 46, 111
Shah of Iran 165

Shakespeare, William 48
shanty towns 138, 139
Shavanti people 138
Sherpa people 170
Shi Huangdi of China 180
Shih Huang-ti of China 181
Shintoism 21, 182, 186
shoguns 186, 187
Shona people 216
Shotoku, Prince 187
Sikhism 21, 49, 172
Silicon Valley 111
Silk Road 180
Sinhalese people 170
Sinn Fein 51
Sino-Tibetan languages 21
Six-Day War 165
skiing 33, 64, 147, 163, 186, 233
skyscrapers 110, 161
slave trade
  Africa 216
  Caribbean 126, 127
  USA 113, 114, 115
  South America 140, 141
  West Africa 209
Slavic people 154, 156
Slovenian people 94
snowmobiles 151, 238
soccer,
  Africa 215
  Brazil 139
  Caribbean 127
  Eastern Asia 179
  Low Countries 43
  Middle East 163
  North Africa 202
  South America 147
  Southeast Asia 193
  West Africa 208
Socrates 97
soil 18, 24, 244
Solar System 8
Solidarity Trade Union 91
solstice 9
Somali people 212
Southern Ape 20
Space Monument 148
Space Shuttles 103
space 8,9
  Brazil 136
  Russia 157
  USA 111
Spanish influence,
  Australia 226
  Central America 120, 121, 126, 127
  Low Countries 43
  North America 114, 115

South America 132, 133, 140, 141, 146, 147
Southeast Asia 194, 195
Spanish language 20
Caribbean 127
Europe 31, 72
South America 131, 138, 146
USA 112
Spanish Main 126
Spanish Riding School 65
spas 87, 89
sphinx 203
Spinoza 43
spirit worship 214, 234
Srivajaya kingdom 194
Stalin, Joseph 156, 157
Statue of Liberty 106
steel bands 127
steppes 19, 244
Asia 149
Europe 30
Middle East 158
Russia 150, 152, 154, 156, 157
stilt houses 205
stock exchange 23, 177
Stone Age 58, 82
stone monuments,
British Isles 50
France 58
Incas, Andes 132
Pacific islands 232, 235
Stonehenge 50
stratosphere 25, 240, 244
subduction zone 13
submersible craft 10
Sultan of Brunei 190
sultans 160
Sumerian civilization 164
sumo wrestling 186
Sun 8, 9, 16, 17, 25
Superbowl 113
supercontinent 13
surfing 225
sushi 184
Swahili language 214
Swedes 36, 113
Swiss Guard 79
Sydney Harbour Bridge 222
Sydney Opera House 219, 225
synagogues 48
Syrians 146

T
tabletennis 179
taiga 150

taijiquan 179
Taipsu festival 193
Taj Mahal tomb 172, 173
Takkakaw falls 101
Tamerlane, Emperor 155
Tamils 170, 173
tanneries 200
Taoism 21, 179
Tarahumara people 121
Tarascan people 121
Tartars 90, 91, 154
Tasman, Abel 227
Tchaikovsky, Peter 154, 155
telecommunications 46, 244
telescopes 9, 124
television 22, 185, 223
Teli-ka-Mandir temple 167
Tell, William 66
Temple of Khajuraho 171
Temple of the Sun 132
tennis 147, 186, 225
Teutonic Knights 90
TGV train 54
Thai boxing 193, 225
theatre 179, 186, 192
Thirty Years War,
Baltic States 90, 91
Germany 66, 67
Scandinavia 36, 37
Tiahuanaco civilization 133
Tiananmen Square 178, 181
Tibetan people 171, 174, 178
time zones 7
Titus, Emperor 82
tobacco 125,126,169, 213
Tokugawa shogunate 187
Tollund Man 36
Tolstoy, Leo 154, 155
Toltecs 99, 117, 118, 120
Tomatina festival 72
tornadoes 17, 26, 108, 109, 245
totem pole 104
Tour de France 57
townships 214
trade unions 91
trade winds 17
traditional costume,
Andes 133
Balkans 96
Baltic States 88
Bavaria 64
Iberia 73

Low Countries 41
USA 113
West Africa 208
traffic jams 20
Trajan, emperor 82
trams 40
Trans-Siberian Railway 152
transform fault 13
transportation 226, 227
Treaty of Paris 115
Treaty of Rome 78
Treaty of Westphalia 66
trenches, ocean 11, 13, 235, 236, 237
Trojan War 164
Tropic of Cancer 6, 9, 10, 219
Tropic of Capricorn 6, 9, 10
tropical forests 18, 19, 98, 116, 117, 135, 218, 220
troposphere 16
Trotsky, Leon 156
tsars 156,157
tsunamis 27, 182, 235
Tuareg people 202
tundra 16, 18, 19
Arctic ocean 238, 239
Asia 148
Canada 100
Russia 150
Tungus people 238
turbans 170
Turkish Cypriots 49, 160
Turkish language 162
Turkish Ottoman empire 165
Turks,
Balkans 94, 97
Baltic States 90
Italy 83
Middle East 160
Tutsi people 212, 214
Tuvinians 154
typhoons 187

U
Uigurs 178
Ukrainians 105
ultraviolet radiation 25, 240, 241
Ulyanov, Vladimir Ilyich 156
Union of Kalmar 37
United Nations 200, 201
Universe 8, 9
Upright Man 20
Uranus 8
Urgup Cones 148
Uru people 131

V
Valentino 79
van Gogh, Vincent 42, 43
Vandals 80
Venus 8
Victoria Falls 211
Victoria, Queen of England 226
Vietnam War 115,195
Vietnamese people 105, 113
Vikings,
Atlantic ocean 236
British Isles 49, 50, 51
Canada 104
France 57, 58
Russia 156, 157
Scandinavia 36, 37
Visigoths 58, 74
Vlaams language 42
Vlad IV of Romania 97
vodka 87
volcanoes 14, 26, 245
gases 12
islands 10, 11, 32, 148
ocean floor 10, 11
volleyball 179, 186
Voodoo 126, 127

W
Wailing Wall 162
Walesa, Lech 91
Wall Street Crash 115
Walloons 42
War and Peace 155
Washington, George President USA 110, 115
water 9
clouds 17
erosion 14
oceans 9, 10, 11
vapour 17, 245
Waterloo, Battle of 59
weather 16, 17, 26, 241
wedding ceremonies 170, 231
Welsh language 48
Welsh people 113, 146
West Australian Current 10
westerlies 16, 17
wharerunanga 232
White Mountain, Battle of 90
Wilhelm I of Prussia 66, 67
William I of England 50
William, Duke of Normandy 50
wind 17, 44, 245
power 25, 34, 35
speed 26

waves 10
windmills 38, 222
Winterlude festival 105
World Cup soccer 43
World Fair 1958 39
World Organisation 62
World War I,
Australia 224, 227
Balkans 97
Baltic States 88, 91
British Isles 51
Canada 105
France 59
Germany 67
Italy 83
Japan 187
Low Countries 43
Middle East 164, 165
USA 115
World War II,
Australia 227
Balkans 97
Baltic States 89, 91
British Isles 51
Canada 105
Eastern Asia 177, 180
France 59
Germany 67
Italy 81, 83
Japan 183, 184, 186, 187
Low Countries 40, 43
Russia 157
Scandinavia 37
Southeast Asia 194
Southern Asia 172
USA 115
Worldwide Web 62
Wounded Knee 115

X
Xhosa people 214, 215
Xingu people 138

Y
yachts 48, 53, 55
Yakut people 154, 238
yams 207, 208, 230
Yanomami people 138
yashmaks 162
year 9
Yeltsin, Boris 157
yodelling 64
Yom Kippur War 165
Yoruba people 208
Yosemite Falls 108
Yuan dynasty 180
yurts 178

Z
Zapotec people 121
Zulu people 214, 216

255

The publishers would like to thank the following sources
for the use of their photographs in this book:

Page 15 (C/R)Rex Features; 15 (C/L) Keith Lye; 34 (B/L) courtesy Legoland; 37 (T/L) AKG,London; 41 (C/L) courtesy Nederlandse Philips Bedrijven BV; 41 (T/L) Frank Spooner; 42 (T/L) AKG,London; 42 (B) Frank Spooner; 42 (T/R) Frank Spooner; 49 (T/L) Rex Features; 50 (C/L) AKG,London; 51 (C) Rex Features; 54 (T/C) Rex Features; 55 (C/L) Spectrum Colour Library; 55 (B/L) & Rex Features; 56 (B/R) AKG, London; 57 (C/R) Rex Features; 57 (T/L) Stock Market; 58 (T/L) AKG, London; 58 (T/R) Spectrum Colour Library; 59 (T/L) AKG, London; 59 (B/R) & (B/L) Rex Features; 62 (B/L) Dover Publications; 63 (B/L) courtesy Volkeswagon; 64 (T/R) Rex Features; 66 (T/L)AKG, London; 67 (C/L) SIPA/Rex Features; 70 (B/L) Stock Market; 70 (B/L) courtesy SEAT; 72 (B/L) Stock Market; 72 (B/R) Stock Market; (72) courtesy Spanish Tourist Office; 72 (B/L) Stock Market; 73 (C/L) Rex Features; 74 (B/L) AKG, London; 75 (T/L) AKG, London, (C/L) SIPA/Rex Features; 76 (C/L) Hilary Fletcher; 78 (B/L) Spectrum Colour Library; 78 (B/L) Stock Market; 78 (T/L) & 79 (B/L) Rex Features; 79 (B/R) D.Parker/Science Photo Library; 80 (T/R) Spectrum Colour Library; 80 (B/L) AKG, London; 81 (B/R) Rex Features; 82 (C/L) Frank Spooner; 82/83 AKG, London; 87 (T/L) & 86 (T/L) Spectrum Colour Library; 89 (C) Panos; 88 (B/L) Mary Evans Picture Library; 91 (T/R) AKG, London; 91 (C/L) Gamma/Frank Spooner Pictures, (B/L) Spectrum Colour Library; 93 (T/L) Spectrum Colour Library; 93 (B/R) & (L/C) Spectrum Colour Library; 94 (C/R) Panos; 94 (B/L) Hilary Fletcher; 95 (T/L) & (C/L) Spectrum Colour Library, (B/R) Hilary Fletcher; 96 (C/L) Spectrum Colour Library; 96 (T/R) & 97 (T/L) Spectrum Colour Library; 97(C/R) SIPA/Rex Features; 103 (T/R) Frank Spooner; 107 (B/R) Graham King, (B/L) Hilary Fletcher;108 (T/R) Hilary Fletcher, (B/R) Keith Lye; 94 (C/R) Panos; 111 (T/L) Stock Market, 110/111 (C) Hilary Fletcher; 111 (T/R) Gamma/Frank Spooner; 112 (B) 113 (C), (T/R) Hilary Fletcher; 112 (C/L) & 113 (C/R) Gamma/Frank Spooner; 115 (C/L) & (C/R) Gamma/Frank Spooner; 117 (B/R) Gamma/Frank Spooner; 118 (T/C) Graham King; 119 (B/L), (T/L) & (T/R) Panos; 120 (C/L) &121 (T/R) Graham King; 122(C) Stock Market; 123 (B/R) Hilary Fletcher; 123 (T/R) Frank Spooner; 125 (T/L) Gamma/Frank Spooner; 125 (B) & (T/R) Hilary Fletcher; 126 (B/R) Mary Evans Picture Library;126 (B/L) Panos; 127 (T/L) Gamma/Frank Spooner; 128 (T/C) & 129 (C) Graham King; 128 (B), 129 (B/L), & (T/R) Graham King; 130 (C/R) Graham King; 131 (B/L), (C/L), Graham King; 131 (T/L) &130 (B/R) & (T/R) Graham King, 131 (R) Panos ; 132 (T/L), (T/R) & 133 (C) (T/Graham King; 132 (B/L) Graham King, 132 (R/C) Jon Keyte; 133 (T/R); 134 (B/L) &135 (T/L) Graham King; 135 (T/R) & (B/L) Graham King; 137 (T/L), 136 (T/C) Panos; & (T/R) Graham King; 137 (B/L) Hutchison Library; 137 (T/C) Hutchison Library; 138 (B/L) & 139 (T/L) Graham King, (C) Panos; 139 (L/C) Frank Spooner, (C/R) Panos; 140 (T/L) AKG, London, (T/L) Panos; 140 (C/R) 141 (C/R) & 141 (B) Panos; 141 (C/L) Hutchison Library; 143 (C/R), (T/R), (T/L) & 142 (B) Graham King; 142 (C/L) Jon Keyte; 143 (C/L) & (B/L) Graham King; 144 (C/R) Hutchison Library, (T/R), (C), 145 (B/L) Graham King; 145 (T/L), 144 (B/L) 146 (T/C) & 147 (B/R); 146 (B/L) & 147 (T/L) Gamma/Frank Spooner, (C) Jon Keyte; 152 (T/L) Rex Features; 153 (T/R) Spectrum Colour Library, 153 (C/L) Spectrum Colour Library; 155 (T/R) Rex Features; 160 (B/L) Keith Lye; 163 (B/R) Keith Lye; 164 (B/C) & 165 (T/R) Keith Lye; 167 (C/R) Keith Lye; 168 (C/L) & 169 (B) Keith Lye; 168 (T/R) Hilary Fletcher, 169 (T/R) Frank Spooner; 170 (B/C) Keith Lye; 171 (C) & (B) Hilary Fletcher; 172 (B) Hilary Fletcher; 177 (T/L) Hilary Fletcher, (T/R) E/T. Archive, (C/R) Hutchison Library; 178 (R/C) Keith Lye, (T/R) Hutchison Library; 179 (R/C) Hilary Fletcher; 181 (T/R) Hilary Fletcher; (T/C) Stock Market; 182 (B/R) & 183 (B/R) Hutchison Library; 183 (L/C) Rex Features; 185(T/R), 184 (B/L) & 184/5 (B) Gamma/Frank Spooner; 185 (C/L) courtesy Sony, (C) courtesy Nikon; 187 (B/L) V & A Museum/E.T.Archive; 194 (C/L) Hutchison Library; (T/C) Gamma/Frank Spooner; 195 (T/R) Hutchison Library, (B/L) Frank Spooner; 198 (B) Hilary Fletcher; 199 (T/L), & (B/L) Hilary Fletcher; 200 (C/R) Hilary Fletcher; 201 (T/L) Hilary Fletcher; 206 (T) Hutchison Library; 212 (B) Keith Lye; 213 (C/R) Hutchison Library; 213 (B/R) Keith Lye; 215 (T/L) Keith Lye; 216 (T/R) & 217 (T/R) Hutchison Library; 222 (C/L) Gamma/Frank Spooner; 223 (C/R) Hutchison Library; 224/5 (C) Frank Spooner, 224 (C/L) Hutchison Library; 226 (B) Mary Evans Picture Library; 227 (T/L) Corbis; 231 (T/L) Gamma/Frank Spooner; 231 (B/L) Hutchison Library; 235 (B/L) Rex Features; 237 (B) Hutchison Library.
All other photographs from Miles Kelly archives.

The publishers would like to thank the following artists whose work appears in this book:

David Ashby/Illustration Ltd; Richard Bonson; Vanessa Card; Kuo Kang Chen; Andrew Clark; Wayne Ford; Chris Forsey; Mike Foster/Maltings Partnership; Terry Gabbey/A.F.A.; Jeremy Gower; Gary Hincks; Sally Holmes; John James/Temple Rogers; Roger Kent/Illustration Ltd; Alan Male/Linden Artists; Jane Pickering/Linden Artists; Eric Rowe/Linden Artists; Peter Sarson; Rob Sheffield; Guy Smith/Mainline Design; Tony Smith; Christian Webb/Temple Rogers; Mike White/Temple Rogers; John Woodcock.